D1594633

A Local Society in Transition
The Henryków Book *and Related Documents*

PIOTR GÓRECKI

This book consists of an annotated translation of a history of a Cistercian monastery known as the *Henryków Book* and of some thirty charters further illustrating that history. A substantial historical essay introduces these materials.

The monastery situated at Henryków, in the duchy Silesia, was founded and consecrated between 1222 and 1228, and endowed with an estate in those years and continuously thereafter. The *Book* was composed at the monastery itself, in three sections: the first and the third by its third abbot, Peter, in or soon after 1268, the second by an anonymous monk, in or soon after 1310. The charters were issued, between 1225 and 1310, by the dukes of Silesia and by others interested in the monastery and its estate: the bishops of Wrocław and Poznań, the monastery's neighbors or donors, and their descendants.

Both the *Henryków Book* and the charters encompass a range of historical topics: the foundation of the monastery, and the resulting political and legal relationships; the history of each of the dozens of holdings included in the monastery's estate; and the full roster of the bishops of Wrocław, the diocese where the monastery was situated. The second occupies most of the work in its entirety, making the *Henryków Book* a history of a substantial population, society, economy, pattern of lordship and power, spanning well over one full century before the work's final redaction – in the words of the title, a local society in transition. The monastery's foundation and its political implications are treated specifically in the first section of the *Book*, which is therefore an excellent entrée into a local world of politics and power centered upon the monastery. Moreover, that section is also highly interesting as a text. It actively negotiates the patterns of lordship and power with which it is concerned, through a variety of rhetorical and forensic strategies; it directly addresses, and reinterprets, the network of memory and of law affecting these issues; and it reflects both the biography and the literary imprint of its principal author, Abbot Peter.

The essay that precedes the translation explores these and related subjects in detail, which is designed as an independent introduction to contemporary medieval Poland as well as to the sources; they are further contextualized by the charters, which offer supplementary, and sometimes explicitly varied, perspectives on the events and relationships described in the *Henryków Book*. The result is a multilayered historical record of a monastery and an author in their local world; a distinct region of medieval Europe; and an interesting fragment of Cistercian history.

STUDIES AND TEXTS 155

A Local Society in Transition

The *Henryków Book*
and Related Documents

PIOTR GÓRECKI

PONTIFICAL INSTITUTE OF MEDIAEVAL STUDIES

Library and Archives Canada Cataloguing in Publication

Górecki, Piotr, 1955–
　　A local society in transition : the Henryków book and related
documents / Piotr Górecki.

(Studies and texts ; 155)
Annotated translation of the Liber fundationis Claustri Sancte Marie
Virginis in Heinrichow.
Includes bibliographical references.
ISBN–13: 978–0–88844–155–3
ISBN–10: 0–88844–155–X

　　1. Liber Fundationis Claustri Sancte Marie Virginis in Heinrichow.
2. Church lands – Poland – Henryków (Wałbrzych). 3. Cistercian
monasteries – Poland – Henryków (Wałbrzych) – History. I. Title.
II. Title: Henryków book. III. Series: Studies and texts (Pontifical
Institute of Mediaeval Studies) ; 155

HD729.5.H45G67 2006　　　　943.8′52　　　　C2006–905995–0

To Alan E. Bernstein and Richard Hellie

Contents

Acknowledgements

This book has been in the making for some time – since autumn 1983, to be exact – and has many more debts than can properly be acknowledged. During the period of its completion at the University of California, Riverside, I have greatly benefitted from a close reading, critique, and encouragement by Lucille Chia, Warren Brown, Patrick Geary, Richard Godbeer, Paul Knoll, Grzegorz Myśliwski, Michele Salzman, and Sterling Stuckey, and by five exceptionally talented students, Christopher Balsz, Claire Clement, Christine Harker, Allison Henry, and Melanie Maddox. I am also very grateful for the comments by the anonymous readers of the Pontifical Institute of Mediaeval Studies, and by the Institute's editor, Fred Unwalla, whose role in substantive and editorial matters has been more helpful than I can begin to say. As on earlier occasions, I thank Linda Bobbitt, associated with the UCR Creative Design Services for producing the genealogical chart and the maps; and am very grateful to the J. Paul Getty Research Institute for permission to use a striking image for the cover of the book.

I am also enormously indebted to a group of students which is, of course, too large to list by name, but whose imprint – collective yet ultimately individual – has shaped everything about this work. As the finished version of the translation took shape, I continuously used it as a primary source in a wide range of survey and undergraduate seminar courses at UCR; in late 1998, as a basis of a graduate seminar at the Department of Medieval Studies of the Central European University in Budapest in late 1998; and as material in a team-taught course in the Summer University at the same institution in July 2005. These experiences have been invaluable, and I want to thank the students and colleagues at both institutions. I am especially grateful to János Bak, who generously invited me to Budapest to teach the graduate seminar at CEU, and encouraged me to teach at the Summer University some years later. On a related note, let me acknowledge an important article concerning a subject bearing on this book, written by a graduate of CEU, Grzegorz Żabiński, "A Pre-Cistercian Settlement of a Future Monastic Site: The Case of Henryków," *Quaestiones Medii Aevi Novae* 10 (2005), 273–302, to which I obtained access after this book went to press.

Renata and Ania, as always, are present here in all kinds of ways, and so this work is yet another modest tribute to them. During the course of its writing and revision, my parents, Danuta and Jan Górecki, were a source of inspiration and strength, and role models of scholarly care and integrity; an earlier version of these ackowledgements was the last piece of prose written by me on which my father commented while confronting his final illness. This brings me to some areas of gratitude that go back to the beginnings – of my work as a medievalist, and of this book. The theme of beginnings that animates so much of the *Henryków Book* prompts me to thank two remarkable teachers and friends, Robert Bartlett and the late Gerald Gunther. Finally, the book reflects my immeasurable gratitude to Alan Bernstein and Richard Hellie – Alan, for enabling me, during one *annus mirabilis* at Stanford University, to switch gears from a career path to a calling; Richard for welcoming me to the University of Chicago in 1983, introducing me to the value of translating historical sources with his own work on the Muscovite *Ulozhenie*, and directly inspiring me to undertake this translation. I am happy and honored to dedicate this book, jointly but to each in its fullness, to them.

Abbreviations

The following list provides abbreviations and sigla used for frequently cited works. Full details can be found in the Bibliography.

Grodecki, *Liber* (1949)	Grodecki, Roman, trans. and ed. *Księga henrykowska*
Grodecki, *Liber* (1991)	Grodecki, Roman, trans. and ed. (with a new introduction by Józef and Jacek Matuszewski) *Liber Fundationis*
Lex.MA.	*Lexikon des Mittelalters*
Niermeyer	Niermeyer, J. F. *Mediae Latinitatis Lexicon Minus*
P.S.B.	*Polski Słownik Biograficzny*
Piastowie	Szczur, Stanisław and Krzysztof Ożóg, ed. *Piastowie Leksykon biograficzny*
Rodowód	Jasiński, Kazimierz, *Rodowód Piastów śląskich.*
S.P.	Plezia, Marian, ed. *Słownik łaciny średniowiecznej w Polsce*
S.U., 1	Appelt, Heinrich, ed. *Schlesisches Urkundenbuch*, vol. 1
S.U., 2–5	Irgang, Winfried, ed. *Schlesisches Urkundenbuch*, vol. 2–5
S.U., 6	Irgang, Winfried, and Daphne Schadenwaldt, ed. *Schlesisches Urkundenbuch*, vol. 6
S.Sp.	*Słownik Staropolski*

The *Henryków Book* and Its Contexts

1 The importance of the sources

Undergraduates interested in the study of the past are invariably perplexed to discover that that past is a subject of strong disagreement among professional historians. Contrary to their initial intuitive sense that, once it has occurred, the past is fixed and accessible as such, our best students promptly learn instead that the conceptual skill driving our discipline is a confrontation of widely divergent interpretations – sometimes by means of outright debate.[1] In turn, the professional historians themselves greatly benefit by placing that fact right at the center of instruction, because teaching inevitably demands from us a rigorous clarification of those contested historiographical issues. One kind of material that may be used in this way is historiography.[2] Another is a sample of primary sources, selected in order to reflect interesting and currently contested historical issues. That is the material presented here.

The primary sources that follow are translated from Latin. They include a narrative history of a Cistercian monastery and of its estate, and a selection of charters further documenting that history. The monastic history and the charters span, at their widest range, the mid-twelfth and the early fourteenth centuries. Their principal subject is the monastery established between 1222 and 1228 at Henryków (Heinrichau) in the duchy of Silesia, currently in southwestern Poland, situated about fifty kilometers to the south of Wrocław, the principal city of that province and the seat of its diocese (see Maps 1–3).[3] The charters were

---

1. An excellent example of this way of framing historical knowledge is *Debating the Middle Ages: Issues and Readings*, ed. Lester K. Little and Barbara H. Rosenwein (Oxford: Blackwell, 1998). For a partial survey of debating in one specialized subject of medieval historiography, see Warren Brown and Piotr Górecki, "What Conflict Means: The Making of Medieval Conflict Studies in the United States, 1970–2000," in *Conflict in Medieval Europe: Changing Perspectives on Society and Culture*, ed. W. Brown and P. Górecki (Aldershot: Ashgate, 2003), 1–35, at 26–33; for a reflection on debating as an intellectual mode in a rather different specialized subject, see Geoffrey Koziol, "The Dangers of Polemic: Is Ritual Still an Interesting Subject of Scholarly Inquiry?" *Early Medieval Europe* 11 (2002), 367–88.

2. This is Little and Rosenwein's approach in *Debating*. Many other works develop it, in various modes. One example is *The Problems in European Civilization Series* initiated in the late 1950s by D. C. Heath and Company – among which see, for instance, *The Pirenne Thesis: Analysis, Criticism, and Revision*, ed. Alfred A. Havighurst (3rd ed., Lexington, MA: D. C. Heath and Company, 1976).

3. A superb introduction to the province of Silesia, especially to the region and duchy of Wrocław, is Richard C. Hoffmann, *Land, Liberties, and Lordship in a Late Medieval*

issued by the rulers of the duchy of Silesia, and, in fewer cases, by their cousins who ruled the other Polish duchies; by the bishops of Wrocław and of Poznań; and by other authors. These sources are interesting for a variety of reasons; as with any good historical material, the exact range of interest is best defined by the readers themselves. As a point of departure let me note three big issues, or problems, that have recently elicited much interest (and much disagreement) among historians, and upon which this monastic history and the related documents shed direct light.

The first is the medieval "frontier." This construct is currently understood by historians in several ways. Some view it principally in spatial terms: either as a type of space, adjoining some other region or situated between two or more other regions; or as a particular region of Europe, the Iberian Peninsula for example. Others consider the frontier above all as a dynamic process: the patterns of interaction – social, political, economic, religious, cultural – within some population or territory thus defined, or between the populations and territories to which it is peripheral. To yet other scholars, the "frontier" is interesting above all as an idea, or a state of mind, held by some historical population, by medieval historians today, or both, and useful for a variety of classificatory purposes.[4]

Countryside: Agrarian Structures and Change in the Duchy of Wrocław (Philadelphia: University of Pennsylvania Press, 1989); for the duchy in general, see Rościsław Żerelik, "Dzieje Śląska do 1526 roku" [The history of Silesia until 1526], in *Historia Śląska* [History of Silesia], ed. Marek Czapliński (Wrocław: Wydawnictwo Uniwersytetu Wrocławskiego, 2002), 14–116. For the origins and history of the Henryków monastery, see Robert Bartlett, *The Making of Europe: Conquest, Colonization and Cultural Change, 950–1350* (Princeton: Princeton University Press, 1993), 139–40, 154–55, 163; a series of studies by Heinrich Grüger: *Heinrichau: Geschichte eines schlesischen Zisterzienserklosters, 1227–1977* (Cologne and Vienna, 1978); "Das Patronatsrecht von Heinrichau," *Cîteaux* 28 (1977), 26–47; "Das Volkstum der Bevölkerung in den Dörfern des Zisterzienserklosters Heinrichau im mittelschlesischen Vorgebirgslande vom 13.–15. Jahrhundert," *Zeitschrift für Ostforschung* 27 (1978), 241–61; Piotr Górecki, "Rhetoric, Memory and Use of the Past: Abbot Peter of Henryków as Historian and Advocate," *Cîteaux* 48 (1997), 261–93; Górecki, "Politics of the Legal Process in Early Medieval Poland," *Oxford Slavonic Papers,* new series 17 (1984), 22–44.

4. Archibald Lewis, "The Closing of the Medieval Frontier, 1250–1350," *Speculum* 33 (1958), 475–83; *Medieval Frontier Societies,* ed. Robert Bartlett and Angus MacKay (Oxford: Oxford University Press, 1989), especially: Bartlett, "Colonial Aristocracies of the High Middle Ages" (23–47); Paul Knoll, "Economic and Political Institutions on the Polish–German Frontier in the Middle Ages: Action, Reaction, Interaction" (151–74); Alfred Thomas, "Czech–German Relations as Reflected in Old Czech Literature" (199–215); Friedrich Lotter, "The Crusading Idea and the Conquest of the Region East of the Elbe" (267–306); and the thematic overview by Robert I. Burns, "The Significance of the Frontier in the Middle Ages" (307–30); *The Transformation of Frontiers: From Late Antiquity to the the Carolingians,* ed. Walter Pohl, Ian Wood, and Helmut Reimitz (Leiden: Brill, 2000); Nora Berend, *At the Gate of Christendom: Jews, Muslims and "Pagans" in Medieval Hungary, c. 1000–c. 1300* (Cambridge: Cambridge University Press, 2001), 6–41; *Medieval Frontiers: Concepts and Practices,* ed. David Abulafia and Nora Berend (Aldershot: Ashgate, 2002),

The second big issue, or problem, is medieval "Europe" – usually viewed as an aspect of an even bigger problem, namely "Europe" in general as a historical entity. Like *frontier*, this construct may be understood principally in spatial terms – that is, as one of the major geographic regions of world history, along with the Near and the Far East, pre-Columbian America, pre-colonial Africa, and others, each of which may be subject to similar analysis. Alternatively, "Europe" may be viewed in dynamic terms, as a cultural unit that in the course of the Middle Ages was either "made," or "transformed," or "unified;" or that, on the contrary, remained, and now remains, irreducibly "diverse." Also like frontier, Europe, too, may be interesting above all as an idea, or an "invention," held by historians and others today, and by the past populations whom the historians study.[5]

The third major issue is the medieval locality, understood broadly as that "small world" which made up the basic parameters of human existence, and which entailed, in a seamless whole, community, production, exchange, spirituality, emotion, power, conflict, and the law.[6] In turn, the locality thus understood is an aspect of yet another kind of history, namely the history of a region – a province, a lordship, a town, or some other substantial unit of space and society. This kind of history has long been represented by substantial, one- or two-vol-

---

especially Grzegorz Myśliwski, "Boundaries and Men in Poland from the Twelfth to the Sixteenth Century: The Case of Masovia" (217–37); Nora Berend, "Défense de la Chrétienté et naissance d'une identité: Hongrie, Pologne et péninsule Ibérique au Moyen Age," *Annales: Histoire, Sciences Sociales* 58 (2003), 1009–27; Martyn Rady, "The Medieval Hungarian and Other Frontiers," *Slavonic and East European Review* 81 (2003), 698–709.

   5. Bartlett, *Making*; Richard W. Southern, *Scholastic Humanism and the Unification of Europe*, vol. 1, *Foundations* (Oxford: Blackwell, 1995); Michael Borgolte, *Europa entdeckt seine Vielfalt, 1050–1250* (Stuttgart: Verlag Eugen Ulmer, 2002); Patrick J. Geary, *The Myth of Nations: The Medieval Origins of Europe* (Princeton: Princeton University Press, 2002); Krzysztof Pomian, *Europa i jej narody* [Europe and its nations], trans. Małgorzata Szpakowska (rev. ed., Gdańsk: Wydawnictwo słowo/obraz terytoria, 2004). On the historiography of one aspect of this subject, see Piotr Górecki, "Medieval 'East Colonization' in Post-War North American and British Historiography," in *Historiographical Approaches to Medieval Colonization of East Central Europe: A Comparative Analysis against the Background of Other European Interethnic Colonization Processes in the Middle Ages*, ed. Jan M. Piskorski (Boulder and New York: East European Monographs/Columbia University Press, 2002), 1–38; see also Górecki, "A View from a Distance," *Law and History Review* 21 (2003), 367–76, and Górecki, "Assimilation, Resistance, and Ethnic Group Formation in Medieval Poland: A European Paradigm?" in *Das Reich und Polen: Parallelen, Interaktionen und Formen der Akkulturation im hohen und späten Mittelalter*, ed. Thomas Wünsch and Alexander Patschovsky, Vorträge und Forschungen 59 (Ostfildern: Jan Thorbecke Verlag, 2003), 447–76.

   6. Wendy Davies, *Small Worlds: The Village Community in Early Medieval Brittany* (Berkeley and Los Angeles: University of California Press, 1988); Susan Reynolds, *Kingdoms and Communities in Western Europe, 900–1300* (2nd ed., Oxford: Clarendon Press, 1997); William C. Jordan, *From Servitude to Freedom: Manumission in the Sénonais in the Thirteenth Century* (Philadelphia: University of Pennsylvania Press, 1986).

ume syntheses of a particular society, economy, and pattern of power.[7] It intersects with yet another major subject, currently being revisited by medievalists after an interlude of relative historiographical disinterest, and that is economic history – a complex of agrarian history, rural and urban demography, technological change, patterns of land use and settlement, the development of towns and of urban and commercial networks, and, perhaps above all, the individual and collective life of the peasantry.[8]

7. The pioneering works of this genre (and its constitutent sub-genres) are: Georges Duby, *La société aux XIe et XIIe siècles dans la région mâconnaise* (2nd ed., Paris: S.E.V.P.E.N., 1971); J. Ambrose Raftis, *The Estates of Ramsey Abbey: A Study in Economic Growth and Organization* (Toronto: Pontifical Institute of Mediaeval Studies, 1957); Raftis, *Tenure and Mobility: Studies in the Social History of the Medieval Village* (Toronto: Pontifical Institute of Mediaeval Studies, 1957); Edward Miller, *The Abbey and Bishopric of Ely* (Cambridge: Cambridge University Press, 1951) – representing, roughly speaking, two different historiographical schools, the francophone and the anglophone. The former has consisted of an enormous number of monographs modelled on Duby's, of which the most synthetic and comprehensive is Robert Fossier, *Enfance de l'Europe, Xe–XIIe siècles: Aspects économiques et sociaux*, 2 vols. (Paris: Presses Universitaires de France, 1982), and of which the explicitly revisionist is Dominique Barthélemy, *La société dans le comté de Vendôme de l'an mil au XIVe siècle* (Paris: Fayard, 1993). An outstanding example of the latter is Eleanor Searle, *Lordship and Community: Battle Abbey and Its Banlieu* (Toronto: Pontifical Institute of Mediaeval Studies, 1974). Among the many historiographical treatments of the francophone variant of regionally based history of society, economy, and power, see above all Thomas N. Bisson, *"La terre et les hommes*: A Programme Fulfilled?" *French History* 14 (2000), 322–45. A major work on a region, related to those "schools," but highly original, is Grzegorz Myśliwski, *Człowiek średniowiecza wobec czasu i przestrzeni (Mazowsze od XII do poł. XVI wieku)* [Medieval man with regard to time and space: Masovia from the twelfth to the mid-sixteenth century] (Warsaw: Wydawnictwo Krupski i S-ka, 1999), of which see the review by Piotr Górecki, *Speculum* 77 (2002), 1368–72.

8. This enormous literature begins with the two classic works by Marc Bloch, *Feudal Society*, trans. L. A. Manyon (Chicago: University of Chicago Press, 1961), and *French Rural History: An Essay on Its Basic Characteristics*, trans. Janet Sondheimer (Berkeley and Los Angeles: University of California Press, 1966). Thereafter, it overlaps with the historiography noted in the preceding note; and in addition includes, among others, the following works in English: Norman J. G. Pounds, *An Historical Geography of Europe, 450 BC– AD 1330* (Cambridge: Cambridge University Press, 1973); Pounds, *An Economic History of Medieval Europe* (London: Longman, 1974); Pounds, *Hearth and Home: A Study of Material Culture* (Bloomington: Indiana University Press, 1993); Richard Hodges, *Dark Age Economics: The Origins of Towns and Trade, AD 600–1000* (New York, 1982); Georges Duby, *Rural Economy and Country Life in the Medieval West*, trans. Cynthia Postan (Columbia, SC: University of South Carolina Press, 1968); *The Fontana Economic History of Europe*, ed. Carlo Cipolla, vol. 1: *The Middle Ages* (Glasgow: Collins/Fontana, 1972); *Towns in Societies: Essays in Economic History and Historical Sociology*, ed. Philip Abrams and E. A. Wrigley (Cambridge: Cambridge University Press, 1978); Edward Miller and John Hatcher, *Medieval England: Rural Society and Economic Change, 1086–1348* (London: Longman, 1978); Kathleen Biddick, *The Other Economy: Pastoral Husbandry on a Medieval Estate* (Berkeley and Los Angeles:

Of course, these major subjects are closely interrelated. For instance, the question of the medieval meanings of *Europe* is explicable, at least in part (and, as always, not without controversy), in terms of Europe's "frontiers," above all their functions and their transitions – a line of analysis which immediately raises the meanings of *frontier* and of its conceptual twin, *core*. Do these words refer to a point of contact? A kind of space? A process? Something else? Such questions may be (and indeed have been) addressed in terms of a close analysis of particular places or regions, peasantries, town populations, merchants and other social intermediaries, ethnically diverse groups, lordships, laws, and much else – in short, in terms of the constituent topics that make up the third big subject just noted, that is, local and regional history.

The sources translated here were produced in a macro-region of medieval Europe whose history raises exactly the three big issues just noted. That macro-region is "Eastern" (or, more currently, "East Central") Europe.[9] Considered in its entirety, the region has long been viewed as a "frontier" of the Continent. Thus, today, it offers us a conceptual and empirical test case of what we mean by

University of California Press, 1989); David Herlihy, *Medieval Households* (Cambridge, Mass.: Harvard University Press, 1985); Jean Chapelot and Robert Fossier, *The Village and House in the Middle Ages*, trans. Henry Cleere (Berkeley and Los Angeles: University of California Press, 1985); Peter Spufford, *Money and Its Use in Medieval Europe* (Cambridge: Cambridge University Press, 1988); Paul Freedman, *The Origins of Peasant Servitude in Medieval Catalonia* (Cambridge: Cambridge University Press, 1991); Piotr Górecki, *Economy, Society, and Lordship in Medieval Poland, 1100–1250* (New York: Holmes and Meier, 1992); Edward Miller and John Hatcher, *Medieval England: Towns, Commerce and Crafts, 1086–1348* (London: Longman, 1995); Thomas N. Bisson, *Tormented Voices: Power, Crisis, and Humanity in Rural Catalonia, 1140–1200* (Cambridge, MA: Harvard University Press, 1998); Freedman, *Images of the Medieval Peasant* (Stanford: Stanford University Press, 1999); Christopher Dyer, *Making a Living in the Middle Ages: The People of Britain, 850–1520* (New Haven: Yale University Press, 2002); Keith D. Lilley, *Urban Life in the Middle Ages, 1000–1450* (Houndmills: Palgrave, 2002). See also the recent historiographical treatments in "La historia rural de las sociedades medievales europeas: trayectorias y perspectivas," Monográfico coord. by Isabel Alfonso, part 1, *Historia Agraria* 31 (2003), 11–83: I. Alfonso, "Presentación" (11–12); Christopher Dyer and Philipp R. Schofield, "Estudios recientes sobre la historia agraria y rural medieval británica" (13–33); Ghislain Brunel and Benoît Cursente, "Tendencias recientes de la historia rural en Francia" (35–56); and José Ángel García de Cortázar and Pascual Martínez Sopena, "Los estudios sobre historia rural de la sociedad hispanocristiana" (57–83); and part 2, *Historia Agraria* 33 (2004), 13–103: I. Alfonso, "Presentación" (13–14); Luigi Provero, "Cuarenta años de historia rural del medioevo italiano" (15–29); Julien Demade, "El mundo rural medieval en la historiografía alemán desde 1930" (31–79); and Piotr Górecki, "Los campesinos medievales y su mundo en la historiografía polaca" (81–103).

9. An important marker of that conceptual shift is Timothy Garton Ash, "Does Central Europe Exist?" *New York Review of Books* 33.15 (9 October 1986), 45–53.

frontier, and by *core*[10] – considerations that inevitably shed light on the bigger question of the existence, formation, and indeed reality, of that Europe whose frontier it (in some sense) was.[11] Yet readers expecting to reach global resolutions of issues that are drawn this broadly will, at first glance, be disappointed, because in these sources East Central Europe is represented in exceedingly local terms. The story the sources tell – the circumstances they narrate, the relationships they describe, the memories they reflect – is circumscribed within a radius of, at the outermost, a bit over ten kilometers around the monastery itself.[12]

These sources also, though less directly, reflect a bigger horizon: the Polish principalities of Silesia, Great Poland, and Little Poland; Germany (mentioned once with that word), including the newly colonized German province of Meißen; pagan Prussia; Polish towns, especially Wrocław, Głogów, Poznań, and Kraków; and (on one occasion, and very obliquely) Rome. One of these wider geographic horizons coincides approximately with medieval Poland between the late twelfth and the early fourteenth centuries. Thus, the sources are among other things, records of Polish history,[13] and may of course be used to teach that subject, or more generally the history of East Central, or Eastern, or northern Europe.[14]

10. Perhaps the most important statement of a historiographical contrast between the approaches to this big problem today – not framed as a polemic or a debate, but a clear and fascinating reflection of conceptual difference – is, on the one hand, Bartlett, *Making*, and, on the other, Berend, *At the Gate*. See the brief remarks (on this and other conceptual issues) by Janet Nelson in her enthusiastic review of Berend, *American Historical Review* 107 (2002), 1279–80; see also Piotr Górecki, "'Tworzenie Europy' Roberta Bartletta w kontekście anglosaskich badań historycznych nad początkami i kształtowaniem się Europy" [Robert Bartlett's *The Making of Europe* in the context of English-language scholarship on the origins and formation of Europe], in Robert Bartlett, *Tworzenie Europy. Podbój, kolonizacja i przemiany kulturowe, 950–1350*, trans. Grażyna Waluga (Poznań: Poznańskie Towarzystwo Przyjaciół Nauk, 2003), 505–15.

11. In contrast to Bartlett's strong confidence, which I share, that Europe and its regions are specifiable constructs in the medieval period and beyond (Górecki, "Tworzenie," 512–14), note the skeptical (and, themselves, strongly differing) views of Borgolte, *Europa*, throughout, and Norman Davies, *Europe: A History* (Oxford: Oxford University Press, 1996), 7–10, 14–56.

12. The particulars in the rest of this paragraph are thoroughly explained in the subsequent, topical sections of the present essay, and illustrated in the chart and the maps.

13. By "Poland," "Polish" towns, peasants, or history, and so forth, I mean (as I have meant throughout my work [*Economy*, 29, n. 1, and *Parishes*, 7, n. 24]), the region of the Continent ruled by the Piast dynasty, inhabited by a Slavic population to which its members and foreigners referred as *Poloni*, and which, at different points between the tenth and the fourteenth centuries, attracted immigrants from elsewhere, above all Germany.

14. In conjunction with the superb series of translated, and tacitly edited, sources concerning this region of Europe, currently underway at the Central European University in Budapest, for which see most recently *Gesta Principum Polonorum: The Deeds of the Princes of the Poles*, ed. and trans. Paul W. Knoll and Frank Schaer (Budapest: Central European University Press, 2003), and the general editors' remarks at vii–viii.

Likewise, because in the course of this period Silesia, and thus the Henryków region, became first a part of Bohemia, then (until 1945) of Germany, they also illustrate Czech and, much more so, German history. However, apart from scholarly audiences specialized in national or in macro-regional terms, these sources should interest general medievalists simply because of the wide range of subjects they address. To illustrate this point, let me return to my three big issues.

First, the "frontier." The Henryków region, and the people who inhabited it at different points between, say, 1160 and 1310, comprised a "frontier" in several senses of that word. Here was an area of both old and new settlement, subject to both old and new lordship. This was also a "frontier" in a local sense – that is, a demographic and economic periphery within Silesia itself, situated in an intermediate zone between old (principally Polish) and new (initially Polish, thereafter increasingly German) subregions of rural and urban settlement. For this reason, the Henryków region was also a stage for interethnic contact and interaction.[15] Moreover, that periphery itself extended, at its own edge, toward a specific boundary perimeter: a segment of a large, deliberately created, defensive border zone encompassing the duchy of Silesia in its entirety, called the *przesieka* (a "clearing") in Polish, and the *hach* (a "hedge") in German.[16] Finally, viewed on the largest scale, the Henryków region was one of thousands of places within East Central Europe, that macro-region of the Continent into which, in the net, foreigners migrated from its other macro-regions (especially, but not exclusively, from Germany), during the century and a half spanned by our documents.

The matter of scale brings me to "Europe." Readers of Robert Bartlett will readily identify in this region some of his indices of a Continent-wide cultural integration. Our story begins with one instance of expansion of the Cistercian Order by filiation, a process long-standardized in regions further to the west, and evidently replicated here in that standardized form.[17] Likewise, the story occurs, right from its outset, within a well-established context of bishoprics, local or parish churches, and practices of possession, assessment, payment, and consumption of tithes. At one moment, crusading enters the picture, as an important actor departs on an expedition against the pagan Prussians.[18] Several more instances add up to a vivid case study of what Bartlett calls the "aristocratic diaspora" that bridged major regions of the Continent, and of its impact upon this local world.

On the other hand, readers of Michael Borgolte will discover here regional, even local, differences, or areas of specificity, that seem to be irreducible and permanent. Examples include the recurring image of the good Piast duke and of his evil counterpart; the statuses, and the collective activities, of the indigenous,

15. Górecki, "Assimilation," 455–75.
16. See nn. 259–60 below.
17. For monastic, especially Cistercian filiation, nn. 133, 301 below.
18. Chapter 46.

Polish peasants, both previously settled in the region, and migrants into it; ethnic classifications, especially the dichotomy between Poles and Germans, and, in one late instance, between both these groups on the one hand and the Jews on the other; legal systems and institutions, especially "Polish" and "German" land law and procedure and their alternatives; and much else. Readers of Nora Berend will find it convenient to view all the types of people and social features just noted, as interrelated, mutually influential, "cells" (in a social sense of that metaphor), engaged, if you will, in a permanent, ongoing negotiation of difference – and neither tending toward, not actually producing, any one unifying, ·systemic outcome. Finally, the material for such considerations inevitably shifts the reader's attention to the concrete: to those hundreds of transactions, and dozens of well-documented people, which and who make up one "small world" of medieval Europe.

In addition, the sources are interesting as texts. They are, of course, two very different types of text. The monastic history is a narrative, although it incorporates charters, whereas the charters are principally records of particular transactions (or sequences of transactions), although they, in turn, incorporate narrative material. Both types of sources have long elicited a specialized, and sometimes highly technical, scholarly interest. The most recent phase of that interest has been underway since about 1990. During this period, the text has emerged as an autonomous object of study, deliberately distinguished from the reality to which it supposedly refers. This recent attention to text on its own terms transcends our profession. It has emerged in the last quarter of the twentieth century out of the "linguistic turn," by which is meant a fascination shared by a long generation of historians, anthropologists, and literary scholars with language and representation; and with the implications of language and representation for objective knowledge.[19]

This intellectual ferment has affected medieval historiography on several levels. Paradoxically, one of its outcomes is a return to a very old historiographical tradition, namely source analysis and criticism in the grand style: a close attention to matters of genre, trope, composition, and other elements of literary form; a renewed, systematic examination of particular fragments of medieval writing, such as preambles of royal charters; an identification of model texts, textual transmission, and textual adaptation; and more. Another outcome is, in every sense, historiographically new. In fact, it is often framed as a strong revision, or an outright rejection, of the aims and assumptions of earlier analysis and

---

19. Medievalists have generally pulled back from the most radical, or skeptical, implications of that last question; two important exceptions to that caution (very different from one another) are Kathleen Biddick, *The Shock of Medievalism* (Durham, NC: Duke University Press, 1998), and Philippe Buc, *Dangers of Ritual: Between Early Medieval Texts and Social Scientific Theory* (Princeton: Princeton University Press, 2001). For an introduction to this subject, see Michael Stanford, *An Introduction to the Philosophy of History* (Oxford: Blackwell, 1998), 183–205, 227–62.

criticism of sources. This is an interest in what might be called the agency behind the text, and the agency embedded within it.

The former kind of agency is reflected in a new search, today, for the meaning of the medieval author.[20] The latter type of agency is an attribute of the text itself. We now recognize that texts themselves work, or – to paraphrase John Austin – that one can do things with texts.[21] One area of reality which texts are understood to affect is memory – especially the kind of memory that is shared by groups, and that historians and others call collective or social memory.[22] Over the past fifteen years, we have experienced an outburst of studies devoted to the ways in which texts function as reflections, or as repositories, or as sources of memory (and of its converse, oblivion) in a variety of past and present societies. In its own turn, this outburst is a result of a fortuitous conjunction of several disparate interests. One, arising directly from psychology, concerns memory's cognitive aspects: the act of remembering, the processes or dynamics behind remembering, and the relationship of remembering to other aspects of cognition.[23] Another, an aspect of the history of ideas, focuses on two cognitive dimensions of memory, as experienced by past populations: mnemonics, meaning active and deliberate approaches to the creation and retention of memory; and theories of memory, that is, the ideas in terms of which memory and oblivion were conceptualized in the past.[24] A third area of interest concerns

20. See nn. 47–59 below.

21. John L. Austin, *How to Do Things with Words* (Oxford: Oxford University Press, 1962); two excellent approaches to this kind of study, specifically concerning charters, are Warren Brown, "Charters as Weapons: On the Role Played by Early Medieval Dispute Records in the Disputes They Record," *Journal of Medieval History* 28 (2002), 227–48, and Brown, "When Documents are Destroyed or Lost: Lay People and Archives in the Early Middle Ages," *Early Medieval Europe* 11 (2002), 337–66.

22. Paul Connerton, *How Societies Remember* (Cambridge: Cambridge University Press, 1989); James Fentress and Chris Wickham, *Social Memory* (Oxford: Blackwell, 1992); Patrick J. Geary, *Phantoms of Remembrance: Memory and Oblivion at the End of the First Millennium* (Princeton: Princeton University Press, 1995); Amy G. Remensnyder, *Remembering Kings Past: Monastic Foundation Legends in Medieval Southern France* (Ithaca: Cornell University Press, 1995); Elisabeth van Houts, ed., *Medieval Memories: Men, Women, and the Past, 700–1300* (Harlow: Longman/Pearson Education, 2001); Rosamond McKitterick, *History and Memory in the Carolingian World* (Cambridge: Cambridge University Press, 2004).

23. Symptomatic of a reawakening of interest is a 1995 reprint of a 1932 classic on the cognitive dimensions of memory, Frederick C. Bartlett, *Remembering: A Study in Experimental and Social Psychology* (Cambridge: Cambridge University Press, 1932, repr. 1995); see also Elizabeth Ligon Bjork and Robert A. Bjork, eds., *Memory* (San Diego: Academic Press, 1996).

24. Again, an important occasion, in the late 1990s, for a reprint, Frances A. Yates, *The Art of Memory* (Chicago: University of Chicago Press, 1966); Mary Carruthers, *The Book of Memory: A Study of Memory in Medieval Culture* (Cambridge: Cambridge University Press, 1990); Janet Coleman, *Ancient and Medieval Memories: Studies in the Reconstruction of the Past* (Cambridge: Cambridge University Press, 1992).

the meanings and the functions of social groups, including the problem of memory (and oblivion) as a type of group experience.[25]

This interest has identified – distilled, as it were, from among other phenomena – memory as a central element of past reality. This outcome is interesting on its own terms: memory is now a dimension of the past no less real, and no less important, than are other cognitive events, such as knowledge, emotion, or belief. In addition, memory usefully frames other phenomena. For example, Mary Carruthers' work on mnemonics in monasteries, or Janet Coleman's essays on ancient and medieval ideas about memory, tell us much about medieval learning – understood as an activity, and as an area of knowledge. Another example concerns memory and groups. Because, as is now clear, memory (and oblivion) may be, and typically are, experienced by groups, memory helps us define what we mean by a group. To put it differently, a group may emerge – indeed, it may meaningfully exist – specifically insofar as its members share common memories (or, which is much the same thing, what they believe to be common memories). Thus, memory relates to group "consciousness," or group "identity."

Because different kinds of groups may experience memory in different ways, memory further serves historians as a criterion for identifying specific medieval groups. We now have a legacy of excellent studies treating memories specific to peasants, to women, to monks or nuns, to families (including ruling dynasties), to "peoples" (*gentes*), and to other types of collectivities.[26] At different moments in its historiography, collective memory has contributed to our understanding of status, gender, institutions, the law, family and kinship, the transition of "the year 1000,"[27] ethnicity, "national" identity or consciousness,[28] and much else. The

25. Once more, we may note here an element of a recent recovery of rather old learning, this time Maurice Halbwachs, *On Collective Memory*, ed. and trans. Lewis A. Coser (Chicago: University of Chicago Press, 1992).

26. Fentress and Wickham, *Social Memory*, 87–143; Geary, *Phantoms*, 62–64, 68–69, 177–79; Remensnyder, *Remembering*, passim; and all the articles in van Houts, *Medieval Memories*, especially: Matthew Innes, "Keeping It in the Family: Women and Aristocratic Memory, 700–1200" (17–35); Patricia Skinner, "Gender and Memory in Medieval Italy" (36–52); Kathleen Quirk, "Men, Women and Miracles in Normandy, 1050–1150" (53–71); Renée Nip, "Gendered Memories from Flanders" (113–31); Fiona Griffiths, "Nuns' Memories or Missing History in Alsace (c. 1200): Herrad of Hohenbourg's Garden of Delights" (132–49).

27. Geary, *Phantoms*, passim.

28. Susan Reynolds, "Medieval *Origines Gentium* and the Community of the Realm," *History* 68 (1983), 375–90; Fentress and Wickham, *Social Memory*, 173–99; and the earlier studies in Poland and the former Czechoslovakia, concerning the subject which the authors usually framed as "national" identity, yet which is identical with one aspect of what is elsewhere conceptualized as collective memory: *Dawna świadomość historyczna w Polsce, Czechach i Słowacji* [Former historical consciousness in Poland, Bohemia, and Slovakia], ed. Roman Heck (Wrocław: Zakład Narodowy im. Ossolińskich, 1978); Jacek Banaszkiewicz, *Kronika Dzierzwy. XIV-wieczne kompendium historii ojczystej* [Dzierzwa's Chronicle: a fourteenth-century compendium of native history] (Wrocław: Zakład Narodowy

reader will readily note that, based on the *Henryków Book*, we may add to the above list: Poles and Germans; the monks of one particular monastery; the cathedral chapters of Wrocław and of Poznań; the courts of the Piast dukes; communities of local knowledge; and (again) more.[29]

For medieval historians, memory is unavoidably mediated by texts. For this reason, another subject that memory helps us frame is the text itself. In my view, memory is the crucial variable behind those dimensions of the text that relate to agency – that is, the dimensions that affect what a text does, or what can be done with it. In order to unpack this rather abstruse proposition, let me begin with a deliberately simplified schema of the relationship of text to memory. First, a text may be a record: a transcription of words actually stated or believed to have been stated, or a narration of events that have actually transpired, or that are believed to have transpired. In that capacity, the text works as an alternative to memory, since it expresses in written form material that is otherwise retained (or lost) by the mind. Second, a text may reflect memory. That is, it may logically assume, or implicitly refer to, some area of knowledge which it does not record, in the sense just noted, on its face.

Third, a text may be a repository of memory. This relationship includes record and reflection, but is not limited to them. The full knowledge conveyed by a text may well extend beyond its explicit content, or its logical assumptions or implications. For example, the *Book*'s frequent references to "the territory of Henryków," or to "the noble and mediocre," presume that these phenomena

---

im. Ossolińskich, 1979); Banaszkiewicz, *Podanie o Piaście i Popielu. Studium porównawcze nad wczesnośredniowiecznymi tradycjami dynastycznymi* [The tale of Piast and Popiel: a comparative study of early-medieval dynastic traditions] (Warsaw: Państwowe Wydawnictwo Naukowe, 1986); *Państwo, naród, stany w świadomosci wieków średnich. Pamięci Benedykta Zientary, 1929–1983* [State, nation, estates in medieval consciousness: in memory of Benedykt Zientara, 1929–1983], ed. Aleksander Gieysztor and Sławomir Gawlas (Warsaw: Państwowe Wydawnictwo Naukowe, 1990), especially the article by Gawlas, "Stan badań nad polską świadomością narodową w średniowieczu" [The state of research concerning the Polish national consciousness in the Middle Ages] (149–194); Banaszkiewicz, *Polskie dzieje bajeczne mistrza Wincentego Kadłubka* [Polish fable history by Master Vincent Kadłubek] (Wrocław: Monografie FNP/Leopoldinum, 1998). For the analogies between this line of inquiry and the subsequent anglophone interest in collective memory (Geary, *Phantoms*, for example), see Piotr Górecki, "Poland: To the 18th Century," in the *Encyclopedia of Historians and Historical Writing* (London: Fitzroy Dearborn, 1999), 929–34, at 931.

29. Piotr Górecki, "Communities of Legal Memory in Medieval Poland, c. 1200–1240," *Journal of Medieval History* 24 (1998), 127–54, at 128–29, 133, 139–40, 148, 151–52; Górecki, "Local Society and Legal Knowledge: A Case Study from the Henryków Region," in *Christianitas et cultura Europae: Księga Jubileuszowa Profesora Jerzego Kłoczowskiego* [*Christianitas et cultura Europae*: A Jubilee Book for Professor Jerzy Kłoczowski], ed. Henryk Gapski, 2 vols. (Lublin: Instytut Europy Środkowo-Wschodniej, 1998), 1: 544–50; with which compare Judith Everard, "Sworn Testimony and Memory of the Past in Brittany, c. 1100–1250," in van Houts, *Medieval Memories*, 72–91.

were generally known and clear, and thus they neither state, nor imply what they encompassed or meant. Finally, a text may be a source of memory. This role, too, includes the above possibilities; the simplest way to use a text as a "source" is to consult it, for its explicit record, or for its implicit information, or for the knowledge it assumes on the part of the audience and does not convey. Rosamond McKitterick opened this whole subject in 1989 by reminding us (very helpfully) that texts are interesting in part because someone actually read them, and, directly or tacitly, drew knowledge from them.[30] In addition, however, the text may be actively structured, or actively used, or both, in order to affect what is remembered – and therefore, in the longer term, what is known.

An intriguing mark of the recent surge of interest in the text is strong scholarly resistance against the simple, or the straightforward, interpretation of these four possibilities. That resistance is usually framed as a rhetorical refutation of several (typically unattributed) propositions: that the text is a "transparent" venue to some reality; that it provides direct "access" to it; that it corresponds with it; or that (to turn to my own metaphor of reflection) it "mirrors" an external reality.[31] Despite (or perhaps because of) their occasional stridency, such critiques have not, at least among most medievalists, successfully undermined the basic, intuitively empiricist notions of reference. Instead, they have complicated, and enriched, our understanding of the link between the text and some real, past world – forcing us (among other things) to devote attention to the four possibilies of my simplified schema, especially to the text considered as a repository of memory about an external world, and as an active source of that memory.

These relationships between text and memory may relate to the text's composition – its arrangement, especially the sequence and relative detail of presentation, its literary (especially rhetorical) emphasis, its mnemonic features, and its visual aspects; or to the earlier sources, oral or written, upon which the text draws; or to the manner in which it draws upon those earlier sources, whether by aural transmission, direct incorporation, paraphrase, new redaction, or elaboration; and to its ultimate form as an accumulation of those earlier sources. A text may thus be a composite document, an "archive" of earlier texts – each of which is related to memory in the ways just noted. Moreover, all these aspects of a text may be products of an intentional design – a purpose, perhaps indeed a strategy – aimed at shaping, modifying, interpreting, and sometimes obliterating what is remembered. This design, the intentionality and the presumed future active use

30. Rosamond McKitterick, *The Carolingians and the Written Word* (Cambridge: Cambridge University Press, 1989), especially for the active consultation of written materials in the *mallus*, 60–75.

31. Nancy Partner, "The New Cornificius: Medieval History and the Artifice of Words," in *Classical Rhetoric and Medieval Historiography*, ed. Ernst Breisach (Kalamazoo: Medieval Institute Publications, 1985), 5–59, at 16–17, 22–24; Górecki, "Rhetoric," 263, 265; most recently, Buc, *Dangers*, especially 9–10, 156, 248–49.

expressed by the text, is exactly what I am calling the text's agency. The *Henryków Book* reflects, and expresses, agency in that sense. In order to illustrate this proposition in depth, let me situate the *Book* in context of its genre, its authorship, and several areas of reality with which it engages, and which it was evidently designed to affect.

2 Purpose, genre, and structure of the Henryków Book

The purpose of the history of the Henryków monastery is quite straightforward, and is explicitly identified by its two identifiable authors.[32] The narrative was written specifically in order to serve the monks as a source of reliable knowledge against current or potential enemies.[33] What is considerably more complicated is the genre of which this particular history is an instance. Like other medieval historical writings, the *Henryków Book* seamlessly incorporates several types of historical prose. It is a local chronicle – that is, a description of a sequence of past events, chronologically arranged, and spanning several generations.[34] It pertains specifically to a monastery, and is therefore a monastic chronicle. It concerns one particular type of monastery, an individual Cistercian community. Thus, it fits into a long tradition of Cistercian historiography extending back to the foundation story of Cîteaux and of the Cistercian Order, elaborated continuously since the first years of the twelfth century.[35]

The *Book* is also a monastic cartulary, that is, a transcription of charters issued to the monks of Henryków by the dukes of Silesia, the bishops of Wrocław, and other authors, intended as a convenient source of access to those documents.[36]

32. For the question of the *Book's* authorship, nn. 47–59 below.

33. See nn. 62–64 below.

34. Elisabeth M. C. van Houts, *Local and Regional Chronicles*, Typologie des sources du moyen âge occidental 74 (Turnhout: Brepols, 1995), 14.

35. For monastic and Cistercian historiography, see Bernard Guenée, *Histoire et culture historique dans l'Occident médiéval* (Paris: Aubier Montaigne, 1980), 46–58, especially 47. Two superb treatments of the Cistercian sub-genre of medieval monastic historiography, in one region of medieval Europe, are Derek Baker, "The Genesis of English Cistercian Chronicles: The Foundation History of Foutains Abbey," *Analecta Cisterciensia* 25 (1969), 14–41, and 31 (1975), 179–212, and Freeman, *Narratives.*

36. For cartularies, see *Les cartulaires: Actes de la Table Ronde organisée par l'Ecole nationale des chartes et le G.D.R. 121 du C.N.R.S. (Paris, 5–7 décembre 1991)*, ed. Olivier Guyotjeannin, Laurent Morelle, and Michel Parisse (Paris: École des Chartes, 1993); Olivier Guyotjeannin, Jacques Pycke, and Benoît-Michel Tock, *La diplomatique médiévale* (Turnhout: Brepols, 1993), 273, 277–81; David Walker, "The Organization of Material in Medieval Cartularies," in *The Study of Medieval Records: Essays in Honour of Kathleen Major*, ed. D. A. Bullough and R. L. Storey (Oxford: Clarendon Press, 1971), 132–50; the range of format and content surveyed in G. R. C. Davies, *Medieval Cartularies of Great Britain: A Short Catalogue* (London: Longman, 1958). For the *Henryków Book* as a cartulary, see Józef Matuszewski, *Najstarsze polskie zdanie prozaiczne: zdanie henrykowskie i jego tło historyczne* [The oldest Polish

It is a rather particular type of a cartulary: the charters transcribed in it are embedded within an extensive historical narrative, and so we have here what medievalists interchangeably call a "historical cartulary," a "cartulary-chronicle," or something equivalent in different languages, always suggesting generic hybridity.[37] Moreover, the *Henryków Book* is a *liber memorandorum* – a "book of things to be remembered" – by which is meant a historical narrative written for the specific purpose of enabling its readers (or listeners) to confront adversity by informing them of important events, circumstances, and relationships, and of their implications.[38] Finally, it is a *liber traditionum* (or *donationum*) – a "book of conveyances" (or "gifts"), that is, a systematic record of landed acquistions by its holder, in this case a monastery.[39]

These classifications of genre vary in importance, depending on one's perspective. Some historians today question the value of these kinds of taxonomies altogether, and emphasize other explanatory features of particular texts – their contexts, for example.[40] This intuitive distrust of classification reflects, I think, a strong reaction to the exaggerated status of taxonomy as a mode of conceptualizing many kinds of historical phenomena, not limited to written sources.[41] Despite this caution, categorization remains important, though for more modest reasons. The type of writing about the past which a given historical work repre-

sentence in prose: the sentence of Henryków and its historical background] (Wrocław: Zakład Narodowy im. Ossolińskich, 1981), 14, n. 40.

37. For this kind of hybrid document, encompassing historical narration and charter transcriptions, see Guyotjeannin, Pycke, and Tock, *La diplomatique*, 276, 278; Guenée, *Histoire et culture*, 34; and the classic article by Jean-Philippe Genet, "Cartulaires, registres et histoire: l'exemple anglais," in *Le métier d'historien au moyen âge: Études sur l'historiographie médiévale*, ed. Bernard Guenée (Paris: Publications de la Sorbonne, 1977), 95–138.

38. For *libri memorandorum*, see Górecki, "Rhetoric," 265, nn. 20–21; Michael Clanchy, *From Memory to Written Record: England 1066–1307* (2nd ed., Oxford: Blackwell, 1993), 133, 147, 171–172; Geary, *Phantoms*, 84–87; Frederic William Maitland, "Introduction," in *Liber Memorandorum Ecclesie de Bernewelle*, ed. John W. Clark (Cambridge: Cambridge University Press, 1907), xliii–lxiii; Rodney H. Hilton, "Introduction," in *The Stoneleigh Leger Book*, ed. R. Hilton (Oxford: Dugdale Society/Oxford University Press, 1960), ix–lvii; *The Chronicle of Battle Abbey*, ed. and trans. Eleanor Searle (Oxford: Clarendon Press, 1980), 1–29.

39. For *libri traditionum* or *donationum*, see Guyotjeannin, Pycke, and Tock, *La diplomatique*, 272–273.

40. Felice Lifshitz, "Beyond Positivism and Genre: 'Hagiographical' Texts as Historical Narratives," *Viator* 25 (1994), 95–113.

41. From my perspective, the most important phenomenon long affected by taxonomy as the principal source of explanation and coherence is agrarian history, in which a rigid classification of settlement into particular types was the decisive mode of making sense of peasant communities and the rural economy in different regions of medieval Europe – with particular emphasis on the European "East," and on the putative contrast in these regards between the Slavs and the Germans; see on this Górecki, *Economy*, 33, n. 23; Górecki, "Medieval 'East Colonization,'" 28–29; and in general Miller and Hatcher, *Medieval England*, 87.

sents tells us quite a bit about the intellectual, cultural, and educational profile of its author and its audience. This knowledge is especially important from the perspective of the three big questions noted at the outset of this essay. For the study of the meanings of "Europe," its "frontiers," its "making," its permanent diversity, and so forth, it is very important that the *Book* belongs in the historiography extending back to Cîteaux in early twelfth-century France; and that, at the same time, it reflects major variations specific to western Poland or eastern Germany one full century later. Genre remains important as an aspect of those big historiographical issues, or problems, which the *Henryków Book* illustrates.

Genre also mattered to the historians active during the Middle Ages – in this case, the authors of the *Book* itself – but it mattered to them for a different reason. They drew on all the genres of historical writing just noted, quite freely and interchangeably, and were not (or at least not evidently) concerned about the taxonomy of their work as we might be today – that is, for the same intellectual reasons. However, this does not mean that they were unaware of generic classification, or or that they were being entirely eclectic: the *Henryków Book* was clearly designed as a particular kind of work, one which we now classify in terms of these several categories – as a rather particular instance of a monastic chronicle, a local chronicle, a cartulary, a treatise of counsel on the law and on matters to be remembered, and so forth. In fact, the *Book* is itself a good example of a similar trait of each of the genres which it embodies. It is quite clear that what we today call cartularies, "historical cartularies," chronicles, "books of things to be remembered," and the others, overlap closely with one another, in terms of substance and arrangement. The entire typology is a flexible spectrum of possibilities rather than a set of discrete categories.[42]

For medievalists (including the present translator) a minor result of this generic complexity has been a search for the best name for this particular source; thus, the *Henryków Book* has variously been called, in the different scholarly vernaculars of today, a "chronicle," a "history," and a "book."[43] Having myself varied in terminology, I now refer to it with that last word, partly because of the authors' own, repeated references to it as a *liber* and a *libellus*, and partly in order to remain consistent with the conventional terminological usage by those Polish and German historians who have written most extensively about this source.

Considered as an example of any one of the genres of historical writing it combines, the *Book* is relatively simple in terms of structure. It consists, in its

---

42. A point most thoroughly demonstrated in work concerning cartularies; see recently Guyotjeannin, Pycke, and Tock, *La diplomatique*, 272–81. Earlier excellent treatments of generic variety include Genet, "Cartulaires," 97–102, 108–11, 113–14, 118–26, and (in their entirety) Walker, "Organization," and Davis, *Medieval Cartularies*.

43. The best formal analysis of this source, and guide to the its classification and related issues, remains Matuszewski, *Najstarsze*, 13–14, 21–29.

entirety, of two sections, to which the text refers as "books" (*libri*),[44] and, as a brief appendix, of a list of the bishops of Wrocław.[45] The manuscript containing the two sections and the bishops' list also include occasional supplementary notes on the margins, or on empty portions of folio, written in an early-fourteenth-century cursive hand.[46] These notes are so similar to the structure of the *Book* itself that historians interested in this source have tended to view them as an integral part of that source. The *Book*'s first portion was composed in or soon after 1268, the bishops' list in or soon after 1276, and the second portion in or soon after 1310. The second portion is explicitly a continuation of the first.

An intriguing issue raised by texts that, like the *Henryków Book*, combine several genres, is the identity (and the meaning) of their author.[47] By author I mean the person, or the group, responsible for the text's content, composition, and expression in written form.[48] This working definition immediately raises three ambiguities. The first concerns that person, or group. On occasion, his, her, or their exact identity is clear from the sources themselves, as happens when we have an autograph, or an explicit self-identification in the first person, or some other unmistakeable attribution of the text's conception, composition, or expression in writing. However, the *Henryków Book* is not that kind of document. Right on its face, the materials that make it up, and the codex into which those materials are transcribed, reflect what must have been a chronologically drawn-out sequence of composition and writing, by a series of persons whom we cannot identify today – apart from two exceptions, to be discussed momentarily.

The second ambiguity concerns the text. That word may refer to the product in its entirety (in our case, the *Henryków Book* in its full, fourteenth-century redaction), but also to the individual components from which that product had been created

44. Chapters 1–123 and 124–96, respectively. The words for the major sub-units of the *Henryków Book* – especially its constituent two *libri* – may be confusing when rendered as "books." Therefore, here and below, I refer to the two halves of the *Book* as "portions." .

45. Chapters 197–211.

46. A short description of urban revenues, written on an empty portion of a folio, at Grodecki, *Liber* (1991), after 225, fol. xxiii^v, and, in the translation, following Chapter 111; a supplementary narrative passage written on the lower margin of Grodecki, *Liber* (1991), after 225, fol. xxxix^r, and, in the edition, bisecting Chapter 170 – presented in this translation at Chapter 170, n. 90. For further discussion of the codex itself, including the implications of the codex itself for the problem of authorship, see below, Section 7, *Transmission and selection of the sources.*

47. For the difficulty (at first glance, the "absurdity") of identifying an author of a cartulary, see Patrick Geary, "*Auctor* et *auctoritas* dans les cartulaires du haut Moyen Âge," in *Auctor et auctoritas: Invention et conformisme dans l'écriture médiévale*, ed. Michel Zimmermann (Paris: École des Chartes, 2001), 61–72.

48. This working definition is indebted, in adapted form, to the criteria for establishing medieval authorship in Alastair J. Minnis, *Medieval Theory of Authorship: Scholastic Literary Attitudes in the Later Middle Ages* (London: Scholars Press, 1984), 5, 28–29, 75–84, and Zimmermann, *Auctor*. For the *Henryków Book*, see Piotr Górecki, "Rhetoric."

at different, and to us largely inaccessible, moments. Such components include the *Book*'s two constituent "books," the bishops' list, and the contemporary marginal notations, but, as we will see, there are other clearly identifiable, discrete components. Each component raises independently the earlier problem of the person or persons responsible for its composition and expression in written form. Moreover, the same problem is raised by the placement of the components in a particular sequence. To us, that placement is most directly (albeit imperfectly) accessible through the *Book*'s manuscript; but, like other elements of authorship, that placement may considerably antedate the making of the manuscript, and so the manuscript may be one step in an ongoing process of new presentation and rearrangement. Finally, because the *Book* consists of discrete components joined together deliberately and over time, it is, among other things, a medieval "archive." That fact, too, raises questions of authorship. As with other medieval "archives," someone, or some group, has in fact assembled it, and thus bears the responsibility for placing it in the sequence in which it is arranged.

The third ambiguity of authorship concerns that responsibility. This is especially problematic for the medieval period, when the relationship between the text and the identity of its actual creator (or creators) was very different than has been the case thereafter.[49] The range of intervention by the creator (or the creators) toward the subject of the text, or toward the earlier texts used in its making, varied greatly. These interventions included – in different combinations – transcription, abbreviation, alteration of sequence and other elements of arrangement, amplification and explanation, and the use of those many literary, compositional, exhortatory, and other devices which I noted above in context of the text's agency.[50] Therefore, the exact sense in which the person who, or the group which, performed one or more of these functions is responsible for the resulting text, also varied.

The *Henryków Book* poses all three ambiguities of authorship. Yet, on this subject, it offers a rare moment of simple clarity. This occurs in two passages, each of which identifies one specific author. These identifications constitute our two exceptions to the overall absence of specifiable authors of the *Book* or of its components. They appear in two phrases of the preamble to the second portion of the *Book*.[51] In the first phrase, the author of the second portion identifies the person who "wrote" the first portion as Peter, the monastery's third abbot. This presumably means that Peter composed, and expressed in writing, that text with which the continuator began his own work. The continuator's attribution is our sole explicit identification of the author of the first portion of the *Book*. I should stress that that first portion itself – "written" by Abbot Peter – never raises the subject of its own authorship, let alone attributes that authorship to anyone.

---

49. Michel Zimmermann, "Ouverture du colloque," in Zimmermann, *Auctor*, 7–14.
50. See nn. 20–31 above.
51. Chapter 126.

In the second phrase, situated toward the end of the preamble, the author of the later portion refers to himself, in the first person, as Abbot Peter's continuator. However, in contrast to Peter, he does not present himself as having engaged in any concrete activity, such as writing. He merely notes in general terms that he had "set out" to continue Peter's work. Moreover, he does not refer to himself by name, or by any other specific trait, monastic office for example. Instead, consistently with medieval conventions of authorial modesty, he refers to himself only as a lesser member of the Henryków community. This, too, is the sole identification, anywhere in the *Book*, of the later author. He emerges as an anonymous monk of Henryków and Peter's continuator, which is how I shall refer to him in the rest of this essay.[52] The double attribution – to Abbot Peter, and to his own self – made by this anonymous monk, is our most straightforward clue to the *Book*'s authorship.

Medievalists have widely accepted the continuator's indentification of Abbot Peter as the earlier author, for several reasons.[53] First, there is simply no reason to doubt the attribution. Peter is independently documented in ducal and epis-copal charters contemporary with the presumed period of preparation, or the writing, of the *Book*.[54] Second, the earlier portion of the *Book*, and the more detailed passages placed in the list of the bishops of Wrocław, repeatedly men-tion a monk named Peter, who advanced from the position of the monastery's cellarer to the office of abbot between the 1250s and 1263, and was during this period a frequent and important actor.[55] These narrations – presumably written by himself – always identify Peter in the third person, by name, by office, and by other attributes. Viewed cumulatively, they seem to be a story of the author's own self – an embedded autobiography. Thereafter, Peter's continuator lists him, by name, among the original, founding group of monks who migrated into Henryków between 1222 and 1227.[56]

Third, the earlier portion of the *Henryków Book*, and the bishops' list, share elements of style, purpose, rhetorical development, and explicit message that recur within those two texts, but that do not appear in the second portion of the *Book*;[57] and that cohere with a considerable degree of inner logic. I do not wish

52. However, with increasing confidence, Polish historians think that this was a later abbot of Henryków, also named Peter, who appears at Chapters 170, 179 and at Supple-mentary Documents no. 30, 32; Rościsław Żerelik, "*Ego minimum fratrum*: w kwestii autorstwa drugiej części 'Księgi Henrykowskiej'" [*Ego minimum fratrum*: concerning the authorship of the second portion of the *Henryków Book*], *Nasza Przeszłość* 83 (1994), 63–75; Stanisław Kozak, Agata Taras-Tomczyk, and Marek L. Wójcik, "Henryków," in *Monasticon Cisterciense Poloniae*, ed. Andrzej Marek Wyrwa, Jerzy Strzelczyk, and Krzysztof Kaczmarek, 2 vols. (Poznań: Wydawnictwo Poznańskie, 1999), 2:64–78, at 66.

53. Matuszewski, *Najstarsze*, 21–29.

54. Chapter 205; Supplementary Documents no. 6–21.

55. Chapter 69, 105, 111, 114, 116, 205, 208.

56. Chapter 126.

57. I refer here to the type of contrast noted in Górecki, "Rhetoric," 266, n. 24.

to overstate; as we will momentarily note, the earlier portion of the *Book* is itself internally quite varied. Yet, that variation is overarched, indeed framed, by those common compositional elements. Moreover, the same literary and compositional elements appear in the more substantial narrative portions of the bishops' list. Therefore, the earlier portion of the *Book*, together with the list, reflect an apparent (that is, a highly plausible) purposeful design, a trait that is at least consistent with a strong authorial presence and intervention. Even if no author were actually identified by the text iself, we would have good reason to think of a specific creative presence behind it. To return to the theme of agency: considered as a text, the portion attributed to Peter and the bishops' list reflects an "authorial function."[58] This feature of the text further substantiates the accuracy of the attribution of authorship to Abbot Peter.

The stylistic and substantive similarities between the earlier part of the *Book* and the bishops' list have led most historians to identify Abbot Peter as the author of that list as well.[59] Therefore – summoning at long last that unfashionable ally, common sense – I squarely accept Peter's authorship of the first half of the *Book*, and, in all likelihood, of the bishops' list; and of his continuator's authorship of the second half of the narrative portion. Of course, even assuming that it is accurate, neither attribution fully resolves the three ambiguities of authorship noted earlier. However, at the very least, we have access to two persons responsible for the shaping of the text at two specific moments of its (presumably much longer) history.

The two portions, or *libri*, are similar to each other in terms of basic arrangement. They are also internally uniform, that is, consist of thematically and compositionally similar units. Each *liber* opens with a preamble, where its author identifies as his basic aim providing the monks with a reliable record of the monastery's acquisitions, and, more broadly, protecting the monastery from oblivion and related dangers. Thereafter, the bulk of each portion is a series of histories, of variable length, of specific places, or holdings, that the monks of Henryków acquired into their estate between the monastery's foundation in the third decade of the thirteenth century and about 1310. The authors typically refer to these histories as "accounts" of (*rationes*), or as "treatises" about (*tractatus*), the individual holdings.[60] The holdings themselves are identified by place names. As reflected in the record, they included a wide variety of settlement, population, and patterns of land use: ranging from individual households and hamlets all the

---

58. Zimmermann, "Ouverture," 7.

59. Matuszewski, *Najstarsze*, 21, 84.

60. And thus – as above to avoid confusion in English concerning the subdivisions of the *Book* – from now on in my own prose I generally refer to the individual *rationes* as "accounts," including the use of quotation marks, but not as "treatises," since that word – acceptable as it is in the text of the source itself – does not seem to work very happily in today's analytical English prose.

way to substantial villages; and encompassing meadow, arable, forest, waterways, notable trees, and other ecological features.

Each "account" is a very local, but also a complicated, history of the following subjects: (1) the original possessors of the holding in question, and its subsequent inhabitants and neighbors, during the period antedating its inclusion into the estate of the monastery; (2) the circumstances of that inclusion: its acquisition, its formal conveyance, the relevant activities, and the modes of prevention or settlement of property dispute; and (3) the persons who either participated in, or were affected by, the acquisition, the conveyance, and the potential or actual dispute. Each such story taken separately, and of course all of them taken together, shed fascinating light on the economic, ecological, demographic, tenurial, ethnographic, and social structure of the individual holdings, their immediate surroundings, and the region in which the monastery was situated – plus, less directly, medieval Silesia and the Piast duchies in their entirety. This wealth of information has led to a certain interesting tension between the *Book*'s manifest purpose and the uses to which historians put it today. The *Book* is a defensive legal treatise, written for the monks' benefit. But it is structured around very specific histories of dozens of places and people, and of hundreds of discrete transactions, and so today conveys an exceptionally focused story of a local medieval society in transition.

Although the primary organization of the history is geographic rather than chronological, the *Book* is very much a history. There is much continuity between the "accounts" of particular holdings (including the actors associated with them), both within each portion of the *Book*, and across the two portions. Moreover, much of the *Book* is structured around overarching chronological schemes that place the individual "accounts" in an overall narrative framework.[61] The "accounts" themselves vary widely in terms of the time span they cover and of the number of generations of possessors and other persons they record. The earliest period to which some "accounts" refer is the mid-twelfth century; the latest is the first decade of the fourteenth century. Within this period, some "accounts" span only a few years, others a better part of one century. However, no "account" spans the entire period covered by the *Book* in its entirety; that is, no narrative about one specific locality stretches all the way from the twelfth century to the fourteenth.

Despite their close relationship to one another, and the similarity in their arrangement, the two "books" are in many respects distinct works, reflecting considerable differences in arrangement, literary technique, historical subject matter, and, perhaps, individual authorial profile. Abbot Peter was much more explicitly concerned than was his continuator about the threat of oblivion and its consequences for the monastery's security. He was also much more emphatic (and to a modern reader repetitive) in his identifications of the exact purpose of

---

61. Such schemes are especially important in Abbot Peter's section of the *Book*; they revolve around the year 1241, the Mongol invasion of Silesia, and the difference between the pre-Mongol past and the narrator's own defined by that year and its events; see nn. 85–88.

his work, in the preamble and throughout the individual "accounts." Although the continuator noted in several places that he shared Peter's concerns, the second "book" is, relatively speaking, unencumbered and unproblematic. Therefore, it is Peter rather than his continuator who is our main informant about the reasons for the *Book*'s compilation, about the political and legal contexts that lend cumulative coherence to its individual "accounts," and about genre and the other textual issues which the *Book* raises.

Abbot Peter identified two closely related purposes for his work: defense of the monastery against proprietary claims by its lay neighbors; and maintenance of a particular relationship between the monastery and the dukes of Silesia.[62] He feared two kinds of threatening proprietary claims: by heirs of those past possessors from whom the monastery had acquired its holdings; and by descendants of other persons, who had in the past affected the security of the monks' possessions in a variety of other ways. The former kind of proprietary claim was based on inheritance, and was, in its broad outlines, similar to legal challenges besetting ecclesiastics throughout medieval Europe.[63] The latter kind of proprietary claim was based on several other grounds.[64]

In order to secure his monastery against both kinds of proprietary threat, Abbot Peter sought to associate the monastery's foundation, endowment, and continuous existence with one especially important actor: the duke of Silesia. This ruler belonged to a branch of the large Piast dynasty that governed the Polish principalities between the tenth century and 1370. Within that dynasty, and within its provincial offshoot in Silesia, Peter was especially concerned with one rather small descent group (see Genealogical Chart). That descent group consisted of five dukes, whose reigns spanned the outer limits of the stories Peter narrated: Bolesław I the Tall (1163–1201), his son Henry I the Bearded (1201–38), the latter's son Henry II the Pious (1238–41), and finally Henry II's two oldest sons, Henry III the White and Bolesław II the Bald, who, between them, ruled portions of the duchy between 1241 and 1278. Other dukes, within

---

62. Górecki, "Politics," 25; Górecki, "Rhetoric," 261–62, 265; Matuszewski, *Najstarsze*, 66–80. For legends and other constructions of the past created in order to enhance institutional security in the present, see Amy G. Remensnyder, *Remembering Kings Past: Monastic Foundation Legends in Medieval Southern France* (Ithaca: Cornell University Press, 1995).

63. For Polish evidence, and broader comparative literature, see Piotr Górecki, "*Ad Controversiam Reprimendam*: Family Groups and Dispute Prevention in Medieval Poland, c. 1200," *Law and History Review* 14 (1996), 213–43, at 217–23, and Górecki, "A Historian as a Source of Law: Abbot Peter of Henryków and the Invocation of Norms in Medieval Poland, c. 1200–1270," *Law and History Review* 18 (2000), 479–523.

64. These other grounds included, among others, raw use of force, skillful use of political maneuver, and tenurial modifications of "German law," or of service to dukes and to other powerholders; Chapters 45–49, 51–57, 74–75, 103–04, 106, 108–11, 154–56, 158–59, 161–62.

and outside the same descent group, also appear in Peter's story, but these five were especially important.

The political history of the Piasts, within Silesia and throughout Poland, is a dauntingly complicated subject.[65] Yet, viewed from Abbot Peter's perspective, it is considerably simplified. From that perspective, the precise significance of the duke was his role as a source of security (broadly defined) for the Henryków monastery against those dangers to which the *Henryków Book* was a response. A good duke, in Peter's view, was a willing and an effective source of that security; a bad duke either refused or failed to provide it. Peter consistently portrayed the five dukes noted above, and their descendants, as the monastery's "advocates," holders of legitimate "authority" (*auctoritas*) over its "foundation," its friends and protectors – in short, as his community's legitimate and exclusive patrons; or, on the other hand, as failures in these roles. Peter's main exemplar of good rule was Henry I the Bearded, while his avatar of bad rule was Henry's oldest grandson Bolesław II the Bald. Peter's repetitiveness and stridency about the dynasty's specifically protective role toward his community suggest that, at the time he wrote, ducal patronage over the monastery was intensely contested, and that his portion of the *Book* was an intervention in that contest.[66] This suggestion is borne out by contemporary documents about this particular subject, some of which are included below,[67] and by Peter's own involvement on the monastery's behalf during times of political stress involving the Piast dukes within the duchy of Silesia and beyond.[68]

Nothing quite like this appears, as a subject or as a theme, in the continuator's portion of the *Book*. In addition, our two authors differ in what might be called the historical depth of their narrations, and in the types of sources they use to gain access to the past. Abbot Peter's portion is more retroactive than his continuator's. Peter attempted to reconstruct the history of each of the holdings that made up the core of the monastic estate in his own time, the 1260s, as far back as he was able to. Several of his histories are attempts to recover origins – of the holding themselves, of their former inhabitants, of the surrounding ecology – going back to a time immemorial, antedating any particular chronological or temporal framework.[69] The earliest specific event to which Peter referes that is datable (although it is not explicitly dated, or otherwise chronologically located, by Peter himself) is the foundation of the Cistercian monastery at Lubiąż

---

65. More on this subject below, in section 5, pp. 57–73. For the genealogy of the Piasts in general, and of the Silesian branch in particular, see Hoffmann, *Land, Liberties, and Lordship*, 16–19; Norman Davies, *God's Playground: A History of Poland* (New York: Columbia University Press, 1982), 1:62–67, 70–75; Jerzy Topolski, *An Outline History of Poland* (Warsaw: Interpress, 1986), 38–44; Górecki, *Economy*, 14–15.

66. Górecki, "Politics," 33; Górecki, "Interpreter," 275–78.

67. Supplementary Documents no. 1–7.

68. Chapters 69, 105, 111, 114, 116, 126, 203, 205, 208.

69. Górecki, "Rhetoric," 275–76.

by Duke Bolesław the Tall, a process that began shortly after that duke's succession to office in 1163, and culminated with his foundation charter of 1175.[70]

Thereafter, most of the histories Peter narrated in their entirety, and most of the datable (or explicitly dated) events in those histories, occur between the second and the late fifth decades of the thirteenth century – in other words, about ten to fifty years into his own past.[71] The continuator's portion is more contemporaneous with the time of his writing. Apart from his reference in the preamble to the year 1227 as the date of the monks' arrival at Henryków,[72] and from his passing mentions of Dukes Henry II the Pious, Bolesław II the Bald, and Henry III the White,[73] the continuator was not concerned with beginnings or origins. Moreover, the histories he narrated, and most of the datable, or explicitly dated, events that make up those histories, occurred between 1278 and 1310.[74] That latter date is the final year explicitly recorded in the *Book*, and presumably (though not certainly) falls within the present, or the very recent past, of Abbot Peter's continuator.

Abbot Peter drew the knowledge for his portion of the *Book* from a wider spectrum of sources than his continuator did. Oral and remembered knowledge were especially important to him, especially concerning those histories, or fragments of histories, that extended deeply into the past and into the time immemorial. Peter drew the earliest history of what later became the monastic estate from the memory of persons who were one or two generations removed from the earliest inhabitants of the region, and who survived into his own lifetime. In an exceptionally interesting passage, he identified as one such informant the old and totally disabled peasant Kwiecik, who spent more than twenty years in residence at the monastic cloister, and, over that substantial period, divulged to the monks of Henryków (presumably including the young Peter himself) an extensive knowledge about early local history.[75] The abbot also relied on the opinion or belief about past events and relationships held by the monks themselves, by secular and ecclesiastical neighbors of the monastery, and by other groups in the locality and the region. He drew on that opinion and belief,

---

70. Chapters 10, 82, 113.

71. The date expressed numerically is 1222 (Chapter 10), but the circumstances narrated in the story where it appears extend back at least to 1202, and implicitly much earlier. The latest date expressed numerically is 1259 (Chapter 73), although another story, noted by subject but without explicit dates, refers either to 1237, or to 1263 (Chapter 37).

72. Chapters 125–26.

73. Chapters 127 (nn. 11–12), 160.

74. Apart from the preamble cited above, the earliest date expressed numerically is 1278 (Chapter 147), while the earliest event mentioned explicitly, but not expressly dated, is 1241 (Chapter 127). The latest date expressed numerically is 1310 (Chapters 185, 189, 191), to which should be added several expressions of the almost-contemporaneous year 1309 (Chapters 177, 179, 183).

75. Chapter 83; see Górecki, "Communities," 140–42, 144–46; Górecki, "Local Society;" Matuszewski, *Najstarsze*, 46.

and he explicitly responded to them.[76] Thus, on the one hand, he used reputation and opinion long held in the surrounding society as an important source of his knowledge, and, on the other, he sought to affect or change that reputation by means of his work.[77] This is the sense in which Abbot Peter's portion of the *Henryków Book* is a text closely engaged with memory.

In all these respects, his continuator differed sharply from Peter. On the sources of his knowledge, he was altogether silent. Whereas for Peter this was an important subject, for his colleague the subject did not even exist. There is one apparent exception: in a few cases, the continuator continued a history Peter had begun, thus implicitly drawing at least its early phases from his predecessor. However, these are not examples of recourse to external, oral or remembered, evidence, so the exception is illusory. The later author relied in constructing his work on charters much more extensively than Peter did – although, likewise in contrast to Peter, he did not address the subject of their value, or the logic of their use. Both in their number, and as a proportion of the text, ducal charters (and occasional supporting documents from officials, judges, and parties to specific transactions) are far more prominent in his text than they had been in Peter's. And, again in contrast to Peter, the author's own comments and interpretations are quite terse.

Utterly absent from the continuator's work is either explicit reliance on memory, or any concern with its significance, political impact, or shaping. Unlike Peter, the continuator simply did not refer to opinion and belief – threatening or otherwise – about past or ongoing facts, or relationships, relevant to the monastery's landholding. Nor did he seek to affect such opinion or belief, or point out to his brethren that his text was intended to save them from difficulty, oblivion, inaccurate recollection, and so forth. How do we explain this difference? First, it may reflect a shift, in Silesia and elsewhere in Piast Poland, from memory to written record.[78] Second, Peter's continuator may have been satisfied by the manner in which his predecessor had dealt with apprehensions about the security of the monastery's estate, and considered Peter's narrative an adequate source of knowledge concerning the broad dangers that had worried the abbot. Third, the selection and presentation of the sources, and the composition of the resulting narrative, many have depended upon authorial decisions – made, above all, by our

76. For treatments of groups and particular persons as sources of knowledge on which Abbot Peter drew, and to which he responded, see: Matuszewski, *Najstarsze*, 44–46; Górecki, "Politics," 43; Górecki, "Historian," 482–84; Górecki, "Rhetoric," 266–67, 287–93; Górecki, "Interpreter," 275–80, 284–85, 287–88.

77. For more on the interrelated subjects of Abbot Peter's use of the past and his access to oral, remembered, and written sources, see the articles by Górecki cited above, and Matuszewski, *Najstarsze*, 37–50, 81–92.

78. Clanchy, *From Memory*; Anna Adamska, "'From Memory to Written Record' in the Periphery of Medieval Latinitas: The Case of Poland in the Eleventh and Twelfth Centuries," in *Charters and the Use of the Written Word in Medieval Society*, ed. Karl Heidecker (Turnhout: Brepols, 2000), 83–100.

two expressly identified authors, and perhaps by those unidentified others who may also have been responsible for the making of the text and its components.

The two portions of the *Book* also differ from one another in terms of their overall structure, and of the particulars of the individual histories included in that structure; that latter difference is further complicated by the considerable variation in the particulars comprising each individual history. In terms of overall structure, the second portion of the *Book* is relatively simple. Here, the seven "accounts" that follow the preamble are not grouped, or classified, in any way. In contrast, Peter himself grouped the *Book*'s individual histories into two sections. That division occurs after the conclusion of the "account" of Głębowice, with a major encomium to the deceased Duke Henry II, a promise of transition in subject matter, and the introduction of a separate numeration of the remaining histories, beginning with the "account" of Schönwald.[79]

Moreover, each of the resulting two divisions of Peter's work consists of two rather different components. Although these components are not explicitly separated from one another by the devices just noted, they are very dissimilar as . texts. The section that precedes the division consists of the long, substantial, and highly crafted "account" of the monastery's foundation,[80] and, thereafter, of the histories of individual localities. The section that follows the division includes only two histories, of Schönwald and of Brukalice,[81] each of which is likewise substantial, highly crafted, and complicated in subject matter – and, in terms of the particulars narrated, quite different from the other. The "account" of Schönwald concerns above all the expansion of settlement within a region that was, from the monks' own perspective, a "frontier."[82] The "account" of Brukalice opens with its own, quite explicit, statement of purpose, in which Abbot Peter reiterated one of his specific aims – namely, shielding his monastery from property claims by difficult neighbors, here by one especially troublesome family group.[83] It closes with a detailed genealogy of that family group and, with a history of the monastery's piecemeal acquisitions of that group's landed holdings. That latter fusion of genealogy and property is a narrative model elaborately developed by Peter's continuator in several "accounts," best exemplified in the history of the old Polish hamlet, Raczyce.[84]

In contrast to his continuator, Abbot Peter framed much of his history in terms of one overarching chronological schema.[85] Throughout his portion of the *Book*,

79. Chapters 91–93, rubric before Chapter 94.
80. Chapters 2–27; see Górecki, "Rhetoric," 272–73, 279–88.
81. Chapters 94–111 and 112–23, respectively.
82. For Schönwald as a terrain of that subject, nn. 219–20, 239 below.
83. Chapter 112.
84. Chapters 121–23 (Brukalice), 165–85 (Raczyce).
85. On Abbot Peter's uses of "the pagans," see: Matuszewski, *Najstarsze*, 29, 39; Górecki, "Rhetoric," 266, 269, 274–78; Górecki, "An Interpreter of Law and Power in a Region of Medieval Poland: Abbot Peter of Henryków and his *Book*," in *Building*

he placed particular events, relationships, or aspects of social reality, either "before" or "after the pagans."[86] This was a very exact chronological marker; "the pagans" were the Mongols, or Tatars, who invaded Silesia in 1241, and killed Duke Henry II the Pious in the disastrous battle of Legnica.[87] Peter considered those two events as the great watershed in the past upon which he was reflecting. They constituted the sharpest demarcation point between the times of good and bad rule – or what he repeatedly calls the age of the "old dukes," and the period of their inadequate, "youthful" successors. They separated a period, in the deep past, of a generalized trust and transcendent justice, from a period stretching into his own present, and defined by conflict and disorder. "The pagans" served Peter as the specific explanation for unjust seizures by the monastery's powerful neighors, and, in one story, for the monks' loss of a charter concerning a property transaction.[88] Finally, "the pagans" served Peter as the benchmark for Duke Henry II's most memorable trait, namely, his heroic death at their hands. Peter's continuator, too, mentioned the Mongols – as "Tatars," not as "pagans" – and recalled Henry the Pious as their victim,[89] but he did so in only one passage, did not return to them elsewhere, and so did not use the events of 1241 as material for explanations, exhortations, or other messages to the monastic community.

In addition to the first portion of the *Book*, Peter compiled the list of bishops of Wrocław.[90] This list is also translated here.[91] Lists of bishops or abbots are a frequent supplementary component of medieval cartularies, histories, and other genres of writing about the past.[92] They also constitute an important genre of ecclesiastical record-keeping in the cathedral and monastic communities of medieval Silesia. Several lists of bishops of Wrocław were fashioned into final redactions during the later thirteenth and the fourteenth centuries.[93] Such lists are arranged by name, in a straightforward chronological sequence. They begin with the founding bishop of a particular see, and culminate during, or close to, the period of their final compilation. The bishops' names are usually glossed by

---

Legitimacy: Political Discourses and Forms of Legitimation in Medieval Societies, ed. Isabel Alfonso, Hugh Kennedy, and Julio Escalona (Leiden: Brill, 2004), 263–89, at 266–67. Compare the analogous functions of the historical-legendary works analyzed by Remensnyder, *Remembering*, 1–7, 215–18.

86. Chapters 15 (n. 21), 16, 28, 44, 47, 54, 61, 71–72, 74, 80, 83–84, 89–93, 98, 100, 102–04, 107, 111.

87. Tomasz Jasiński, *Przerwany hejnał* [The interrupted bugle call] (Kraków: Krajowa Agencja Wydawnicza, 1988), 56–61; Stanisław Kałużyński, *Dawni Mongołowie* [The former Mongols] (Warsaw: Państwowy Instytut Wydawniczy, 1983), 41.

88. Chapter 90.

89. Chapter 127, n. 11.

90. For Peter's authorship of the list, n. 59 above.

91. Chapters 197–211.

92. For examples, see Genet, "Cartulaires," 98, 100–01, 105.

93. Roman Heck, "The Main Lines of Development of Silesian Medieval Historiography," *Quaestiones Medii Aevi* 2 (1981), 63–87, at 65 (n. 9), 73 (n. 32).

short notes, or by fuller accounts of the deeds of the individual bishops, especially those most important to the ecclesiastical community or milieu where a particular list was produced. Thus, in his list, Abbot Peter commented in detail on Lawrence and Thomas, the two bishops of Wrocław who were particularly important in the foundation and the endowment of his monastery;[94] and he appended his comments with transcriptions of several charters issued for his community by Thomas.[95] He was also attentive to several unusually helpful canons in the Wrocław cathedral chapter.[96] Overall, his comments about this group of clergy make up another detailed local history, similar in its form and emphasis to the "accounts" comprising the *Book* itself.

3 The contexts of power and of writing
Apart from what the two authors actually say on this subject, we have considerable external evidence about the reasons why the *Henryków Book* was composed specifically at the turn of the 1260s and the 1270s, and then again soon after 1310. During these two periods the Henryków monastery seems to have experienced either continued, or renewed, pressure from some of the heirs of those powerful neighbors whose legal claims each author wished to lay to rest. This pressure interacted with transitions in the meaning and the exercise of ducal power, in Silesia and throughout Piast Poland,[97] and thus in the relationship between the dukes and the monastery. Second, the *Book* was composed in the course of another transition, of which it is itself an example, namely a dramatic shift throughout Piast Poland away from oral and remembered toward written forms of authoritative record.

Among the potentially difficult neighbors, Abbot Peter was explicitly concerned about the family that traced its descent to a Czech immigrant, Boguchwał.[98] The concluding story in his narrative is the "account" of Brukalice (see Map 5), this family's former holding, whose central subject is the family's persistent and troublesome claims against the monastery around the mid-thirteenth century.[99] This story is quite distinctive within Peter's work as a whole. It is prefaced by an unusually strong warning to his monks about a threat posed by this kindred; it is situated compositionally rather apart from the rest of the

94. Chapters 198–99.
95. Chapters 201, 207.
96. Chapters 205–06, 208–11.
97. For an overview of the Polish duchies, the Piast dynasty that ruled them between the tenth and the fourteenth centuries, and the significance of Piast politics for the Henryków monastery, nn. 242–47 below.
98. Chapters 113. On the interesting eponym, see Górecki, "*Viator* to *ascriptitius*: Rural Economy, Lordship, and the Origins of Serfdom in Medieval Poland," *Slavic Review* 42 (1983), 14–35, at 22–24, and Gerald Stone, "Honorific Pronominal Address in Polish Before 1600," *Oxford Slavonic Papers*, new series 17 (1984), 45–56, at 46.
99. Chapters 112–23.

narrative; and its tracing of property fragmentation, kinship, and their implications for the monastery is excepionally thorough.[100] The author's concerns with Boguchwał's descendants resonate with a considerable increase in the 1260s and 1270s in the output of detailed ducal charters specifically concerning this kindred and its relationship with the Henryków monastery. Several of these charters are enclosed below.[101]

Similarly, the continuator refers (among other subjects) to successors of actors whom Abbot Peter had previously identified as adversaries, or at least as problematic. Another group of such actors, or of their successors, is documented by charters issued during the years separating Abbot Peter's completion of his portion of the *Book*, and the resumption of the work by his continuator. In addition to the descendants of Boguchwał Brukał, this group of actors includes the descendants of four powerful and important neighbors of the monastery: Albert the Bearded, Peter Stoszowic, Michael Daleborowic, and Stephen Kobylagłowa.[102] This population is further enhanced by the continuator himself, who describes several other kin groups that posed similar difficulties, requiring similar attention. Among the most important were the descendants of John Osina,[103] of Michael Daleborowic,[104] and of the four joint holders of Raczyce: Żupczy, Gniewko Woda, John Rzeźnik, and Cieszko.[105] These individuals and families, and others like them, also elicited a substantial diplomatic output.[106] Collectively, the stories about these descendants nicely exemplify the medieval narrative commonplace of the evil kindred.[107] The recurrence of these concerns implies one strong area of continuity in the issues, difficulties, and relationships of the monastery with its secular neighbors, between the seventh decade of the thirteenth century and the first decade of the fourteenth – a fact that explains the continuator's decision to return to the work begun by Abbot Peter.

Throughout the period spanned by the *Henryków Book*, the monks navigated major transition and fluidity in ducal power, especially in its relationship to its competitors: the autonomous world of knights, peasants, ecclesiastics, and (increasingly) townspeople. The constituent elements of this proposition are the subject of the rest of this essay. At present, let me frame the significance of those elements specifically for the making of the *Book* itself; a significance that is,

100. See nn. 81, 83–84 above.

101. Supplementary Documents no. 19–23.

102. Supplementary Documents no. 8–10, 13–14, 24–27.

103. Chapters 127–31, 133–38.

104. Chapters 186–89.

105. Chapters 165–81, 184–85.

106. See the remainder of Supplementary Documents, sections II and III.

107. Piotr Górecki, "Violence and the Social Order in a Medieval Society: The Evidence from the Henryków Region, ca. 1150–ca. 1300," in *The Man of Many Devices, Who Wandered Full Many Ways: Festschrift in Honor of János M. Bak*, ed. Balázs Nagy and Marcell Sebők (Budapest: Central European University Press, 1999), 91–104, at 94–95.

as usual, especially well-reflected by Abbot Peter's work. For all his complaints about the winds of political fate, economic and political crisis, post-Mongol devastation, failure of ducal rule, and so forth, Peter's own text, and the contemporary documents, suggest that, upon this difficult terrain, he and his monks were in no sense helpless. Sometime before 1268, certainly during Peter's abbacy, the monastery elicited from Pope Clement IV a letter describing, with considerable clarity and detail, the relationship between the dukes of Silesia, the monastery, and other significant people, in terms that bear a suspicious resemblance to Peter's much expanded image of the same subjects throughout the *Book*.[108] Nearly simultaneously, in 1263, Duke Bolesław II the Bald described those same relationships in similar terms in a lengthy diploma,[109] whose issuance presumably closed (or at least calmed) that long period of bad relations between himself and the monastery to which Peter devoted lavish attention throughout his narrative. The years when Peter wrote were a period of intense negotiation and positioning of the monastery within a difficult and fluid regional political scene.[110]

In Piast Poland, Silesia included, the shift toward written modes of record-keeping and authoritative knowledge occurred between the mid-twelfth and the early fourteenth centuries – exactly the time span encompassed by the histories narrated in, and the making of, the *Henryków Book*. Now, in Poland as elsewhere, it is difficult to specify watersheds of this process in terms of precise dates or events. Nevertheless, Abbot Peter was aware of this transition, located it chronologically at a specific moment, and used it as one of the framing themes of his work. In fact, he cast the entire long history of his monastery and its estate between the mid-twelfth century and his present as a case study in the transition from memory to written record. Quite apart from the rhetorical use to which he put that transition, his discernment of it was, as a matter of fact, accurate. During the period upon which he reflected, the use of written documentation in Poland shifted from the exceptional toward the routine.[111] That fact specifically

108. Supplementary Document no. 6. For the significance of the papal letter, see Górecki, "Interpreter," 277–79.

109. Supplementary Document no. 5.

110. Since Peter's continuator was far less sensitive to, or vocal about, the implications of power and politics for his story, it is difficult to note any analogous agenda in the later segment of the history. However, he too may have been motivated by considerations of regional politics in what was yet another period of political uncertainty and competition among dukes, and between dukes and their powerful subjects, in Silesia and the other Piast duchies.

111. The subject of writing and literacy, and their implications for the legal and political culture of medieval Poland, awaits the kind of treatment now offered for other regions of medieval Europe by Clanchy, *From Memory*; Rosamond McKitterick, *The Carolingians and the Written Word* (Cambridge: Cambridge University Press, 1989); *The Uses of Literacy in Early Medieval Europe*, ed. R. McKitterick (Cambridge: Cambridge University Press, 1990); and Brian Stock, *Implications of Literacy: Written Language and Models of Inter-*

explains why, in the late 1260s, he viewed writing as an especially serviceable source of legal security for his monastery.

The written record continued to rise in importance, in Silesia as in the other Piast duchies, throughout the thirteenth and the fourteenth centuries. This meant, first of all, a continued output of charters, by dukes (after 1320, kings), bishops, abbots, and others, in substantial quantities, and at an accelerating rate. In addition, it meant the appearance around 1300 of several new types of written record. One was the cartulary, in the full complexity of that genre.[112] Among the earliest communities in Piast Poland to arrange their charter archives in this way were the monasteries at Lubiąż and at Henryków itself.[113] The Lubiąż monks compiled a relatively large dossier of 146 documents around the mid-thirteenth century, while the community at Henryków began with a compilation of 65 diplomas toward the end of the same century, which they subsequently expanded in a series of redactions, the first between 1317 and 1319, the second in 1344, the third in the later fourteenth century. Also in the course of the fourteenth century, the Cistercian community at Krzeszów likewise compiled the charters received since its foundation in 1292.[114]

Another type of document new around 1300 is the close survey of specific elements of estates – populations, fields, mills, units of settlement, and much else – known in English as a rental.[115] Surveys of this kind were not, strictly speaking, new in the early fourteenth century, but were until then almost always embedded

---

pretation in the Eleventh and Twelfth Centuries (Princeton: Princeton University Press, 1983); see, however, the superb studies in that direction by Anna Adamska – "From Memory," especially 92, 96–97, 99; "Dieu, le Christ et l'Église dans les préambules des documents polonais au Moyen Âge," *Bibliothèque de l'École des chartes* 155 (1997), 543–73; and *Arengi w dokumentach Władysława Łokietka. Formy i funkcje* [Preambles in the charters of Władysław the Short: forms and functions] (Kraków: Towarzystwo Naukowe Societas Vistulana, 1999) – and by Tomasz Nowakowski, *Idee areng dokumentów książąt polskich do połowy XIII wieku* [Ideas in the preambles of the documents issued by Polish dukes through the mid-thirteenth century] (Bydgoszcz: Wydawnictwo Uczelniane Wyższej Szkoły Pedagogicznej w Bydgoszczy, 1999). More briefly, with some reference to Henryków, see Górecki, "*Ad Controversiam*," 218, n. 18; Górecki, "Communities," 153–54; Górecki, "Historian," 518; Górecki, "A View from a Distance," *Law and History Review* 21 (2003), 367–76, at 370–73.

112. Above, nn. 36–37, 42, 47.

113. Rościsław Żerelik, "Średniowieczne archiwa cysterskie na Śląsku" [Medieval Cistercian archives in Silesia], in *Cystersi w społeczeństwie Europy Środkowej*, ed. Andrzej Marek Wyrwa and Józef Dobosz [Cistercians in the society of Central Europe] (Poznań: Wydawnictwo Poznańskie, 2000), 353–62, at 358; Artur Bruder, *Najstarszy kopiarz henrykowski* [The earliest Henryków cartulary] (Wrocław: Wydawnictwo Uniwersytetu Wrocławskiego, 1992); Andrzej Walkówski, *Najstarszy kopiarz lubiąski* [The earliest Lubiąż cartulary] (Wrocław: Wydawnictwo Uniwersytetu Wrocławskiego, 1985).

114. Żerelik, "Średniowieczne," 358.

115. Clanchy, *From Memory*, 94–96.

in the narrations or dispositions of diplomas, and therefore relatively short and fragmentary. In exceptional cases, they were quite substantial, and charters containing them may be viewed as a separate sub-genre, resembling short Carolingian polyptyques; the most important example is the remarkable set of diplomas issued by Duke Henry I the Bearded to the monastery of Lubiąż, and especially to the newly established Cistercian convent in Trzebnica, between 1202 and 1218.[116] However, this adaptation of the ducal diploma was early and fleeting. It is really an example of the variety of uses of writing in an early phase of that particular mode. What is notable is the relationship of this type of survey to the earliest two Cistercian monasteries in Silesia, one of which, Lubiąż, was directly involved in the establishment of Henryków a short time later.[117] That relationship was renewed nearly a century later. In 1292, Duke Bolko I explicitly invoked his ancestors during his own new Cistercian foundation at Krzeszów, which he confirmed by an exceptionally long diploma consisting largely of a detailed survey,[118] and, in 1299, by a further expansion of that diploma in two variants. The survey portions of both variants were enhanced and elaborated into geographically arranged descriptions of a monastic estate.[119]

Let me emphasize that this type of source was as unusual around 1300 as it had been a century earlier. We are not on the cusp of the formation of yet another hybrid genre, in this case a diploma fused with a rental. Instead, the 1292 and 1299 Krzeszów documents reflect an emergence of the survey as a type of document distinct from a charter, and arranged according to different, above all geographic, criteria. Each portion of the *Henryków Book* is, among other things, that kind of document. Thus, quite apart from the many differences in their form and subject, the *Book* and the two Krzeszów charters reflect a common, underlying transition in the nature of the written record. Another symptom of that transition – very different, in its own turn, from the *Henryków Book* and from the Krzeszów charters – is the survey of the very large estate of the diocese of Wrocław compiled soon after 1300.[120] This is of course not a charter at all, but, by contemporary standards, a very large rental, consisting entirely of several dossiers, each structured around an important town in Silesia, and recording in the resulting district dozens of places, land units, and objects, but not, in this

---

116. On the evidentiary aspect of the Trzebnica documents, see Górecki, *Economy*, 23–26.

117. It was the "mother house" of Henryków, on which n. 301 below.

118. *S.U.*, 6:no. 65 (1292), 51–54, of which the survey comprises 52, line 24–53, line 38.

119. *S.U.*, 6:no. 418 (1299), 320–24, of which the two enhanced surveys comprise 321, line 18–324, line 17.

120. *Liber fundationis episcopatus Wratislaviensis (Codex Diplomaticus Silesiae*, vol. 14), ed. Hermann Markgraf and J. W. Schulte (Breslau: Max, 1889), for which see briefly Hoffmann, *Land, Liberties, and Lordship*, 7.

case, enumerated inhabitants.[121] Several surveys of type were produced for various landholders in the course of the fourteenth century.[122]

Another type of document that was not strictly speaking new, but newly important near the turn of the fourteenth century, was forgery – by which I mean a document (typically a diploma) either fully created or substantially redacted by its own beneficiary, and which contains inaccurate and anachronistic attribution of authorship, criteria of authentication, or both. Quite significantly, a spike in forging activity began just after the mid-thirteenth century and into the early fourteenth, and specifically in the two Cistercian monasteries which are most important from the *Henryków Book*'s perspective, Lubiąż and Henryków itself. During this period, the Lubiąż monks produced three substantial expansions of Duke Bolesław the Tall's foundation charter of 1175,[123] one similar embellishment of the first extant diploma issued to them by Henry the Bearded in 1202,[124] and redactions of two other early diplomas, concerning more specific transactions.[125] Meanwhile, their Henryków brethren produced three (known) forgeries: a document not related to any known original (and thus perhaps entirely fabricated), putatively issued in 1229,[126] and two documents expanding and amplifying a charter issued to them by Duke Henry II the Pious in 1239.[127] All three Henryków documents are quite specific. Neither reiterates Henry the Bearded's 1228 foundation charter, but all add detail and variation to Abbot Peter's narrations in two "accounts" of the *Book*.[128]

---

121. Markgraf and Schulte, *Liber*, 3–38 (Nysa), 41–88 (Wrocław), 91–112 (Ujazd), 115–40 (Legnica), 143–64 (Głogów), and two very short surveys, 165–67 (Grodków), 168–74 (Kreuzburg and Byczyna).

122. See in general Hoffmann, *Land, Liberties, and Lordship*, 7–9.

123. *S.U.*, 1:no. 325–27 (putatively 1175), 239–46, compiled, respectively, at the turn of the thirteenth and fourteenth centuries (239), in the "early" fourteenth century (242), and in the first half of the fourteenth century, possibly after 1319 (244–45).

124. *S.U.*, 1:no. 333 (putatively 1202), 254–56, compiled "in the last decade" of the thirteenth century (254).

125. *S.U.*, 1:no. 332 (putatively 1202), 251–54, compiled after 1295, possibly around 1310, in any case "at the outset of" the fourteenth century (252); no. 350 (putatively 1213), 274–75, compiled at the very end of the thirteenth century (274).

126. *S.U.*, 1:no. 371 (putatively 1229), 295–96, compiled in "the late" thirteenth century (295). I should note that, specifically concerning this document, Heinrich Appelt's definitive pronouncement that it is a forgery has not been universally accepted; twenty years later, Józef Matuszewski specifically referred to it as genuine – that is, as in fact issued in 1229, by Duke Henry the Bearded, to the monks of Henryków; see Matuszewski, *Najstarsze*, 63–64.

127. *S.U.*, 2:no. 429 (purportedly 1239), 271–73, and no. 431 (purportedly 1239), 274–75, both compiled "in the last quarter" of the thirteenth century (272, 276, respectively).

128. The document putatively (or, in Matuszewski's view, in fact) issued in 1229 adds detail to Chapters 85–89, discussed at Górecki, "Historian," 480–84, 487–88, 490–91, 511–18; the two documents supposedly issued by Henry II in 1239 add detail to Chapters

Traditionally, historians have tended to devalue such documents – or at most to excavate them, so to speak, for fragments apparently copied from authentic originals[129] – because, in one sense, such documents are false. However, over the past twenty years or so, fabrication has elicited a more nuanced view from medievalists. It is now quite clear that, like other constructs generated by historians, *forgery*, whether understood as an activity or as a document, is a fluid category. To be sure, it encompasses the production of documents explicitly intended to deceive. Medieval actors certainly thought so; they were quite aware that documents were sometimes designed as sheer fabrications, and they viewed this kind of activity as illicit, and its product as void.[130] Truth and falsehood are therefore not anachronistic criteria for evaluating the significance of medieval forgery, but, contrary to traditional diplomatic scholarship, they are not adequate. Quite simply, forgery included documents produced for other reasons. It is at least plausible that documents which diplomatists today, for good reason, detect as in-house productions, express attempts by their authors to reconstruct a past which these authors viewed as accurate[131] – or, in the plain meaning of that unfashionable word, truthful.[132]

The subject of such reconstructions may have been either the past reality itself – the events or relationships thought to require a fuller record in the present – or the written documents which were in fact issued, or, in the view of the fabricators, ought to have been issued, in the past. It seems needlessly restrictive to reduce this kind of enterprise exclusively to purposeful deception. The three Henryków forgeries are an excellent example. Of course, we cannot rule out that they were created specifically in order to mislead; but there is no positive reason

---

98–102, especially Duke Henry's authentic charter on the same subject of 1240, Chapter 102, and *S.U.*, 2:no. 196 (1240), 124.

129. A good example in Polish scholarship has been the use of a handful of documents widely recognized as, themselves, relatively late interpolations, for access to presumably much earlier – and no longer extant – texts, and thus to a period of Polish history that is otherwise entirely undocumented, for example, Karol Maleczyński, "Uwagi nad dokumentem legata Idziego biskupa tuskulańskiego dla klasztoru w Tyńcu rzekomo z roku 1105" [Remarks on the document of Legate Guido, bishop of Tusculum, for the monastery in Tyniec, supposedly of 1105], *Collectanea Theologica* 17 (1936), 339–65, repr. in K. Maleczyński, *Studia nad dokumentem polskim* [Studies in the Polish document] (Wrocław: Zakład Narodowy im. Ossolińskich, 1971), 150–69.

130. For this concern, see Clanchy, *From Memory*, 323–24.

131. Especially important in this regard is Clanchy, *From Memory*, 318–27.

132. The word is unfashionable because the interest in the text as an autonomous subject of inquiry noted earlier has complicated, in important and interesting ways, the question of correspondence between the text and the realities to which it refers; I do not mean here to return to the kind of naïve view of that correspondence that was long ago criticized by Partner, "New Cornificius;" but I do mean to state that particular medieval authors may have been aiming at texts that did in fact, to the best of their abilities, correspond to a past reality – even with an ulterior, or interpretive, or otherwise selective purpose.

to think that they were. Instead, on their face, and in conjunction with Abbot Peter's stories, they appear to have been intended to shed additional light upon what had in fact occurred on those occasions. Likewise, it is possible that, by means of those several redactions of their 1175 foundation charter and of its renewal of 1202, the monks of Lubiąż sought, in the late thirteenth and the early fourteenth centuries, to transcribe, enhance, clarify, and update – in other words, to continue in written form – those authoritative prototypes.

Over a decade ago, Michael Clanchy observed that, quite apart from the question of its intent or legitimacy, intensive fabrication reflects an expansion of the importance of writing. Although it emerges from materials concerning a very different part of Europe, this view closely matches the transition from memory to written record in medieval Poland, in Silesia, and in Abbot Peter's world. In-house enhancement, or outright creation, of diplomas at Lubiąż, at Henryków, and, about half a century later, at Trzebnica, was one aspect of that transition. The creation of the *Henryków Book* itself was another. The *Book*, too, is both a reconstruction and an interpretation of past events and relationships, along particular, partisan, but plausible lines.[133] This conjunction, especially in the final years of the thirteenth century, is further strengthened by yet another constellation of documents: the two Krzeszów charters of 1292 and 1299; and three large diplomas issued jointly by Bishops John of Wrocław and Conrad of Lubusz in 1296, on the same day and before the same group of witnesses – and thus as one coherent sequence of activity.[134]

These documents directly concern the Henryków monastery. In addition to their interest as a type of source, the Krzeszów charters refer in detail to that monastery, and to the dukes who had founded it. The newly created monastery is identified as Henryków's "daughter."[135] The association resonates a few years later in the *Book* itself, when Abbot Peter's continuator referred to Duke Bolko as the founder of the Krzeszów community.[136] The three documents issued by the two bishops all share a common goal, explicitly enunciated in a standardized formula:[137] to transcribe a series of charters granted to the Henryków monastery. Additional text by the two bishops is very sparse, consisting solely of the opening and the closing protocols; thus, most of each document is a transcription of

---

133. For the constraints preventing Peter from complete fabrication, i.e., lying, see Górecki, "Rhetoric," 292, n. 175.

134. See nn. 117–18 above, and *S.U.*, 6:no. 248–50 (1296), 199–200.

135. For the relationship between "mother" and "daughter" monasteries, of which Henryków and Krzeszów are here an example, n. 301 below. The passages appear at *S.U.*, 6:no. 65 (1292), 52, lines 6–7, 10–12, 15–18, and in an exact transcription at no. 418 (1299), 320.

136. Chapter 157, n. 57.

137. *S.U.*, 6:no. 248 (1296), 199, lines 10–13; no. 249 (1296), 199, lines 38–41; no. 250 (1296), 200, lines 29–33.

charters.[138] These documents do not provide, or aim at, an exhaustive transcript-tion of charters granted to the monks; far from it.[139] They are, however, interest-ing for a different reason, in conjuction with the text of the *Henryków Book*, and in the broader documentary context of the later thirteenth and the early four-teenth centuries.

The total number of diplomas reproduced by the two bishops is unusually large. To be sure, one transcription is brief, including only two diplomas,[140] but the remaining two are substantial, encompassing twelve diplomas in one docu-ment, nine in the other.[141] The overall total of 23 diplomas is clearly intended to constitute a single dossier concerning one particular monastery. This is yet another very unusual type of document, as distinct in its own way as were the great endowment charters for the communities of Lubiąż and Trzebica at the start of the thirteenth century, and the two Krzeszów documents at its close. It resonates with the *Henryków Book* on two levels. The persons active in their mak-ing – the bishops and the cathedral clergy of Wrocław and Lubusz[142] – reflect a long and close association between the Henryków monastery and the prelates and clergy of those two bishoprics, a subject to which Abbot Peter devoted considerable attention.[143] Moreover, one of the witnessing canons of Lubusz, John, was simultaneously the parish priest in Münsterberg – by the 1290s, an important regional town, a center of ducal power and jurisdiction, amply treated by Abbot Peter's continuator.[144] John's presence reflects the close economic, legal, and institutional relationship between that town and the monastery around the turn of the fourteenth century. Therefore, the 1296 dossier suggests a pur-poseful perpetuation of some of the same institutional memories with which the *Book* is concerned.

The dossier and the *Book* also concern several common issues. Of the three transcriptions, the longer two constitute compilations of considerable coherence. One begins with a transcription of the 1228 foundation charter,[145] and thereafter includes documents contemporary with, and further illustrating, several stories

---

138. At this point, the editors Winfried Irgang and Daphne Schadewaldt cross-refer to their editions of the charters included here elsewhere in *S.U.*; the cross-references appear at *S.U.*, 6:no. 248 (1296), 199, line 14; no. 249 (1296), 199, lines 1–2; no. 250 (1296), 200, lines 34–35.

139. The number of charters transcribed in the *Book* itself, and the number of the charters concerning the monastery but not transcribed in the *Book* (a selection of which appears as Supplementary Documents below) are each much larger than the number consolidated on this occasion.

140. *S.U.*, 6:no. 248 (1296), 199, line 14.

141. *S.U.*, 6:no. 249–50 (1296), 200, lines 1–2, 35–35.

142. *S.U.*, 6:no. 248 (1296), 199, lines 17–20; no. 249–50 (1296), 200, lines 5–8, 38–41.

143. Chapters 2, 4–9, 21, 37, 51, 68, 100, 197, 198–211.

144. See nn. 211, 217 below.

145. Supplementary Document no. 2.

that Abbot Peter and his continuator described as in some sense problematic: the complicated property transactions concerning Głębowice;[146] the troublesome descendants of Boguchwał Brukał,[147] of Stephen of Skalice,[148] and, later, of John Osina;[149] confiscation of a formerly granted holding, Jaworowice, by Duke Henry III;[150] and other, more or less challenging, events. The other longer document relates to something rather different, namely, the regional outliers of the monastic estate. It includes charters issued by the duke of Great Poland, Przemysł I, and by his bishop Paul of Poznań,[151] plus an early diploma concerning (what became) one of the monastery's holdings in the duchy of Little Poland, near Kraków.[152]

The stories reflected in all the documents incorporated into the dossier, the persons in whose names they were issued, the persons whom they identify as actors, the localities they mention, and the issues they address, were all central to the work of Abbot Peter and of his continuator. Although we cannot know the specific relationship – if any – of this consolidation of charters to the writing of the *Henryków Book* – either by Abbot Peter thirty years before 1296, or by his continuator about a decade afterwards – what is unmistakeable, and surely not coincidental, is the conjunction of the documentary output, and of its specific and contemporaneous focus on the Henryków monastery. That fact specifically explains why, soon after the years 1292, 1296, and 1299, the anonymous "least of the brothers" viewed the completion of his predecessor's work as pressing and timely.

4 . Agriculture and towns

One of the big historiographical issues reflected by the *Henryków Book* is the medieval "frontier." This construct may, among other possibilities, be understood in spatial and societal terms. Viewed from that perspective, the monastery was situated within a frontier region in two senses. First, before, during, and (with increasing intensity) after the monastery's foundation and endowment, the duchy of Silesia, along with the remaining Polish provinces, were a destination of immigration and settlement by peasants, knights, and clerics from other regions

---

146. Chapters 82–92; one of the two included charters on this subject is Supplementary Document no. 12.

147. Chapters 112–23; of the two included charters, one is Supplementary Document no. 23, the other is Chapter 115.

148. Chapters 71–73; the single included charter is Supplementary Document no. 17.

149. Chapters 127–38; the three included charters are Chapters 133, 142–43.

150. Chapters 78–79; the single included charter is Supplementary Document no. 11.

151. Neither of the two included charters by Duke Przemysł or the one included charter by Bishop Paul, is translated in the Supplementary Documents; see, however, Supplementary Documents no. 4–5.

152. Chapter 24; the single included charter (*S.U.*, 1:no. 200 [1220], 148) is not translated in the Supplementary Documents.

of medieval Europe, above all Germany, who settled under ducal and ecclesiastical lordship or protection. This is a good example of what Robert Bartlett calls a "diaspora" out of one region of Europe and into another.[153] Second, like other major regions of medieval Europe, and like each of the remaining Piast provinces, thirteenth-century Silesia itself included sub-regions that had long been settled and integrated into coherent structures of power and lordship, and sub-regions of relatively new and expanding settlement. In other words, Piast Poland, and each of its major provinces, had their own, as it were internal, "cores" and "frontiers."[154]

The Henryków monastery and its estate were situated upon one of the "frontiers" internal to the Polish duchies, in that latter, regional sense: between the core, lowland region of Lower Silesia, which had long been settled by a Slavic population, and a relatively sparsely populated, forested, and somewhat higher region situated to the southwest, near the foothills of the Sudetes, which attracted new settlement during the later twelfth century and all of the thirteenth.[155] The new settlers migrated from within Silesia itself, other Polish duchies, in small groups from Bohemia and Flanders, and, by far most importantly since the first decades of the thirteenth century, from the western regions of Germany, and from regions of more recent German settlement between the Elbe and the Odra (see Map 1).[156] Within this migratory and demographic context, Germans were by far the most numerous and important. The specific destinations of their settlement varied – including, at different times and places, the lowlands and hilly

153. Bartlett uses this word specifically toward the knightly, or noble, participants, or, as he puts it, the "aristocratic diaspora" within Europe, *Making*, 24–59. Its German knightly component in Silesia is well described by Tomasz Jurek, *Obce rycerstwo na Śląsku do połowy XIV wieku* [Foreign knighthood in Silesia until the mid-fourteenth century], (2nd ed., Poznań: Wydawnictwo Poznańskiego Towarzystwa Przyjaciół Nauk, 1998) (German summary, 441–50). For the Polish duchies in general, see also Górecki, *Economy*, 69, 87–91, 101–05, 124, 127–28, 196–97.

154. This aspect of the frontier in Poland and elsewhere is East Central Europe – that is, the differentiation between local, or regional, centers and peripheries and the resulting intra-regional dynamic, during a period long antedating exogenous, especially German or German-influenced, variables, has been noted long ago by Pounds, *Historical Geography*, 242–44, 261, 263, 272, and subsequently largely neglected in favor of viewing all sub-units of the European East as one large frontier zone in the other sense just mentioned. For the framing, and the aftermath, of Norman Pounds's more nuanced vision, see Górecki, "Medieval 'East Colonization,'" 47–52.

155. Henryk Łowmiański, *Początki Polski* [The origins of Poland], 6 vols. (Warsaw: Państwowe Wydawnictwo Naukowe, 1963–85), 3:39, map 1.

156. In addition to Abbot Peter's and his continuator's records of specific migrants from and to other regions of Silesia, other Piast duchies, and Bohemia, see Bartlett, *Making*, 24–59, 111–16; Hoffmann, *Land, Liberties, and Lordship*, 34–44, 61–82; Górecki, *Economy*, 16–17, 168, 194, 278–79; Benedykt Zientara, "Walloons in Silesia in the Twelfth and Thirteenth Centuries," *Quaestiones Medii Aevi* 2 (1981), 127–50.

areas, previously settled and sparsely populated spaces, the towns and the countryside. Within central Silesia, they migrated into the midst of earlier Polish settlement, as well as speficially into the relatively sparse, upland, forested foothill subregion of the Sudeten mountains to the south and to the west of the Henryków region. These processes are well reflected in both sections of the *Henryków Book*.

Perhaps because these transitions were so dynamic, so well-documented, and so significant in their overall impact, they tend to obscure the fact that, at the time they began around the turn of the twelfth and thirteenth centuries, the settlement and the economy of the Piast duchies, Silesia included, were very old. Here, as throughout East Central Europe, the beginnings of intensive agriculture and urban settlement antedated the migration of the Slavs into this region during the fifth and sixth centuries that accompanied the crisis of both halves of the Roman Empire, and continued thereafter.[157] As far back as the archaeological evidence extends, populations long settled in the region had sustained themselves primarily from several domesticated grains, including wheat, rye, oats, barley, and millet, in conjunction with animal husbandry and other sources of sustenance, such as fishing, beekeeping, and hunting. The earliest written evidence pertaining to this region reflects complex societies with highly-articulated hierarchies of settlement, a significant agricultural sector, and élites that sustained themselves from warfare, plunder, exchange, and agriculture, and were based in or near fortified urban complexes characteristic of the earliest period of the Middle Ages.[158]

In these very general contours, the history of agriculture and towns at the beginning of the Middle Ages in East Central Europe was similar to the patterns that obtained across the Continent as a whole – especially the regions distant from the frontiers of the Roman Empire. There were, however, regional differences – differences whose origins are uncertain, but which are clearly docu-

---

157. Graeme Barker, *Prehistoric Farming in Europe* (Cambridge: Cambridge University Press, 1985), 135–60; Witold Hensel, *Słowiańszczyzna wczesnośredniowieczna. Zarys kultury materialnej* [Early–medieval Slavic peoples: an outline of the material culture] (4th ed., Warsaw: Państwowe Wydawnictwo Naukowe, 1987), 33–37; Jerzy Lodowski, *Dolny Śląsk na początku średniowiecza (VI–X w.). Podstawy osadnicze i gospodarcze* [Lower Silesia at the beginning of the Middle Ages (the sixth through the tenth centuries): the settlement and economic base] (Wrocław: Zakład Narodowy im. Ossolińskich, 1980), 60–76, 129–36.

158. Górecki, *Economy*, 18–19, 45–46, 54–56, 65; Paul Knoll, "The Urban Development if Medieval Poland, with Particular Reference to Kraków," in *The Urban Society of Eastern Europe in Premodern Times*, ed. Bariša Krekić (Berkeley and Los Angeles: University of California Press, 1987), 63–136; Lech Leciejewicz, "Early–Medieval Sociotopographical Transformations in West Slavonic Urban Settlements in the Light of Archaeology," *Acta Poloniae Historica* 34 (1976), 29–56; Barker, *Prehistoric Farming*, 152–56; Hodges, *Dark Age Economics*, 20–25; Robert Bartlett, "Technique militaire et pouvoir politique, 900–1300," *Annales: Économies, Sociétés, Civilisations* 41 (1986), 1135–59, at 1140.

mented over several centuries preceding the foundation of the monastery, and, with it, the memories later (distantly) reflected in the *Henryków Book*. During the tenth, eleventh, and twelfth centuries, a substantial proportion of agriculturalists supported itself from activities additional (or peripheral) to agriculture, including hunting, fishing, beekeeping, brewing, small-scale rural crafts, as well as licit or illicit use of force against other inhabitants.[159] Despite much controversy on this subject, historians continue to explain this proliferation of specialized groups in terms of a deliberate initiative by the earliest Piast dukes in the tenth century to organize resources – including human groups – as an economic base for their rulership.[160] A few intriguing if obscure details in Abbot Peter's earliest stories may reflect the long aftermath of this regional distinction. Peter recalls that at least some of the earliest inhabitants of the Henryków region had possessed or wielded "power," that they had been based in small forts or castles (*castella*), and that they had "dominated" substantial territories nearby.[161]

Although historians have strongly disagreed about the frequency, overall economic significance, and (above all) origins of these directions of specialization within the rural population, what is clear is that between the mid-twelfth and the fourteenth centuries these directions of specialization largely disappeared. During the expansionary period spanning the twelfth, thirteenth, and early fourteenth centuries, agriculture emerged in the Piast duchies as (virtually) the sole component of rural sustenance strategies, and of the revenues sought from the peasants in rent, tax, and tithe.[162] Over the same centuries, towns expanded substantially beyond the old fortified centers, the surrounding suburban settlements, and ecclesiastical establishments, and (as elsewhere in medieval Europe) emerged as spatially discrete localities where most of the population sustained itself from activities other than agriculture. During the same period, rural estates and towns acquired liberties – that is, grants of autonomy from

159. Górecki, *Economy*, 3, 7, 26, 67–101.

160. Making up what Thomas Bisson has recently called "the system of local production and supply that was a distinctive feature of the early Slavic polity," in his "Princely Nobility in an Age of Ambition (c. 1050–1150)," in *Nobles and Nobility in Medieval Europe: Concepts, Origins, Transformations*, ed. Anne Duggan (London: Boydell and Brewer, 2000), 101–13, at 107. The original statement of this model of economic specialization is Karol Modzelewski, "La division autarchique du travail à l'échelle d'un état: l'organisation 'ministériale' en Pologne médiévale," *Annales: Économies, Sociétés, Civilisations* 19 (1964), 1125–38; Modzelewski's last word on some of the ensuing disagreements is *Organizacja gospodarcza państwa piastowskiego, X–XIII wiek* [The economic organization of the Piast state between the tenth and the thirteenth century] (2nd ed., Poznań: Wydawnictwo Poznańskiego Towarzystwa Przyjaciół Nauk, 2000), 5–10.

161. Chapters 29, 31, 34, 36, 76, 96, 103, 111.

162. Bartlett calls this process "cerealization," in *Making*, 152–56, citing mostly Polish (and Polish-German) evidence.

ducal and seigneurial power, of varying scope and significance – and corresponding rights of jurisdiction, taxation, and internal governance.[163]

The long history of land use in the Polish duchies is, in its broad contours,
the counterpart of the history of land use throughout the Continent – that is, it is
a story of a gradual intensification of the use of available land, especially of
strategies to replenish its chemical nutrients through alternating periods of cultivation and fallow.[164] As elsewhere, these strategies included the swidden, or "slash-
and-burn" technique, whereby arable cultivated for a single growing season was
allowed to revert to forest, which was burned down decades afterwards to replenish the level of nutrients in the soil; planting the arable with crops that re-
plenished the nutrients (especially legumes); fertilizing some portion of the arable
(e.g., the "infield," or a garden near a household) especially intensively; and, most
importantly, establishing some kind of organized, communal régime of crop rotation, usually a system of two or three fields with an annual or semi-annual rotation
of the grains sown. The written sources are quite intractable on the question of
whether there was any one such "system" in this region during the Middle Ages;
but they clearly document increasingly routine planting of spring and winter grains,
especially from the early thirteenth century onward, and so imply some kind of
collective strategy for alternating crops and the use of rural arable. This strategy
may or may not have approximated, or with time tended toward, the "classical" (or
perhaps the textbook) three-field system.

The gradual transition in field systems and crops planted was accompanied,
and to an extent driven, by technological change, especially in cultivation and
milling. Considerable change in cultivation techniques antedated the medieval
period, and continued long into it and beyond. Over that very long period,
sickles were supplemented, and to some extent replaced, with scythes; the structure of a harrow changed from a cylinder consisting of a portion of a tree trunk
with sharpened branch stumps, to a rectangle with vertical sharpened stakes; and
the plow replaced the adze as the primary instrument for breaking up the soil
prior to cultivation on the rural arable (apart, perhaps, for the garden plots of the
individual peasant households). Of these, plowing technique is the most significant, because of the plow's intrinsic importance in cultivation, and because of its

163. Benendykt Zientara, "Socio-Economic and Spatial Transformation of Polish
Towns during the Period of Location," *Acta Poloniae Historica* 34 (1976), 57–83; Maria
Bogucka, "The Towns of East-Central Europe from the Fourteenth to the Seventeenth
Century," in *East-Central Europe in Transition: From the Fourteenth to the Seventeenth Century*, ed.
Antoni Mączak, Henryk Samsonowicz, and Peter Burke (Cambridge: Cambridge Univer-
sity Press, and Paris: Éditions de la Maison des Sciences de l'Homme, 1985), 97–108.

164. For what follows on land use, techniques, and implements, see Hensel,
Słowiańszczyzna, 18–66; Barker, *Prehistoric Farming*, 135–60; Bartlett, *Making*, 133–66;
Górecki, *Economy*, 5–6, 81, 113, 252–54. On the historiographically thorny issue of plow-
ing techniques, see the subsequent footnotes; and on the historiography in general, see
Górecki, "Los campesinos."

conceptual importance for the understanding of the transformation of medieval agriculture in general, and of the "Eastern" and "Western" variants of that transformation in particular.[165]

A wide variety of plowing implements had been used by the cultures of East Central Europe since well before the migration of the Slavs throughout the region, and continued to be employed by the Slavic, Magyar, and German populations into the medieval period.[166] Historians, following difficult and scarce sources, generally assimilate the several kinds of early plows into one type, the ard (*aratrum* in Latin, *radło* in several Slavic vernaculars), and in addition sometimes inaccurately identify the ard with a wooden scratch-plow, best known under its Russian name *sokha*. Archaeological evidence suggests that, ever since Antiquity throughout the Middle Ages, the ard included several different kinds of plow, with different and differently positioned metal tips or blades. (These differed from the wooden *sokha*, which is most frequently documented in use among the Eastern Slavs.)[167]

Technological change within the mix of plowing implements, and specifically the diffusion of the moldboard plow (*aratrum magnum*, *pług*) in Polish sources, is difficult to trace with confidence. Although, in contrast to comparable evidence from Western Europe, the sources do not explicitly identify the "large" plow with the usual designation for a moldboard plow (*carruca*), considerable circumstantial evidence indicates that the *aratrum magnum* was designed to be pulled with eight oxen; and that when, at the turn of the twelfth and thirteenth centuries, landlords planned or established agrarian estates, they conceived of the basic farming unit as a team of animals (oxen and horses) sufficient to pull a single moldboard plow.[168]

The ultimate source – that is, the origins – and the overall frequency of use of the moldboard plow in the Polish duchies are very sparsely documented, and cannot be traced to any single factor. Whatever its "origins" in this region of Europe, German immigrants were especially important as agents of its diffusion.[169] The transformation in milling technique in the Polish duchies in some respects parallels the changes in plowing, but the cumulative results are better documented.[170] Throughout the medieval period, grain in much of this

---

165. Bartlett sorts out the evidence from the historiographic controversies and anachronisms in *Making*, 133–66.

166. Hensel, *Słowiańszczyzna*, 36, 40–42, 44–57.

167. Hensel, *Słowiańszczyzna*, 45–49.

168. Górecki, *Economy*, 113, 252–54.

169. Bartlett, *Making*, 133–66; Górecki, *Economy*, 80–81, 252–54.

170. On this subject, see most recently Grzegorz Myśliwski, "Utilisation of Water in Central Europe (12th–16th Cents.)," in *Economia e energia secc. XIII–XVIII: Atti della "Trentaquattresima Settimana di Studi" 15–19 aprile 2002*, Serie II – Atti delle "Settimane di Studi" e altri Convegni 34, ed. Simonetta Cavaciocchi (Florence: Le Monnier, 2003), 321–333.

region was ground in hand querns.[171] In addition, the powered mill was introduced at the turn of the twelfth and thirteenth centuries, and gained very widespread acceptance thereafter – a transition well-reflected by both portions of the Henryków history. Prior to the appearance of written documentation, querns underwent several transformations in the shape and the positioning of the millstones, in the structure of the mechanism that directly turned the millstones, and in the overall construction of the quern.[172] During the Middle Ages, querns were used in individual peasant households, where they were operated by women, and possibly on larger estates (as suggested by a Polish reference from the mid-thirteenth century to the operation of millstones by women slaves).[173] Indeed, the most vivid single instance of the use of hand-querns in Poland, and of milling as women's work, is Abbot Peter's story about the wife of Boguchwał the Czech, situated around 1200.[174] Evidence of the use of hand querns continues into the fourteenth century, suggesting that querns continued to be used throughout the medieval period.[175]

The diffusion of the powered mill was rapid, and is documented much more explicitly than the diffusion of the moldboard plow. It is also much more clearly and demonstrably related to German migration.[176] In the course of the thirteenth and fourteenth centuries, the watermill became a standard feature of the village and the agrarian estate in the Polish duchies. The German rural entrepreneurs, or village bailiffs,[177] who recruited and settled German migrants into and within the Polish duchies were frequently entrusted with construction, repair, and maintenance of mills for the lords whose estates they were expanding; and thereafter also served as millers for the peasants whom they recruited, and for the indigenous and German lords upon whose estates they settled. As in Western Europe, the powered mill emerged as a central element of the estate economy, but, in contrast to regions further west, the rights and obligations associated with it were in several respects distinctive.

First – quite apart from controversies on this subject concerning Western European rural societies – in the Piast duchies the peasants were not compelled to use manorial mills in preference to the domestic hand querns. The rural entrepreneurs who acted as millers were remunerated for this part of their responsibilites with a multure payment, but there is no evidence that they, their lords, or anyone else compelled the peasants to use the powered mills they operated as their only source of flour, or that they prohibited the use of domestic hand querns. The

171. Górecki, *Economy*, 108–11; Hensel, *Słowiańszczyzna*, 77–82.

172. Hensel, *Słowiańszczyzna*, 77–82.

173. Górecki, *Economy*, 110, n. 165.

174. Chapter 113.

175. Górecki, *Economy*, 109–10; and elsewhere, Richard Holt, *The Mills of Medieval England* (Oxford: Blackwell, 1988), 1.

176. Górecki, *Economy*, 207–08, 210–13, 218–19, 225–28, 288–89.

177. See nn. 194–96 below.

estate mill was not a part or an aspect of a seigneurial monopoly, and of fines or legal sanctions designed to enforce that monopoly.[178] Second, the powered mills were held in tenure – that is, on condition of payment of rent or performance of an obligation, to the lord of the estate of which the mills were a part. The usual holder of the mill, a German rural entrepreneur, owed the lord of the estate payment in coin, or, alternatively, directly in flour intended for the lord's consumption. Abbot Peter's continuator implied that this kind of obligation was attached to a landed estate, and that it bound its subsequent possessors – hence his intriguing example, late in the thirteenth century, of a landholder destroying a previously existing mill in order to avoid paying rent on it.[179]

An important element of the history of agriculture in medieval Poland is the formation and the transformation of the agrarian estate, that is, the regional counterpart of the Western manor. In its broad contours, the history of the agrarian estate in medieval Poland is similar to its history in medieval Europe as a whole. First, the agrarian estate was a fundamental source for the sustenance of the secular and ecclesiastical élite, clearly displacing – in this macro-region of Europe, between the tenth and the twelfth centuries – other sources of revenue, such as booty, tribute, and the bundle of movable commodities involved in gift exchange. Second, agrarian estates throughout medieval Poland, including Silesia, entailed a complicated mix of direct (or demesne) exploitation, tenure, and rent. Third, the structure, the population, and the modes of management of agrarian estates in the Polish duchies varied widely throughout the medieval period.

Fourth – and this part is in sharp distinction to regions of Europe further to the west – the early history of the Polish agrarian estate is exceedingly sparsely documented during the entire period that preceded Abbot Peter's story, that is, the mid-tenth through the later twelfth century.[180] The earliest relatively ample documentation, produced after 1200, reflects the estate (or rather, a rather substantial group of particular estates) in the process of transition. One especially important variant of that transition, from about 1220 onward, is "German law" and its systemic impact.[181] Thus, for reasons that are quite specific to this region of medieval Europe, and to the nature of its surviving documentation, we cannot speak of a "typical" estate, or "manor," in this region between the tenth and the late thirteenth centuries, any more than we might with respect to other regions.

---

178. The basis for comparison here are Holt, *Mills*, 36–53, and Pierre Dockès, *Medieval Slavery and Liberation*, trans. Arthur Goldhammer (Chicago, 1979), 174–96.

179. See the story of John Zeruch and Poltko in the "account" of Wiesenthal, Chapter 155.

180. For early Polish agrarian and seigneurial history as a story without a clear beginning, and the resulting paradoxes of scarcity of evidence explaining a barely-glimpsed but undeniable past complexity, see Górecki, *Economy*, 2–3, 45, 67; Górecki, *Parishes*, 8–9, 21, 49, 97–98.

181. See nn. 194–96 below.

One area of variation among estates in medieval Poland was the directions of their specialization of production, and of the revenues drawn from them.[182] Most estates included a settled, agriculturally-based population; however, the importance of grain as a form of revenue (and presumably as a type of output) varied from estate to estate. Despite the limitations of the written record just noted, it appears that this variation was especially prononunced during the earliest period documented by that record, that is, over the many decades – up to two full centuries – culminating in the turn of the twelfth and the early thirteenth centuries. Thus, between the tenth and early thirteenth centuries, and to some extent thereafter, in addition to (or sometimes instead of) grain, inhabitants of estates were often subject to obligations in small craft output, in animal skins and furs, in fish, in wheels, in bundles of flax, and other specialized commodities or products. One recurrent such payment in earlier medieval Poland – which remained important quite late, well into the thirteenth century – included honey and wax. Moreover, some small estates, or components of larger estates, were exploited especially intensively as sources of these other, non-agricultural forms of revenue.

Another area of variation among estates was the relative importance of agriculture and animal husbandry. Although the better-documented early estates clearly show a close relationship between animal husbandry and grain-based agriculture – again, matching the patterns usual in medieval Europe – some estates were primarily devoted to keeping and maintaining herds of animals, especially breeding horses or herds of cattle intended specifically for slaughter.[183] The relative importance of this sector of estate economy varied with place and time. Although this direction of estate specialization in no sense displaced the agricultural component of economic output anywhere within this region of Europe, some particular estates, clusters or components of estates, and market towns specialized in this

---

182. For the subsequent generalizations on the structure, specialization, and management of estates in medieval Poland, and specifically Silesia, in the twelfth, thirteenth, and early fourteenth centuries, and for a comparative perspective with other regions of Europe, see: Górecki, *Economy*, 48–51, 67–101, 241; Hoffmann, *Land, Liberties, and Lordship*, 93–113; István Kiss, "Agricultural and Livestock Production: Wine and Oxen – The Case of Hungary," in Mączak, Samsonowicz, and Burke, *East-Central Europe*, 84–96. The implicit and explicit comparisons to other regions of Europe are indebted, among other works, to: Biddick, *Other Economy*; Annie Grant, "Animal Resources," in Astill and Grant, *Countryside*, 149–87; and Michael M. Postan, "The Famulus: The Estate Labourer in the XIIth and XIIIth Century," *Economic History Review*, Supplement 2 (1954). In addition, more specific points are accompanied by more specialized references.

183. Kazimierz Tymieniecki, "Majętność książęca w Zagościu i pierwotne uposażenie klasztoru joannitów na tle dorzecza dolnej Nidy. Studium z dziejów gospodarczych XII w." [The ducal estate in Zagość and the original endowment of the house of the Hospitallers of Saint John in the context of the settlement of the lower Nida river system: A study in twelfth-century economic history], in K. Tymieniecki, *Pisma wybrane* [Selected writings] (Warsaw: Państwowe Wydawnictwo Naukowe, 1956), 35–126; Górecki, *Economy*, 48–50.

type of animal husbandry with a relative intensity – especially with the rise of international demand for cattle and horses toward the end of the Middle Ages. Cattle and horses were among the important commodities traded through the major urban markets in late medieval and early modern East Central Europe, and raised at estates in some of its sub-regions, notably in Hungary.[184]

A third area of variation among agrarian estates in the Piast duchies was their management, their exact tenurial structure, and the criteria for assessing the obligations (whether agricultural, or other) due from their inhabitants. On these subjects, the early documentation, spanning the tenth through the early thirteenth centuries, sheds exceedingly limited light. Quite simply, we do not know how the estates were managed, and specifically who, if indeed anyone, mediated the contact between the lords and the people subject to them. In these instances, it is tempting to assume that the recorded holdings were demesnes, that is, estates held and exploited under direct seigneurial supervision, without mediation by seigneurial agents, and without a significant component of true tenurial landholding.[185] However, this interpretation would exaggerate uniformity in the early period. Despite the difficulties of the documentation, around 1200 at least some agrarian estates were quite clearly inhabited, and worked, by tenants, who were subject both to rents (chiefly in grain, and in orther commodities) and to a variety of labor obligations (plowing, threshing, mowing, and cartage). Moreover, in the best-documented instance – of the estate centered at Trzebnica, situated to the north of Wrocław[186] – those labor obligations were to be performed within one specific location central to the estate – a demesne in another sense of that word.

The criteria for assessing the inhabitants' obligations also varied – or, at the very least, they are variously expressed in the written record. In some cases, no explicit criteria are noted at all. Obligations are expressed as a specified amount of grain, flax, honey, or something else, and placed on "each" person, or on some locality indicated by name – suggesting that the units subject to obligations were known implicitly, well enough not to require specification in the written record. At other times, obligations were set according to the wealth of a productive unit (presumably a household, possibly a larger group) – assessed, in varying combinations, according to: the number of draught animals available to the productive unit; its possession of its own land, or cultivation of someone else's land; and the degree of its pooling of techical resources with other units.[187] Finally, several kinds of payments (specifically due to the duke) were assessed in terms of

184. Laszlo Makkai, "Economic Landscapes: Historical Hungary from the Fourteenth to the seventeenth Century," in Mączak, Samsonowicz, and Burke, *East-Central Europe*, 24–35, at 33–34.

185. This is what Hoffmann appears to mean by "demesne farming," especially in the period antedating the impact of "German law," in *Land, Liberties, and Lordship*, 93–113.

186. For the Trzebnica estate in general, see Górecki, *Economy*, 23–26, 76–78, and below, pp. 78, 80–3 with nn. 305, 308, 328.

187. Górecki, *Economy*, 75–76, 79–80, 82–84, 93–94, 96–98.

the "household" or "dwelling" (*dwór*), the "hearth" or "smoke" (*dym*), and the light plow (*radło*)[188] – further reflecting the use of people, dwellings, and cultivation tools as conceptually standardized criteria for assessing obligations.

Conspicuously absent from among these early criteria are concepts that refer, on their face, to abstract units of space, or of land surface. Several decades later, as Abbot Peter looked back at the inhabitants of the Henryków region in the final years of the twelfth century, he placed some of them within localities which he called *sortes* (plural of *sors*), a word I translate uniformly as "holdings."[189] Although the literal meaning of this word in Latin is "lot" – a unit of space allocated to its possessor at random – on the occasions when Peter used that word he never noted that mode of conveyance; nor did he, even implicitly, associate this conceptual unit with obligations – let alone some specific set of obligations – to anyone. Instead, he presented this unit as a rather open-ended, undifferentiated complex including, at its core, the dwelling or household, and, moving outward, land (arable or otherwise), and, at least implicitly, the nearby environment. The specific attributes which he did associate with the "holding" were quite different: this unit was subject to inheritance (that is, it normally passed across generations, as a matter of course); and it was designated by a place name, and thus reflected, or embodied, those ideas of property which place names conveyed in the earliest society upon which he reflected.[190] This conceptual and spatial unit most closely approximates a *terra unius familiae* – in that same open-ended, yet ultimately clear, sense in which many centuries earlier the Venerable Bede had defined the Anglo-Saxon hide.[191]

Even though he wrote in the later 1260s, Peter was not inventing this conceptual unit retroactively or anachonistically. The "holding" (*sors*) indeed appears, albeit rarely, in ducal charters contemporary with the earliest period to which the *Henryków Book* extends. However, these documents, too, do not present the "holding" as either a basis for obligations, or as a unit of land surface. Moreover – and contrary to its apparent meaning in Latin – in medieval Poland this conceptual unit was not, or at least is never documented as having been, allocated by lot. In fact, all that we actually do know about the mode of its conveyance takes us back

188. The root words for the obligations called *podworowe, podymne* and *poradlne* – which might be translated as household tax, hearth tax and plow tax, respectively – about which, along with a bundle of similarly conceptualized payments, see Karol Buczek, "Powołowe – poradlne – podymne," *Przegląd Historyczny* 63 (1972), 6–9; Karol Modzelewski, *Chłopi w monarchii wczesnopiastowskiej* [The peasants in the early Piast monarchy] (Wrocław: Zakład Narodowy im. Ossolińskich, 1987), 66–84; Modzelewski, *Organizacja*, 60, 90, 97, 147, 229.

189. Chapters 26–29, 32–35, 61, 63, 72, 78, 81, 84, 89, 112–17, 122–23.

190. For the relationship between place names and ideas of property, see Górecki, "Communities," 141–46.

191. Frederic William Maitland, *Domesday Book and Beyond: Three Essays in the Early History of England* (2nd ed., Cambridge: Cambridge University Press, 1987), 358–60; Dieter Hägermann and Andreas Hedwig, "Hufe," *Lex.MA.*, 5:cols. 154–56, at 154.

to Abbot Peter himself, as he recalled that several of the early landholders in the Henryków region had obtained their holdings from Dukes Bolesław the Tall and Henry the Bearded, during that period long ago when these two dukes were distributing holdings to their "peasants," or to "the noble and the mediocre."[192] Because the concept to which the word *sors* referred was rather broad and open-ended, it ought, in my view, to be translated with a word that is at the same time simple and inclusive. Hence my preference for *holding*.

The overall evidence available from the period during which Abbot Peter started his story – the turn of the twelfth and thirteenth centuries – is so fragmented in its particulars, and so modest in its overall size, that it is quite difficult to generalize any particular model of the agrarian estate as typical or paradigmatic. What is being suggested for the reader of the sources presented here is intellectual caution, perhaps indeed agnosticism, concerning some of these background issues. To complicate matters, since approximately the second decade of the thirteenth century, the structure and the management of agricultural estates were strongly affected, transformed, and to a large degree standardized, by German immigration and by the widespread establishment of villages and agrarian estates "according to German law" (*iure Teutonico*). Abbot Peter records that process, and several specific individuals who participated in it, in a handful of passages of his portion of the *Book*,[193] whereas his continuator clearly implies that it had had a continuous, transformative impact in the Henryków region and beyond for several generations.

In sharp contrast with the fragmentation, and the scarcity of the written record, concerning the arrangements and practices upon estates settled by the indigenous, Polish inhabitants, the meaning of "German law" is well-documented in the charter evidence from the late twelfth, all of the thirteenth, and the early fourteenth centuries.[194] "German law" defined, and regulated, two features of the agrarian estate: the tenurial obligations of peasants settled "according to German law;" and the management of the estate on behalf of its lord. Charters that record grants of "German law" always provide for a division of the estate arable into two (or more) kinds of tenure; and describe in detail the position of the village bailiff (*Schultheiss, villicus,* or *scultetus*), the German rural entrepreneur who recruited, established, managed, and judged the peasants of the

192. Chapters 3, 82, 113; nn. 30 above, 233 below.

193. Chapters 49, 51, 80–81, 94–96, 102–03, 109–11.

194. For what follows on "German law," and for further literature, see Hoffmann, *Land, Liberties, and Lordship,* 104, 114–23; Bartlett, *Making,* 118, 128–32, 139, 163, 179, 205, 208–09, 218–20, 302; Górecki, *Economy,* 213–14, 215–19, 220, 239–42, 255; and, in its entirety, Jan M. Piskorski, *Kolonizacja wiejska Pomorza Zachodniego w XIII i w początkach XIV wieku na tle procesów osadniczych w średniowiecznej Europie* [Rural colonization of Western Pomerania in the thirteenth and the early fourteenth centuries in the context of settlement processes in medieval Europe] (Poznań: Wydawnictwo Poznańskiego Towarzystwa Przyjaciół Nauk, 1991).

agrarian estate on behalf of the lord of the estate. The estate arable was allocated into two portions – sometimes (in ironic contrast with the indigenous *sors*) in fact by means of an allottment. One portion was peasant tenures, with the tenants subject to substantial payments in three or four kinds of grain, and in coin, but to no other payments in kind, and, most importantly, to no labor obligations. The other portion was the tenure belonging to the village bailiff, which was free from the grain and coin payments and from tithe, and which constituted a reward to the bailiff for his entrepreneurial, judicial, and rent-gathering responsibilities.

Also in contrast to the widely varied agrarian estates settled by the indigenous population, the estate established "according to German law" uniformly entailed a clear, and standardized, criterion for the assessment of obligations placed upon its inhabitants. The tenants' payment of grain and coin was clearly and explicitly tied to the *mansus* – a conceptual unit of landholding recorded ubiquitously in the *Henryków Book*, the ducal charters, and the other documents noted earlier in this essay,[195] translated here (with some hesitation, to be addressed shortly) as the *hide*. This conceptual unit was standardized in a sense that the indigenous "holding" was not. It served as the precise basis of obligations – or, on the other hand, of freedom from obligations. The tenures of the bailiff, and of the peasants, all were all held, and assessed, in some number of "hides," of which each was subject to the specified grain or coin payment, and of which some were exempted from payment. An early example of a plan to reorganize land, obligations, and lordship in this way is Abbot Peter's story about the recruitment of the village bailiff Menold by Duke Henry the Bearded between 1221 and 1227.[196]

The translation of the *mansus* as *hide*, rather than with some other word (*manse*, for example), or no translation at all, requires an explanation. Right on its face, the word *hide* pulls the anglophone reader toward concepts of landholding, obligation, and assessment appropriate to an entirely different medieval universe: England between the times of Bede and the Norman Conquest, when and where both that word, and the concepts to which it referred, had a rather specific history. Furthermore, its transposition into the Silesian, Polish, and Polish-German context via this particular translation of *mansus* masks one actual correspondence between words and things; as we have seen, in Poland the open-ended conceptual shorthand encompassing residency, exploitation, and environment which most closely resembles Bede's *terra unius familiae* – "the hide" in one early, and precise, sense – was not the *mansus*, but the *sors*, which I nevertheless translate as *holding*.[197] Here, perhaps, is a better candidate for this particular translation.

These semantic caveats reflect needless caution. I now render *mansus* as *hide*, as I have done throughout my work, in order to present as much prose as

195. For the other documents, see section 3 above, "The contexts of power and of writing," nn. 111–14, 117–27, 132–33.
196. Chapters 94–96.
197. See nn. 189, 191 above.

possible in English, and not clutter up the text with matter that is, on its face, inaccessible, and which would, in any event, require its own cautioning commentary. The alternatives are unpromising: the word *manse* is barely a part of active vernacular in today's English, and its meanings are now more or less archaic. *Hide*, in contrast, continues to be understood, at least in a general sense, as a unit of land. Moreover, its application to a medieval world very distant, in every sense, from the realities of Bede, or of the surveyors of Domesday, is not intrinsically anachronistic. The word itself, its equivalents in different historical and historiographical vernaculars,[198] and its range of relationships to spatial, proprietary, seigneurial, and fiscal realities, have a long history, of which Anglo-Saxon or Anglo-Norman developments are one fragment.

In the Continental phase of that history, two early moments are especially important: during the Carolingian period, the use of the *mansus* as a conceptually standardized criterion for obligations to the king;[199] and, over the long twelfth century, its use as a similar criterion for assessment of obligations to lords, rulers, and bishops, from peasantries engaged in "colonizing" the European East.[200] This is the capacity, so to speak, in which the word *mansus* arrives in the Piast duchies, shortly after 1200 – a part of the long history of the *huba*, *Hufe*, *mansus*, *sors*, and similar expressions, of which the unit known in English as the *hide* was one variant. In short, when viewed from a vantage point other than the world of Bede, *hide* works for *mansus* in English at least as well as does any alternative.

The German-law estates were clearly, and quite uniformly, based on tenure and rent. Within this context, the village bailiff's tenure was rather ambiguous. The bailiff was, typically, a peasant entrepreneur, and thus his farm was essentially one of the peasant tenures; but the farm was usually much larger than were the individual tenures of the peasants whom he recruited, and he possessed it as a reward for exercising seigneurial power over these peasants on behalf of the lord. The bailiff's privilege is sometimes further underscored by references to his farm as "feudal hides" (*mansi feodales*), and by their association with the bailiff's military service to his lord.[201] In some respects, the bailiff's estate also resembles the demesne in one sense of that word, the *mansus indominicatus*: the portion of total village arable that is not farmed out as tenures but retained by the lord (or, in this case, the lord's agent) for direct exploitation.[202] Not surpri-

198. Hägermann and Hedwig, "Hufe," col. 154.

199. Christoph Sonnlechner, "The Establishment of New Units of Production in Carolingian Times: Making Early Medieval Sources Relevant for Environmental History," *Viator* 35 (2004), 21–37.

200. Hägermann and Hedwig, "Hufe," col. 156; Walter Kuhn, *Vergleichende Untersuchungen zur mittelalterlichen Ostsiedlung* (Cologne and Vienna: Böhlau, 1973), 89–90.

201. Górecki, *Economy*, 239–40, 248, 266.

202. Duby, *Rural Economy*, 34–35, 197–204; Michael Postan, *The Medieval Economy and Society* (Harmondsworth: Penguin, 1975), 82, 105–21; John Langdon, *Horses, Oxen and*

singly, the village bailiff was a very privileged tenant, who seems to have enjoyed a considerable power toward the lord of the estate, and within the local and regional society in general. In some exceptionally interesting case studies, Abbot Peter and his continuator recall the political difficulties their monks confronted from several German rural entrepreneurs of this kind.[203]

The German-law estate consisted of two portions allocated among the peasants and the seigneurial agent. Some German-law grants also envisioned a third portion portion of the arable, held directly by the lord. In this cases, the result was a plan for a kind of tripartite manor – and the portion possessed by the lord might be directly comparablc to the demesne if we knew who labored for the lord on his own reserve. However, we do not know who labored on either the village bailiff's or the lord's farms until about the sixth decade of the thirteenth century, at which time peasants on German-law estates began to be subjected to labor obligations on them, though in this early period very rarely, and at the very light level of a few days per year. The gradual expansion of the frequency of these obligations in Silesia, in Poland, and indeed in East Central Europe as a macro-region, is, in its entirety, a much later story, not yet reflected, or even anticipated, in either portion of the *Henryków Book.*[204]

As is the case with agriculture and agrarian estates, several features and functions of Polish towns show strong continuity throughout the Middle Ages in many respects, dramatic discontinuites and changes in others. As far back as the archaeological and written evidence extends, towns were, above all, regional centers of several interrelated and mutually reinforcing processes: authority and power; monumental or defensive construction (in stone, earthwork, and wood); cult; relative population density (and sometimes a planned layout); social stratification and intensive specialization and exchange (through trade or forced redistribution) – all in varying combinations.[205]

Technological Innovation: The Use of Draught Animals in English Farming from 1066–1500 (Cambridge: Cambridge University Press, 1986), 2, n. 5.

203. Chapters 103, 109–11, 160.

204. Leonid Żytkowicz, "Trends of the Agrarian Economy in Poland, Bohemia and Hungary from the Middle of the Fifteenth to the Middle of the Seventeenth Century," in Mączak, Samsonowicz, and Burke, *East-Central Europe*, 59–83.

205. For the working definition of the town as a regional center, see Robert Fossier, *Enfance de l'Europe*, 2:980–1047 (specifically for early medieval Slavic Europe, 1035–48), and the review essay of that book by Léopold Génicot, in *Révue d'histoire de l'Église* 78 (1983), 400; for various approaches to the conceptual issues posed by that and alternative working defintions, see Tadeusz Rosłanowski, "Comparative Sociotopography on the Example of Early-Medieval Towns in Central Europe," *Acta Poloniae Historica* 34 (1976), 7–27, at 9; Leciejewicz, "Early-Medieval Sociotopographical Transformations," 33–41, 44–52; Susan Reynolds, *An Introduction to the History of English Medieval Towns* (Oxford: Clarendon Press, 1977), 18–21, 24–34, 52–62, 87–90; Hodges, *Dark Age Economics*, 20–25. Recently, Keith D. Lilley returns to those conceptual issues in *Urban Life*, 3–8, 45–46, on which, however, see n. 208 below.

Historians and archaeologists disagree on the period of the origins of the relatively dense clusters of settlement, specialization, power, and cult in those locations that are documented as the core Polish urban centers from the tenth century onward. However, the histories of Kraków, Wrocław, Poznań, Gniezno, and Płock as urban centers (see Maps 1–2) antedate, and were affected by, the rise of the Piast kingdom and the conversion of its rulers in the tenth century; and thus long preceded the gradual appearance of the written record over the subsequent 300 years.[206] In the early twelfth century, Poland's basic political and ecclesiastical organization rested on a network of "the principal seats of the kingdom" – the fortified main cities and their surrounding districts, each of which in turn included dozens more modest fortified settlements and hundreds of villages. This network of central places provided the basic territorial and administrative unit for the Polish duchies throughout the Middle Ages. Each duke sought to control the most imporant town or towns in a particular Piast province, and from there to project authority to the entire hierarchy of outlying settlement.[207]

The structure, size, range of functions, and legal status of the cities and towns within this network underwent enormous change between the tenth and the fourteenth centuries. Several directions of this change were counterparts to the dynamics of urban change in other regions of medieval Europe. Geographically, the Polish medieval towns evolved from clusters of one or more rings of fortifications, housing the principal ecclesiastical buildings, palaces of rulers and their chief officials, and a population of unspecified size consisting of knights, ecclesiastics, small communities of merchants, and other socially open-ended groups, all in the midst of a dense settlement blending into, and overlapping with, the rural countryside[208] – toward "new towns," situated within, near, or at some dis-

206. Leciejewicz, "Early-Medieval Sociotopographical Transformations," 44–47, 50–52; Knoll, "Urban Development," 62–71, 78–86; F. W. Carter, *Trade and Urban Development in Poland: An Economic Geography of Cracow, from Its Origins to 1795* (Cambridge: Cambridge University Press, 1994), 2–17, 42–62; Jerzy Wyrozumski, *Dzieje Krakowa* [A history of Kraków], vol. 1: *Kraków do schyłku wieków średnich* [Kraków until the end of the Middle Ages] (Kraków: Wydawnictwo Literackie, 1992), 35–146; *Miasto zachodniosłowiańskie w XI–XII wieku. Społeczeństwo – kultura* [The Western Slavic town in the eleventh and twelfth centuries: society and culture], ed. Lech Leciejewicz (Wrocław: Zakład Narodowy im. Ossolińskich, 1991); Marta Młynarska-Kaletynowa, *Wrocław w XII–XIII wieku: przemiany społeczne i osadnicze* [Wrocław in the twelfth and thirteenth centuries: social and settlement changes] (Wrocław: Zakład Narodowy im. Ossolińskich, 1986), 15, 17–99.

207. Tadeusz Wasilewski, "Poland's Administrative Structure in Early Piast Times," *Acta Poloniae Historica* 44 (1981), 5–31; Karol Modzelewski, "The System of the Ius Ducale and the Idea of Feudalism: Comments on the Earliest Class Society in Medieval Poland," *Quaestiones Medii Aevi* 1 (1977), 71–99.

208. Without wishing to re-engage in the kinds of polemics and reassessments on early medieval towns that have, in a conceptual sense, crested in the mid-1980s, I would like to signal here my strong disagreement with Lilley's designation, in his otherwise very fine book, of such complexes as "proto-towns" – with the "new towns" making up the

tance from these earlier complexes, but distinguished from them, and from the surrounding rural settlement, by some combination of the following features: a street layout; an encompassing fortification or boundary (in the later medieval period, the town wall); at least one marketplace, with or without specialized buildings; and a distinctly high concentration of churches. The populations of the early fortified cores, and of the surrounding "new towns," expanded substantially. They became increasingly specialized in mediating local and regional exchange, in craft production, in high-skill construction, and in several other pursuits sharply divorced from one another, and from agriculture. Apart from their wide variation in size, the sheer number of towns with these features increased dramatically in the course of the medieval period.[209]

In the Polish duchies, and throughout East Central Europe, these transformations were closely related to immigration of Germans, and to widespread use by dukes and lords of "German law" to define the legal, jurisdictional, spatial, and economic structure of the towns situated within their duchies or estates.[210] As in the case of agricultural and demographic expansion, the contours of this relationship are complicated. While Germans, or "German law," were perhaps not the essential cause, or driving force, of the expansion of towns in the Polish duchies between the tenth and the fourteenth centuries, Germans very actively participated in these processes, and crucially affected their dynamics and their results. One result was the appearance of Germans among, and, in a global sense, indeed the "Germanization" of, the wealthiest groups of townspeople, and of civic institutions. Another was the formulation and use of "German law" as yet another formal blueprint for human organization, in this case of urban settlement.[211]

The specific terms of this adaptation of "German law" were drawn, in a process of deliberate and complicated imitation, from a handful of especially important cities that had been settled (or resettled) by Germans within two regions of intensive German settlement among Slavic populations. Lübeck,

---

real thing. This seems to me a turn back to mid-twentieth-century thought, revised thoroughly later, and now grounded by Lilley in an unexplained dismissal, at *Urban Life*, 6, n. 29, of the arguments on this subject by Richard Hodges. The result, though expressed in passing, is a very flat and unsatisfactory treatment of twelfth-century Szczecin, at 46, as a supposed instance of a "proto-town" – with no conceptual room for considering early Wrocław, for example, or Płock a century later. Compare the far more nuanced and sophisticated treatment of early Kraków in Carter, *Trade*, 52–62.

209. Bogucka, "Towns of East-Central Europe," 97–98.

210. This subject apparently continues to require considerable historiographical unpacking; Lilley notes, albeit in passing, the residual political implications of this subject in 2002, in *Urban Life*, 23–25.

211. Bartlett, *Making*, 172–73, 179–81, 191–96; Górecki, *Economy*, 203–08; Lilley, *Urban Life*, 83–93, 131–37. An excellent piece of evidence about urban expansion and transformation, and the significance of Germans and German law in these processes, is the history of the town of Münsterberg, reflected in several passages of the *Henryków Book*, especially the second section.

Magdeburg, and – somewhat later and more regionally – Halle were especially important in the region between the Elbe and the Odra, which had attracted German settlement in the course of the tenth, eleventh, and twelfth centuries (see Map 1). Środa, an early and important Slavic market center to the northwest of Wrocław that attracted German settlers (and subsequently acquired the German name Neumarkt [see Map 3]), served as a model for one variant of the German "laws" of dozens of towns (of varying size and importance) in the Polish duchies throughout the thirteenth and early fourteenth centuries.[212]

Although these patterns of imitation undoubtedly entailed informal migration and complicated networks of information and recruitment among generations of settlers, in a formal sense the "German law" of urban settlement was granted through a written charter, usually issued by a duke.[213] Like its rural counterpart, the urban "law" included two elements: a "liberty," or an immunity – that is, an exemption for the inhabitants and the space defined as part of the city from a wide range of traditional obligations to dukes, lords, and ecclesiastics; and a blueprint of the urban economy and law.[214] The latter included, in varying detail, elements of the urban political and social structure (such as membership in guilds or in communal assemblies); of the urban economy (such as regulation of cloth production, or of the central marketplace); of substantive law (such as inheritance, criminal procedure, or marriage involving the citizens); and of the management and administration of the town (such as the competence of a town council, assessors, "burgraves," or advocates).

The resulting "German law" of urban settlement was closely related to its rural counterpart in several ways. The tenures and the responsibilities of the highest officials of German-law towns – called advocates in Silesia – were similar to, and in some cases indistinguishable from, those of the rural village baliffs. In fact, the substance of the "German law" of rural settlements was itself, in varying degrees, explicitly drawn from the town "laws" of Środa–Neumarkt, Halle, or Magdeburg. The most ambitious plans formulated by Piast rulers for recruitment of Germans during the early thirteenth century envisioned future hierarchies of settlement and authority, centered on "cities" surrounded by substantial clusters of villages, in which city-based "advocates," and the civic institutions

---

212. Zbigniew Zdrójkowski, "Miasta na prawie średzkim (materiały)" [Towns established according to the law of Neumarkt – the sources], *Sobótka* 41 (1986), 343–51; Górecki, *Economy*, 203–08, 214–17, 219, 260–61 (n. 53), 276, 278–79; Lilley, *Urban Life*, 89.

213. The formal grant of liberty, and some degree of spatial transformation and planning with respect to the town encompassed by it, are in this context called "location"; see Benedykt Zientara, "Socio-Economic and Spatial Transformation of Polish Towns during the Period of Location," *Acta Poloniae Historica* 34 (1976), 57–83; Knoll, "Urban Development," 64, 70, 86–89.

214. See Górecki, *Economy*, 27, 36 (n. 38), 123–203, for charters of "liberty," or immunity, in Poland in general, and 203–08, 237, for the adaptation of such charters for towns and their populations.

over which they presided, exercised jurisdiction, and other areas of authority, over all the inhabitants of the districts surrounding each "city."[215]

Despite the rather mixed degree of success of the particular early initiatives of which these plans were a part, regions of especially intensive German settlement in the Polish duchies closely conformed to them during the subsequent century. Above all, Silesia included several districts in which city advocates and courts exercised very broad jurisdiction concerning peace, property issues, inheritance, and a wide range of other matters, over the rural as well as urban population.[216] The broad jurisdictional role of cities in the region of Henryków is well reflected by the involvement of the town judges, assessors, and council of Münsterberg in property transfer and litigation, and in criminal cases. Abbot Peter notes the importance of that city briefly and in passing, whereas his continuator consistently notes the central position of Münsterberg, and to a lesser extent other new towns, in the legal life of the Henryków region during the first years of the fourteenth century.[217] Münsterberg and its civic institutions recur as actors so frequently that the second part of the *Henryków Book* can usefully be viewed as a history of a town and the world around it – with the monastery as a part of that world.

To return to the broad sweep of time between the later twelfth century and the early fourteenth, the Henryków monastery itself, and the most important part of its estate, were situated within a region in which these agrarian, urban, seigneurial, ethnic, and demographic changes are very well-documented – by the *Book* itself, by the charters translated here as Supplementary Documents, and by a much larger volume of diplomas (and, since the fourteenth century) cartulary and rental evidence. In its entirety, the monastery's endowment was scattered across three Polish provinces: Silesia (Maps 4–5), Great Poland (Map 2), and Little Poland (Map 2). However, the estates situated in Silesia were by far the most important, both as a proportion of the total endowment, and as a subject of record by the two Henryków authors, as well as by other evidence.

The monks' endowment in Silesia in turn encompassed three distinct spaces: (1) the "territory of Henryków," by which Abbot Peter meant a compact area of settlement, old but in the process of transition, within which the monastery, the

---

215. Górecki, *Economy*, 214–15, 237, 244, 263–70, 272.

216. The current generation of Polish and German scholars note that, in the regions of intensive German settlement (Silesia above all), by the fourteenth century the emerging towns and their districts became the most important units of the administrative and judicial network on which ducal power rested, and in these capacities replaced the older structure of fortified Polish towns and their districts ("castellanies"); see Sławomir Gawlas, *O kształt zjednoczonego królestwa. Niemieckie władztwo terytorialne a geneza społecznoustrojowej odrębności Polski* [Toward the shape of the united kingdom: German territorial lordship and the origins of the socio-political distinctness of Poland] (Warsaw: Wydawnictwo DiG, 1996), 53–58, 89–90.

217. Chapters 80–81, 115, 127, 131, 133, 135, 138, 147–49, 152, 156, 158–59, 162–64, 169–70, 172, 175, 177–79, 184–87, 189–92.

cloister, and the core of the monastery's estate, were established (Map 5);[218] (2) Schönwald, by which Peter meant an area of more recent settlement, especially by German immigrants, situated between twenty and thirty kilometers to the southwest of the "territory of Henryków" near the foothills of the Sudeten mountains (Map 4);[219] and (3) two adjacent forests elsewhere in the foothills of the Sudeten mountains, which Peter and his continuator also identified with German place names, *Richnow* and *Quolsdorf*, and which were also destinations of early German immigration (Map 4).[220] Schönwald and the two forests were the territories that, together, situate this monastery and its estate within a "frontier" within Piast Poland, and within Silesia. The monastery's possessions in Great and Little Poland were far more modest – one of them situated near another kind of liminal space, namely the region between Great Poland and Silesia, and peripheral to each (Map 2). In addition, the monks were endowed with rights of lordship over a future, planned district of (presumably German) settlement in the far northern periphery of Great Poland (Map 2),[221] but these ambitious plans do not appear to have succeeded.[222]

Taken as a whole, the *Henryków Book* focuses overwhelmingly on the one cluster of localities and population that had, from the very beginning, been the core of the monastic estate: the "territory of Henryków" (see Map 5). (In addition, Peter, but not his continuator, included a detailed history of Schönwald, and more cursory references to one of the Great Polish possessions of the monastery.)[223] The "territory of Henryków" was compact; the localities within it were all situated between two and ten kilometers of the monastic church.[224] The geography and ecology of the region was defined by three features: a system of streams and local rivers, draining ultimately to the Odra in the north; a lowland, relatively flat terrain, rising gradually but perceptibly into gently rolling hills in the upper reaches of these streams, about fifteen kilometers to the west and southwest of the monastic church; and several stretches of forest both in the lowland and in the higher regions, once again especially in the southwest, where it blended with a substantial and wide belt of highland forest that spanned the foothills of the Sudetes, the mountains themselves, and the district of the Czech frontier (see Maps 4–5).

Perhaps the most conspicuous, in some respects defining, ecological feature was the northward flow of the Oława river, draining into the Odra near Wrocław (see Map 4). For all of its demographic, ethnic, economic, and political

---

218. Chapters 34, 39, 83.
219. Chapters 94–111.
220. Chapters 21–22, 157–60; Supplementary Documents no. 2, 6.
221. Supplementary Document no. 1.
222. On the context, and the results, see Górecki, *Economy*, 263–67.
223. Chapters 94–111, 114–119.
224. Łowmiański, *Początki*, 3:39.

changes in the course of the thirteenth century, the "territory of Henryków" remained clustered within the system of streams that drained eastward into the Oława along its middle course, over the span of about seven to ten kilometers, gently downward from the slightly hilly terrain further west (see Map 5).[225] It also included localities situated on the right bank of the Oława, but no further than about two kilometers to the east. At the time of the monastery's foundation between 1222 and 1228, this region included a settlement (or group of settlements) which Abbot Peter identified as "Old Henryków," and several other localities to which he devoted especially detailed historical reconstruction in the first geographic "account" of his portion of the *Book*.

The "territory of Henryków," its partly-settled, partly-forested outliers, and its network of streams and rivers, were situated approximately within the center of a much larger complex of well-irrigated settlements and forest to the south of Wrocław that was encompassed – and, in an ecological sense, defined – by the wide arc of the river Nysa, which flows from the northern reaches of the Sudetes about seventy kilometers to the southwest of Wrocław, due eastward, northeastward, and and then, in a relatively smooth loop of a radius of about forty kilometers, northward to the Odra halfway between Brzeg and Opole in the southeast of the province (see Map 4). The large region encompassed by the Nysa was a setting of several of the broad processes and changes that characterized Silesia and the Polish duchies in general, and that are especially well-documented in the Henryków history in particular.

Its lowland north and northeast had, for at least several centuries before the foundation of the monastery, been settled by a dense network of Polish villages, fortified towns, and other forms of settlement. It included a former important center of pagan cult, Mount Ślęża (or Sobótka) – a location of an early monastic foundation in the twelfth century – and a substantial cluster of villages. It also included a series of Slavic towns that remained significant in the expanding urban network of the province throughout the demographic, ethnic, legal, economic, and political changes that affected Silesia during the later twelfth, thirteenth, and early fourteenth centuries. These old and early towns within the Nysa–Odra arc included the chief city of Wrocław itself, as well as Oława, Ryczyn, Brzeg, Niemcza, and Strzelin; and they were a part of a much longer string of localities along or near the Odra, extending from Lubusz, Krosno, and Głogów in the northwest, to Opole in the southeast, that had for centuries provided the administrative and defensive skeleton of the province (see Maps 3–4).

In contrast, the slightly higher and relatively forested region to the south and southwest of the Nysa–Odra region had in the preceding centuries been relatively unsettled. From the late twelfth century onward, it had been an early desti-

---

225. For more detail on the ecological and topographical setting of this region, see Jerzy Kondracki, *Geografia regionalna Polski* [The regional geography of Poland] (Warsaw: Wydawnictwo Naukowe PWN, 1998), 218–22.

nation for German settlers, and an early venue for the foundation of a large, ambitious, and carefully planned estate of the diocese of Wrocław, relying specifically on German settlers, in and around Otmuchów and the emerging town of Nysa (Neiße). In the course of the thirteenth century, this southwesterly region near the upper Nysa river experienced a dramatic expansion of new German towns, including Reichenbach, Löwenstein, Frankenstein, and Münsterberg. Somewhat like their Polish counterparts closer to the Odra and within the Silesian Plain, these localities were part of a series of German towns that extended throughout the province along the foothills of the Sudetes, from Löwenberg and Goldberg in the northwest to the town of Nysa and beyond in the southeast (see Maps 3–4). These towns were also local centers of a dramatic expansion in the number of German villages in this region. The "territory of Henryków" to a significant extent straddled the lowland northeast and highland southwest. To return to one of the three big subjects I noted at the outset: this is why it was a frontier region in one, higly precise, sense of that word.

5 Lords, counts, knights, and dukes
The *Henryków Book* is a history of two closely interrelated subjects: the individual localities that became part of the monastery's estate in the course of the thirteenth and the early fourteenth centuries; and the relationships of political power in the Henryków region and beyond. Both subjects were crucially important for Abbot Peter and for his continuator. The proprietary history of the monastery's estate protected the monks from legal challenges concerning their landholdings, whereas an accurate interpretation of power relations positioned the monks with regard to a number of other actors who wielded political power in ways that mattered to the monastery. These actors included: the Piast dukes; ducal judges and other officials; other powerful landholders, established in and near "the territory of Henryków," and elsewhere; ecclesiastical institutions and the people who staffed them – bishops, cathedral clergy, abbots, monks, and parish priests; and, especially during the later thirteenth and early fourteenth centuries, towns, urban institutions, and individual townspeople.

All these categories of actors were important. Power within this society can best be understood as an outcome of their interactions. Two categories should be noted right at the outset. The first is rather amorphous and open-ended, especially when viewed from today's perspective; it consists of the populations just classified as the "ducal officials" and as the "other powerful landholders." As elsewhere, "office" in medieval Poland was at the same time a symptom and a source of the social standing for the person who exercised it.[226] Another

226. By office, I mean a specialized function that was performed, at least in a formal sense, on behalf of a duke, or (more seldom in the sources) of someone else generally recognized as holding legitimate authority, e.g., a bishop – by persons specifically designated with a particular word (e.g., *castellanus*), who otherwise enjoyed a wide range of power and

symptom and source of social standing was possession of landed estates, which encompassed the wide range of resources described in the preceding section, and included one or more rural localities, or *villae* – uniformly, though a bit problematically, translated here as *villages*.[227] A third determinant of social standing was the possession of seigneurial powers over the inhabitants of such estates. A fourth was access to active participation in several areas of important activity: making gifts to the saints and to their temporal agents, the clergy; litigating important matters, directly before the duke or his highest officials; and other kinds of action reflecting a distinct level of social privilege.[228]

All these determinants of status affected particular persons in varying combinations. The subset of this general population that did not hold office comprises, in my classificatory schema, those "other powerful landholders." Viewed from the present perspective, the "officials" and those "others" partly overlap, because over their life-cycles particular individuals held office, at least for a time, as part of a wide range of these attributes; the stories in the *Henryków Book* swarm with actors who conform to this profile. However, viewed from the perspective of the contemporaries – including Abbot Peter, his continuator, and the authors of the diplomas – my two conceptually overlapping categories are quite clear and precise. First, whatever their other attributes, officeholders are

privilege, and who may or may not have in fact acted under the principal's effective control. The notion of *office* is currently somewhat complicated; its understanding relates to ongoing reassessments of the medieval, especially the early medieval, state, specifically the relationship between rulers and their agents, for which see: Susan Reynolds, "The Historiography of the Medieval State," in *Companion to Historiography*, ed. Michael Bentley (London: Routledge, 1997), 117–38; Matthew Innes, *State and Society in the Early Middle Ages: The Middle Rhine Valley 400–1000* (Cambridge: Cambridge University Press, 2000); Warren Brown, *Unjust Seizure: Conflict, Interest, and Authority in an Early Medieval Society* (Ithaca: Cornell University Press, 2001), above all the exemplary study of one official at 102–23; Stephen D. White, "Tenth-Century Courts at Mâcon and the Perils of Structuralist History," in Brown and Górecki, *Conflict*, 37–68, at 51–52, 64–65. In the Polish context the subject raises related, additional issues of Piast power which I cannot address here; for now, please see my discussions of office in Górecki, *Economy*, 125–26, 134, 173–74, 176–80. A recent treatment is Janusz Kurtyka, "Hofämter, Landesämter, Staatsämter und ihre Hierarchien in Polen im mittleleuropäischen Vergleich (11.–15. Jh.)," in Wünsch and Patschovsky, *Das Reich und Polen*, 129–213.

227. *Villa* in Polish documents poses an ambiguity similar to that same word in regions further to the west, especially in the earlier medieval period – the word may also designate what we would call an estate, or, alternatively, a small number of households. An interesting example of this ambiguity is Abbot Peter's reference as a *villa* to Budzów at a time when it was a piece of land where Duke Henry the Bearded intended to establish a village in the ordinary sense of that word (a plan that, notably, failed) – for which see Chapters 94, 96–97. Nevertheless, *villa* did, among other things, mean a village, and I so render it with that word, in order not to clutter the text with untranslated words.

228. For privileged activities as a source and reflection of social standing, see Piotr Górecki, "Words, Concepts, and Phenomena: Knighthood, Lordship, and the Early Polish Nobility, c. 1100–c. 1350," in Duggan, *Nobles and Nobility*, 115–55, at 122, 125, 128–30, 133.

clearly and explicitly classified as such in the written sources, the *Henryków Book* included. Thus, underlying the written record is an assumption that these classifications, and the functions to which they refer, were clear and well understood at the time – even though they may be less accessible to us today. Second, the population which I lump together as those "other powerful landholders" is identified in the surviving written record by three recurring epithets which, on their face, appear to express high social standing, and which, like the words associated with office, must have been clear to the contemporaries, even if they are not entirely clear to us.

The most recurrent such epithet is *dominus* – which I always translate as *lord*. This word is used hundreds of times in the *Henryków Book*, and thousands of times in the diplomatic record of Silesia and the other Piast duchies. It usually precedes the first name of some lay or clerical actor. Less often, it is used by itself, as a full substantive noun. In that latter case, it is sometimes used in the vocative, that is, as a form of address to a group of "lords" employed in direct speech;[229] or, in order to express a relationship between a subordinate and a superior, especially the duke;[230] or (but this uniquely by Abbot Peter) as a synonym for the monks of Henryków.[231] In the *Henryków Book* and elsewhere, the word *dominus* appears so often that it seems to work, at the same time, as an expression of general respect – as we today might interchangeably use *lord*, *sir* or *sire*, *monsieur*, or *mister* – and as a marker of high standing, combining at least some of the attributes of privilege noted above: landed property, lordship, and a capacity to engage in important activities.

A less frequent epithet marking high standing is *comes* – in this translation always rendered as *count*. This seems to have been a more specific or restricted word than *dominus*. It always precedes a first name, and is never combined with *dominus*. It is therefore more specifically an individual attribute of a particular person, and an expression of respect and social standing fully alternative to *dominus*. Because it is less frequent, it may also be more exclusive, and thus reflect that respect and social standing more strongly.[232] It is applied only to lay persons; to my knowledge, there is not a single indentification of an abbot, a bishop, or any other ecclesiastic, as a *comes*, in the *Henryków Book* or elsewhere. To complicate things a bit, in medieval Poland, as in other places, the word *comes* relates to office: on rare occasion, it is used as a synonym for one of the two highest ducal officials, the palatine and the castellan.[233] However, this is very much an excep-

---

229. Chapters 6–7, 9, 11, 69, 74, 85, 87, 106, 111, 114, 116, 119–21, 200, 202–03, 206.
230. Chapters 2, 5–7, 9, 11, 13, 74, 82, 101, 105, 111, 135, 142–43, 152, 159, 164, 170, 183, 189, 194, 200.
231. Chapters 65, 91–92, 111–13, 119–21, 164, 176, 202, 205–06, 210.
232. All of the uses of this epithet (not the specialized uses concerning *dominus* above) are: Chapters 48–49, 55, 60–61, 63, 70, 75, 78–79, 81, 86, 90, 96, 98, 102, 107–09, 115, 117, 119, 133, 146, 148, 159.
233. For these two offices, nn. 269–71 below.

tion. Almost always, *comes* stands alone as a personal attribute, with no indication that it meant any differentiated function on anyone's behalf. Its relationship to office is therefore semantic, and, by the mid-twelfth century, perhaps historical. We may have here an analogy with the English *earl* after the Anglo-Saxon period.[234] All this makes my decision to render the word *comes* as *count* a bit problematic to modern English readers, yet, with this particular caveat, I do so.[235]

The third frequent expression of high social standing is the epithet *miles*, which is always translated here as *knight*. Like "lord" (*dominus*) and "count" (*comes*), that word is used, in the *Book* as elsewhere, in conjunction with a first name, that is, as an individual attribute. Moreover, also like *dominus*, but unlike *comes*, it is sometimes used in the vocative in direct speech, as a form of address.[236] In contrast to *comes*, it seems interchangeable with *dominus*, and indeed with *comes* itself. It is consistently used for lay persons – although, like a layman, a cleric may be of a "knightly" background.[237] This last, adjectival usage reflects an important difference between this epithet and the other two – and, by the way, a moment of relative precision in the Polish early terminology of high social standing. During the first years of the thirteenth century, *miles* was well-established as a designation of a specific status – that is, a rather precise bundle of privileges for (and perhaps obligations by) the persons designated by that word.[238] *Knight* was a specific social category in a way that the *dominus* or the *comes* were not. The word *miles* was therefore available as a rather precise criterion of social classification, as well as a more general epithet of distinction. Accordingly, both authors of the *Book* repeatedly classify particular

234. David Crouch, *The Image of Aristocracy in Britain, 1000–1300* (London: Routledge, 1992), 41–83.

235. My decision to translate this word reflects a general preference, whenever possible, not to overload the English text with Latin words, and to save interpretations that turn on the meanings of the Latin word to reference matter. However, for the reasons just noted, others (now notably including Knoll and Schaer, *Gesta*, 17, n. 6) prefer to leave *comes* untranslated.

236. Chapter 74.

237. Chapter 2.

238. On the elements of this privileged status, and the social group (or groups) that benefitted from it, see: Górecki, "Words"; Janusz Bieniak, "Knightly Clans in Medieval Poland," in *The Polish Nobility in the Middle Ages*, ed. Antoni Gąsiorowski (Wrocław: Zakład Narodowy im. Ossolińskich, 1984), 123–76; Bieniak, "Clans de chevallerie en Pologne du XIIIe au XVe siècle," in *Famille et parenté dans l'Occident médiéval*, ed. Georges Duby and Jacques Le Goff (Rome: École française de Rome, 1977), 321–33; Jan Wroniszewski, "*Proclamatio alias godło*. Uwagi nad genezą i funkcją zawołań rycerskich w średniowiecznej Polsce" [*Proclamatio alias godło*: remarks on the origins and function of the knightly battle cry in medieval Poland], in *Społeczeństwo Polski średniowiecznej* [The society of medieval Poland], ed. Stefan Kuczyński, vol. 4 (Warsaw: Państwowe Wydawnictwo Naukowe, 1990), 147–70. For German knights in particular, see above all Jurek, *Obce rycerstwo*.

actors as "a knight," "a certain knight," "a rather powerful knight,"[239] and particular collectivities as "knights," or "senior knights."[240]

Again, our authors clearly knew what they meant by these three (and some other) epithets of status, and they knew the population to which such epithets were applicable; we know much less. However, even these relatively firm classifications were fluid and subject to negotiation.[241] An important party to that negotiation was another major actor, or agent: the duke. In contrast to the privileged groups just described, this particular actor was back then, and appears in the record today, sharply distinguished from everyone else. Right from the twelfth-century beginnings narrated by Abbot Peter, until the most recent events narrated by his continuator, the ruler is a visible and prominent actor in the monastery's history. As noted earlier, the nature of the office of the dukes of Piast Poland, and their full political and dynastic history, are exceedingly complicated subjects.[242] For present purposes I offer here only a skeletal outline that may serve as a context for the interpretation of the *Henryków Book* and related sources.

Like the society and economy over which he presided, by the later 1260s the duke, now considered as an abstract figure, was very old. His formal position – that is, this one especially important "office" – had been well entrenched across about three centuries of history, ideology, and practice before Abbot Peter began to write. He was a member of a single dynasty that traced its descent to a legendary founder believed to have that name. The dynasty ruled Poland continuously between the mid-tenth century, when Duke Mieszko I united several West Slavic peoples into a single Polish principality, until the death of King Casimir the Great in 1370. The public authority of the Piast dukes survived the division of the united Polish principality, after 1138, into the duchies of Silesia, Great Poland, Little Poland, and Masovia (see Map 2), and the subsequent continued

239. Chapters 2, 29, 31, 34, 45, 74, 78, 85, 111, 114, 127–28, 133, 138, 146, 151, 154–55, 158–59, 161–62, 168, 183, 186, 189, 191.

240. Chapters 47, 74, 77, 101–02, 111, 116, 127, 153, 160, 167, 170, 196.

241. Górecki, "Words," 135–37, 146.

242. The literature on the difficult question of ideological authority, and the effective power, of the Piast dukes is vast in Polish and German, much sparser in English; for the former, see now, as an introduction, Stanisław Szczur, *Historia Polski – Średniowiecze* [A history of Poland: the Middle Ages] (Kraków: Wydawnictwo Literackie, 2002), 132–61, 210–18, 257–326; for the latter, see: Malcolm Barber, *The Two Cities: Medieval Europe, 1050–1320* (2nd ed., London: Routledge, 2004), 326–33; Jerzy Lukowski and Hubert Zawadzki, *A Concise History of Poland* (Cambridge: Cambridge University Press, 2001), 3–32; Thomas N. Bisson, "On Not Eating Polish Bread in Vain: Resonance and Conjuncture in the *Deeds of the Princes of Poland* (1109–1113)," *Viator* 29 (1998), 275–89; Norman Davies, *God's Playground: A History of Poland* (New York: Columbia University Press, 1982), 1:61–105; Paul Knoll, *The Rise of the Polish Monarchy: Piast Poland in East Central Europe, 1320–1370* (Chicago: University of Chicago Press, 1972); Knoll, "Polish-German Frontier," 158–59, 165–66; Hoffmann, *Land, Liberties, and Lordship*, 16–22; Górecki, *Economy*, 14–15, 29 (n. 1).

subdivisions of those duchies (including Silesia) into a considerable number of smaller political units, all ruled by branches of the Piast extended family.[243] Within each generation of the proliferating dynasty, and of the proliferating number of principalities over which it presided, a few particular dukes stood out in importance, regional success, and power, and managed to dominate their cousins and their principalities while at the same time consolidating power within their own domains. These relatively powerful and successful dukes accomplished those goals in several ways: by controlling the most important Polish cities, Kraków, Gniezno, Poznań, Wrocław, and Płock; by skillful exercise of patronage over monastic foundations and other kinds of ecclesiastical endowment; by encouragement and protection of new settlers, new lordships, and urban expansion; by grants of immunity to ecclesiastical and secular lords; and, from the later thirteenth century onward, by diplomatic efforts to acquire the crown of a reunified Polish kingdom.

Overall, the Piast dukes (and, after 1320, kings) confronted (or perhaps merely confront us with) an interesting political paradox. On the one hand, they were very active, indeed central, in all these and many other areas of political endeavor, and were clearly recognized as uncontested holders of a special, hereditary authority. On the other hand, their effective power was severely constrained by their competition with one another, and by a dependence on those powerful groups of laymen and ecclesiastics who, as we saw, had access to distinct social privilege – those "counts," "lords," "knights," and privileged others who, among other things, populate the *Henryków Book*. For each Piast duke, ruling therefore meant a constant process of domestic and interregional negotiation, interrupted by periodic outbursts of warfare.[244]

243. Davies, *God's Playground*, 1:62–67, 70–75; Knoll, *Rise*, 1–5; Knoll, "Polish-German Frontier," 153, 158–59, 165–66. This process of division, spanning the years 1138–1320, has traditionally been referred to in Polish historiography as the period of "fragmentation," "feudal fragmentation," or "disintegration"; Topolski, *Outline*, 38–41; Henryk Łowmiański, "Rozdrobnienie feudalne Polski w historiografii naukowej" [The feudal fragmentation of Poland in the historiography], in *Polska w okresie rozdrobnienia feudalnego* [Poland during the period of feudal fragmentation], ed. H. Łowmiański, (Wrocław: Zakład Narodowy im. Ossolińskich, 1973), 7–34. Although labels of this sort are currently a bit old – see Nelson's approving remarks about Berend's approach to "feudal" matters in Hungary (*American Historical Review* 107 [2002], 1279–90) – "feudal fragmentation" does at least point to an irreducible problem of proliferation of Piast principalities, and of the political relations among and within them.

244. We lack a study focusing on Piast power considered in its entirety, of the kind John Fennell has provided for another fragmented dynasty, the Riurikovichi in Russia in a comparable period, in *The Crisis of Medieval Russia, 1200–1304* (London: Longman, 1983). Two studies of the dynasty as a wider group include Jerzy Mularczyk, *Władza książęca na Śląsku w XIII wieku* [Ducal power in Silesia in the thirteenth century] (Wrocław: Zakład Narodowy im. Ossolińskich, 1984), and Roman Michałowski, *Princeps fundator. Studium z dziejów kultury politycznej w Polsce X–XIII wieku* [*Princeps fundator*: a study in the history of

The *Henryków Book* directly reflects three specific aspects of this history: the dynastic, the ecclesiastical, and the economic. Abbot Peter and his continuator refer to a period of ascendancy of three especially important and skilled dukes within the Silesian branch of the Piast dynasty: Dukes Bolesław I the Tall, Henry I the Bearded, and Henry II the Pious. In addition, they refer to two phases in the gradual division of the duchy and province of Silesia among the descendants of Henry I into smaller duchies, ever since the death of Henry II in 1241. The earlier phase of that division occurred between 1241 and the 1260s, and involved the grandsons of Henry I the Bearded. The later phase involved his great-grandsons, and took place approximately between 1280 and 1300.[245]

Each of these two generations of Henry I's descendants was quite numerous.[246] However, within each generation, two dukes were especially significant for that

---

political culture in Poland between the tenth and the thirteenth centuries] (Warsaw: Arx Regia, 1993). We do, however, have a series of excellent biographies of individual Piast dukes, of which the great prototype is Stanisław Smolka, *Mieszko Stary i jego wiek* [Mieszko the Old and his age] (Warsaw: Gebethner i Wolff, 1881, repr. Warsaw: Państwowe Wydawnictwo Naukowe, 1959) – see especially Aleksander Gieysztor's postscript to the 1959 reprint, at 645–72; other works in the genre include Benedykt Zientara, *Henryk Brodaty i jego czasy* [Henry the Bearded and his times] (Warsaw: Państwowy Instytut Wydawniczy, 1975; 2nd ed., Warsaw: Wydawnictwo TRIO, 1997); Tomasz Jurek, *Dziedzic Królestwa Polskiego Książę głogowski Henryk (1279–1309)* [The heir of the Polish Kingdom, the duke of Głogów, Henry (1279–1309)] (Poznań: Wydawnictwo Poznańskiego Towarzystwa Przyjaciół Nauk, 1993); Janusz Kurtyka, *Odrodzone Królestwo. Monarchia Władysława Łokietka i Kazimierza Wielkiego w świetle nowszych badań* [A restored kingdom: The monarchy of Władysław the Short and Casimir the Great in light of recent research] (Kraków: Towarzystwo Naukowe Societas Vistulana, 2001); Paweł Żmudzki, *Studium podzielonego królestwa. Książę Leszek Czarny* [A study in a divided kingdom: Duke Leszek the Black] (Warsaw: Wydawnictwo NERITON, 2000); and, for a comparable analysis of Pomerelia and its non-Piast dukes, see Marek Smoliński, *Polityka zachodnia księcia gdańsko-pomorskiego Świętopełka* [The western policy of the duke of Gdańsk Pomerania, Świętopełk] (Gdańsk: Wydawnictwo Uniwersytetu Gdańskiego/Officina Ferberiana, 2000).

245. Both phases are illustrated in the Genealogical Chart in this volume, where the names of the dukes mentioned in the *Henryków Book* are expressed in bold; and, for genealogical works in Polish, see the reference to that Chart, and the references in the notes throughout the translation of the *Book* and the Supplementary Documents. In varying degrees, and with a varying periodization, the other major Piast provinces underwent similar division into more local duchies – and, like Silesia, were also intermittently led by relatively capable, or relatively aggressive, rulers. Of that complicated story, the *Henryków Book* directly reflects only two dukes of Great Poland, Władysław Odonic and Przemysł I – and that only in the earlier section written by Abbot Peter. The best guide in English to the actual dynasty (including the Silesian branch, and the four generations of dukes with whom Abbot Peter and his continuator were concerned) is the genealogical chart in Davies, *God's Playground*, 1:64.

246. Individual dukes – including the seven discussed below – are fully situated in time, in dynastic succession, and in the relevant genealogical literature, within the body of the *Henryków Book*, and at the Supplementary Documents.

region of Silesia where the "territory of Henryków," the bulk of its estates, and of course the monastery itself, were situated. In the early generation, the crucial pair were Duke Bolesław II the Bald and his brother Henry III the White; their later counterparts were Henry IV the Righteous and Bolko.[247] Altogether, Peter and his continuator consistently specify these rulers as the Piast dukes who were the most active in the Henryków region. They are the individuals who, for better or worse, affected ecclesiastical foundation and patronage; managed the economic and demographic expansion of rural and urban resources discussed in the preceding section; and (especially since the final decades of the thirteenth century) presided over an increasingly complicated system of coinage.[248]

247. Importantly for the English reader, Davies, *God's Playground*, 1:64, renders the ducal titles somewhat differently, in Polish for Henry I (*Brodaty*), Henry II (*Pobożny*), and Bolesław II (*Łysy*), and in Latin for Henry IV (*Probus*).

248. This last subject may be especially confusing to readers of the second portion of the *Book*, which reflects the apperance in Silesia of so many different kinds of currency around the turn of the thirteenth and fourteenth centuries that it seems questionable to talk about a coinage "system" here at all. At a general level, however, the picture in this region of Europe is far more straightforward than it seems, especially given special political significance of the first decades of the fourteenth century. Until the later thirteenth century, the coinage of the duchy (after 1241, the duchies) of Silesia, and of the remaining Piast duchies, and of most of Europe, had been based on the silver pence (*denarius*), a relatively small coin, which here as elsewhere varied considerably from region to region, and across different political units, in its silver content, stability, degree of public or seigneurial control, and degree of exclusion of competing coinages. After the mid-thirteenth century, following the example of Louis IX of France, rulers of the re-emerging kingdoms and principalities throughout Europe began to reform coinage systems based on a new, "fat" pence (*denarius grossus*), a coin that was more substantial it terms of silver content and nominal value, but which, like its "thin" prede-cessor, varied widely along analogous lines. Unlike its precessor, the *grossus* was sometimes subdivided into smaller coins, or perhaps only units of account, in order to accommodate relatively modest transactions. The result was the appearance, throughout Europe, of several different kinds of "groat," and its constituent coinages (or units of account). The resulting degree of systematization depended crucially on the effectiveness of the central authority that issued a particular coinage. The proliferation of the different systems of coinage in later medieval Silesia directly reflects an absence of an effective issuing authority in the region, coupled with the emergence of strong, centralized nearby principalities (Bohemia, Hungary, Brandenburg, and what later became the reunited Polish kingdom), which competed for political and economic control over that Piast province. See Peter Spufford, *Money and Its Use in Medieval Europe* (Cambridge: Cambridge University Press, 1988), especially 136, 224–33; Hoffmann, *Land, Liberties, and Lordship*, 400–04; Ryszard Kiersnowski, *Wstęp do numizmatyki polskiej wieków średnich* [Introduction to Polish numismatics of the Middle Ages] (Warsaw: Państwowe Wydawnictwo Naukowe, 1964), 116, 128–31; Kiersnowski, "W sprawie genezy kwartników śląskich" [Concerning the origins of the Silesian *quartenses*], *Wiadomości Numiz-matyczne* 10 (1966), 197–220; Kiersnowski, "Kwartniki śląskie i czeskie grosze" [The Silesian *quartenses* and the Czech groats], *Wiadomości Numizmatyczne* 6 (1962), 225–44; Kiersnowski, "Złoto na rynku polskim w XIII–XIV w." [Gold in the Polish market in the thirteenth and

Characteristically, Peter was more sensitive than was his continuator to the difficulties posed to the Henryków monastery by dynastic politics, especially after the death of Henry II the Pious in 1241. Curiously, although war was an important aspect of intra-dynastic relations during the thirteenth century, Peter did not identify warfare among the dukes as a problem from which his monastery actually suffered. Instead, the core problem was the duke's absence from the monastery's political horizon. Throughout his portion of the *Book*, Peter repeatedly described the failure, or the unwillingness, of Duke Bolesław II, and to a lesser extent his younger brother Henry III, to perform the wide range of legal, political, and ethical roles which, in the abbot's view, had traditionally defined good ducal rule, and which, despite the difficulties of their applications in practice, had worked as a central source of order and security for the monastery. In particular, the second Bolesław emerges in Peter's image as a ruler deliberately indifferent to, and unavailable to rectify, the grievances inflicted upon the Henryków monastery by its enemies.

Abbot Peter's portrait of this duke is especially severe; indeed it constitutes one of the two literary paradigms of bad rule in the historical writing produced in Piast Poland.[249] However, in the broader context of Peter's own present, his portrayal of Bolesław is somewhat paradoxical. In 1263, a few years before the abbot began to write, Bolesław issued a diploma for the monks that strongly reasserted the same pattern of ducal protection and patronage over the Henryków monastery which Peter sought to recover and reconstruct by means of the *Book*.[250] It is therefore quite possible that, after three decades of difficult relations, the 1260s were a time of a tentative reconciliation between the monastery and Duke Bolesław. If accurate, this conjecture further explains why Peter undertook to write the *Book* on the cusp of the seventh decade of the thirteenth century, and why he repeatedly explained Duke Bolesław's considerable shortcomings in terms of the ruler's youth – thereby implicitly situating them in the deep past.

In contrast, the abbot used the two earlier dukes, Henry I the Bearded and Henry II the Pious – both of whom he credited with founding the monastery – as a joint paradigm of good rule. Although his portraits represent an idealized vision of the past, the particular areas of practice and ideology upon which he focused when constructing that vision are consistent with the impressions from diplomatic and other narrative evidence, issued by or about those two rulers, and indeed by their Piast relatives. In conjuction, the result is a good sketch of the traits that were expected, at least among ecclesiastics, of a good and successful ruler in thirteenth-century Poland. The Piast duke was a source, indeed the em-

---

fourteenth centuries], *Wiadomości Numizmatyczne* 16 (1972), 129–56. For the particular types of coin explained generally by this footnote, see the notes at the text.

249. The other being the hagiographical image of King Bolesław II the Bold, the executioner of Bishop Stanisław of Kraków; see Jacek Banaszkiewicz, "Czarna i biała legenda Bolesława Śmiałego" [The black and the white legend of Bolesław the Bold], *Kwartalnik Historyczny* 88 (1981), 353–90 (French summary, 390).

250. See Supplementary Document no. 5.

˙ bodiment, of legitimate authority within society, even at the very local level with which the authors of the *Book* are concerned. Unless he abdicated his responsibilities or failed, he sought to express, and strengthen, his authority and prestige by the performance of several important roles.

Perhaps basic to the others was that of a social mediator; by which is meant here a function extending well beyond the conventional sense of that word, that is, a third-party actor engaged in prevention or settlement of dispute.[251] To be sure, the duke was a mediator in this narrow sense too, but, much more broadly, he formally facilitated significant transactions – above all, gifts to the saints, which were made by a wide variety of donors, including the duke himself. As Henry the Bearded put it in his 1208 diploma for the nuns of Trzebnica, their recently formed "manor" (*praedium*) consisted of holdings that had formerly belonged either to the duke himself, or to "knights," or to individual clerics, or to previously existing ecclesiastical institutions. Regardless of their provenance, the duke acquired all these goods into his own hands, and subsequently conveyed the consolidated estate to the nuns, with his own blessing, and implicitly on his own terms.[252]

In this sequence of events, the duke's role as a mediator of property transfer was at the same time central and, in a substantive sense, somewhat ambiguous. Henry positioned himself as simultaneously a facilitator of property transfer from several kinds of former possessors, and as himself the donor of all of the properties transferred. Although this may appear to have been another paradox of ducal authority, it was not. The duke was important precisely because his central role in property transfer was ambiguous, and thus politically malleable and negotiable by all sides concerned. Abbot Peter's elaborate reconstructions of Duke Henry's and his descendants' formal relationship to the properties transferred into the estate of the Henryków monastery both reflected, and themselves were a part of, just this process of political negotiation about the central position of the duke in legal transactions, and within the political world upon which those transactions impinged.[253]

The duke was, among other things, an especially important type of donor to the saints and to their earthly custodians. He was also a source of gifts to a variety of other recipients.[254] In Poland, as elsewhere, a central element of the image of good

251. For the basic working definition of mediation in this sense, see Peter Stein, *Legal Institutions: The Develoment of Dispute Settlement* (London, 1984), 5–6.

252. Of the several remarkable charters for the convent at Trzebnica Henry issued on these matters, see especially *S.U.*, 1:no. 115 (1208), 81.

253. The political importance, and the substantive vagueness, of the duke's proprietary position with respect to the foundation of the monastery and the monastic estate are reflected in Abbot Peter's elaborate discussion of the relationship of Duke Henry to the active founder, his notary Nicholas, right at the outset of the *Book* in, in his reiterations of ducal property and patronage throughout the *Book*, and in the competing memories of the same issues reflected in documents from Great Poland; Chapters 2–21, and Supplementary Documents 1, 3, and 4; see Górecki, "Interpreter," 70–75, 81–82.

254. Górecki, "*Ad Controversiam*," 218–19.

rulership (in theory and in practice) was generosity with land, coin, and other valuable resources in favor of monasteries, bishoprics, collegiate churches, parish and other local churches, as well as to individual ecclesiastical figures. In addition, during the demographic and economic expansion of the twelfth and thirteenth centuries, the Piast dukes distributed land and other resources to an open-ended range of lay recipients – "the noble and the mediocre," "middling knights," and "peasants in diverse places," as Abbot Peter called them at several points of the earliest phase of his story about the "territory of Henryków."[255]

These patterns of giving positioned the Piasts in two closely-related roles. On the one hand, the dukes played an essentially distributive role as sources of gifts, and as nodes of complicated networks of resulting relationships.[256] On the other, they established, or helped establish, substantial territorial units of new lordship and authority: directly their own, ecclesiastical, or secular. The distributive, gift-based role of the Piast dukes remained important into the fourteenth century. However, over time that role became complicated with the proliferation of the network of other lordships (ecclesiastical and secular), of parishes, of new categories and communities of peasants, and of towns. Especially difficult were patterns of coexistence between dukes, the ecclesiastical beneficiaries of their generosity, and the lay landholders. The three sides competed vigorously over physical access to the labor, revenue, and grain of the peasants who inhabited ecclesiastical, ducal, and knightly estates; over access to forests, fisheries, and hunting resources; over peasant labor obligations related to construction, defense, transport, and similar "public" roles; and over jurisdiction.[257] Both authors of the *Book* either allude to, or relate outright, several conflicts over population and resources of this kind, involving the Henryków monastery, the dukes, and other holders of power, land, and lordship.[258]

In the course of the later thirteenth and early fourteenth centuries, population pressure and the proliferation of lordships began to limit the dukes' ability to distribute land and other resources. Land scarcity during the second half of the thirteenth century is reflected by settlement pressure, especially from German immigrants, against that reserved frontier belt of ducal forest called "the clear-

255. Chapters 2, 82, 113.

256. Georges Duby has used the Piasts of the tenth and eleventh centuries, especially Bolesław I the Brave, as exemplars of the ruler as a source of gifts in a society in the earlier Middle Ages, in *The Early Growth of the European Economy: Warriors and Peasants from the Seventh to the Twelfth Century*, trans. Howard B. Clarke (Ithaca: Cornell University Press, 1974), 128–29.

257. On these subjects, which require further inquiry over the full period of Piast rule at least until 1320, see Górecki, *Economy*, 123–88.

258. Chapters 47–49, 103–04, 106–08, 111, 155, 158, 161, 192; on the role of violence in such conflicts, see Górecki, "Violence."

ing" (*przesieka*) and the "the hedge" (*hach*) in the two vernaculars.[259] Abbot Peter reports that between 1241 and his own present, peasant clearing in this forest, carried out without ducal permission and under the leadership of German village bailiffs and of "knights," had become routine, and, interestingly, that it posed a great political risk of ducal retribution against his monastery.[260] Scarcity of land after the mid-thirteenth century is also reflected by occasional ducal confiscations of estates that had previously been granted to monasteries and other recipients. In contrast to ducal gifts, the specific circumstances of this practice are sparsely documented. Abbot Peter obliquely explained Duke Henry III's confiscations of formerly granted estates as a special case of the more general problem of heirs attempting to regain their inheritance.[261] The practice presumably reflects a combination of a depletion of land after several generations of intensive cultivation, and thus a dwindling of ducal reserves of the basic resource that had initially enabled the dukes to perform all of their traditional roles.[262]

Apart from making (and, in a later period, occasionally voiding) their own gifts, the Piast dukes mediated gifts by a variety of other donors, including gifts which those donors themselves made to ecclesiastical recipients. The dukes routinely participated in, and consented to, gifts, exchanges, and sales, effected by (and among) that rather amorphous group of lay and ecclesiastical landholders whom Abbot Peter identified as "the noble and the mediocre" – and who, to a degree, overlap with my own "other powerful landholders." The dukes emerge from the sources as very much a third party in the process of alienation – as they bridged, confirmed, and secured particular alienations. Although, as I noted, the exact meaning of this central position is a bit elusive, the specific activities entailed in it are clear. Acting by themselves, or through designated deputies, the dukes frequently perambulated the boundaries of individual localities included into larger estates, or of those estates in their entirety; and they physically marked out those boundaries with several kinds of "signs." In medieval Poland, perambulation was carefully recorded as a ritual that expressed and formalized a conveyance, as well as affirmed the exact physical extent of the holding or

259. See n. 16 above. The leading study of the *przesieka/hach* is Walter Kuhn, "Der Löwenberger Hag und die Besiedlung der schlesichen Grenzwälder," in W. Kuhn, *Beiträge zur schlesischen Siedlungsgeschichte* (Munich: Delp, 1971), 32–66; see also Ewa Maleczyńska and Karol Maleczyński, *Dzieje Śląska* [The history of Silesia] (Warsaw: Wiedza Powszechna, 1955), 151, 240.

260. Chapter 111.

261. Chapter 78; Supplementary Documents no. 11–12.

262. Ducal confiscations of previously granted land are treated by Jurek, *Dziedzic*, 89, and Mularczyk, *Władza*, 28. Jurek explains ducal revindications as a Polish counterpart of the later medieval royal demands for written or other proofs of past grants of estates (or liberties attached to estates), in the absence of which rulers claimed the right to confiscate estates. Mularczyk does not explain ducal revindication, but rather uses its evidence as part of an interesting reassessment of proprietary relations in Silesia.

estate conveyed. Parties to this activity included, in various combinations, the duke himself or his deputy, leading members of his entourage (variously called, in this context, his "barons" or his "nobles"), "neighbors" of the transferred holdings, the parties to the transfer or their representatives, and clerics.[263]

The dukes also settled, or prevented, disputes – by which I mean adversarial conflicts among specifically defined parties – about property transfer, and about other subjects.[264] Ducal charters frequently include notices of settlement of disputes about particular properties, including boundary disputes; clarify property rights, including those aspects of the relationship between the duke and the past and present possessors that affected these rights; and record specific actions aimed at securing a property transaction from conflict or dispute in the future.[265] Our two authors present several interesting instances of the duke's involvement in this broad range of activities – including, as one such activity, the compilation of a written record in the form of charters.[266] Nearly all the charters transcribed in the *Book* are ducal confirmations of property transfer; and several of those include records of dispute.

Taken cumulatively, these roles of the Piast dukes seem to have added up to rather more than the sum of their parts; for example, they extend considerably beyond prevention or settlement of dispute. In property transfer, the dukes formally defined, and clarified, the rights of all the parties involved in an alienation toward the alienated holdings, toward the resulting estate, and toward one another – before, during, and after the alienation. As a result, the more elaborate

263. Myśliwski, *Człowiek*, 40–67; Myśliwski, "Boundary Delimitation in Medieval Poland," in *Perspectives on Central-European History and Politics (Selected Papers from the Fifth World Congress of Central and East European Studies, Warsaw, 1995)*, ed. Stanislav Kirschbaum (Houndmills: Macmillan, 1999), 27–36; Myśliwski, "Boundaries and Men in Poland from the Twelfth to the Sixteenth Century: The Case of Masovia," in Abulafia and Berend, *Medieval Frontiers*, 217–37; Górecki, "Communities," 137, 146–51.

264. Górecki, *"Ad Controversiam*," 214 (n. 6), 218–19.

265. To put this somewhat differently: the Piast dukes were central actors in what Emily Tabuteau has, in the context of another medieval European society, called the "modes of assurance" of the permanence of alienations, that is, the wide range of activities that enhanced (though did not guarantee) their future security; Emily Z. Tabuteau, *Transfers of Property in Eleventh-Century Normandy* (Chapel Hill: University of North Carolina Press, 1988), 112–210.

266. Chapters 8, 10, 29 (ducal gift), 32 (ducal gift), 58–62 (ducal criminal trial, confiscation of property, alienation to the monastery, two charters, ducal trial concerning property) 66–67, 69–70, 72 (ducal consent, charter), 74–79 (ducal consent, ducal revindication, charters), 81 (charter), 85, 87–90 (ducal revindication, ducal trial concerning property, ducal consent, perambulation of the boundaries, charter), 98, 101–02, 106–07 (ducal participation in exchange and sale, ducal consent, charters, ducal trial concerning property), 115–19 (charters, ducal consent), 129–30, 132–35 (ducal trial concerning property, criminal execution, ducal revindication, perambulation of the boundaries, charters, ducal consent), 142–43 (ducal charters).

ducal charters concerning property transfer include instantaneous, though perhaps highly idealized, constructions of a social and political order.[267] By means of these constructions, the dukes positioned themselves (or the ecclesiastical authors of the documents positioned the dukes) in an ultimate, overarching role of political and legal mediation. Abbot Peter's portion of the *Book* is, among other things, a detailed reconstruction of this kind of social and political order. Peter sought to portray, evaluate, and influence a multilateral network of relationships, involving the monastery, its powerful neighbors, and the rulers. His portrait of Henry I the Bearded is a carefully crafted image of the duke's centrality in the local political order of which the monastery was (or of which Peter wished it to be) a part.

The dukes performed these roles directly, or with the assistance of officials.[268] The highest territorial official in the Polish duchies throughout the medieval period resembles his counterpart in other parts of medieval Europe.[269] He was the ruler's deputy in a wide variety of matters. His authority extended over a substantial territory, that is, the duchy in its entirety, or some major subdivion of it. In these regards, he was much like the Carolingian count (*comes*) – and indeed, as noted earlier, *comes* is one of the terms occasionally used for the chief royal deputy in the Polish duchies in the early period between the tenth and twelfth centuries.[270] Nominally a military leader, like his Carolingian prototype he also performed broad judicial, enforcement, and revenue-gathering functions. The military core of his functions is encapsulated his Polish vernacular name, *wojewoda* – literally "leader of the army" – a term which was apparently employed interchangeably with the Latin "count palatine" (*comes palatinus*) or "palatine" (*palatinus*).

During the long course of territorial division of the Piast duchies after 1138, these highly aggregated functions tended to devolve upon more local officials. The most important among them were the castellans, ducal deputies based (typically) in the more important towns of each duchy. Strictly speaking, the castellans did not replace the *wojewodowie*, but in varying degrees supplemented them. In some duchies, the *wojewoda* disappeared; elsewhere, he remained the nexus between the ruler and the castellans. In any event, each office was an apex of a subordinate official hierarchy staffing the Polish duchies. Attempts at a reunification of the kingdom at the turn of the thirteenth and fourteenth centuries entailed the introduction of a new type of royal governor, aimed at providing a measure of control over these two high officials. This new governor

267. This is especially visible in the early-thirteenth-century charters for the Cistercian convent at Trzebnica. In a very different region, the function of ducal diplomas as political images, or constructions (again, in another region and period of medieval Europe), is well analyzed by Remensnyder, *Remembering*, 14, 117, 134–37, 139–40, 142–43, 147, 194.

268. For my working definition of *office* and related concepts, n. 226 above.

269. For what follows on the palatines and castellans, see Hoffmann, *Land, Liberties, and Lordship*, 20, and Górecki, *Economy*, 164, 171–72, 175, 183, 188 (n. 3), 196, 198.

270. See nn. 232–35 above.

was the *capitaneus* (*starosta* in Polish), initially established by the kings of Bohemia and the princes of Brandenburg, as these two powers vied for control over major regions of the Piast inheritance during the later thirteenth century.[271] Abbot Peter's continuator portrays the *capitaneus* in Silesia specifically in his capacities as the vicegerent of the prince of Brandenburg, and as a military commander.[272]

Several categories of officials subordinate to the palatines, castellans, and their fourteenth-century successors were involved in the governance of the Polish duchies. Although their areas and lines of competence cannot always be reconstructed with precision, lower-level officials, considered as a total population, performed three broad roles.[273] One was what today would be called taxation, that is exaction, in the duke's name, of several kinds of resources and services, which included (among others) dues in coin, grain, labor, hospitality, construction and maintenance of roads and fortifications, assistance with the hunt, and limited obligations to participate in warfare. Another role was jurisdiction, that is, the right to prevent or to resolve dispute, to hold court and (at least theoretically) to compel parties to appear before it and to abide by its sentence, and to select the body of law appropriate to particular types of parties and subjects in controversy. A third role was what might today be called police power, that is, enforcement of all kinds of commands by the dukes, their highest deputies, the lower-level officials concerned with revenue and jurisdiction, and a host of authoritative decisions made by other persons – ecclesiastical or secular lords, mediators of especially difficult disputes, town authorities, and so forth. In several "accounts," Abbot Peter and his continuator refer to officials who exercised that third area of competence.[274]

In the course of the twelfth and thirteenth centuries, we can clearly observe a formal network of ducal courts.[275] These courts included judicial sessions of the duke and of his entourage, generally in large assemblies; similar sessions presided by "judges of the [ducal] court," which were in turn sometimes entrusted to the judges' own deputies ("sub-judges"); and courts held by the palatines and castellans, and staffed by their own "judges" and other subordinate officials. In addition, we have important glimpses of lower-level officials who opened or guarded court sessions, seized and transported prisoners, delivered summonses,

271. Knoll, *Rise*, 26–27.

272. Chapter 153.

273. On officials below the level of palatine and castellan, and their areas of competence, see Górecki, *Economy*, 123–54, 173–74, 163–88, 195–202; Górecki, "*Viator* to *ascriptitius*," 28.

274. Especially notable examples are Chapters 106, 111, 129 (n. 15), 165.

275. On what follows, see Juliusz Bardach, *Historia państwa i prawa Polski* [History of the state and law in Poland], vol. 1 (Warsaw: Państwowe Wydawnictwo Naukowe, 1964), 271–74, 331–32, 338–40, 345–46, 475–81; Bartlett, *Making*, 173–77; Hoffmann, *Land, Liberty, and Lordship*, 20; and Górecki, *Economy*, 172–74, 176–78, 203–08.

exacted fines, imposed other punishments, or who physically assisted in effecting compromise settlements – for example, by helping trace out new boundaries between contested properties. Moreover, by the early fourteenth century, town courts acquired jurisdiction over two subjects that were very important in conflict at a local level – violence and property – within substantial administrative districts associated with each town. Because in this later period towns were typically established, or restructured, "according to German law," the procedure and substance of the law administered by these urban courts was either directly borrowed from German law or influenced by it.

The two portions of the Henryków history neatly reflect these transitions. Abbot Peter situates judicial procedure within ducal courts, which were staffed by the dukes themselves, their officials (including ducal judges, castellans, boundary perambulators, lower enforcement officials, and other persons). On the other hand, Peter's continuator consistently places disputes before the city council of Münsterberg, and specifically its "assessors" (*scabini*) and their leader, whom he variously identifies as "hereditary judge" and "advocate" – titles adapted in the fourteenth century from the areas of competence of the German settlement entrepreneurs who had been recruiting German settlers into the Polish duchies, and wielding jurisdictional and other authority over them, for much of the preceding century.[276] The reader will readily note that the names of most of the assessors and town judges were German; that the procedure of their court was explicitly different from that used in other courts; and that the administration of "Polish law" was the responsibility of a category of urban judge specifically different from ordinary town-based courts.[277] At least some Piast dukes actively fostered this expanding jurisdictional significance of German towns in the Polish duchies, and relied on them as an additional resource in the maintenance of peace and dispute settlement. The second portion of the *Book* therefore reflects, right around 1300, the entrance of German towns and their districts into a central position among the proliferating (and to some extent overlapping) hierarchies of ducal, seigneurial, ecclesiastical, and urban jurisdiction.

The effectiveness of the ducal judicial system is difficult to gauge. At the very least, the dukes were able to threaten the use of force against violent offenders. Abbot Peter and his continuator recall several executions of violent neighbors of the monastery, or penal confiscation of estates in lieu of execution, in the thirteenth and fourteenth centuries.[278] On the other hand, the Piast dukes of the twelfth, thirteenth, and early fourteenth centuries negotiated their effective

276. For the terminology of German settlement entrepreneurs (*villicus, scultetus, advocatus, locator*), see Górecki, *Economy*, 198–202, 212–21; Górecki, *Parishes*, 98–99, 102–03, 109–12; for its adaptation in the urban context in East Central Europe in general, see Lilley, *Urban Life*, 131–37.

277. Hoffmann, *Land, Liberty, and Lordship*, 20.

278. Chapters 29, 58, 63, 108, 129, 136–37, 154–55,186; Górecki, "Violence," 97–99.

power against a dynamic and self-assertive aristocracy and knighthood, a vigorous institutional Church, and increasingly independent lordships and towns. Ever sensitive to local politics, Peter noted that, even in the good times of Duke Henry the Bearded, only parts of the outlying region which in due course became Schönwald were securely subject to effective ducal power. Elsewhere, powerful landholders, whom he identified variously (and obliquely) as knights, robbers, and bandits, possessed areas of settlement and lordship, and frustrated or prevented peasant settlement under "authority" of the dukes and the Henryków monastery. A recurring subject of both portions of the *Book* is several such landholders, their ruthless strategies of social climbing and upward mobility, the conflicts they provoked (or settled), and their relationships with one another, with the monastery, and with the dukes.[279]

The Silesian Piasts also competed with the dukes of Great Poland, and with their political allies in Great Poland, Little Poland, and Silesia itself, for that same protective relationship with the Henryków monastery which Abbot Peter sought to reconstruct in favor of Henry the Bearded and his successors. Especially active supporters of the monastery were Władysław Odonic and his son Przemysł I of Great Poland, as were groups of clerics and knights in Poznań and Gniezno. Abbot Peter recalled these connections in considerable detail, and the two dukes reiterated them in their own diplomas for the monastery,[280] along lines that sharply differ from the image which Peter sought to construct, and that reflect yet another geopolitical challenge to his project of locating his community within a clear and politically secure context.

6 *Religious communities, ecclesiastical institutions* ·

Abbot Peter and his continuator wrote their history against a background of ecclesiastical communities and institutions that were at the same time well-established and in the process of dynamic transition.[281] In their general contours, throughout the period antedating and fully encompassing the history narrated in the *Book*, the religious groups and institutions present in the Piast duchies were similar to their counterparts throughout Europe. On the other hand, the parti-

---

279. Chapters 31, 33–35, 45–49, 51–57, 74–75, 85–87, 89, 96, 103–04,106, 108–09, 111, 154–56, 158–59, 161–62, and Supplementary Documents no. 7–10. I have explored some of those dynamics in more detail in: "Politics," 37–42, "Words," 135–37, and "Interpreter," 66–70, 75–80. See also Anne Duggan, "Introduction," in Duggan, *Nobles and Nobility*, 1–14, at 6.

280. Chapters 114–18; Supplementary Documents no. 1, 4. For treatment of the varied records of these dukes in documentary records and traditions, see Górecki, "Interpreter," 72–73, 81–82.

281. In addition to the more specific literature cited at particular points below, see above all Jerzy Kłoczowski, *A History of Polish Christianity* (Cambridge: Cambridge University Press, 2000), and Kłoczowski, *Dzieje chrześcijaństwa polskiego* [A history of Polish Christianity], vol. 1 (Paris: Nasza Rodzina, 1987).

culars of their significance, of their relationships to dukes and lords, and of their transformations, were distinct, along lines directly reflected by the *Book* itself.

The most important ecclesiastical official in the Polish duchies was the bishop.[282] As elsewhere, he performed specifically ecclesiastical or spiritual transactions, such as presiding over local or provincial councils, refining canon law jurisdiction, granting tithe revenues, or imposing ecclesiastical sanctions in order to protect estates belonging to the clergy.[283] However, his competence extended beyond formal ecclesiastical capacities. The bishop also participated in many of the same legal transactions which defined the authority and the power of the duke. Bishops, and high officials of cathedral chapters, consistently served as witnesses to all kinds of transactions. In terms of raw numbers, the frequency of their apperance in the witness lists of ducal diplomas is second only to that of the dukes personally and of the highest ducal officials. Moreover, bishop and chapter occasionally joined in ducal perambulations of boundaries, or in the other activities that accompanied, expressed, and strengthened property transfer.[284] Finally, as Abbot Peter recalled, the bishop – or, rather, three particular Polish bishops – facilitated the foundation of the Henryków monastery, and it appears that bishops played a similar role elsewhere.[285]

As of the first years of the thirteenth century (and presumably earlier), Polish bishops and cathedral clergy constituted an interregional political network – one that could be mobilized across the boundaries of individual duchies in order to mediate significant events, and one that affected the balance of political and seigneurial power within particular localities and regions of each duchy.[286] Abbot Peter repeatedly noted the importance of the chapters of Wrocław, Poznań, and Gniezno as milieux of useful contacts for the abbots of Henryków, and the close relationships between those milieux and the courts of the dukes of Silesia and of Great Poland.[287] His insights are supported by considerable circumstantial record of a geographic and social mobility of particular clerics within and among the Polish duchies, within the ecclesiastical hierarchy, as well as within the ducal courts.[288] For some time before 1208 – the year of the first written record of a canonical election of a Polish bishop – Polish bishops, and the urban ecclesiastical groups over which they presided, functioned as autonomous agents of power and influence, and as an important resource to others in a wide range of legal transactions.

282. Józef Szymański, "Biskupstwa polskie w wiekach średnich. Organizacja i funkcje" [Polish bishoprics in the Middle Ages: organization and functions], in *Kościół w Polsce* [The Church in Poland], ed. Jerzy Kłoczowski, 4 vols. (Kraków: Znak, 1966), 1:127–236.

283. James Brundage, *Medieval Canon Law* (London: Longman, 1995), 8–10, 12, 15, 23, 28–29, 41–43, 72–76, 120–22.

284. Górecki, "Communities," 134, 146–49.

285. Chapters 6–10, 21; Supplementary Document no. 2.

286. Szymański, "Biskupstwa," 191–231.

287. Chapters 2, 4–5, 116, 200, 205–06, 209–11.

288. Górecki, *Parishes*, 59, 65, 67–69.

The later twelfth and all of the thirteenth and fourteenth centuries are a period of continuous expansion of a parish network throughout Piast Poland.[289] This process is reflected in the *Henryków Book*, because, on the eve of the monastery's establishment in its original, "wooden church," Abbot Peter remembered Henryków and the surrounding settlement as a prosperous parish.[290] In addition, Piast dukes, bishops, and other benefactors presided over a strong expansion of monastic and mendicant presence throughout the Polish duchies. Between the tenth and the fourteenth centuries the archdiocese of Gniezno experienced all the major European currents of monastic religiosity.[291] Before the mid-twelfth century, the number of monasteries was very modest. During the subsequent expansionary period, encompassing the second half of the twelfth and all of the thirteenth century, four types of communities of "the religious"[292] emerged as especially important in Poland: canons secular, canons regular, Cistercian monks, and mendicants. Of these four types, the mendicants do not bear on the present sources, either in the sense of appearing in the narrative, or in the sense of affecting the spiritual or institutional scene affecting the Henryków monastery.[293]

289. Heinrich Felix Schmid, *Die rechtlichen Grundlagen der Pfarrorganisation auf westslavischen Boden und ihre Entwicklung während des Mittelalters* (Weimar: Böhlhaus, 1938); Julia Tazbirowa, "Początki organizacji parafialnej w Polsce" [Origins of the parish organization in Poland], *Przegląd Historyczny* 5 (1963), 369–86; Eugeniusz Wiśniowski, "Rozwój organizacji parafialnej w Polsce do czasów reformacji" [The development of the parish organization in Poland until the Reformation], in Kłoczowski, *Kościół*, 1:237–274; Wiśniowski, "Parish Clergy in Medieval Poland," in *The Christian Community of Medieval Poland: Anthologies*, ed. Jerzy Kłoczowski (Wrocław: Zakład Narodowy im. Ossolińskich, 1981), 119–48; Stanisław Litak, "Rise and Spatial Growth of the Parish Organization in the Area of Łuków District in the Twelfth to Sixteenth Centuries," in Kłoczowski, *Christian Community*, 149–81; Górecki, *Parishes*, 21–48.

290. Chapters 21, 65; Górecki, *Parishes*, 90–95.

291. On those major currents, see the works of C. H. Lawrence, *Medieval Monasticism: Forms of Religious Life in Western Europe in the Middle Ages* (3rd ed., Harlow: Longman /Pearson Education, 2001), and *The Friars: The Impact of the Early Mendicant Movement on Western Society* (London: Longman, 1994); and the earlier synthesis by Richard W. Southern, *Western Society and the Church in the Middle Ages* (Harmondsworth: Penguin, 1970), 214–99. On Poland in particular, in addition to the materials cited elsewhere in these notes, see Marek Derwich, *Monastycyzm benedyktyński w średniowiecznej Europie i Polsce. Wybrane problemy* [Benedictine monasticism in medieval Europe and Poland: selected problems] (Wrocław: Wydawnictwo Uniwersytetu Wrocławskiego, 1998); Kłoczowski, *A History*; Kłoczowski, "Zakony na ziemiach polskich w wiekach średnich" [Monastic orders in the Polish lands during the Middle Ages], in Kłoczowski, *Kościół*, 1:375–494.

292. Here and in the body of the text, "the religious" (*religiosi*, in the masculine, or *religiosae*, in the feminine) always refers to monastic and mendicant clergy. This word, rather than "monk," "friar," "nun," and so forth, was the most general term for the clerics who lived according to a rule; Southern, *Western Society*, 214.

293. On mendicants, or begging orders (including, but not limited to, the Dominicans and the Franciscans), see Lawrence, *Medieval Monasticism*, 238–78; Lawrence, *The Friars*;

On the other hand, the two categories of canons, and of course Cistercian monks, are directly important in both senses as a context for the *Henryków Book*.

Canons secular were groups of clergy attached to particular churches, but either not living in common according to any particular (or today specifiable) rule, or living according to the relatively early Rule of Aachen, attributed to Chrodegang of Metz.[294] In the Polish duchies, such groups usually consisted of three or four clerics, staffing churches of varying size, importance, and location.[295] Canons regular were also clerics attached to specific churches, but living according to a relatively rigorous rule, typically some variant of the Rule of Saint Augustine in one of its twelfth-century redactions.[296] The earliest, twelfth-century foundations of canons regular in Poland were all ambitious, large-scale endowments of large religious communities, with cloisters situated in the countryside. In that sense, they were indistinguishable from the Benedictine and, later on, the Cistercian foundations. During the later twelfth and the thirteenth centuries, important communities of canons regular were founded in or near major towns. Furthermore, small groups of canons adopted rules, received property, and organized themselves as priories.[297] This process is directly reflected in the opening chapters of the *Book*. In his story of the circumstances preceding his monastery's foundation, Abbot Peter remembered that one serious, actively considered alternative to the establishment of the Cistercian monastery shortly before 1222,

---

and, for Poland and East-Central Europe in particular, the remarkable *oeuvre* of Jerzy Kłoczowski, including, among much else: *Dominikanie polscy na Śląsku w XIII–XIV wieku* [Polish Dominicans in Silesia in the thirteenth and fourteenth centuries] (Lublin: Wydawnictwo Katolickiego Uniwersytetu Lubelskiego, 1956); "Zakony," 458–81; "Dominicans of the Polish Province in the Middle Ages," in Kłoczowski, *Christian Community*, 73–118. See recently Szczur, *Historia*, 236–40.

294. Lawrence, *Medieval Monasticism*, 160–62, 165–66; Colin Morris, *The Papal Monarchy: The Western Church from 1050 to 1250* (Oxford: Clarendon Press, 1989), 77; Szczur, *Historia*, 179–81. "Secular" is an old-fashioned adjective formed from the Latin noun *saeculum*, meaning "the world," that is, the ordinary pattern of interactions and relationships, which, in contrast to monks and those canons who adopted a rule, these clerics did not abandon.

295. Józef Szymański, *Kanonikat świecki w Małopolsce od końca XI do połowy XIII wieku* [Canons secular in Little Poland from the end of the eleventh to the mid-thirteenth century] (Lublin: Agencja Wydawniczo-Handlowa AD, 1995); Szczur, *Historia*, 179–82. Morris considers the network of secular canons especially important in the earlier history of the medieval Polish duchies, that is, in the late eleventh and twelfth centuries; *Papal Monarchy*, 276.

296. Lawrence, *Medieval Monasticism*, 160–66; Morris, *Papal Monarchy*, 77–78, 247–250, 259–61, 405–07; Szczur, *Historia*, 186–87. "Regular" is an old-fashioned adjective from the Latin noun *regula*, meaning "rule."

297. The large, early communities of canons regular included the Hospitaller house at Zagość, house of the canons regular of the Holy Sepulchre at Miechów, and the houses of canons regular of Saint Vincent's and Saint Mary's in Wrocław. See Górecki, *Economy*, 15–16, 19–20, 48–54, 56; Górecki, *Parishes*, 16, 26, 33, 45–46, 58–67. Abbot Peter recalls a foundation of a smaller community of canons regular in Kamieniec (Chapters 68–69, 86).

had been the formation of a "priory," that is, a group of canons endowed with "prebends," to be carved out of the estate encompassing Henryków and its "territory."[298]

Nevertheless, the Cistercian option prevailed – for reasons which Peter also carefully presented in the opening chapters.[299] The creation of the Henryków monastery fully conforms to one of the two basic patterns of Cistercian expansion throughout Europe, ever since the establishment of the five earliest Cistercian monasteries in the early years of the twelfth century.[300] According to the two authors, that creation entailed two parallel steps: (1) the endowment, which at the outset in 1228 included the earlier "wooden" church in which the new monastic altars were consecrated, and the original estate, consisting of "the territory of Henryków" and of the largely forested region which subsequently became Schönwald; and (2) the recruitment of a group of monks from a previously existing Cistercian monastery, which in this case was Lubiąż, situated to the northwest of Wrocław along the Odra river (see Maps 3–4). That latter step is known as "filiation," a parental metaphor expressing the relationship between the model, or originating, monastery – the "mother," as Peter himself called Lubiąż – and the new, "daughter" community.[301] These two steps in the creation

298. Chapter 4.

299. Chapter 5.

300. The other pattern being incorporation of a previously existing community into the Cistercian Order; this is not relevant to the Henryków monastery, but conforms to the early history of the women's community in Trzebnica, among other communities in Piast Poland. For what follows, see in general Lawrence, *Medieval Monasticism*, 172–74, and, regarding Poland, Józefa Zawadzka, "Fundowanie opactw cysterskich w XII i XIII wieku" [The founding of Cistercian monasteries in the twelfth and thirteenth centuries], *Roczniki Humanistyczne* 7 (1958), 121–50; Jerzy Kłoczowski, "Les Cisterciens en Pologne, du XIIe au XIIIe siècle," *Cîteaux* 28 (1977), 111–34; Andrzej Marek Wyrwa, "Powstanie zakonu cystersów i jego rozwój na ziemiach polskich w średniowieczu" [The origins of the Cistercian Order and its development in the Polish lands during the Middle Ages], in Wyrwa, Strzelczyk, and Kaczmarek, *Monasticon*, 1:27–54; Wyrwa, "Cystersi. Geneza, duchowość, organizacja życia w zakonie (do XV wieku) i początki fundacji na ziemiach polskich" [The Cistercians: origins, spirituality, and organization of life in the Order (through the fifteenth century), and the beginnings of foundations in the Polish lands], in *Cystersi w Polsce* [The Cistercians in Poland], ed. Daniel Olszewski (Kielce: Wydawnictwo Jedność w Kielcach, 1990), 11–39; Kłoczowski, "Cystersi w Europie Środkowowschodniej wieków średnich" [The Cistercians in East Central Europe during the Middle Ages], in Wyrwa and Dobosz, *Cystersi*, 27–53; Kłoczowski, "Zakony," 406–32.

301. That is, the establishment of Henryków as a "daughter" monastery of Lubiąż. A "daughter" monastery means a monastery established on a pattern of, by monks or nuns recruited from, and supervised by, another, older monastery, which is called the "mother" monastery. This is standard medieval language of relationships among older and newer monasteries, which formed enormous networks, ultimately centered on the founding houses of entire orders. The process of establishing monasteries in this way, and the

of the Henryków monastery are important subjects of both portions of the *Book* – and the *Book* is, in turn, the central source in today's scholarship for the history of that creation, and of the early aftermath.[302]

Neither author notes the third step in this monastery's foundation, which, by 1222, was also standardized throughout Latin Europe. This was the approval of its creation, especially the egress of the founding group out of Lubiąż and into Henryków, by the Cistercian general chapter and by the pope. These steps, too, in fact took place, but they are documented entirely outside of the *Henryków Book*.[303] In fact (and in sharp contrast with several other European examples of Cistercian historiography), the *Book* refers to the bishop of Rome only once, and that exceedingly obliquely.[304] Likewise, the two authors' vision of the Cistercian Order as an institution is entirely domestic. It is limited to three other monasteries in Silesia – Lubiąż, the women's convent at Trzebnica, and, much later, Krzeszów.[305] Also noted is the community at Kamieniec, which was a house of canons regular for much of the period narrated by Abbot Peter, and is so identified by him, but was appropriated by the Cistercian Order, after much controversy, in 1248.[306]

This narrowness of geopolitical optic closely reflects the modest place of all of Poland, Silesia included, in the medieval Cistercian world. It is almost a cliché among Polish medievalists today that, at the beginnings of the story told by the *Book* around the the mid-twelfth century, when the Cistercian establishment in Western Europe consisted of almost 350 monasteries, the foundations in all of Poland included exactly two communities, Jędrzejów in Little Poland, and Łekno in Great Poland; and that in the course of that century the overall number of male houses here reached six, to ascend by another sixteen during all of the thirteenth.[307] These numbers increase somewhat when we include women's monasteries, which, however, are more difficult to classify as Cistercian or otherwise than are their male counterparts; and when we add those communities (male or female) that were merely planned, or that were actually brought into existence, but, for whatever reason, did not survive.[308] Those additions enhance the overall

---

resulting system of "mother" and "daughter" houses, are called filiation; Lawrence, *Medieval Monasticism*, 173–74, 180–81, 183–86, 298. For eastern and northern Europe in particular, showing Lubiąż and Henryków, see Bartlett, *Making*, 259, map 12, and Olszewski, *Cystersi*, pocket supplement, figure 6.

302. The early part of the narrative told by Kozak, Taras-Tomczyk, and Wójcik, "Henryków," 65–66, is virtually a paraphrase of Abbot Peter's story.

303. Kozak, Taras-Tomczyk, and Wójcik, "Henryków," 65.

304. Chapter 199.

305. Lubiąż: Chapters 1, 4, 10, 82, 113, 125; Trzebnica: Chapters 10, 98, 127 (n. 11); Krzeszów: Chapter 157, n. 57.

306. Chapters 68–69, 86.

307. Kłoczowski, "Zakony," 408; Kłoczowski, "Cystersi," 33; Wyrwa, "Powstanie," 49; Wyrwa, "Cystersi," 35–36.

308. Kłoczowski, "Cystersi," 35; Wyrwa, "Powstanie," 39–41, 50; Marian Kanior, "Zakon cysterek i jego rozwój w Europie Środkowej w XII–XVI wieku" [The Order of

Cistercian presence in the Piast duchies during the period spanned by the *Book* by perhaps one-third – hardly an order of magnitude.

Yet, an emphasis on quantity – that is, on the raw numbers of particular communities, the frequency of their establishment, the geographic areas serviced by them, and so forth – obscures other criteria of interest and importance. These criteria sometimes emerge from a perspective that is very big, and in other cases, on the contrary, from a local or regional vantage point. For example, in his recent survey of the Cistercians in East Central Europe, Jerzy Kłoczowski situates the expansion of the Order in Poland within the much larger perspective provided by this macro-region in its entirety, between the beginnings of Cistercian presence here in the second decade of the twelfth century and the end of the most dynamic monastic expansion just over two centuries later.[309] Kłoczowski estimates that during this period, the number of Cistercian monasteries within this macro-region increased to about 200 by 1200, and to about 850 in the first years of the fourteenth century.[310]

Kłoczowski's study is part of his fundamentally important long-term project concerning the "occidentalization" of East Central Europe, by which he means the gradual convergence of this macro-region's culture, institutions, and societies with their counterparts in the European West[311] – a process formerly, and much more schematically, described as one instance of the "closing" of medieval Europe's "frontier."[312] Viewed from the perspective of Cistercian history, Kłoczowski's synthesis places the (quantitatively modest) proliferation of the Cistercians in Poland in a broad and dynamic regional perspective. This macroregional dynamism converges with Abbot Peter's expression of confidence

---

women Cistercians and its development in Central Europe between the twelfth and the sixteenth centuries], in Wyrwa and Dobosz, *Cystersi*, 109–22, at 113–16; Krzysztof Kaczmarek, "Nieudana fundacja cysterska księcia Władysława Odonica z 1210 roku" [A failed Cistercian foundation by Duke Władysław Odonic in 1210], in Wyrwa and Dobosz, *Cystersi*, 273–89; Gerard Kucharski, "Początki klasztoru cysterek w Ołoboku" [The beginnings of the monastery of women Cistercians in Ołobok], in Wyrwa and Dobosz, *Cystersi*, 314–38.

309. Kłoczowski, "Cystersi."

310. Kłoczowski, "Cystersi," 33.

311. A project most fully expressed in: Kłoczowski, *Europa słowiańska w XIV–XV wieku* [Slavic Europe in the fourteenth and fifteenth centuries] (Warsaw: Państwowy Instytut Wydawniczy, 1984); Kłoczowski, *Młodsza Europa. Europa Środkowo-Wschodnia w kręgu cywilizacji chrześcijańskiej średniowiecza* [The younger Europe: East Central Europe in the ambit of medieval Christian civilization] (Warsaw: Państwowy Instytut Wydawniczy, 1998). On Kłoczowski's views, and on their resonances with subsequent anglophone scholarship, see Górecki, "Tworzenie," 511, 513–14, and Górecki, "A View from a Distance," *Law and History Review* 21 (2003), 367–76, at 369–70.

312. An expression coined by Lewis, "Closing," for whose subsequent fate as a concept see Burns, "Significance," 313–18, Górecki, "Medieval 'East Colonization,'" 25–27, 48, 58, and Górecki, "Tworzenie," 509.

about the strength of the Cistercian option among the possibilities for the religious life available near Wrocław in the early decades of the thirteenth century.[313] In other words, despite all the limitations of his geopolitical vision, Peter may have been aware of that dramatic increase in the presence of the Cistercians throughout Europe, its "East" included, which occurred exactly during the century with which he was concerned in his work. Therefore, considered in terms of the major historiographical issues raised at the outset of this essay, Kłoczowski's analysis, in conjunction with the *Book*, locates the Cistercians in general, and Henryków in particular, in medieval Europe as a whole, in one of its macroregions, and upon one of its "frontiers."

On a somewhat lower level of scale, the particular features, or profiles, of individual Cistercian monasteries, or groups of monasteries, in the Piast duchies appear to have been quite distinct. The beginnings of the Cistercian presence in Poland relate specifically to early plans by Polish dukes, bishops, and others to convert the pagan Prussians; and, although this is strongly debated, they may also reflect plans to proselytize among the orthodox Rus'.[314] Prussian conversion resonates directly (if fleetingly) in the *Book* itself, as Abbot Peter recalled that, in 1229, an important early neighbor and benefactor of his monastery embarked on a Prussian crusade.[315] Moreover, as has by now been noted in several contexts, the foundation of the three earliest Cistercian houses in Silesia – Lubiąż, Trzebnica, and Henryków – relates closely to ducal power, and to the prestige of three branches of the Piasts: the Silesian, the Great Polish, and quite possibly the Little Polish. This relationship is especially well attested by Abbot Peter and by the diplomatic record.[316]

Likewise, the lines of filiation within the Polish duchies are interesting and distinctive. Apart from the houses in western Pomerania, the Cistercian monasteries in Poland were all affiliated specifically with the French abbey of Morimond – indirectly in Great Poland and Silesia, through German intermediary

---

313. Chapter 5.

314. Brygida Kürbis, "Cystersi w kulturze polskiego średniowiecza: trzy świadectwa z XII wieku" [Cistercians in the culture of the Polish Middle Ages: Three twelfth-century sources], in *Historia i kultura Cystersów w dawnej Polsce i ich europejskie związki* [History and culture of the Cistercians in old Poland and their European connections], ed. Jerzy Strzelczyk (Poznań: Wydawnictwo Naukowe UAM, 1987), 321–42; Wyrwa, "Powstanie," 45–46; Dariusz Aleksander Dekański, "Cystersi i dominikanie w Prusach – działania misyjne zakonów w latach trzydziestych XIII wieku. Rywalizacja czy współpraca?" [Cistercians and Dominicans in Prussia – missionary activities in the 1230s: Competition or collaboration?], in Wyrwa and Dobosz, *Cystersi*, 227–50; Jan Powierski, "Aspekty terytorialne cysterskiej misji w Prusach" [Territorial aspects of the Cistercian mission in Prussia], in Wyrwa and Dobosz, *Cystersi*, 251–70.

315. Chapter 46; n. 18 above.

316. Supplementary Documents no. 1–7.

mother houses, directly in the early cluster of monasteries near Kraków.[317] This tells us something about the dynamics of trans-European cultural contact of which (among other processes) Cistercian filiation was an aspect. It also relates quite closely to a diffusion of a well standardized pattern of Cistercian architecture, especially into and within Little Poland.[318]

Another feature of Cistercian monasteries specific to twelfth- and thirteenth-century Poland was their endowment, by which I mean the estates from which the communities drew their support, and the process whereby these estates were created. This aspect of regional distinctness is well illustrated by the three houses most important to Abbot Peter and his continuator, but is it also reflected in the later establishments at Kamieniec and at Krzeszów, and by the Cistercian monasteries in the remaining Piast duchies and in Pomerania. To be sure, in several respects, endowment here resembles the patterns that obtained throughout contemporary Europe, especially after the pioneering generation of the Order that passed with the death of Saint Bernard. Right from their mid-twelfth-century beginnings, Cistercian houses in the Piast principalities acquired a wide variety of estates and revenues, from a wide variety of donors; and they used and transformed such estates and revenues so as to enhance profit, according to a well standardized program.[319] The estates consisted of land that had either been previously settled and cultivated by a peasant population, and of land that had been relatively underpopulated, and thus comprised a local "frontier." Also included were other sources of revenue, into which the monks or nuns skilfully tapped – or, as Robert Fossier put it some years ago in describing Cistercian endowment elsewhere, of which they "grasped the development."[320] Finally, the estates included tithe revenues, both from the landed endowment and from the remaining spectrum of productive resources.

Once obtained, these landed and other resources were, in various degrees, transformed or reshaped. The creation of our two best-documented Cistercian estates, Trzebnica and Henryków, was an elaborate example of what Constance Berman calls "compacting," by which she means a territorial and a proprietary

317. Wyrwa, "Powstanie," 35–37 (figs. 4–7); Wyrwa, "Cystersi," 28, fig. 2.

318. Zygmunt Świechowski, "Architektura polskich cystersów w kontekście europejskim" [The architecture of Polish Cistercians in a European context], in Strzelczyk, *Historia*, 137–47; Świechowski, "Architektura cystersów w Polsce, Czechach i na Węgrzech" [Cistercian architecture in Poland, Bohemia, and Hungary], in Wyrwa and Dobosz, *Cystersi*, 54–77.

319. Lawrence, *Medieval Monasticism*, 174–79, 190–92; Constance H. Berman, *Medieval Agriculture, the Southern French Countryside, and the Early Cistercians: A Study of Forty-three Monasteries*, Transactions of the American Philosopical Society 76.5 (Philadelphia: American Philosophical Society, 1986); Morris, *Papal Monarchy*, 244, 255, 261–62; Southern, *Western Society*, 257–69; for further literature, see Górecki, *Economy*, 34–35, n. 32.

320. Robert Fossier, "L'Économie cistercienne dans les plaines du nord-ouest de l'Europe," *Flaran* 3 (1983), 53–74, at 66–69.

consolidation of holdings that had originated from several sources, typically in more or less fragmented form, into larger units of land use and exploitation.[321] The principal subject of Duke Henry the Bearded's great early-thirteenth-century charters for the nuns of Trzebnica is the hundreds of individual transactions that led to a "compacting" of several dozens larger-scale units, and, thereafter, of one large, territorially coherent estate. Similar consolidation of individual holdings, either for reasons of geographic proximity and convenience, or of piecemeal acquisitions from kin groups, is a central subject of the *Henryków Book*. Excellent examples of "compacting" include Abbot Peter's "account" of the making of "the territory of Henryków" from its constituent "holdings," or "parcels," and both authors' stories concerning the painstaking gatherings of properties formerly possessed by the kindreds of Boguchwał Brukał and of John Osina.[322]

At least part of the newly acquired estates was restructured into granges – those distinctive farms established upon Cistercian estates throughout medieval Europe, typically (though not always) worked by monastic lay brothers, or *conversi*, and in Poland sometimes alternatively recorded as "farmsteads" (*curiae*).[323] Both Peter and his continuator noted, in their respective present, the existence in and near the "territory of Henryków" of several monastic "farmsteads" (*curiae*), situated in specified places.[324] Apart from granges, a portion of the newly acquired estates either remained, or newly became, settled by several kinds of subject populations, including, in various combinations, peasant tenants, hired laborers, and (more or less explicitly) unfree *famuli*.[325]

All these basic components of Cistercian estates, in their general contours, resemble the Europe-wide patterns of Cistercian estate-building. However, what seems regionally distinct in Piast Poland in general and in Silesia in particular, is their relative importance, and their relationship to the broader patterns of economy, of lordship, and of deliberate strategies to reorganize and enhance estates. What distinguished the Cistercian monasteries in the Piast duchies from their counterparts elsewhere was the great range of these components, and the eclectic, highly complicated organizational structure of the resulting estates – even allowing

321. Berman, *Medieval Agriculture*, 43–50.

322. Henryków: Chapters 29, 31–35, 37–39, 44; Brukalice: Chapters 112–23, and Supplementary Documents no. 20–23; Muszkowice: Chapters 128–39.

323. For a superb definition of the grange, see Berman, *Medieval Agriculture*, 61–63. For the equivalence of *curia* and the grange in the Cistercian context in Poland, see: Górecki, *Economy*, 57; Kozak, Taras-Tomczyk, and Wójcik, "Henryków," 66; Kłoczowski, "Cystersi," 37. What was included in an individual "farmstead," or "grange," and how that unit was managed, are, for Silesia and the Piast duchies in general, quite difficult and elusive questions; for instance, actual *conversi* appear in the sources very seldom. The content of one monastic "farmstead" is well recorded in Chapter 81.

324. Chapters 36, 52, 80–84, 89, 186, 193, 207.

325. In addition to what follows below, principally with reference to the estate at Trzebnica, see Postan, "The Famulus."

for those internal transformations of "compacting" and grange creation just noted. The estates and the revenues of Cistercian monks and nuns spanned the full range of rural and urban resources outlined in an earlier section of this essay.[326] Right from the outset of their foundations, all three major Cistercian monasteries in Silesia were endowed with arable, peasant population, urban space, coin revenue, specialized markets and workshops, animals, mineral resources, forest, rents, and tithe revenues – in various combinations; and all three transformed and reorganized those resources piecemeal, if at all. The result was consistently a monastic régime of economic exploitation in which those elements that were standardized elsewhere, above all granges and "lay brothers," were so interspersed with many other units of space and population as to be almost invisible.

To complicate matters, these patterns of endowment were not limited to Cistercian monasteries, but characterized all ecclesiastical establishments in twelfth- and thirteenth-century Poland – the archbishopric of Gniezno, the bishopric of Wrocław, the houses of canons regular of Saint Mary's and Saint Vincent's in Wrocław, and, near Kraków, the major communities at Tyniec, Zagość, Miechów, and Staniątki, among many other examples. All ecclesiastical establishments were supported by estates consisting of a broadly similar bundle of elements, with some degree of relative specialization, or varying intensity, among them.[327] In course of the thirteenth and early fourteenth centuries all underwent several common spectral shifts, along the lines described in the earlier section concerning the economy and its significance: "cerealization," that is, a relative intensification of the production and use of grain; increasing recruitment of Germans, and an adaptation of indigenous grants of immunity with reference to "German law"; formation of "farmsteads" (*curiae*) of various kinds of which the Cistercian grange (itself, by the way, quite varied) was one subset; and monetization, both of obligations, and of protocols for the procurement of commodities.

What distinguished between the estates of Lubiąż, of Trzebnica, and of Henryków itself was the precise mix within that range of resources, and within the outcomes of their deliberate modification, especially as that range evolved over time. At their foundation, documented between 1202 and 1218, the nuns of Trzebnica were granted a large, indigenous population of dependent rural tenants, subject to an elaborate set of rents and labor payments, and settled principally within one territorially large district of dense agricultural settlement. In addition – and no less importantly as a source of revenue – they received a substantial income in coin from several loci of rural and urban exchange.[328] The monks of Lubiąż

326. Górecki, *Economy*, 8, 23–26, 47–48, 51–55, 57–58, 75–88, 91–101; see section 4 above, "Agriculture and towns."

327. Górecki, *Economy*, 18–21, 45–46, 48–51, 67–75, 79, 83, 88–91, 98, 123–29 141, 144–45, 162, 195, 208–09, 215–19, 238–40, 245–47.

328. Górecki, *Economy*, 23–26, 51–56, 58, 75–88, 91–101, 108–09, 127–30, 137, 140, 165–66, 194, 238; Górecki, *Parishes*, 29–30.

were among the earliest recruiters of German and Polish tenants into their estate; received generous tithe revenues from a large and diffuse number of villages; appropriated several parish churches, which they then staffed as an autonomous parochial network; and received long-distance trading privileges, especially for the procurement of salt, spanning Silesia with the Baltic.[329]

How does the third Cistercian monastery in Silesia, at Henryków itself, fit into this overall picture? Modestly. The scale of its endowment, at the foundation itself – as noted by Henry the Bearded in his diploma of 1228[330] and by Abbot Peter in his "account" of the "territory of Henryków"[331] – and thereafter, as recorded by Peter and by his continuator, was far smaller than was the case with the large and varied estates granted to the monks of Lubiąż in 1175 and 1202, to the nuns of Trzebnica between 1202 and 1218, and to these two communities throughout the thirteenth and early fourteenth centuries.[332] This fact is reflected by the survey portions of the diplomas concerning Lubiąż, Trzebnica, and Henryków; and by Abbot Peter's worries about income and other resources, some expressed in his own voice, others attributed to his predecessor Abbot Bodo, to Bishop Thomas, and to other friends of the monastery. These concerns are especially audible in the abbot's passages about the inadequacy of the monastery's tithe revenues during the 1230s, the impact of the Mongol invasion after 1241, and the economic hardship posed by a recurrent need to pay out large sums of cash in order to secure individual holdings, or fragments of holdings, from several kinds of proprietary and political threat.[333]

While such complaints may express a trope of Cistercian monastic historiography – a myth of great hardship placed on the holy community by a hostile surrounding political universe – they gain plausibility in light of the relative modesty of this monastery's initial endowment. Yet here again, questions of scale, and the impressionistic glimpses of stress and difficulty, mask otherwise interesting and distinct patterns. However modest this estate was in relation to the much larger endowments of the "mother" community, or of the convent at Trzebnica, everything about Abbot Peter's history of this particular foundation indicates that it was in fact, and was remembered as having been, a generous act, worthy both of his own elaborate "account" at the outset of the *Book*, and of that strongly contested, competitive tradition about the identity of Henryków's true benefactor which affected the ducal courts of Wrocław, Poznań, and Kraków, and in which the *Book* itself was an intervention.[334]

329. Górecki, *Economy*, 47–48, 56–57, 124, 143, 173, 193–97, 199–203, 262–75; Górecki, *Parishes*, 32–45.

330. Supplementary Document no. 2.

331. Chapters 28–44.

332. Kozak, Taras-Tomczyk, and Wójcik, "Henryków," 66.

333. Chapters 47, 68, 78–81, 90–91, 103–04, 108, 111, 114–19.

334. Górecki, "Interpreter," 72–73; Supplementary Documents no. 1–7.

Quantitative considerations may be a misleading criterion for the actual resources represented by a gift for another reason. Precisely in the 1220s, the kind of large, extensive, and varied estate, consisting of a whole spectrum of revenues which the communities of Lubiąż and Trzebnica acquired in the first years of the thirteenth century, was becoming unusual. Grants smaller in scale, but perhaps more lucrative in revenue, were emerging as the norm in ecclesiastical endowment. The "territory of Henryków," the core of the original estate granted to the monks between 1222 and 1228, appears to fit this pattern. Although Abbot Peter's continuator remembered the first generation of the monks of Henryków as heroic cultivators of a forested and empty wilderness,[335] Peter himself clearly described this "territory" as an area of cultivation, settlement, and lordship for at least one full generation before the monastery's appearance.

Thus, here as elsewhere in Europe, the image of a primeval wilderness misidentifies, at least to a degree, the economic and demographic significance of the arrival of the Cistercian community. The Cistercians appeared at Henryków after, and in the midst of, that considerable period of local and regional expansion of settlement and land use described in general terms earlier in this essay.[336] However the monks in turn affected that process while constructing their cloister and – at least to a degree – reorganizing the productive resources of the "territory of Henryków" and of Schönwald into their own estate. In these respects, the monks of Henryków were similar to many Cistercian communities throughout Europe; and, as their many critics noted throughout the twelfth and the thirteenth centuries, they implicitly diverged from their own biblical self-image of cultivators of the desert.

At this point, let me switch perspective, and sum up. When the *Henryków Book* is viewed, against its explicit intent, as a survey, it records the following components of the monastery's estate. One is the granges, or (in this case, interchangeably) "farmsteads." Another is tithes. This component was especially important to Abbot Peter, who described acquisition of tithes with considerable care, and morally evaluated the two bishops of Wrocław actively involved with the monastery, Lawrence and Thomas, specifically in terms of their generosity with this form of income.[337] The third component, relatively new by 1268, but implicitly ubiquitous by about 1300, is a population of German peasant tenants, settled "under the authority" of the monastery and of other lords.[338] The fourth

---

335. Chapters 124–26. This observation may also well be a fourteenth-century Cistercian literary commonplace that recurs in other writings by German Cistercians about the "Polish" prehistory of the localities in which Cistercian monasteries and their estates were subsequently situated; Bartlett, *Making*, 152–56; compare Bartlett, *Gerald of Wales, 1146–1223* (Oxford: Oxford University Press, 1982), 158–67. The appearance of this tradition relatively late in the *Henryków Book* and elsewhere is a fascinating glimpse of the Cistercian collective identity in the Piast duchies.

336. Above, nn. 153, 155–56, 162–66, 168–72, 176, 208–10.

337. Chapters 198, 200–01, 206–07.

338. Chapters 49, 51, 80, 94–96, 103, 109–11.

is not so much a single component as a varied range of dozens of small but cumulatively lucrative things or spaces: an orchard, a cabbage-patch, a garden, a recent forest clearing, an adler-wood, a sheep-barn, a sand-pit used for building material, and (surprisingly seldom, and late) a powered mill. The fifth component, new as of 1310, is the economy of the newly emerged German town of Münsterberg, with which, as Peter's continuator shows, the monastery interacted on several levels by the turn of the fourteenth century.[339]

On the other hand, much that was specific to the other two Cistercian communities, is, relatively speaking, invisible. The indigenous, Polish specialized peasants or crafspeople, so important to the Trzebnica nuns in 1204 and for some decades afterwards, are here (perhaps) represented by a grand total of two "carpenters of [the] village" (*carpentarii villae*) of Jaworowice.[340] Also in contrast to the two earlier monasteries, and despite its close relationship with Wrocław through the cathedral milieu, the Henryków monastery did not acquire at its foundation any interest in urban space, market activity or its profits, or long-distance trade.[341] Its economic involvement with Münsterberg was a late development. Now, to explain the differences in the endowments of these three (and indeed the other) monasteries, and the dynamics in the changes of that endowment over time, at a satisfactory level, requires a study in the economy of the Piast duchies between the later twelfth and the early fourteenth centuries far broader than is possible here.[342] Thus, for present purposes, let me simply assert, not explain, the persistence of a permanent, complicated variety of resources and uses, and situate the sustenance of the Henryków community within that general context.

7 *Transmission and selection of the sources*

After placing the Henryków monastery within one material framework – the economy – let me close by placing it within another, namely the text, now considered as a physical object. The two "books" of the Henryków history, and the list of bishops of Wrocław, have come down to us in a single codex, written in its present form at the monastery of Henryków in the early fourteenth century. The codex is currently situated in the archive of the archdiocese of Wrocław.[343] It has been edited, along with a selection of sixty charters relevant to the history

---

339. Above, nn. 144, 211, 217.

340. Chapter 76.

341. Of the kind that made up, ever since their respective initial endowments, important sources of revenue to the communities at Lubiąż and at Trzebnica (and of other, non-Cistercian, monasteries); see Górecki, *Economy*, 45–62, 85–88.

342. A study extending at least half a century beyond the period covered in my *Economy*. Two superb studies that cover long periods, but that, in turn, do not encompass all the Piast duchies, and are otherwise differently specialized, are Hoffmann, *Land, Liberties, and Lordship*, and Carter, *Trade*.

343. Matuszewski, *Najstarsze*, 10.

it narrates, by Gustav A. Stenzel in 1854.[344] The subsequent edition by Roman Grodecki and Józef Matuszewski in 1949 corrects Stenzel's text, but, unlike the prototype, does not possess a full apparatus.[345] Their edition was reprinted in 1991 without change in the text, or enhancement of the apparatus, but with the addition of a useful preface written by one of the original editors and his son.[346] The 1991 reprint is also appended by a facsimile of the Wrocław codex itself.

The charters are extant in their orginals, in copies, or in photographs, at a variety of archives in Poland, Germany, the Czech Republic and elsewhere. Between 1963 and 1998, the entire corpus of charters from Silesia, until the end of 1300 as the year of issue, was edited in a definitive, six-volume edition, the *Schlesisches Urkundenbuch*. This edition culminated several decades of preparatory work by a group of German scholars associated with the Historical Commission for Silesia under the leadership of Heinrich Appelt and Josef Joachim Menzel. The editor of the diplomas published between 1963 and 1971 as the first volume was Appelt himself, while the remainder of the enterprise proceeded under the editorship of Winfried Irgang – who, in turn, was assisted in the preparation of the final, sixth volume by Daphne Schadewaldt.[347] The Commission has also produced a distinguished body of source criticism of the edited charters.[348] An incidental outcome of the Commission's, and the three editors', work, has been to reedit, and re-evaluate, the substantial number of charters concerning the Henryków monastery published by Stenzel as an appendix to his edition of the *Book*.[349]

The sources that follow in this book are annotated translations of these most recent editions: Grodecki and Matuszewski's edition of 1949, as reprinted (with the facsimile) in 1991; and Appelt, Irgang, and Schadewaldt's edition of 1963–1998. Let me emphasize that the following materials are not themselves translated original editions – that is, they are not based on the original manuscripts,

344. *Liber Fundationis Claustri Sanctae Mariae Virginis in Heinrichow*, ed. Gustav A. Stenzel (Breslau: Josef Max & Komp., 1854), with a detailed codicological analysis on v–xi. This remains the full edition of the *Book*.

345. *Księga henrykowska. Liber Fundationis claustri sancte Marie Virginis in Heinrichow*, ed. and trans. Roman Grodecki (Poznań and Wrocław: Instytut Zachodni, 1949); hereafter Grodecki, *Liber* (1949).

346. *Liber Fundationis claustri sancte Marie Virginis in Heinrichow, czyli Księga henrykowska* [The *Liber Fundationis claustri sancte Marie Virginis in Heinrichow*, or the *Henryków Book*], ed. Józef and Jacek Matuszewski (Wrocław: Muzeum Archidiecezjalne we Wrocławiu, 1991); hereafter Grodecki, *Liber* (1991).

347. *Schlesisches Urkundenbuch*, ed. Heinrich Appelt et. al., 6 vols. (Vienna, etc.: Various imprints, 1963–1998), cited throughout as *S.U.*, with the volume number.

348. Appelt, "Die Echtheit der Trebnitzer Gründungsurkunden (1203/18)," *Zeitschrift des Vereins für Geschichte Schlesiens* 71 (1937), 1ff; Appelt, *Die Urkundenfälschungen des Klosters Trebnitz* (Breslau, 1940); Appelt, "Zur schlesischen Diplomatik des 12. Jahrhunderts," *Zeitschrift für Ostforschung* 2 (1953), 568ff; Winfried Irgang, "Das Urkundenwesen Herzog Heinrichs III. von Schlesien (1248–1266)," *Zeitschrift für Ostforschung* 31 (1982), 1–47.

349. Stenzel, *Liber*, 146–212.

and they do not rest on independent source criticism or evaluation by me. In translating the *Henryków Book*, I have consulted the facsimile appended to the 1991 reprint of Grodecki and Matuszewski's edition, but solely in order to shed light on some questions of composition and meaning of particular passages which that edition leaves unanswered because it lacks a full apparatus. All such uses of the fascimile by me are indicated in the footnotes. The texts of all the charters issued until 1300 (including those transcribed by Abbot Peter and by his continuator into the *Book*), and the remaining charters presented as Supplementary Documents, are translations from the six-volume, definitive German edition. A small handful of post-1300 documents are translated either out of the text of the *Book*, or, when not enclosed in the *Book*, out of Stenzel's supplement to the 1854 edition. For convenience, I have cross-referred to the new German edition all the charters that were issued until the year 1300, and that are included in the *Book*.[350]

Apart from the incorporated charters and a few other exceptions, the entire text of the Wrocław codex containing the *Henryków Book* consists of narration. The charters incorporated into the text are almost always reproduced in their entirety, that is, with the opening and closing protocols. They are almost always introduced, and afterwards interpreted, by the narrative itself – although, as noted earlier, in the later portion of the *Book* that narrative is relatively sparse.[351] Visually, the charters flow continuously with the narration, from which they are however marked off by rubrics – short introductory passages which serve as lengthy titles, or as commentary on the text that follows or precedes them, or as repetitions or elaborations of what is said in the text. Rubrics also subdivide, or otherwise appear in, that text. The rubrics are written in the codex in red ink (hence their name), whereas the narration itself and the charters embedded in it are expressed in black. Furthermore, some rubrics begin with enlarged or ornate initials. Apart from the rubrics, and from these occasional variations in size or in design, the original text has no visual subdivisions or markers.

The rubrics raise, anew, the interesting question of authorship. Here, substantially following Roman Grodecki, I assume that the specific agent – the person or the group – to whom, or to which, the composition and the incription of the rubrics ought to be attributed may be the scribe, or the group of scribes, responsible for the actual making of the codex itself; or, that agent may be the author, or authors, of the discrete portions, or segments, out of which the codex was compiled – including the two explicitly identified authors, Abbot Peter and his continuator.[352] Moreover (and

350. My first cross-reference of this type occurs at Chapter 60, as a gloss to Abbot Peter's account of Bobolice. The reason for the cutoff date 1300 is that the six volumes of the *Schlesisches Urkundenbuch* – the completed project – include documents extending through the end of that year.

351. See nn. 77–78 above.

352. Roman Grodecki, *Liber* (1991), xxxii–xxxiv; see also Józef and Jacek Matuszewski, "Wstęp do wydania drugiego" [Introduction to the second edition], in Grodecki, *Liber* (1991), ix–xv, at xiv–xv.

this is going somewhat beyond Grodecki), it is quite possible that Abbot Peter was himself the author – that is, either the conceptual originator, or the actual writer, or both – of those rubrics which explicitly reiterate the messages and the statements interspersed with the main body of the narration of the earlier portion of the *Book*. At the very least, apart from the color of their transcription, these passages appear to have been composed by one specific author – whom, as I noted earlier, it would be needlessly skeptical simply to dismiss as Abbot Peter.[353]

The visual presentation of my translation follows the composition of the codex itself, coupled with the approach adopted by Grodecki and Matuszewski in the 1949 edition, and reproduced without change in the 1991 reprint. In the manuscript itself, the characters used in the rubrics and the narrations are usually of the same size, except that the first rubric of the codex as a whole is set out in relatively quite large characters. Accordingly, Grodecki and Matuszewski adopt that particular rubric as the title for the portion of the *Book* written by Abbot Peter; and they similarly use the rubric that opens the portion written by Peter's continuator, and the rubric the opens the bishops' list, as titles for these two sections.[354] Furthermore, they adopt the rubrics that open the "accounts" of the individual holdings as separate titles for each of those "accounts."

Because this arrangement is more convenient to the reader than a continuous flow of rubrics and narration, I follow it here. Accordingly, in this book I set out the rubric material as follows: (1) the rubrics that open the three major parts of the codex are expressed in italics, as short passages before each part; (2) the rubrics that open the individual "accounts" or histories are expressed in italics as titles; and (3) the rubrics interspersed with the narrations are placed wherever they occur in the text, and expressed in italics.

No part of the text in the original codex is numbered. Accordingly, in order to facilitate reference, Grodecki and Matuszewski number the passages in the codex consecutively, including (in that order) in the two "books" that make up the Henryków history, and in the bishops' list, both in the Latin original, and in their Polish translation. (However, this numeration does not encompass those first rubrics of the two "books" and of the Wrocław bishops' list which the editors adopt as titles.) Grodecki and Matuszewski position the numbers in places which they consider as convenient logical or visual breaks in the story – most notably, but not always, to the left of each rubric, which in turn sometimes means at the beginning of an "account," at other times within the body of an "account." Quite simply, I retain their original numeration, and express the numbers in brackets before the passage at which Grodecki and Matuszewski place it. However, I omit the editors' identifications of divisions between the folios of the codex which are placed at the margins of their Latin edition.

353. See nn. 57–59 above.
354. Respectively: before Chapter 1; between Chapters 123 and 124; between Chapters 196 and 197.

In contrast to the documents contained in the codex, the charters lend themselves to a wide variety of arrangement and presentation. Although the charters included here may be used in conjunction with the narrative sources in several different ways, they are selected and grouped here according to two criteria. First, I include only those documents that refer specifically to the issues which Abbot Peter or his continuator explicitly defined as important; or documents that refer specifically to the particular holdings to which the two authors devoted their "accounts." Second, I arrange the resulting selection of 33 documents into three thematic sections – whose topics, in my view, best reflect the most important concerns articulated and addressed by Abbot Peter and by his continuator. These topics include: (1) ducal patronage over the Henryków monastery; (2) the relationships between the monastery and several powerful neighbors in its region; and (3) specific proprietary transactions involving the monastery.

Accordingly, Subsection I, titled "Politics of the monastic foundation: Alternative views," conveys the diversity of views concerning the original, defining relationship between the Piast dukes and the Henryków monastery – a diversity which Abbot Peter was so concerned to construe in one particular direction. Subsection II, titled "Powerful neighbors of the Henryków monastery: Coexistence, conflict, alliance," throws additional light on the relationships between the monastery and several potentially difficult nearby lords whom Abbot Peter and his continuator also describe in their stories. Finally, Subsection III, "Family histories, property divisions, alienations, and disputes," supplements (and occasionally contradicts) some of the individual "accounts" that are the main subject of the Henryków history. Within each subsection, I try to reconcile chronology with a clear thematic arrangement. Thus, the documents in the first subsection are almost entirely in chronological order, those in the second are arranged to shed light on specific neighbors and their kindreds, while those in the third follow the geographic arrangement of the monastic history. I preface each subsection with a short introductory paragraph, intended to bridge for the reader the documents, persons, and issues reflected in it with the text of the *Henryków Book* itself.

The *Henryków Book*: Book One

Here begins the treatise introducing the first book about the foundation of the cloister of Saint Mary the Virgin in Henryków.

[1] Because the deeds of the mortals grow old and are dimmed by a fog of oblivion in the course of time and with the long succession of posterity, it has wisely been decreed to entrust them to the memory of succeeding generations by a record of letters. Therefore we, the first monks transferred from the holy and venerable community of the monastery of Lubiąż to plant the flower of divine service in Henryków, have decided to reveal to our successors by the present writing in what way – meaning from what persons and for what reason – this house has assumed the beginnings of its foundation.

And because through the succession of diverse times and persons the good deeds of the faithful are sometimes violated by the malice and iniquity of some among those who come after them, we have expressed in the present booklet, by a truthful narration, how – meaning from what persons and by what authority – the gifts of all the inheritances which this cloister has peacefully possessed since the beginnings [of the rule] the first Abbot Henry until the most recent times of the fourth Abbot Geoffrey,[1] have accrued to this church, and been confirmed in its eternal possession: so that the knights of Christ who slave for Almighty God in this place for a long time to come may be able to refute any claim levelled against them and answer the adversaries of their house with reasoned reflection, because, thanks to this book, they know the origins of each gift and the cause [of the monks' possession] of each inheritance.

However, it is now fitting to omit this for a while, and first to write down the knowledge about the foundation of the cloister, and a little later to demonstrate in truthful narrative the reason of the gift and the confirmation of each inheritance in its proper place.

About the person of the founder and the course of the foundation.

[2] There once was a certain cleric by the name of Nicholas, born of parents neither very noble nor completely base but from among middling knights in the province of Kraków. In the days of the celebrated Duke Henry, son of the late

---

1. Abbots of Henryków during the years 1227–34 and 1269–73, respectively; Grodecki, *Liber* (1991), 1, n. 2.

old Duke Bolesław,[2] this same Nicholas entered the province of Silesia in modest circumstances. At that time he did not have a single pace of ground either in patrimony or in any [other type of] property in this land. But early on, he adhered to a certain canon of the [cathedral] church of Saint John [in Wrocław] by the name of Lawrence. At that time Lawrence was the highest notary of the said great Duke Henry.[3] Because Nicholas had an able hand for writing, and maintained himself under a great rigor of discipline, the aforesaid Lawrence received him into an increasing familiarity, and gradually, little by little, distinguished him in the duke's matters, until at last he began quite often to praise him to the duke in secret. While this was going on, and Nicholas was serving his lord with a faithful obedience, a few years later it happened that Lawrence was raised by a divine nod to the dignity of ruling the bishopric of the holy church of Lubusz,[4] and that the office of the highest notary – and, to tell the truth, the rule of the entire land of Silesia – were entrusted upon Nicholas by this duke, on unanimous counsel of the highly born.

Oh, the Providence of the divine decree of Almighty God, Who, as formerly with Joseph in Egypt,[5] has sublimely raised this Nicholas for the glory of His name – but the former [i.e., Joseph] so that He might come to the aid of his parents' circumstance of need,[6] and the latter [i.e., Nicholas] so that He could materially augment the way of salvation and the eternal joys for the souls of the many faithful serving God in this cloister! As those who knew him in his youth have testified, from the beginnings of his life Nicholas strove for discipline with an unceasing exertion, and after reaching mature age, was distinguished by an honesty of habits, and, because of his constant uprightness, was much cherished by the noble, the mediocre, and the base. So he was venerated with a wonderful fondness by the duke himself and by all the people.

[3] While this was going on and Nicholas became enriched with a certain opulence in things, he began, by the duke's will, to procure for himself posses-

2. Duke Bolesław I the Tall was born in 1127, succeeded to the rule of Silesia between 1159 and 1163, and died in 1201; his son Henry I the Bearded was born in the 1160s, succeeded Bolesław to the rule in 1201, and died in 1238; *Rodowód*, 1:45–49, 74–81; Andrzej Marzec, "Bolesław I Wysoki" [Bolesław I the Tall], *Piastowie*, 363–68; Marzec, "Henryk I Brodaty" [Henry I the Bearded], *Piastowie*, 375–86.

3. The chief notary, sometimes called the protonorary, was the head of the Silesian chanceries in the later twelfth and thirteenth centuries; Karol Maleczyński, Maria Bielińska, and Antoni Gąsiorowski, *Dyplomatyka wieków średnich* [Diplomatics of the Middle Ages] (Warsaw: Państwowe Wydawnictwo Naukowe, 1971), 176–82.

4. Lawrence was bishop of Lubusz from 1209 through 1233; Pius Bonifacius Gams, *Series episcoporum ecclesiae catholicae* (1886, repr. Graz: Akademische Druck- u. Verlagsanstalt, 1957), 285.

5. Gen. 39:2–6, 21–23; 41:40–45; 42:6.

6. Gen. 45:7–8; 50:19–21; the "need" might also refer to the temporary barrenness of Joseph's mother Leah, and of her sister Rachel, for which see Gen. 30:1–24.

sions and inheritances in various places. The duke believed that after the end of Nicholas's days he and his successors would possess all these inheritances. But the duke thought one thing, while Almighty God illuminated the breast of his servant with a certain holy intention. As the outcome of things showed later, and as the grace of Almighty God revealed, the intention in Nicholas's soul led toward the honor of his Creator. Although this man did not offer an example of a life of any [particular] religiosity,[7] yet, since he rarely or never did anything by his behavior or actions to offend anyone's sight or hearing, he seemed adorned on the inside in the image of a pearl, gleaming most brightly from four angles. Hence, because external action is understood to proceed from the intention of a man's interior, Nicholas carried a certain holy intention within himself, and prudently pondered it to himself internally in the midst of [attending to] the duke's great matters which he conducted externally among men.

He shone forward with the eye of prudence, because through reflection he wisely foresaw the good and the bad in the future. He was served at the rear by the eye of justice, because each day he cleansed his past errors, if he had committed any, by works of mercy. On his right he shone no less with the eye of temperance that was present in him, because although before or after him no cleric ever rose to such power near the dukes in this land, yet in all his good fortune he prudently kept himself in a posture of great humility. On his left he likewise shone with the eye of fortitude, because although he was sometimes oppressed by misfortunes, he never abandoned his good intentions.[8]

[4] While this man shone with those and many other virtues, with which he was so well illuminated, a religious and holy intention (very pleasing to God, we believe) was born in the secret chamber of his heart. He contemplated how he might initiate some religious house, and bring this about through his [own] capacity and out of his own expenses, for the honor of God and Saint John. After weighing this and similar things inside himself for a long time by a quiet reflection of mind, and just when, as if by a certain deliberation of his heart, the plan to do this became stronger and stronger every day, it happened that he revealed his heart's intention to certain religious men with whom he was very familiar. One of them was called Peter, at that time provost of the [episcopal]

---

7. *Sed licet vir iste non in religiositate aliqua exemplum vivendi non preberet*, a phrase Grodecki reads as stating that he was not some kind of monk, evidently considering *religiositas* as an equivalent of *religio* (observance), or a state of being a *religiosus* (n. 12 below). I think he over-reads the text.

8. This paragraph metaphorically describes the four cardinal virtues; see Grodecki, *Liber* (1949), 68 n. 8, and Piotr Górecki, "Rhetoric, Memory and Use of the Past: Abbot Peter of Henryków as Historian and Advocate," *Cîteaux* 48 (1997), 262–93, at 273.

church of Wrocław,[9] and the other was Guido, formerly archdeacon of that church, but at the time when these things were taking place a monk of our Order in our mother [monastery of] Lubiąż.

With these two alone, Nicholas discussed the plan he had in mind, and first obtained advice from them about what he should do, that is, how he might capture the will of the duke in this matter. After these things were done, these men sat together and discussed this and many similar things among themselves, and Provost Peter said that it would be best to establish some prebends in honor of the church of Saint John in the place called Henryków, and for lord Nicholas to be entrusted here with the guidance over this priory.[10]

[5] To which Master Guido answered that over the course of times and persons, various tribulations often come to pass in many provinces, and princely quarrels often turn the land into waste, and so it is clear that a divine office cannot be stabilized by canons in such a place; but that if Nicholas wished to fulfill the vow of his soul, he should plant in this place the vine of the Cistercian Order, because once this Order puts down root someplace, it is not easily eliminated by adversity. After Master Guido said these words, Nicholas answered,

"Truly, since the Order of the Cistercians, also commonly called the Order of grey monks,[11] appears to be the mirror and the flower of all the religious,[12] it was and is my heart's intention to plant the flower of that Order in this place, if this should please God, and if the consent of my lord the duke should be well inclined toward it. After this plan began to press upon my soul, I felt the steadiness of this Order within me more and more every day. So, because we see the vines of the Order blooming so splendidly throughout all the Christian lands, I ask that this now be resolved among ourselves, and that my heart's plan be shrouded by silence

9. A provost was one of the officials of the cathedral chapter. The canons in the chapter were led by several such officials. The most important were the archdeacon and the dean, but there were a number of others.

10. A prebend was an estate that served as a source of support for an individual cleric (priest, monk, or canon regular). A priory was a group of clerics who lived in common, either according to a monastic rule or otherwise. In the context of regular clergy, a priory was either a community of clerics smaller than a monastery, or a community of canons regular, or a community of monks in groups of monasteries presided by one abbot, specifically the Cluniacs; thus, Cluniac monasteries were headed by priors. A community of canons regular was one of the meanings of priory. C. H. Lawrence, *Medieval Monasticism: Forms of Religious Life in Western Europe in the Middle Ages* (3d ed., Harlow: Longman/ Pearson Education, 2001), 91–92, 302; Colin Morris, *The Papal Monarchy: The Western Church from 1050 to 1250* (Oxford: Clarendon Press, 1989), 237–50; Richard W. Southern, *Western Society and the Church in the Middle Ages* (Harmondsworth: Penguin, 1970), 217–30.

11. The Cistercians were called "grey" (or "white") monks from the color of their habit, which was made of coarse and undyed wool; Lawrence, *Medieval Monasticism*, 174.

12. "The religious" (*religiosi* or *religiosae*) was a collective term for monks, nuns, friars, and sisters; see the introductory essay above, n. 292.

until, for the honor of God and of Saint John, by the authority of my lord the duke, I am able to fulfill the agreed-upon advice through deeds."

After these things were done, and the three men were confirmed in this holy plan as if by a single agreement, they left each other.

[6] Not much time after that, Nicholas held a solemn feast in the village of Henryków itself, for his lord the duke and for all the highly-born of this land, to which feast he invited lord Lawrence, at that time bishop of the church of Wrocław,[13] lord Paul, in those days bishop of the diocese of Poznań,[14] and also lord Lawrence, at that time bishop of Lubusz,[15] through whom this Nicholas had first reached the summit of such honor. Before the hour of the feast, Nicholas also most secretly revealed his heart's desire to these three bishops, and diligently asked them to try to incline the consent of the duke's will regarding that deed, whenever the time seemed right. After these things were done, the said bishops arrived at the feast, together with the lord Duke Henry the elder and his son the younger duke, also Henry,[16] and ate and drank joyfully. After the feast ended, and the duke seemed a bit happier, the bishops approached the duke and said to him secretly,

"Lord, we have a certain request of the magnificence of your dignity, but we will not willingly reveal it unless you first promise to hear us out gladly, according to the grace of your goodness."

But the duke, who was a most prudent prince, guarded by a shield of great discernment, said,

"It is unjust for the prince to promise anything unless he first knows the cause and the reason for the request."

And they said,

"Lord, you should know that we so cherish the honor of yourself and of your [relatives] that we strive to request nothing other than that which will enhance your honor in this life, and the salvation of your soul in future life."

[7] Then the duke answered by saying,

13. Lawrence was bishop of Wrocław from 1207 through 1232; Gams, 264; Ewa Maleczyńska and Karol Maleczyński, *Dzieje Śląska* [The history of Silesia] (Warsaw: Wiedza Powszechna, 1955), 331, 335–36; Grodecki, *Liber* (1949), 70 (n. 12), 102 (n. 37).

14. Paul was bishop of Poznań between 1211 and 1242, the first canonically elected bishop of that see; Maleczyńska and Maleczyński, *Dzieje*, 331–36; Grodecki, *Liber* (1949), 70 n. 13; Gerard Labuda, "Paweł, biskup poznański" [Paul, bishop of Poznań], in *P.S.B.*, 25:363–5.

15. See n. 4 above.

16. Duke Henry II the Pious, son of Henry I the Bearded, was born shortly before 1200, succeeded his father to the rule of the Duchy of Silesia in 1238, and died in 1241 at the battle of Legnica, in a vain attempt to repel the Mongol invasion; *Rodowód*, 1:94–9; Piotr Rabiej, "Henryk II Pobożny" [Henry II the Pious], *Piastowie*, 393–400. The dukes of Silesia named Henry are hereafter identified by their regnal number in brackets.

"I believe and firmly know that you seek nothing other than the enhancement of my honor, and so don't be afraid to reveal your requests to me, because if, as you say, the requests are meant to advance the salvation of my soul in any way, you shall undoubtedly be heard out today."

Happy and thankful to God and to the duke, they said,

"Lord, your chaplain Nicholas once came to your land poor and very modest in things, but you have made him wonderfully great in the church of Saint John and near yourself, for which he returns to you, his lord and father, enormous thanks. He proposes, if your goodness give consent, to initiate in this place a cloister of grey monks, by your authority, toward the advancement of the salvation of your soul, and to move it forward as best he can out of the goods which have accrued to him by the gift of your grace. Therefore, lord, prostrate at the feet of your dignity, we humbly request on bended knees that you gladly deign to admit your chaplain's vow into the grace of a hearing, according to the mercy of your rule."

Then the duke was silent for a long time. He deliberated for nearly one hour, and at last he finally said,[17]

"Although I had a plan in my heart to establish something else in this place, yet, because your holy request will, it is hoped, help advance the salvation of many souls, may the boldness of my presumption not stand in the way of your requests, so pious and devoted; and, for the honor of Almighty God, the Holy Virgin, and Saint John, I receive these prayers into a favorable hearing. Provided, however, that if a cloister is built in this place, Henryków, then the authority of this cloister's foundation shall be ascribed not to Nicholas, but to me and my successors."

Upon hearing this, the bishops said with a great joy of heart,

"We offer cries of praise to the dispenser of all goods, the Almightly God – Who has granted you, His devoted servant, the rule of this province for the honor of His name – and we also give thanks to you, lord, because through your feeling of devotion you always seek to enhance the ornament of the Holy Mother Church. Now therefore, lord – if your consent regarding this deed be so inclined by a spontaneous will – make your son, our younger lord [Henry II], and the other nobles in your presence come forth, and reveal to them your chaplain's vow and our requests."

[8] When these things were completed in this way, lord Henry the younger duke, and all the nobles who were then in attendance there, were summoned. With all of them gathered before the lord duke, and all listening, lord Henry the elder duke said,

---

17. The final Latin phrase here is *tandem ultimo dixit*, which is as repetitive in the original as it is in the translation. Thus, the English is not my editing error, but an attempt to convey Abbot Peter's strong emphasis, just here, on delay and on the fact of awaiting the duke's response.

"The more excellent a place we hold over others in the duchy under our rule, the more we are exposed to the sight of all. Hence, because all the vows or rights of the subjects of our dominion depend upon our 'we wish' or 'we do not wish' for their eternal confirmation, may our 'we wish' never inhibit anything that pertains either to the salvation of souls or to the adornment of our Venerated Mother Church – but may it always seek to confirm pious deeds in praise of Almighty God and Saint John. Therefore, let it be known to you, my son, and to all of you who have come together into our presence just now, that lord Nicholas, our notary, is proposing to build a cloister of grey monks in this place, Henryków. But because this Nicholas has all that he has by our gift and grace, he asks that we give our consent to God and to himself concerning this deed. Hence – even though this will considerably diminish the utility of our dominion for a time[18] – nevertheless we, inclined by the prayers of the father bishops, agree by our spontaneous will, in honor of Almighty God and of Saint John, that a cloister be built here in Henryków, but on this condition: that the authority of the foundation of this cloister shall be ascribed to me and to my son and to our successors, because when Nicholas first entered our province, he had no property in it. Thus, let present and future persons know that whatever is accomplished or done here in Henryków, occurs within our property and inheritance. Hence, the authority of this cloister's foundation shall not be ascribed to anyone more justly than to me and my successors. Truly, by a spontaneous will I permit and wish that a cloister of grey monks be founded in this place, Henryków, for the eternal salvation of myself and of my successors."

[9] Upon hearing this, the bishops and nobles said to the duke in a unanimous voice,

"Lord, because we fully discern the kind flourish of feeling of your devotion to the exaltation of the Holy Mother Church, we splendidly give thanks to Almighty God, and to you, our lord, for having given us, subjects of your magnificence, joy beyond belief, in that today, as we hope and firmly know, you have offered God a pleasing and welcome sacrifice, by lavishly giving to such a venerable Order a place where God can be served for the salvation of yourself and your successors, and where, God willing, we hope that eternal salvation of many faithful will be augmented every day."

[10] After these things were done, at the nod of the bishops and nobles lord Nicholas took off his cowl, knelt before the dukes, and resigned all his possessions to them. After this and many similar things were done there in God's praise, the elder lord Duke [Henry I] said,

"My father, Duke Bolesław [I] of happy memory, founded the monastery of the church of Lubiąż as a remedy for his sins. After his death, I founded the

18. The Latin word is *temporaliter*, which can also mean "in the physical world," i.e., "temporally," or "with respect to temporal matters"; Niermeyer, 1016, *s.v. temporaliter*; Du Cange, 8:53, *s.v. temporaliter*.

cloister of the nuns of Trzebnica for the honor of God and of Saint Bartholomew. Hence it seems, if it please God and all of you, that my son Henry should accept the care of the foundation of this cloister of Henryków – because just as the memorial of the monks of Lubiąż shall henceforth be assigned to my father, and that of the nuns of Trzebnica to me, so I wish that this cloister of Henryków should be the foundation and memorial of my son Henry [II] and his successors."

After the elder lord duke said this and many other similar things in praise of God and for the honor of the Holy Church, lord Nicholas once more reverently came up to the knees of the younger Duke [Henry II], and there received from him the power and authority to found the cloister in this place. This feast was celebrated in the village of Henryków in the year of the Lord 1222, and those deeds were accomplished there at that time. After these things were done, the dukes and bishops departed from one another.

[11] Upon receiving from the lord duke the power to build the cloister here, Nicholas strove with all the strength he could muster to recruit the convent to this place as quickly as possible. The convent arrived here in the year of our Lord 1227, on the fifth [day before the] calends of June [May 28]. That same year, on the day before the calends of December [November 30], the oft-mentioned Nicholas of revered memory died. As he was reaching his end, lord Henry, abbot of this place, asked him if he wished to choose the burial for himself in this cloister. He answered by saying,

"Lord abbot, allow my body to be buried in the cemetery [of the cathedral church] of Saint John, because He raised me from a poor cleric to the height of great honor. After a long deliberation of mind with myself, I have resolved that my bones, asleep in the dust of death, will nowhere better await the Trumpet of the Final Resurrection than in that place where I was first sublimely installed in a canonical see, not by my own merits, but by the free grace of God and of Saint John. In addition, the presence of my dead body might not cause your church temporal advantage, but, I fear, might cause it great disadvantage, because although I may be the efficient cause of the initial foundation of your cloister, yet you shall in no way describe me as the author of this foundation, but the duke. Whatever I had amounted to in this land, and was able to accomplish in temporal matters,[19] I possessed it all by the grace and the gift of my lord the duke."

[12] *About the final end of lord Nicholas.* After he said this and many other similar things for the cloister's benefit to lord Abbot Henry, he was strengthened by the *viaticum* of the Sacrosant Body of Christ[20] and by other ecclesiastical sacraments, and he left this world.

19. *Temporaliter*, again, for which see the preceding footnote.
20. That is, the eucharist administered to the dying; Niermeyer, 1085, *s.v. viaticus*; F. L. Cross, *The Oxford Dictionary of the Christian Church* (London: Oxford University Press, 1958), 1416, *s.v. viaticum*.

[13] *About his humility.* Here, brothers, you see by what devotion and effort this man labored so that the divine office may flame up and be celebrated in this place forever. Even when he was on his last breath, he urged that the authority of this monastery's foundation be ascribed not to himself, but to his lord the duke.

[14] *That he should be prayed for.* In this matter, we urge ourselves and our successors that the memory of this pious man, Nicholas, be forever solemnly celebrated on the anniversaries [of his death] and in other obsequies.

[15] *That the Duke Henry, killed by the pagans,*[21] *be assiduously prayed for.* And the memory of Duke Henry, killed by the pagans, as the true founder of this cloister, shall forever be solemnly sustained on the anniversaries [of his death] and in other prayers and obsequies.

[16] *The death of this same lord duke.* This lord duke fell in battle for his people at the hands of the pagans, in the year of the Lord 1241, on the fifth [day before the] ides of April [April 9].

[17] *Admonition to prayers.* Thus, we admonish ourselves and our successors to implore, with inclined minds, the mercy of God's immense goodness, so that when the Final Trumpet sounds to arouse the whole human kind, He Who on the said day and hour has led this duke out of the prison of the body, may rescue him from the prison of death; and that, for the good deeds expended by him upon this cloister, and for his other pious deeds, he may earn entrance among the ranks of the saints forever. Amen.

[18] *Here ends our account of the cloister's foundation.* Here, brothers, the cause and reason for this cloister's foundation has been set out for you, so that you may that much more eagerly and promptly return thanks and praises to Almighty God, Who inspired the advancement and the beginning of this cloister through the aforesaid dukes and your other benefactors. We wrote down all these things in order that our successors may not regard any man [as patron of the monastery] by reason of the foundation, but that they honor, with a due reverence, only those who issue, or shall [in the future] issue, from the stock of the aforesaid dukes.

[19] *That all the aforesaid and noted things are true.* If anyone among men in the future says or thinks that these statements are frivolous, let the present and future [persons] know that we have described all the things noted and written down above in a truthful narration, just as we heard them from the aforesaid revered father bishops, and from many others who had been present at these events together with the lord duke. Hence we have inserted [this knowledge] into the present booklet for the memory of our successors.

[20] *Here begin the accounts of the gifts of the individual inheritances of the cloister of Henryków.* Enough said about the reason for the cloister's foundation. Now we begin to record the events that followed, that is, the accounts of the gifts of in-

---

21. This is the first of Abbot Peter's many references to the Mongol invasion of 1241 as "the pagans," for which see the introductory essay above, nn. 85–88.

heritances to the cloister, so that the servants of Christ who shall long hence do battle for the True God in this place may know the reason for the gift of each inheritance from this booklet; and in order that if someone from among men should raise a claim against them for any cause, after perusing the present [writings] they may be able to answer correctly and reasonably.

[21] *The account of the foundation of the monastery.* Let it be known that in the days when the cloister was being initiated, there was a certain bishop of the church of Poznań who had been present at the aforesaid events with the lord duke from the beginning. He was an old man and a revered person, and was from the kindred of the aforesaid lord Nicholas. This lord Bishop Paul had baptized lord Henry, the younger duke, and raised him from the holy font, and hence was joined by a certain special familiarity to lord Henry the elder duke, [nicknamed] the Bearded.

On the counsel and direction of lord Henry the elder duke, during the second year after lord Nicholas's death, this Bishop Paul held a large feast for the lord duke and all the great [persons] of this land in this very same Henryków. At this feast, lord Henry the younger, the celebrated duke, founded the monastery here by the will and under the direction of his father. Three bishops were present here at this foundation at that time, that is to say, the same lord Paul bishop of Poznań, and lord Lawrence, at that time bishop of Wrocław, predecessor of lord Thomas, bishop of Wrocław.[22] On that day, the two aforenamed bishops consecrated two altars here in the sign of truth, one in honor of Saint Mary the Virgin, the other of Saint John the Baptist, in the wooden church. At this feast was also present lord Lawrence, at that time bishop of Lubusz and the father of Master Przemysł, a man most famous in his days. And there was then a great rejoicing, and a most solemn divine service here.

This foundation of the monastery was accomplished in the year of the Lord 1228, on the eighth [day before the] ides of June, Saint Vincent's Day [June 6]. At this foundation and feast, the elder duke, together with his son, confirmed for the [Cistercian] Order and for this cloister all the possessions which Nicholas had held during his life by the duke's gift. Also on that day and at that hour the lord duke granted to this cloister a hundred large hides of forest, fifty of which hides are in Budzów and fifty in Quolsdorf.[23]

[22] *The names of lord Nicholas's villages.* These are the manors (*praedia*) which Nicholas held during his life, and which the lord duke then [i.e., in 1228] confirmed for the cloister. First, Henryków with its circuit, in which the cloister was founded. Second, Nikłowice near Ręków. Third, Osiek near Żmigród. Fourth, Richnow with its region (*ambitus*) that is to say [an area] in the amount of a hundred large hides.

---

22. Thomas was bishop of Wrocław between 1232 and 1267 or 1268; Maleczyńska and Maleczyński, *Dzieje*, 331; and n. 39 below.

23. Supplementary Document no. 2.

[23] *That he had held these villages.* Lord Nicholas possessed those inheritances in this province during his life by the grace and gift of the lord duke, and the lord duke confirmed them for the cloister, as was said.

[24] *About lord Nicholas's inheritances in the region of Kraków.* Nicholas also held two inheritances in the land of Kraków, that is to say Glewo and Głęboka, which in his days he granted to this cloister, to be possessed forever.

[25] *That some of the inheritances have been alienated from the cloister.* But because some of the aforesaid inheritances, Nikłowice and Osiek, are now alienated from the cloister, we shall also describe the reason why this was done in the appropriate place.[24]

[26] *If anyone from among men ever raises a claim against the cloister concerning any holding, the brothers may inspect the modest record below and immediately find out how they should answer.* Now begin the treatises about the reasons for the gift of each of the inheritances of the cloister of Henryków, describing in what way or from which persons each inheritance and holding has accrued to this cloister, and been confirmed in its eternal possession.

[27] *First, about Henryków.* First, about Henryków: the small parcels from which it was collected and expanded into a proper inheritance. *Second, about Bobolice.* About Cienkowice and by what reason the cloister may hold that parcel. About the parcel of Bobolice. *Third, about Skalice.* About Skalice: in what manner, or in what way, this holding accrued to the cloister and was confirmed in its eternal possession. *Fourth, about Jaworowice.* About Jaworowice. *Fifth, the account of Michael's exchange.* About Michael's holding, [which was] exchanged for Nikłowice. *Sixth, about Głębowice.* About Głębowice. *Seventh, about Brukalice.* About Brukalice. *Eighth, about Dębnica in [Great] Poland.* About Dębnica in [Great] Poland. *Ninth, about Grodoszów.* About Grodoszów.

Here begins the account of Henryków.

[28] These aforenamed holdings were joined to our [estate of] Henryków and to the cloister, some before the pagans, some after.

[29] *That Henryków was gathered from many parcels.* Let it be known about Henryków that at first it was called Januszowe, for the reason that long ago two small knights (*militelli*), full brothers,[25] possessed [land] in the place where the stream

24. Neither Abbot Peter nor the continuator describe Osiek; for the alienation of Nikłowice, see Chapters 80–81.

25. *Germani fratres*, a term used by Abbot Peter repeatedly, in contrast to *fratres uterini*. In Polish medieval usage, *germanus* could mean a number of relationships, but when used about siblings it referred to descent from at least one common parent, whether mother or father. In general medieval usage, "uterine brothers" (*fratres uterini*) were sons of the same mother, though of different fathers. The term was used specifically to designate male offspring of successive marriages by the same mother, and to distinguish them from male

which flows through the village has its spring. The older was called Janusz, so this place was called Januszów at that time.²⁶ The younger brother was called Dobrogost. Because this Dobrogost practiced robbery, he was expelled from the land, without yet having taken a wife, and his brother Janusz died there without an heir. Hence, because in the days when this was going on our Nicholas served the duke, and saw that this holding of Januszów was empty, he requested the lord duke that it be given to him.

[30] *Lord Nicholas's first possession.* This was the first [holding] given to lord Nicholas in possession in this land. This Januszów was a modest territory (*modicum territorium*) in those days.

[31] *The reason for the name Henryków.* At that time there was a certain Henry who possessed [land] near the spring whose stream now flows through [the estate of] the cloister together with the Morzyna.²⁷ This Henry held himself out as a knight, and had borders up to the stream which the old Poles call Jaworzyca, and which takes its name from its spring. This stream now flows through the village of Henryków itself; at that time, it divided Januszów from the small knight Henry. This Henry was an ancestor²⁸ of those who are now called Czesławice.²⁹

[32] *About the place where the cloister is [today, and about] what was here earlier.* In those days there were certain ducal peasants (*ducis rustici*) on the other side of Januszów who had a good quantity of land. Those peasants held [land] in the place where the cloister now stands. Let it truly be known that among those peasants there were two who surpassed the others by a certain [degree of] power. One of them was called Żuk, the other Krzepisz, and hence this place was formerly called Żukowice. A quarrel erupted between Krzepisz and Żuk, so that they mutually killed one another.³⁰ When they were dead, all the other peasants

---

offspring of successive marriages by the same father: see Du Cange, 8:392, *s.v. uterinus* (this dictionary does not have the entry *germanus*), and Plezia, 4:524–25, *s.v. germanus*. For the derivation of the modern English meanings of german and uterine brothers, see *Oxford English Dictionary* (Oxford: Clarendon Press, 1933), 1:1133, *s.v. brother*; *germani fratres* are here defined as male descendants of the same father and mother, while *fratres uterini* are male descendants of the same mother.

26. Please note the slight discrepancy in the ending of the place name (*-ów* and *-owe*). Both versions refer to the name of an early settler, and Abbot Peter clearly uses them interchangeably, here and in some other passages, annotated below.

27. One of the small streams crossing the area of settlement included in the monastic estate; see Map 5.

28. *Attavus*, which can also mean grandfather, which is how Grodecki translates it.

29. This locality is the subject of the final story of Abbot Peter's continuator, most clearly dated to the years 1297, 1301, 1303, and 1305, and narrated at Chapters 126, 151, 170, 192–96.

30. The Latin here states *ita ut alterutrum se invicem occiderent* – another phrase I choose to render in its glorious redundancy.

living here dispersed. Hence lord Nicholas, seeing the arable fields (*agri*) of Żukowice empty, joined them to his holding of Januszów by the will of the lord duke. Let it also be known that the aforesaid peasants had boundaries up to the road which now divides Czesławice from Muszkowice.[31]

[33] *About lord Nicholas's exchange with Henry.* Lord Nicholas made an exchange with the aforesaid Henry – who held [land extending] from the Morzyna up to the stream – by accepting the same Henry's holding for himself, and by giving him the same amount [of land] on the other side of the Morzyna, between Kojanowice and the Morzyna [stream]. Hence the cloister [now] possesses the said Henry's holding, and this is the reason why Czesławice (that is, the heirs of the aforenoted Henry)[32] now possess [land] between the cloister and Muszkowice. Enough said about that.

[34] Now we will say why this entire territory in which the cloister was founded is at present called Henryków. The knight Henry mentioned above held [land] between the Morzyna and the stream that crosses the village of Henryków. So this knight's modest holding of that time was called Henryków, whence this entire territory is called Henryków. In the old days a certain tree – a large beech, a tree called *jawor* in Polish – stood in the village of Januszów. At the root of the tree originated a spring, which was at that time called Jaworzyca, after that tree. From this spring issues a stream which at present crosses the village of Henryków, and the stream itself is called Jagielno, for the reason that long ago the Poles have often sown millet in its ravine.[33] So the small fort (*castellum*)[34] which is now [situated] between Wadochowice and the cloister, is also called Jagielno.

31. Muszkowice is the subject of the first story of Abbot Peter's continuator, dated implicitly to 1266, and explicitly to the years 1282, 1288, 1298, and 1303, and narrated at Chapters 126–39, 142–43, 145, 153.

32. A name in the form *Czesławice* refers grammatically to the descendants of Czesław (presumably some heir of Henry), and physically to the village they inhabit (or have formerly inhabited); see the preceding chapter.

33. The name *Jagielno* comes from *jagły*, Polish for millet; *S.Sp.*, 3:90, *s.v. jagielny, jagły.*

34. In general medieval and in Polish usage, the term *castellum* is ambiguous. It may refer to any fortified place, whether a castle in the strict sense of a keep, motte, and bailey, or a town with a fortified core or perimeter, or (as in this case) to some much more local structure. Note from Chapter 36 below that a *castellum* might also be a dwelling for an inhabitant of the locality with which this portion of the *Book* is concerned. The military functions of the two *castella* mentioned in the *Book*, if any, are entirely inaccessible. Niermeyer, 154, *s.v. castellum*; Witold Hensel, *U źródeł Polski średniowiecznej* [At the sources of medieval Poland] (Wrocław: Zakład Narodowy im. Ossolińskich, 1974), 184–92; for *castella* as networks of towns and their outlying fortified settlements in the earlier twelfth century, see Piotr Górecki, *Economy, Society, and Lordship in Medieval Poland, 1100–1250* (New York: Holmes and Meier, 1992), 19, 40, 45–46; Górecki, *Parishes, Tithes, and Society in Earlier Medieval Poland, ca. 1100–1250*, Transactions of the American Philosopical Society 83.2 (Philadelphia: American Philosophical Society, 1993), 14–16, 23–25.

[35] *About the cutting of the famous tree.* After lord Nicholas made the exchange with the said Henry, he caused the said tree to be cut down, and thereby obliterated the name of this holding, Januszów. Because he joined [the acquired holding] to his holding of Żukowice, he named the whole [estate thus formed] Henryków, out of reverence for the elder lord duke.

[36] *About Kołaczów and its territory.* Also in the old days, a certain old ducal peasant (*rusticus ducis*) who was called Kołacz possessed [a dwelling] in a small fort (*castellum*)[35] which is [situated] beyond the Oława, between the farmstead[36] [called] Gurów and the cloister. Because in those days the land here in the circuit was forested and empty, this same peasant dominated many forests and woods in the circuit at that time. So this territory is called Kołaczowe[37] ever since long ago. And let it be known that in this territory of Kołaczowe there are now certain hamlets (*villulae*), whose names are these: Witostowice with its circuit, Raczyce, Skalice, and Jaworowice.[38]

[37] *The account of tithe from this territory.* Because the tithe from these villages, confirmed by the reverend father Thomas bishop of Wrocław and his chapter,[39] belongs to our cloister in Henryków, we have unavoidably judged [it appropriate] to pass this onto the memory of our sucessors in writing.

[38] *In what way lord Nicholas obtained the parcel of Kołaczów.* Because, for the future utility of the cloister, we have moved onto a written description of the boundaries [of the estate] of Henryków, let us now return to those things from which we have turned away. Let it be known that after a long succession of generations, the aforesaid peasant Kołacz diminished [in wealth] more and more, and Nicholas found this peasant's heirs holding in the said small fort, very sorely lacking in things.

35. For a plausible similarity in the dwellings of isolated families elsewhere in much earlier medieval Europe, see Richard Hodges, *Dark Age Economics: The Origins of Towns and Trade, AD 600–1000* (New York: St. Martin's, 1982), 135.

36. Here and elsewhere, "farmstead" is a translation of *curia*, which can, depending on the context, be translated as "court" (in the sense of a substantial individual holding, a rendition of the Polish *dwór* or the Russian *dvor*), or a "grange," that is, a specialized farm belonging to a monastery, especially common among the Cistercians; Lawrence, *Medieval Monasticism*, 177, 298; introductory essay above, nn. 323–24.

37. This is one of those cases in which a place name refers to the same feature (here the earliest known settler), but varies slightly.

38. These four localities, which represent, as it were, the territorial and social succession to Kołaczów, are important subjects of the rest of the *Book*, in the following passages and times: Witostowice in 1263 (Chapter 207); Raczyce in 1263, and over three generations culminating in 1305, 1309, and 1310 (Chapters 126, 167–85, 207); Skalice in the years culminating in 1227, then in 1233, 1239, 1259, and 1263 (Chapters 27, 65–73, 207); Jaworowice in 1243, 1255, and 1263 (Chapters 27, 57, 74–79, 207).

39. Abbot Peter has more to say about Bishop Thomas and this grant of tithes in Chapters 201 and 207.

Because they were poor, he gave them gifts, and eliminated them with [their] good will. And he joined their arable fields, whatever they then had, to his Henryków.

[39] *Here ends the reason why this cloister is called Henryków.* Now, brothers, you know from how many small parcels this territory of Henryków has been gathered, and the reason why it is called Henryków.

[40] *That all the aforesaid [holdings and gifts] should be [considered] the duke's.* Brothers, we have described the preceding events for this reason: so that present and future [persons] may know that [the monks] possess nothing at all around the cloister other than the estate (*fundus*) of the elder Duke Henry nicknamed the Bearded and his successors.

[41] *That no one beside the dukes may be honored by reason of the foundation.* Now is recorded the reason why you may not honor any man whatsoever on account of this cloister's foundation, except only those who have issued or may issue from the stock of this celebrated duke Henry the Old.[40]

[42] *About the duke's farmstead in Henryków.* Hence [the same argument is accurate] because this glorious duke had earlier proposed to build in the village of Henryków a royal farmstead (*regalis curia*) for himself and his successors, but by God's will was diverted from that intention by the bishops, and, out of love for divine things, resigned the earthly conveniences here to foreign men, the future monks serving God in this cloister forever.

[43] *About prayer for the dukes.* So we exhort ourselves and our successors to pray and to entreaty, with the most ardent devotion, and with the most immediate and assiduous prayers, for the souls of this old Duke Henry and of his son, also Henry, killed by the pagans. This is because, although lord Nicholas was, as it were, the efficient cause of this cloister's foundation, nevertheless whatever this cloister holds in its circuit, it possesses everything by the alms and the generosity of those dukes. Hence, because lord Henry, the younger duke killed by the pagans, knew these things, if he had lived, he might in the course of time have brought this cloister to a good state.

[44] *Enough said about Henryków.* This statement suffices [for knowledge] about Henryków and its piecemeal gathering.

Second, about Cienkowice.

[45] We will say about Cienkowice how and why the cloister may possess part of it. In the days when the cloister of Henryków was being founded, there was a certain rather powerful knight by the name of Albert, and by the nickname of

---

40. When used in the singular, "the Old," "the elder," and similar adjectives are Abbot Peter's alternative nicknames for Henry I the Bearded. When used in the plural ("the old dukes," for example), they identify Henry I, Henry II the Pious, and (perhaps) Bolesław I the Tall. For stylistic reasons, whenever Peter identifies Henry I by one of his alternative nicknames in the text below, I do not consistently gloss his name with his regnal number.

Łyka in Polish, who possessed [land] in Ciepłowoda. This same Albert took as wife a daughter of a certain noble by the name of Dzierżko, and begat a daughter by her. When she was born, the wife herself died at once.[41] After her death, Albert granted to the cloister a part of his inheritance of Ciepłowoda, in the amount of two plows (*ad duo aratra*), to be possessed forever for the soul of his father, then dead, and for his own sins.

[46] *About the gift and the alms of Albert with Beard.* Albert made this gift in the year of the Lord 1229. That same year, Albert went to Prussia for the sins of his father and for his own sins.[42] But before he embarked on that journey, he ordained before the lord duke and the barons that if he should not return, the cloister of Henryków was to possess the entire territory of Ciepłowoda; while if he did return, the closter was to keep that part which he had granted earlier, in the amount of two plows. But because in those days men were simple, without the bile of malice, no privilege was requested from the duke about this deed at that time. Albert returned from Prussia healthy and whole, and later took a German wife by whom he begat sons and daughters. Yet, the cloister possessed from him and from his sons the land which he had granted out of his Ciepłowoda, peacefully and for many years.

[47] *What happened in the land after the pagans.* However, as soon as the pagans entered this land, and did much in it that was worthy of lament, and after the celebrated Duke [Henry II] was killed, this land was dominated by knights, each of whom seized whatever pleased him from the duke's inheritances. Hence the said Albert procured for himself from the boyish Duke Bolesław[43] two ducal inheritances adjoining his [estate], Cienkowice and Kubice, for a modest sum of money.

41. Presumably in childbirth.

42. Presumably as a crusader against the Baltic Prussians; for the background, see Eric Christiansen, *The Northern Crusades: The Baltic and the Catholic Frontier, 1100–1525* (Minneapolis: University of Minnesota Press, 1980), 70–78; Karol Górski, *L'Ordine teutonico alle origini dello stato prussiano* (Turin: Einaudi, 1971), 13–15, 22–37; Marian Biskup and Gerard Labuda, *Dzieje Zakonu Krzyżackiego w Prusach. Gospodarka – społeczeństwo – państwo – ideologia* [History of the Teutonic Order in Prussia: economy, society, state, ideology] (Gdańsk: Wydawnictwo Morskie, 1986), 80–95; *Crusade and Conversion on the Baltic Frontier, 1150–1500*, ed. Alan V. Murray (Aldershot: Ashgate, 2001).

43. Duke Bolesław II the Bald (or "the Fat") was the oldest son of Henry II the Pious, born between 1220 and 1225. He succeeded his father to the rule of the Duchy of Silesia in 1242, a year after the battle of Legnica. In 1248, he divided up the inheritance into two duchies with his brother, Henry III the White. He died in 1278. *Rodowód*, 1:109–11; Tomasz Jurek, "Bolesław II Rogatka (Łysy)" [Bolesław II Rogatka (or the Bald)], *Piastowie*, 408–12; Jurek, "Henryk III Biały" [Henry III the White], *Piastowie*, 415–17; Grodecki, *Liber* (1949), 98, n. 34. As noted in the introductory essay above, p. 65, he has furnished Abbot Peter, and Polish chroniclers and hagiographers, with one of their paradigms of bad rule.

[48] *About the purchase.* In order, then, that [the sum of] this money, and the extent of the said inheritances, may be more fully known: this same Albert measured out in the said two villages thirty large hides (*mansi magni*), for which hides he gave the juvenile Duke Bolesław thirty silver marks;[44] and, after eliminating the heirs of these villages, he joined these hides to his village of Ciepłowoda. Hence the names of the said villages were completely obliterated, and changed to the name of Count[45] Albert's village, Ciepłowoda.

[49] *A further account of this.* While this and many similar evils, very harmful to the dukes, were taking place in the land, the said Albert began to settle (*locare*) his Ciepłowoda, together with the aforesaid [two] villages, with Germans.[46] But because that portion [of Ciepłowoda] which he had given to the cloister lay in the kind of place that prevented him from establishing a German village in one piece there unless he redeemed the cloister's arable fields for himself, he

---

44. A mark is a weight of silver, and an amount of pence, which varied in both respects throughout medieval Europe, and in the Piast duchies usually corresponded about 240 pence. The pence relevant for this passage is the "thin," silver variety that was current in Silesia and the other Polish duchies before the reform of coinage in favor of the "fat" pence after the mid-thirteenth century (see the introductory essay above, n. 248); it is not itself a coin, but a unit of account, that is, a simple multiple of the physical coin that makes it up. For the mark as a unit of account in Europe in general, see Peter Spufford, *Money and Its Use in Medieval Europe* (Cambridge: Cambridge University Press, 1988), 223–24; for Poland in particular, see Ryszard Kiersnowski, *Wstęp do numizmatyki polskiej wieków średnich* [Introduction to Polish medieval numismatics] (Warsaw: Państwowe Wydawnictwo Naukowe, 1964), 152–53.

45. See the introductory essay above, nn. 232–35.

46. Here and elsewhere in the context of planning future settlement and land use, "settlement" is one of the two translations of *locatio* – "establishment" is another, used depending as stylistically appropriate in a given context – with the verb form varying accordingly. See also the story of Menold at Budzów, at Chapters 94–96 below. (I prefer to avoid the terms "location" or "to locate," in order to make the translation as clear as possible.) Regardless of the English translation in a particular place in the text, *locatio* refers to: (1) the recruitment of new (in the thirteenth century, German) settlers, under the leadership of the village bailiff, (2) the plan for their settlement and arable arrangement, and (3) the resulting village itself. On this subject, see the introductory essay above, nn. 177, 181, 193–96, 210–12; Richard C. Hoffmann, *Land, Liberties, and Lordship in a Late Medieval Countryside: Agrarian Structures and Change in the Duchy of Wrocław* (Philadelphia: University of Pennsylvania Press, 1989), 62–64, 73–76; Górecki, *Economy*, 212–23; Robert Bartlett, *The Making of Europe: Conquest, Colonization and Cultural Change, 950–1350* (Princeton: Princeton University Press, 1993), 121–23; Paul Knoll, "The Urban Development of Medieval Poland, with Particular Reference to Kraków," in *The Urban Society of Eastern Europe in Premodern Times*, ed. Bariša Krekić (Berkeley and Los Angeles: University of California Press, 1987), 63–136, at 64, 71–76; Benedykt Zientara, "Socio-economic and Spatial Transformation of Polish Towns during the Period of Location," *Acta Poloniae Historica* 34 (1976), 57–83, especially 62–67.

repeatedly asked lord Bodo, abbot of this cloister at that time, to resign to him the land which he had earlier given to the cloister for his sins, and to receive the same amount [of land] near the cloister's old boundaries, that is, in the corner (*angulum*) of Cienkowice. Weary of his repeated insistence and prayers, at last the abbot finally – albeit reluctantly – consented to him, and made the exchange with him, receiving near the cloister's boundaries in Cienkowice as much [land] as he had held in Ciepłowoda; and he resigned to Count Albert what he was asking for. Hence the name of Cienkowice lives on today for the parcel which we have there.

[50] *Here ends the reason why the cloister possesses Cienkowice.* Here, brothers, the reason why you possess Cienkowice has been set out to you. But because we have described the reason why the cloister may possess Cienkowice, it seems fitting that we also state the reason for the [cloister's] right to receive tithe from it.

[51] *Here begins the account of the tithe from Cienkowice.* Let it thus be known to all who read this book that when the said Albert settled the said thirty hides, together with his Ciepłowoda, with Germans, he agreed with lord Thomas, bishop of Wrocław of happy memory, that Albert should pay the lord bishop or his canons eight silver *scoti*[47] annually from each hide of those thirty hides that had been measured out in Kubice and Cienkowice. Therefore, because this parcel which the cloister possesses in Cienkowice contains two and a half hides in furnished arable fields and one *iugum*,[48] and is reckoned among the said [thirty] hides, lord Abbot Bodo agreed with Albert that Albert himself should receive from the cloister as tithe 21 silver *scoti* annually from our hides in Cienkowice.

[52] *More about the same.* A bit later, when Albert died, his sons considered that tithe payment as some kind of rent (*census*), payable to them from our farmstead there, and said that it was not a payment not of tithe, but of rent. So the first-born among them, because he was a tyrant, greatly molested the cloister in things.[49] But as he lay dying, he relaxed the rent, believing that he was furnishing God with a great favor by this. But you should know, brothers, present and

47. A *scotus* is another unit of account, usually consisting of 14 pence in the Polish duchies, and variable throughout Europe in general; Kiersnowski, *Wstęp*, 152–53; Spufford, *Money*, 223.

48. The Latin originals are *ager paratus* and *iugum*; I assume *ager paratus* is a cleared field, ready for cultivation. In traditional classical and medieval Latin, the *iugum* was a unit of land that could be cultivated with two oxen over one day, and this is how this term was presumably used in Poland. Witold Kula, "Miary i wagi" [Measures and weights], in *Encyklopedia historii gospodarczej Polski do 1945 r.* [Encyclopedia of the economic history of Poland until 1945], ed. Antoni Mączak et al. (Warsaw: Państwowe Wydawnictwo Naukowe, 1981), 1:510–18; Kula, *Measures and Men*, trans. Richard Szreter (Princeton: Princeton University Press, 1986), 29–30, 33–34.

49. Supplementary Documents no. 9–10, issued by Albert's grandson and namesake, and no. 8, issued by a papal legate, shed circumstantial light on this figure and on the nature of the grievances involved.

future, that you shall never pay any rent to anyone at all from this or any other farmstead of yours, except as tithe [that is due] there in Cienkowice and in some other places.

[53] *The reason why the cloister of Henryków may not be subject to any advocate.*[50] Although we are prolonging the treatise about the aforesaid Albert and his activity, it is appropriate and very necessary for our successors to say a bit more in writing about the said Albert's person and shrewdness.

[54] *More about the same.* In those days when the aforesaid lord Nicholas shone blessed with an opulence in things, and, as was said, was a newcomer in this land,[51] this Albert joined himself to him by a certain special familiarity, saying that he was his kinsman. Hence, when lord Nicholas was dead, and when, after the pagans, our founder lord Duke Henry [II] was also dead, Albert often said that by reason of kinship with Nicholas he was this cloister's advocate. The sons of a certain Siegród said and say the same thing. That is to say, this Siegród also reputed himself to be Nicholas's kinsman because he was formerly a neighbor of Henryków.

[55] *That Albert may not be [considered] joined to Nicholas by any tie of kinship.* But let it be known that on his father's side Count Albert was from the Czurbani clan from Germany,[52] and on his mother's side he was a Walloon from the Street of the Walloons of Wrocław,[53] while Nicholas, as was said, was born in the province of Kraków. This is the kindred.

50. The term "advocate" had several meanings during the Middle Ages. In the context of this account, the term meant a lay protector of a monastic, parish, or other church, who had the obligation to defend its interests in secular courts (and, more generally, protect it from hostile power in general), and who, in return, benefitted from a close spiritual and economic relationship with the church and its estate, and in addition (in some parts of Europe) could affect the appointment of the clerics who staffed the church. Since the early twelfth century, this bundle of rights was also called patronage over a church. In England, for example, the rights of advocacy in this sense, or patronage, were called "advowson"; see Frederick Pollock and Frederic William Maitland, *The History of English Law before the Time of Edward I*, 2 vols. (2nd ed., Cambridge: Cambridge University Press, 1968), 1:125–26, 497–98, 2:136–39. This passage is one of many examples of Abbot Peter's effort to portray the dukes of Silesia as the legitimate patrons of the Henryków monastery.

51. Chapters 2–3.

52. For Albert's paternal lineage see the prosopographical study in Tomasz Jurek, *Obce rycerstwo na Śląsku do połowy XIV wieku* [Foreign knighthood in Silesia until the mid-fourteenth century] (2nd ed., Poznań: Wydawnictwo Poznańskiego Towarzystwa Przyjaciół Nauk, 1998), 194–96, supplementing and correcting Marek Cetwiński, *Rycerstwo śląskie do końca XIII w. Biogramy i rodowody* [Silesian knighthood until the end of the thirteenth century: biograms and genealogies] (Wrocław: Zakład Narodowy im. Ossolińskich, 1982), 63–65.

53. This is an early example of that multiethnic immigration into the Polish duchies in the course of the twelfth, thirteenth, and fourteenth centuries, of which the two most important groups were the Germans and the Jews. On this group in Silesia during the twelfth century, and specifically its identification as Walloons, see Benedykt Zientara, "Walloons in Silesia in the Twelfth and Thirteenth Centuries," *Quaestiones Medii Aevi* 2

[56] *The [accurate] knowledge of kinship between Nicholas and Albert.* Therefore, after they have viewed these writings and statements, we again and again persuade our successors that they shall not place any man over themselves by reason of any kinship, except only those who issue or may issue from the stock of the glorious duke of revered memory, Henry the Bearded.

[57] *That [only] the dukes may by law be the cloister's advocates.* Although for the cloister's future utility we may have said in writing certain contrary things about the person of the aforesaid Albert, nevertheless he is not to be segregated from the brothers' common prayer, but is to be very much associated in it, because thanks to him the cloister possesses two inheritances: one, that is Cienkowice, by his gift; the other, that is Jaworowice, from Duke Bolesław as a result of his first request.[54] We shall describe the reason for that request in its [appropriate] place.[55]

Third, it is treated about Bobolice and its reason [for inclusion in the monastery's estate].

[58] Enough has now been said about these things. Here begins a treatise about Bobolice. Let it thus be known that formerly in the days of the glorious dukes, that is, lord Henry [I] the elder and his son, also Henry [II], there were four men in Bobolice, heirs of this village, whose names are these: Przybysław, Boguchwał, Wojsław, and Gostach. These four were accused of committing robbery before lord Duke [Henry II], who ordered that they be captured and imprisoned. Afterwards, by the lord duke's order, they were all defeated in a [judicial] duel. Hence, according to Polish custom, they were obliged either to sacrifice their necks to the duke, or to redeem themselves at the duke's will. When they had nothing with which to redeem themselves, the duke ordered [them] to sell their inheritance and [in this way] to redeem their necks. When, according to Polish custom, they offered their inheritance to their relatives for sale, the kinsmen said,

"Sell to whomever you want, because we have nothing with which we may redeem your necks."

For this reason the lord duke ordained and established by the counsel and judgment of the barons that whoever redeemed their necks by buying out their inheritance may forever possess their inheritance, [free] from any claim by their kindred. Hearing this, lord Bodo, abbot of Henryków, bought [the inheritance]

(1981), 127–50; Grodecki, on the other hand, thought that the *Romani* were Italians, at *Liber* (1949), 20 n. 32.

54. The Latin original is *prima petitione*, which means, most exactly, a request that was the first in a sequence of several; and indeed the circumstances described in Chapter 74 below are consistent with this act as having taken place early in Albert's post-1241 career. However, the phrase may also more simply mean an earlier, or prior, request.

55. Abbot Peter describes the circumstances of the monastery's acquisition of Jaworowice in Chapters 74–79 below.

of these four men, that is to say, Przybysław, Boguchwał, Wojsław, and Gostach, for nineteen silver marks, by the counsel and the direction of the lord duke.

[59] *The privilege issued about Bobolice.* Concerning this event, the following privilege, given to the cloister by the celebrated Duke [Henry II], [reproduced here] word for word, is kept [by the monastery].

[60] *The truth of the words of the privilege.*[56]

In the name of the Holy and Indivisible Trinity, amen. The deeds of the present time are wont to disappear unless strengthened with a due protection of letters, and with a memorable witness of righteous men.

Therefore we, Henry, by the grace of God duke of Silesia, Kraków, and [Great] Poland, wishing to guard against such [consequences], make it known to all present and future [persons] that by our good will the four heirs of Bobolice sold their inheritance with its entire circuit to the religious men of the Cistercian Order, that is to say Abbot Bodo and his convent of Henryków; and that they received from them for it nineteen silver marks in Polish weight. Of these marks, the said men [i.e., the abbot and the monks] gave seven marks to the one of them who is called by the name Przybysław for his portion, and twelve marks to the remaining three, that is to say Boguchwał, Wojsław, and Gostach, subject to this condition: that the aforesaid inheritance may never in the future be redeemed by any of them, or by any of their successors.

In order that this deed may remain firm and inviolable, we ordered the present page to be written down about it, and marked by the placement of our seal. Done in the year of the Lord 1239, in the presence of the following [persons]: Bolesław [II] the young lord,[57] Count Stephen castellan of Niemcza, his son Master John, Count Albert of Karczyn, Siegród, and many other righteous men.

[61] *That afterwards the survivors [of the four heirs] of Bobolice were making claims against the cloister.* More about the same. Let it be known that after the pagans the surviving heirs of the men of Bobolice recorded above came up to lord Duke Bolesław [II] in Leśnica, and complained that the lord abbot of Henryków and his brothers were retaining their kinsmen's holding of Bobolice unjustly and violently.[58] After this [allegation] was produced into the middle [of the proceed-

---

56. *S.U.*, 2:no. 172 (1239), 110–11.

57. *Domicellus*, which Grodecki translates as "the young duke," thus identifying this witness as the future Duke Bolesław II the Bald.

58. The Latin formula *iniuste et violenter* does not imply physical violence was used to acquire the contested area but, more generally, that possession was acquired illegitimately. *Violenter* was often used to render the Old Polish *nasile*, an illegitimate or violent act, and its adjectival form, *nasilnie*: see *S.Sp.*, 5:98, *s.v. nasile, nasilnie,* and the related terms *nasilnik, nasilno, nasilny,* 98–99. This meaning of *violenter* seems the exact counterpart of the later meaning of *nasil'stvo* in Russian; I would like to thank Professor Richard Hellie for this suggestion.

ings], Duke Bolesław himself rose, and placed in his stead and on his behalf as judge a certain noble man, Count Racław of Strzelin, at that time castellan of Wrocław. And the duke himself spoke the cloister's word there, explaining to the judge and the barons all the activity of these men of Bobolice described above; and among other things he added,

"I am the true founder of this cloister, so I am bound to answer on the cloister's behalf against any man and for any cause in any place."

[62] *That Duke Bolesław said that he was the true founder.* About this deed, the following privilege was given right there by the lord Duke Bolesław himself.

[63] *Duke Bolesław's second confirmation of the same.*[59]

In the name of the Lord, amen. We, Bolesław, by the grace of God duke of Silesia and [Great] Poland, make it known to present and future [persons] that certain brothers from Bobolice, that is to say Sieciesław and Witosław, with all their kinsmen, complained before us that the abbot of Henryków was retaining certain holdings of their inheritance unjustly. To which the said abbot answered that not unjustly, but that, at the direction of the celebrated Duke Henry [II], our father of happy memory, he had redeemed their brothers from Bobolice, namely Gostach, Boguchwał, Wojsław, and Przybysław, from hanging; and he produced into the middle [of the proceedings] the [written] instrument of confirmation issued by our father about this to his church. Hence, by unanimous counsel of our barons, the aforesaid men from Bobolice, that is to say Sieciesław and Witosław with all the kindred, are forever ousted from the holdings just mentioned.

In order therefore that the house of the Holy Virgin of Henryków may possess these holdings of Bobolice forever in peace, we strengthen the present charter with the protection of our seal. This was done in the year of the Incarnation of the Lord 1247, on the third [day before the] calends of May [April 29], in the assembly which was held at Leśnica, in the presence of these [persons]: Count Bogusław castellan of Niemcza, Count Racław castellan of Wrocław, Count Mroczko castellan of Ryczyn (who spoke the abbot's word there), Count Cieszęta castellan of Oleśnica, Count Peter judge of the court, and very many others.

[64] *Here ends the exposition of the account of Bobolice.* Here, brothers, the reason why the cloister of Henryków should possess part of the arable fields of Bobolice has been adequately and truthfully set out.

Fourth. Here begins the account of the gift of Skalice.

[65] Here begins a treatise on the reason why the cloister of Henryków possesses a third part of the inheritance of Skalice.

---

59. *S.U.*, 2:no. 323 (1247), 190–91.

A preliminary treatise about this. In those days when the convent was first transferred to Henryków,[60] there were certain uterine brothers, heirs of Skalice, of whom the older was called Nicholas, the younger Stephen. These two men were holding a third part of the whole inheritance of Skalice of that time.[61] Nicholas was a priest, and was in those times the legitimate parish priest in the church of Old Henryków,[62] while his brother Stephen was a layman, then living in his inheritance of Skalice, but very modest in temporal things. Let it then be known that in those days Nicholas, the aforesaid parish priest of Henryków, used to receive tithes throughout the whole field (*campus*) of Henryków[63] – that is to say, [from the area situated] against Skryboszów, and from the other part of the village

---

60. Chapter 11.

61. The original Latin text states *tocius hereditatis tunc temporis de Scaliz,* which implies that that locality had been quite different – in terms, perhaps, of settlement, size, land use, and other attributes – in the past which Peter was describing that it was in his present. This is hardly surprising in view of Peter's own narrations concerning immigration, settlement expansion, and transformations of estates included into the monastic estate in the course of the thirteenth century.

62. The original Latin text states *in ecclesia Antiqua Heinrichov,* which could also mean "the old church of Henryków," and this is how Grodecki translates it. In either case, this was a parish church endowed with tithe revenues from the locality included in the monks' estate between 1222 and 1228, and appropriated by the monastery thereafter.

63. The original Latin text states *campus de Heinrichow.* In this context, *campus* seems to mean the estate or district of Henryków. This use may be a Latin rendition of the Polish *opole,* or "neighborhood." The *opole* is sparsely documented, and its functions have been hotly debated in recent years. It is believed to have included a group of villages, and to have constituted the basic community involved in dispute settlement, enforcement of peace, and fiscal liability to lords and rulers. In this respect, it was a Polish variant of the numerous rural neighborhoods of Europe in the earlier and central Middle Ages. On this subject, see Susan Reynolds, *Kingdoms and Communities in Western Europe, 900–1300* (2nd ed., Oxford: Clarendon Press, 1997), 101–54; Grzegorz Myśliwski, "Boundary Delimitation in Medieval Poland," in *Perspectives on Central-European History and Politics (Selected Papers from the Fifth World Congress of Central and East European Studies, Warsaw, 1995),* ed. Stanislav Kirschbaum (Houndmills: Macmillan, 1999), 27–36; Karol Modzelewski, *Chłopi w monarchii wczesnopiastowskiej* [The peasants in the early Piast monarchy] (Wrocław: Zakład Narodowy im. Ossolińskich, 1987), 160–92; Jacek Matuszewski, *Vicinia id est ... Wposzukiwaniu alternatywnej koncepcji staropolskiego opola* [*Vicinia id est*: in search of an alternative conception of the Old Polish neighborhood] (Łódź: Wydawnictwo Uniwersytetu Łódzkiego, 1991); Górecki, "Local Society and Legal Knowledge: A Case Study from the Henryków Region," in *Christianitas et cultura Europae. Księga Jubileuszowa Profesora Jerzego Kłoczowskiego* [*Christianitas et cultura Europae*: A Jubilee Book for Professor Jerzy Kłoczowski], ed. Henryk Gapski, 2 vols. (Lublin: Instytut Europy Środkowo-Wschodniej, 1998), 544–50; Górecki, "Communities of Legal Memory in Medieval Poland, c. 1200–1240," *Journal of Medieval History* 24 (1998), 127–54.

up through [the stream called] the Morzyna – from the arable of Nicholas, at that time patron of this inheritance.[64] Hence his church in Henryków flourished with great revenues at the time. He received this tithe from the cloister's plows for a few years after the arrival of the convent at this place. So, after the arrival of the brothers at this place, he was quite happy, thinking that he was always going to receive the tithe from the cloister's plows for himself. For which reason he said to his brother Stephen,

"I see that thanks to the arrival here of these brothers and my lords, my prebend is increasing quite a bit. So I wish to assign the part of our inheritance which belongs to me to the cloister in eternal possession."

[66] *About the first gift of Skalice.* A few days after these things happened, this [parish priest] Nicholas, together with his brother Stephen, came up to the elder Duke [Henry I] in Niemcza, and before him granted to this closter the two parts of their inheritance which belonged to them among their other brothers in Skalice, to be possessed forever, for their sins. And the third part Stephen then retained for himself, toward his needs.

[67] *In what year the gift of the same [donor] was made.* This gift was made before lord Duke Henry the elder in the year of the Lord 1233. But a privilege about this was not requested from the lord duke at that time.

[68] *About the removal of the tithe of the village chapel.* After these things happened and a few days passed, lord Thomas of venerated memory – then bishop of the church of Wrocław – entered this cloister with his retinue, and, upon noting that the brothers then dwelling here lived in the most acute poverty, asked lord Henry, abbot at that time, and the brothers about the cloister's revenues and external wealth.[65] Upon hearing from the abbot and brothers that the cloister's plows were paying tithe [only] to the cloister's own chaplain, the lord bishop became very angry, summoned the same Nicholas chaplain of Henryków to himself, and told him,

"You sit here by yourself and do nothing but sing with sparrows![66] So I want these brothers to receive tithe from this part of the village of Henryków for themselves, toward the aid of their bodies."

Upon hearing these words, Chaplain Nicholas was distressed by a great sadness of mind, but did not answer anything right there. But later, after two years went by, he resigned the chapel of Henryków into the abbot's hands, and trans-

---

64. *That* Nicholas had been Duke Henry I's notary and initiator of the monastery's foundation between 1222 and 1227, as described by Abbot Peter at length in Chapters 2–12. This is the only passage where, perhaps inadvertently, Abbot Peter refers to Nicholas as the *patronus* of the lands he had amassed by 1222, and to his estate as a *hereditas*.

65. Grodecki translates this cryptic phrase as "revenues" and "the rest of the endowment."

66. *Tu es solus et cantas sepius cum passeribus*, evidently a thirteenth-century proverb for idleness; or, perhaps, a pejorative comparison of a parish priest to a monk.

ferred himself to the Order of the [canons] regular in Kamieniec.[67] From that hour and time, the large revenue of the chapel in the village of Henryków was removed by the venerable lord Thomas, bishop of Wrocław, and given to the cloister. We shall describe the good deeds which this happily remembered bishop bestowed upon the cloister in an appropriate place.[68]

[69] *The first confirmation of Skalice.* When Duke Henry the elder died later [in 1238], and when his son Henry the younger ruled in his father's stead, and the said [priest] Nicholas was already confirmed in the aforesaid Order [of the canons regular in Kamieniec], his brother Stephen came up with a certain monk of Henryków by the name of Peter (sent by his father Abbot Bodo) to the said lord duke in Oleśnica, and there confessed before the duke and his barons that for their sins he, together with his brother, Priest Nicholas, earlier gave two parts of their inheritance to the cloister of Henryków before the elder duke, to be possessed forever. And the same Stephen added before the duke and barons, as if to repeat and renew the entire deed,

"Lord duke, I again make it known to your majesty in the audience of these nobles that my brother Nicholas and I granted before your father two parts of our inheritance, for the remedy of our souls, to be possessed forever by the cloister of Henryków. The third part I, Stephen, sold to this cloister for 27 silver marks. So because your father did not give a privilege about this, I – together with my fellow Peter, sent with me here by the lord abbot – ask and request that you deign to extend the privilege of your confirmation to the cloister of Henryków [in this matter]."

That hour, on the duke's order, a certain lord Conrad, chaplain of the court and parish priest in Löwenberg,[69] wrote a privilege about this deed, word for word, in the following way.

[70] *The privilege of confirmation.*[70]

In the name of Our Lord Jesus Christ, amen. Inasmuch as over the course of time matters that have not been firmly committed to memory are easily lost to oblivion, we, Henry [II], by the grace of God duke of Silesia, Kraków, and [Great] Poland, wishing to provide a remedy against such

67. A community of canons regular that had been established around 1208, then appropriated by the Cistercians, and changed into a Cistercian monastery in 1248; Grodecki, *Liber* (1949), 102 n. 39. Abbot Peter narrates an important story concerning the founder of the original community in Chapters 86–87.

68. Chapters 199–210.

69. A chaplain of the court is a priest in regular attendance on the duke or duchess, or both. On this occasion, the cleric who held both of these position also functioned as a scribe. There is considerable evidence from the Polish duchies of this kind of aggregation of clerical and courtly responsibilites (and its implications for their performance), for which see Górecki, *Parishes*, 86.

70. *S.U.*, 2:no. 167 (1239), 108–09.

defects, make it known in writing and offer full witness to present and future [persons] that, in the presence of the illustrious Duke Henry [I], our father of happy memory, certain brothers of Skalice, Nicholas and Stephen, granted out of the three parts of their inheritance which belonged to them among their other brothers, two parts to Saint Mary and to the brothers serving God there in Henryków, for the remedy of the souls of [their] father and mother, and for their own [souls], to be possessed [forever]; while after his brother took the habit and accepted [a monastic] observance, Stephen sold the third part to the house [of Henryków] for 27 silver marks, to be possessed by hereditary right. Provided that, by the direction and decree of our aforenoted father, and with our [own] agreement to this, neither he nor his successors shall henceforth have any power to redeem [Skalice].

In support of this matter, so that no-one may ever by some bold deed dare to contradict this agreement, we ordered that the present page be strengthened with the protection of our seal. The witnesses of this matter are Count Stephen castellan of Niemcza, Count Bogusław castellan of Ryczyn, Count Racław castellan of Wrocław, Albert of Karczyn, Berthold the village bailiff (*scultetus*) of Piława, and very many others. Done in the year of the Incarnation of the Lord 1239, on the fourth [day before the] calends of October [September 28].

[71] *How after the pagans Abbot Bodo dispatched John, Stephen's son, in various ways.* In those days when these two brothers, that is to say Nicholas and Stephen, confirmed the things written down above for the cloister of Henryków, Stephen had a single very small son, John by name.[71] As soon as this John reached a responsible age, he often tried by Polish custom to revoke his uncle's and his father's deeds. But because he was always poor and modest in things, his malice achieved nothing of what he wanted.

[72] *That John resigned from the right to demand the father's inheritance.* Finally, lord Bodo, abbot of Henryków, seeking to avert future evil to this house, by giving John modest gifts brought it about that after the pagans this John came up to Duke Henry [III], who ruled in this land at that time,[72] and before him and his nobles resigned from every right and every jurisdiction which he had, or may have had, in the said inheritance of his father, Skalice. For the good of the peace

---

71. John and the other heirs involved in these potentially conflictual transactions concerning Skalice are further recorded in Supplementary Documents no. 16–18.

72. Abbot Peter is here referring to the portion of the formerly united Duchy of Silesia that came under the authority of Henry III after the division of the duchy with his older brother, Bolesław the Bald, in 1248; *Rodowód*, 1:109–11; Grodecki, *Liber* (1949), 98 n. 34; Jurek, "Bolesław II," 409; Jurek, "Henryk III," 415.

and out of his good will, at that hour the said abbot of Henryków bought before us for the said John out of the cloister's wealth [...].[73] This renunciation by the same John was effected before us and our barons in Wrocław in the year of the Lord 1259, on the tenth [day before the] calends of March [February 20], in the presence of these men, that is to say John of Wierzbno, Master Gocwin the physician, Michael judge of our court, and the many others who were in our presence there. At that hour, by witness of the same men, the said John received the aforesaid two hides from the abbot, to be held forever; and right there he promised by a spontaneous will never again to contest or to revoke his father's deeds. Concerning this deed, we gave the privilege of the original renewal, so that previous deeds may always be held as ratified. And may these most recent deeds [effected] before us, namely the deeds of the lord abbot of Henryków and of John, serve as protection of eternal confirmation for the cloister regarding the holding of Skalice, and for John regarding the said hides.

[73] *That in the privilege issued by Duke Henry [III] to the cloister at the said time nothing was written other than what is contained in the original privilege,[74] from which [renewal of the original] we have made a record in this booklet. And let it be known [...][75]*

Five. Here begins the account of the gift of Jaworowice, which was obtained by many labors and tribulations.

[74] In those days when, after the pagans, our young dukes first began to reign,[76] many things occurred which were unheard of under the glorious ancient dukes. Hence the first-born brother among them, lord Bolesław, did many juvenile things at tournaments and in other amusements during his youth. Among other things, one time he gathered many knights in Löwenberg on Saint Matthew's Day, and ordered that a tournament be held. The knights said all together,

"Lord, we will not enter the tournament today unless you offer God a solemn and joyful sacrifice."

The lord Duke Bolesław answered them by saying,

73. A part of the phrase is missing; there is a gap in the manuscript, and the chapter ends with the final protocol of a ducal privilege; see Grodecki, *Liber* (1991), after 225, fol. xii[v]. The full diploma Henry III issued concerning this transaction is translated here as Supplementary Document no. 17. For the relationship between that diploma and the fragment that follows in this chapter, see Chapter 73.

74. That is presumably the text presented as Supplementary Document no. 17.

75. The text breaks off.

76. The "young dukes," Bolesław the Bald and Henry III, ruled Silesia jointly between 1241 and 1248. Henry III was the third son of Henry II the Pious, born between 1227 and 1230; he died in 1266. *Rodowód*, 1:109–11, 118–22; Grodecki, *Liber* (1949), 98 n. 34; Jurek, "Bolesław II"; Jurek, "Henryk III."

"I promise all of you to offer some cloister one small inheritance, in honor of God, and for all my sins and yours."

Upon hearing these words, Albert with Beard said to the greater knights before they entered the tournament,

"Glorious lords and knights, listen to my words. There is a certain cloister in my lord's land, not far from Nysa, very poor in things and in substance, Henryków by name. Before the doors of this cloister, my lord has a certain tiny manor by the name of Jaworowice. So I ask you, for your sins, to obtain this manor for this exceedingly poor cloister from my lord [the duke]."

Those same knights unanimously said to the duke,

"Lord, if you promise us to give your cloister the manor which Albert has indicated to you by name – [exactly] according to the words of Albert, your knight and our friend – we will delight you by engaging in the tournament today."

Upon hearing these [requests], the duke, with hand raised, promised before all that whatever the aforesaid Albert might request for the cloister of Henryków, he would cheerfully give, in honor of God.

[75] *Here is the first cause and reason for the gift of Jaworowice.* After these things happened and a few days passed, Duke Bolesław came to Niemcza, sent for lord Bodo, abbot of this place, and, in response to the said Count Albert's request, granted Jaworowice to this cloister and its servants [i.e., the monks] in its entirety, to be possessed forever. At that hour he gave the following privilege about this deed.

[76] *The privilege of this gift and of its confirmation was written down, word for word, on the duke's order.*[77]

In the name of the Lord, amen. We, Bolesław, by the grace of God duke of Silesia and [Great] Poland, make it known to present and future [persons] that, for the remission of our own and our brothers' sins, and for the redemption of the soul of the illustrious Duke Henry [II], our father of happy memory, we have forever granted to the house of the Holy Virgin of Henryków of the Cistercian Order, and to the brothers of the same house, the inheritance which is called Jaworowo[78] (situated next to the cloister itself, with [the holding of] Michael Daleborowic[79] on the side, from the farther part of Kunzendorf, which belongs to [the convent of] Trzebnica), to be possessed by the said house and by its servants forever.

In order, then, that this gift may be firm and remain stable, we ordered that it is worth strengthening by the placement of our seal. Given in Niemcza, on Saint Gregory's Day [March 3], in the year of the Lord 1243,

77. *S.U.*, 2:no. 241 (1243), 145.

78. This is another instance in which the name of a particular place varies slightly.

79. For Michael Daleborowic, see Chapter 27 above and Chapters 80–81, 186–91 below.

in the presence of these [persons]: lord Sobiesław our uncle, Bogusław castellan of Niemcza, lord Gunther of Biberstein, Peter judge of the court, Bogusław castellan of Bytom, Andrew castellan of Szydłów, Milej the chaplain, and very many others. We also gave the cloister two carpenters of that village, Dobrosza with his brother.

[77] *After those deeds, the house possessed these [holdings in Jaworowice] peacefully for a few years while the said lord Duke Bolesław reigned.*[80] After these things were done and a bit of time passed, the knights captured their lord Bolesław, the said duke, and this was done supposedly in the name of Henry [III], his brother born after him. But let it be known that at that time this young lord, lord Henry, had not yet attained the years of responsible age. Hence, because the disorder and damage of the entire province [of Silesia] began at that time, let it be known that this captivity was perpetrated not by the counsel of the young lord Henry, but of certain others, whose names shall not be inscribed in this booklet.[81]

[78] *Here begins a treatise about how afterwards, in the reign of lord Henry (the third duke of that name in this land), Jaworowice was taken away from the cloister, and was [later] once again confirmed for this cloister by the same Duke Henry in eternal possession.* Let it thus be known that when this lord Duke Henry [III], confirmed in the rule, began to revoke his first-born brother's deeds in diverse places, he removed from us and from this cloister the village of Jaworowice, among others.[82] He said on every occasion and at every gift that was sat aside,

---

80. This rubric is ambiguous. Its text states, in the entirety, *Post hec acta possedit domus ista regnante domino duce dicto Bolezlao pacifice aliquot annis*, which could also mean "After those deeds the house possessed these [holdings in Jaworowice] while the lord duke, the said Bolesław, reigned peacefully for a few years." The story that follows immediately is consistent with either interpretation.

81. As Grodecki notes, Abbot Peter is handling this conflict, and the question of Henry III's culpability in it, with tactfully obscure brevity. The conflict concerned claims to the inheritance to rule of the entire Duchy of Silesia, as it was exercised by Henry II the Pious upon his death in 1241. It involved Henry II's four sons: Bolesław II the Bald, Conrad, Henry III the White, and Władysław. Several years of civil war culminated with the division of the duchy in 1248. According to the treaty, each of the resulting two duchies was to be ruled by two of the brothers. Bolesław the Bald and Conrad acquired Lower Silesia, consisting of the districts of Legnica, Głogów, Krosno, and Lubusz; Henry the White and Władysław acquired the district of Wrocław, the future Duchy of Wrocław in the narrow sense. Bolesław II and Henry III rose to preeminence in their respective duchies; however, the subdivision of the duchies continued into the subsequent generations. Grodecki, *Liber* (1949), 110 n. 47; Jurek, "Bolesław II"; Jurek, "Henryk III"; Jurek, "Władysław," *Piastowie*, 418–19; Jurek, "Konrad I," *Piastowie*, 613–15.

82. Supplementary Documents no. 11–12 record two repurchases by the Henryków monastery from Duke Henry III of holdings that had formerly been part of the monastic estate; no. 11 concerns Jaworowice. The possible explanations for ducal revindication are presented in the introductory essay above, n. 262.

"I wish to regain my forefathers' inheritances."

Upon hearing this, lord Bodo, abbot of this place, said with a certain sadness,

"If this holding, Jaworowice, should be granted to some powerful knight, the cloister will have nowhere to procure sand for [building] work. The cattle pastures around this cloister will also be greatly diminished."

So for six weeks, with whatever strength he could muster, he continuously worked around Henry, the said duke, by [intercession of] the nobles and by himself, until at last the duke finally requested for the said holding a certain sum of money. Hence the abbot was advised that it would be better for the cloister to be indebted by money in the present than to be deprived of the aforesaid holding forever. For this reason, lord Abbot Bodo promised and paid lord Duke Henry eighty silver marks and a horse which had been bought for ten marks; Count John of Wierzbno, for arranging this matter, a horse [bought] for ten marks; and Master Walter, notary at that time, a horse [bought] for ten marks. The lord abbot paid out this money to the duke and his officials recorded in the privilege below, within two weeks, with damage to the cloister. Duke Henry [III] then gave a privilege about this deed to the cloister, written in this way.

[79] *The second privilege of Jaworowice.*[83]

We, Henry, by the grace of God duke of Silesia, recognize and acknowledge to all present who inspect this letter, that lord Bodo, abbot of Henryków, gave us eighty silver marks for the purchase of the inheritance of Jaworowice, and, according to our mandate and direction, paid out this money to these persons: to our first scholar[84] Master Walter, 26 marks; to Lawrence our key-keeper, nineteen marks; to Paul Słupowic, 35 marks. This eternal purchase was made in Wrocław, in the year of the Lord 1255, on the nearest Sunday before the eve of [Saints] Peter and Paul [June 27], with these [persons] present: lady Anne our mother, Count John of Wierzbno, Master Gocwin the physician, Master Walter who composed this letter, and very many others.

Here ends the account of the first gift and of the second purchase of the inheritance of Jaworowice.

Sixth. Here begins a treatise about the reason [for the loss] of Nikłowice, and about the exchange with Michael.

[80] Among the many inconveniences which the cloister underwent at various times after the pagans, a certain Michael, son of the late Dalebór, had

---

83. *S.U.*, 3:no. 150 (1255), 106. Duke Henry III's fuller description of the process of conveyance of this holding back to the monks, issued a few days later, is edited as no. 151 (1255), 106–07, and translated as Supplementary Document no. 11.

84. *Primo scolari nostro*, a rather obscure designation which Grodecki interprets to mean a chancery official; Grodecki, *Liber* (1949), 112 n. 48.

borders with the cloister from the side on which Münsterberg is now situated.[85] These borders touched the bank of the stream which flows between Kojanowice and Czesławice into the Oława [river]. This stream once passed through our vegetable garden, so the said Michael at that time had the boundaries of his inheritance up to our vegetable garden. Because the same Michael repeatedly tried to disturb the cloister, he settled his inheritance with Germans. For which reason, while this was going on, women and girls danced in our orchard on holy days. Upon noticing this, lord Bodo, abbot at that time, became distressed with a great affliction, saying in his heart,

"If over a long passage of time this dancing ripens into a habit here, that will lead to a most dangerous loss of many souls in this cloister."

So in order to eliminate this filth from the monastery, he discussed, repeatedly and whenever he could, some kind of exchange with the said Michael. While the abbot and Michael repeatedly spoke among themselves about this and many similar things, at last Michael, together with his boys, received the entire inheritance of the cloister, and a well-built farmstead, in Nikłowice; and [in exchange] he gave the cloister, in his inheritance [situated] here near the cloister, the same amount [of land] in length and in width (according to [standard] measure), to be possessed forever. Many things were added for this Michael during this exchange, which are plainly recorded in the privilege prepared on that occasion.

[81] *Here is the account of the exchange with Michael. Concerning this exchange, a privilege, most lucidly prepared in these words, was then issued to this cloister by the third lord Duke Henry:*[86]

In the name of the Lord, amen. We, Henry [III], by the grace of God duke of Silesia, make it known to present and future [persons] that Count Michael, son of the late Dalebór, has exchanged with the brothers of Henryków the part of his inheritance which is situated near the cloister itself, and has received from them for it an inheritance of this cloister which is called Nikłowice (and which is [situated] near Ręków), in an amount of each other's land to which the abbot of Henryków and Michael have agreed among themselves by a good and spontaneous will. And because Michael had settled this inheritance of his with Germans, the abbot of Henryków and his brothers bought out these Germans piece-

---

85. This is an early reference, by Abbot Peter, to a German town that he here implies had appeared (or at least dramatically expanded) after the events narrated here, and which by 1300 had emerged as the most important regional center of judicial authority, and perhaps economic exchange, impinging on the monastery and its estate. Münsterberg's central role is documented throughout the second section of the *Henryków Book*. It is an excellent example of a German town in Silesia, of the kind described in general terms by Keith D. Lilley, *Urban Life in the Middle Ages, 1000–1450* (Houndmills: Palgrave, 2002), 131–37.

86. *S.U.*, 3:no. 125 (1254), 90–91.

meal, by individual hides,[87] giving [them] eighty silver marks there, in addition to the land which they [also] gave [them]. In addition to all that, the abbot of Henryków and his brothers gave this Michael the aforesaid inheritance of Nikłowice, sown with 69 measures[88] [of grain] in the winter, and with 48 measures in the summer; a well-built farmstead and in it twenty heads of horned cattle, thirty pigs, carts, plows (*aratra*), pans, jars, iron tools, and whatever useful things there had been in the same farmstead.

Let it also be known that, concerning the remaining part of the aforesaid inheritance of his – which he has retained between the cloister and Münsterberg – the aforesaid Michael has so decreed it, and by his good and spontaneous will ordained, before ourselves and our barons, that neither Michael himself nor any one of his successors may ever sell it to, or exchange it with, anyone among men other than the aforesaid cloister of Henryków. After all these things were done, the abbot of Henryków, with his brothers' unanimous consent, added for this Michael a mill in Krasice, to be possessed forever by the same right by which the cloister has held this mill since the time of our grandfather [Henry I].[89] In witness of this matter, he [i.e., the abbot] specially placed his seal on this letter.

In order, therefore, that this exchange of theirs, and each other's (that is to say, the abbot's and Michael's) gift, may always remain firm and fixed in the future, we caused the present charter to be strengthened by the placement of our seal. And in order that this [exchange] may be made stronger and more solemn, and never be disturbed by the succession of times and persons, in response to our petition, our brothers the illustrious Dukes Bolesław [II] and Conrad[90] also placed their seals on this charter, in the witness of truth and of eternal confirmation.

The witnesses of this exchange are: our venerable father lord Thomas, by divine will bishop of Wrocław, who also placed his seal in order to confirm the truth of what has been written down above; lord Rambold, chancellor of Duke Conrad; John Osina; Paul Słupowic; Stanisław our *subcamerarius*; Sulisław, son of the late Bartholomew, who by our authority, together with our *camerarius* Zabrat, performed a circuit around this holding of Michael and fixed certain boundaries [around it] for the cloister; and very many others. This was done in the year of the Incarnation of the Lord 1254, on the day before the nones of June [June 4], in the assembly which was held in Wrocław when the liberation of Count Mroczko [from captivity] was discussed, and the construction of castles was arranged. In addition, let it be known that the aforesaid Count

87. The Latin text states, rather ambiguously, *exemerunt ... particulatim per singulos mansos*.
88. The Latin word for "measures" in this sentence is *modii*.
89. *Avus*, which might refer to a more distant ancestor.
90. Conrad of Głogów; n. 81 above, and Chapters 74, 77.

Sulisław, called Irdzek, assigned to the said Count Michael the inheritance of Nikłowice mentioned above, and the aforesaid mill; and that he strengthened [the resulting estate] with certain and legitimate boundaries by performing a circuit [around it].

Here ends the privilege about the exchange with Michael of Nikłowice.

Seventh. Here begins the treatise about Głębowice. Much is to be said about the reason why the cloister should possess this corner and the wood adjoining it.

[82] In those days when Nicholas, whom we mentioned at the beginning of this book, became renowned for an opulence in things, and first obtained Januszów from his lord the duke, as was said,[91] the land here in the district was deserted and very wooded. Hence by the permission and good will of the lord duke he subjugated for himself the forest which is now called by the name Bukowina among the moderns. But in order that the origin and the earliest name of this forest may be known among our successors, let it be noted that in those days when the old lord Duke Bolesław (that is to say, the founder of the church of Lubiąż) was distributing land to his peasants in diverse places, he gave this forest to a certain own peasant of his, Głąb by name. This same peasant Głąb first cleared that place which is now called the Great Meadow, or in Polish *Wiela Łąka*. Hence the entire district of this forest was long ago called Głębowice, after the name of the said peasant, which name this forest retains among some Poles today. Afterwards, this peasant's heirs, oppressed in this place by the grandfather of a certain Mojko, moved to the mountain where the orchard now stands next to a farmstead of the cloister. *These things were written so that those who always serve God in this cloister may know that they do not possess a single furrow here around the cloister other than the inheritances of the dukes, ancient as well as modern.*

[83] *More about the same.* Among the heirs of the aforesaid peasant Głąb, there was later a certain peasant exceeding the others in power[92] by the name of Kwiecik – that is, "flower," or "pertaining to a flower." This same Kwiecik often moved lord Duke Henry the elder and his entourage (*familia*) to great laughter with his trickery and wonders. So he was esteemed at the duke's court above all his kinsmen in his days.

When this same Kwiecik first departed with his heirs from the said Great Meadow, he established a village where the cloister's farmstead stands now. Hence this place was at that time called Kwiecikowice, which name is still used by some until now. This same Kwiecik was a peasant, son of the son of the

91. Chapters 29–30.

92. Kwiecik is described as *quidam rusticus ceteris potentia eminentior*. This is another vague but interesting reference to peasant leadership as "power," echoing Abbot Peter's description of the peasant group in Żukowice, a part of his account of Henryków (Chapter 32).

aforesaid Głąb, and was very old, so he recalled the events of many years. In the days when the cloister was already founded here [i.e., 1227 or 1228], this peasant lacked one hand, and had the other so damaged by a sword that he was unable to move it for his needs at all. Hence, because he was extremely poor in body and in things, and was, as was said, very old, lord Abbot Henry (the first of this cloister) and his successor lord Bodo sustained this peasant with victuals until his death. He lived until the fourth year after the departure of the pagans from this land [i.e., 1245].[93] Because, as was said, this same peasant Kwiecik lacked one hand and had no use of the other, the Poles at that time called him "the Stump." Because this peasant quite often ate bread here after the cloister's foundation, before and after the pagans, he narrated to us all the antiquities of the inheritances [situated] around the territory of the cloister.

[84] *That our successors may deem it worthy to pray for this peasant Kwiecik. Let it be known that after the pagans the cloister obtained through him the forest which is called Bukowina and the holding of Głębowice, where the [cloister's] farmstead now stands.[94] Likewise, [we will describe] by how much labor the second abbot of this cloister, lord Bodo, retained the said forest of Bukowina for this cloister after the pagans.*

[85] In the days of the old Duke Henry, a certain knight, Stephen by name, and by the nickname of Kobylagłowa, possessed [land] not far from this forest. After lord Nicholas's death, this same Stephen incited certain peasants, who were at that time called Piroszowice, to demand the forest of Głębowice for themselves. And because these peasants were the duke's own [peasants], were rich, and were the heirs of Cienkowice, they said to the duke,

"Lord, this forest was violently taken away from us by the power of your notary, lord Nicholas. But, if this be your grace, we ought to possess it by hereditary right, because the old Głąb was the uterine brother of our grandfather Pirosz."

The duke believed them, as his own peasants, took away the forest from the cloister right then, and gave it to the peasants. Upon seeing his shrewdness prevail by means of these peasants, the aforesaid Stephen of Kobylagłowa[95] came up to

93. For the broader context of the fascinating demographic detail concerning Kwiecik, see Grzegorz Myśliwski, "Old Age and Longevity in Medieval Poland against a Comparative Background," *Acta Poloniae Historica* 86 (2002), 5–45.

94. Apart from this fleeting passage in the rubric, Abbot Peter says nothing about Kwiecik, or any other relative of Głąb, as a party to the monastery's acquisition of the localities under narration. In Chapter 85 Peter implies that that kin group had had meaningful property rights in those localities, but does not develop that subject thereafter. Continued property rights of Głąb's descendants, as late as the last decade of the thirteenth century, are strongly suggested (but not further illuminated) by Supplementary Document no. 19.

95. *Kobylagłowa* is a place name as well as a nickname, and Abbot Peter variously links it to Stephen's first name with a nominative or with a genitive case.

the duke and offered him a war-horse, which was then appraised before the duke at 28 silver marks. The lord duke happily accepted the horse, and said to Stephen,

"For this favor and for your gift, if you ask me for something, you will get it."

Upon hearing this, Stephen reverently and happily came up to the duke, saying,

"Lord, you know that I serve you with the utmost pleasure, but I have modest possessions. So I ask that, in order that I may be able to serve you, my lord, that much better, you may deign to grant me the forest which has just now reverted to you."

After hearing these words and summoning the said peasants, the lord duke granted the forest to this Stephen, much mentioned.

[86] *Here is the reason why Stephen's sons and heirs threaten to take away this forest from the cloister. But in the following we shall show how the said forest was later confirmed in the cloister's eternal possession, and that Stephen's sons and their heirs have no jurisdiction to demand or to redeem*[96] *the said forest.*

This forest was lost in the aforesaid manner during the first year after lord Nicholas's death [i.e., 1228]. But after the oft-mentioned Stephen held this forest for a modest length of time, he offered it for sale to diverse persons, and this is because he was poor, and because at that time [people] cared very little about [keeping] some deserted possession. In those days, there was a certain prior in Kamieniec, Vincent by name. This prior was a noble man, paternal uncle of Count Mroczko, and was the founder of this cloister of Kamieniec[97] [of which he was prior]. Several times, Stephen offered the forest of Głębowice to this prior for sale. But the same prior, as he was an aged and a very cautious man, refused to deprive our cloister of the forest. He sent a suitable emissary to lord Henry, abbot of this place, advising him to redeem this forest for his cloister in any way he could. Upon hearing this, the lord abbot came up to the prior in person, and said to him,

"If I buy this forest, Stephen's heirs will later demand it according to Polish law."

To which the prior said in answer,

"Not at all. But you ought to know, lord abbot, that it has been established long ago among our ancestors and forefathers that if anyone from the stock of the Poles sells any patrimony of his, his heirs will be able to redeem it later. But perhaps you Germans do not fully understand what a patrimony is. Therefore, in order that you may fully understand, let me give you an explanation. If I possess anything which my grandfather and my father have left me in possession, this is my true patrimony. If I sell this to anyone, my heirs have the power to demand it according to our law. But whatever possession the lord duke may have given to me for my service or by grace, that I [may] sell to whomever I wish, even against

---

96. In the use of the expression "jurisdiction to demand," I literally follow the Latin original, in order to render the writer's legal language as closely as possible. Jurisdiction here does not mean judicial authority, but simply what we would today call a right.

97. Chapters 68–69; see also the introductory essay above, nn. 297, 306.

the will of my friends,[98] because my heirs do not have the right to demand such a possession. Hence, because it is known and established that the forest of Głębowice just mentioned neither was nor is Stephen's patrimony, but is the duke's gift, you can therefore buy it securely, freely and without fear, because none of Stephen's heirs has or ever will have any right to demand it – as long as there are, or as there will be, in your cloister those who know how to defend themselves with Polish law and with this argument."

Here, brothers, consider from the treatise written above how you ought to answer the heirs of Stephen of Kobylagłowa.

[87] *Here now begins the account of the purchase of this forest.* Upon hearing these words from the prior, the lord abbot bought the forest from Stephen of Kobylagłowa for 28 silver marks for this cloister, in eternal possession. After he bought it and Stephen resigned it before the duke in favor of the cloister, the lord duke – as he was a very circumspect and cautious prince – said to Stephen,

"I wish this deed to remain firm for the cloister from now on. Hence, know that at first it [i.e., the forest] was, by my gift, lord Nicholas's, who, by my authority, [later] confirmed all of his possessions for the cloister of Henryków. Come and resign to the cloister, before me and my barons, that which had at first been its [property]; and let the lord abbot of Henryków restore to you [the value of] your horse, in the same sum of money at which it had then been appraised, that is, [you will get] 28 marks for it."

After Stephen of Kobylagłowa accepted this sum of money right there, the lord duke said again,

"You, lord barons, and all who are now present here, should know that for his sins Stephen has now resigned from, and restored to the cloister of Henryków, his forest of Głębowice – which he held, albeit by our gift, yet unjustly, because it had earlier been [the property] of the cloister."

[88] *This purchase and restitution was[99] effected before the said lord Duke Henry the elder in Niemcza, with many nobles then appearing there before the duke, in the year of the Lord 1234. But a privilege was not then requested or given about this. Why this was the case, we will state in the following, [where we also note] that during the following week the same duke personally performed a circuit around this forest in order to fix certain boundaries for the cloister.*

[89] First, we will state here why a privilege concerning the deed described above was not requested there and then. In those days when these glorious

---

98. The word used here, *amici*, meant in Polish usage, as generally in medieval Latin, relatives, as well as friends in today's conventional sense; Plezia, 1:478–79, *s.v. amicus.*

99. Although it sounds awkward in English, this use of singular is not an error, but a deliberate reproduction for the reader of the original phrase, *[h]ec emptio et restitutio facta est,* describing this property transfer as essentially one single transaction, consisting in its essence of two reciprocal components. This kind of usage is similar to (and may have been directly influenced by) the expression for sale in Roman law as an *emptio venditio*; see Barry Nicholas, *An Introduction to Roman Law* (Oxford: Clarendon Press, 1962), 171–82.

dukes – that is to say Henry the elder and his son also Henry, later killed by the pagans – reigned in this land, their deeds were so fixed and stable that seldom did anyone care to receive a privilege concerning any deed. Furthermore, lord Henry, the first abbot of this cloister, was a simple man, and, fearing God, considered the princes' deeds always to remain good and inviolate. When the said forest was returned to the monastery for the reason just described, during the following week on the abbot's request the lord duke personally performed a circuit around the said forest, and added for this cloister to that which had been redeemed from Stephen eight large hides from his own forest, to be possessed forever. And then the name of the forest, Głębowice, was changed to another name, Bukowina, and it is so called by the Poles today. But that holding where the cloister's farmstead now stands is called Głębowice, on account of the heirs of that ancient peasant who was called by that name, because long ago his heirs held [land] on the mountain near the farmstead.

Here, brothers, has most clearly been shown to you the reason whereby you can answer the heirs of Stephen of Kobylagłowa if they should ever raise a claim against you regarding this forest.

[90] *How after his father's death, but before the pagans, Duke Henry the younger performed a circuit around the said forest through his emissaries, and confirmed it for this cloister.* In those days when lord Duke Henry [II] was already confirmed in the reign after his father's death [in 1238], on the request of lord Bodo, the second abbot of this place, he likewise performed a circuit around the forest, through [his representative] Count Bogusław of Strzelin, then castellan of Ryczyn; and he confirmed this monastery within the same boundaries by which his father had done earlier. About which a privilege was then issued by the duke. But because it was lost in the flight from the pagans, all adversaries regarding this forest should be answered according to the account recorded above.

[91] *How after the pagans it was established and decreed that the deeds and the confirmed [actions] of the ancient dukes in this land – that is to say, of lord Henry the elder and of lord Henry, his son killed by the pagans – may never be revoked.* While the sons of the duke killed by the pagans [Henry II] reigned in the land,[100] many quarrels and jeers arose among the people every day about things that had been effected in the times of the ancient dukes. Hence, when – after the death of his brother, the third Duke Henry[101] – a certain younger son of the killed duke, Władysław by name, began to rule, he established and ordained that all the deeds of his grandfather and father should be held as ratified and firm and, as it were, buried[102] –

100. See n. 43 above.

101. Władysław, the youngest son of Henry II, was born in 1237, succeeded to the rule of the Duchy of Wrocław upon Henry III's death in 1266, and died in 1270. His brief rule was preceded by a longer tenure as archbishop of Salzburg. See Chapters 74, 77 above; *Rodowód*, 1:129–32; Grodecki, *Liber* (1949), 123, n. 50; Jurek, "Władysław."

102. *Quasi sepulta.* Settlement or prevention of dispute in medieval Poland is sometimes expressed with a metaphor of burial – either of conflict, or of transactions subject

so that no one among men may ever presume to say, or judge, or ordain anything regarding ancient deeds. Hence let it be known to our successors serving
God in this cloister in a future time that they are not bound to answer anyone
concerning anything, large or small, that was confirmed for this cloister before
the pagans. We thus admonish our lords and brothers diligently to inspect this
writing and all the things said in this book, and repeatedly to commit to memory
the ways in which they may reasonably be able to answer their attackers.

[92] *Here, lords and brothers, the deeds of this cloister in this land before the pagans
appear to be adequately and most lucidly exposed. Let it truly be known that the pagans
entered this land of Silesia in the year of the Lord 1241, and that year, on the fifth [day before
the] ides of April [April 9], killed lord Henry, the celebrated duke of this land of happy
memory, [in a battle] before Legnica. This duke, while he was alive, also reigned powerfully in
[Great] Poland and gloriously in Kraków. On the day recorded above, that is, the fifth ides of
April, his [death] anniversary is forever to be solemnly celebrated in this cloister.*

[93] *Because this cloister's deeds before the pagans now appear to be adequately exposed, we
shall now try to explain [the circumstances of] those [localities] which were given to and
confirmed for this cloister after the pagans, [and] how our successors may be able to answer their
adversaries without error and with reason. The first is the treatise about Schönwald. The second
is about the parcel of Głębowice which was given [to the cloister] after the pagans.*[103] *The third
is about Brukalice.*

First.[104] *About Schönwald.*

[94] About Schönwald, and the reason why the cloister possesses this village.[105] Let it be known that the stream which is called Budzów originates at the
foot of the Czech Mountain, and flows through sloping places into the river
which is called the Węża. Hence in the days long ago the forest near this stream
was called Budzów. Before the cloister was founded here, lord Henry, the
ancient duke by the nickname the Bearded, had established a village in this forest

---

to conflict – which is really an aspect of a broader image of eternal rest; see Piotr Górecki,
"*Ad Controversiam Reprimendam*: Family Groups and Dispute Prevention in Medieval
Poland, c. 1200," *Law and History Review* 14 (1996), 213–43, at 214–15.

103. Abbot Peter does not provide this part of the story.

104. This appears in the modern text as a new numbering sequence, which is in turn
inexplicably discontinued by Abbot Peter after his account of Schönwald. However, the
facsimile of the codex shows that this numbering sequence refers to the three accounts
promised in the text immediately above; see Grodecki, *Liber* (1991), after 225, fol. xviii^v.
There is no break of any sort before the words "first about Schönwald." The compilers of
the codex were simply continuing the story, not opening a new section.

105. This sentence is not part of a rubric – that is, not rendered in distinct color or
character size – but in the same character as the rest of the text. See Grodecki, *Liber*
(1991), after 225, fol. xviii^v.

which he called by the name of the stream, Budzów. Concerning this establishment (*locatio*),[106] he gave a certain Menold, the first village bailiff,[107] a privilege written as follows.

[95] *The first privilege of the village bailiff of Budzów.*[108]

In the name of the Savior, amen. We, Henry [I], by the grace of God duke of Silesia, wish it to be known to men of present and future time that we gave Menold a village which is called Budzów, to be established out of fifty hides, [in exchange] for [every] sixth hide, which [hide] shall be free of all payment of rent and tithe. And if anything [in the land area cleared] of the forest exceeds fifty hides, we joined that to the said village according to the same law. We also granted to Menold a mill and a tavern, to himself and to his heirs, or to whomever he will wish to sell in the future, with the aforesaid sixth hide, to be possessed by hereditary right forever. Conceding to the aforesaid village a liberty of fourteen years for the aid which is called the *hollunge*,[109] we also wish that the said village shall exist according to the same law and [terms of] payment by which the privileged villages [situated] near Salzborn are known. Done in Niemcza, in the year of [the Lord's] Grace 1221.

[96] *For how much time Menold was village bailiff in Budzów.* This same Menold ruled this village bailiwick under the duke's authority for six years before the cloister was founded [i.e., 1221–1227],[110] but he accomplished very little because he was much impeded by the father of Count Peter of Piotrowice and his brother, who were referred to by the nickname *Scriwazona*. Much could be said about the violence and evil of these two;[111] but because they have just been snatched by God through the finger of death, let us leave them alone and write down those things which are more pressing.

106. See n. 46 above.

107. "Village bailiff" translates *villicus* throughout both portions of the *Henryków Book* (likewise, "village bailiwick" translates *villicatio* in Chapter 96 below). The other official names for German village headmen are rendered as follows: *scultetus*, which is left untranslated in Book One; and *advocatus*, which is translated as "advocate" throughout. In Book Two, the usual name for the German village headman is *scultetus*, so, for convenience in reading, "village bailiff," or "bailiff," translate *scultetus* specifically in Book Two.

108. *S.U.*, 1:no. 210 (1221), 153–54.

109. This passage is a bit obscure; the new village is obtaining freedom for fourteen years from a kind of payment (an "aid," in Latin *iuvamen*) which has this name in the vernacular; *Matthias Lexers Mittelhochdeutsches Taschenwörterbuch* (Stuttgart: S. Hirzel Verlag, 1966), 45, 92, *s.v. erholn, holunge*.

110. Chapters 10–11, 21.

111. Abbot Peter discusses Peter Stoszowic himself extensively, and his father and uncle in passing, in his account of Schönwald (Chapters 103–10); see also Supplementary Documents no. 13–14.

[97] *That lord Duke [Henry] the Bearded truthfully granted Budzów to the cloister.* After these things were done, in the course of the foundation of the monastery in this cloister, the aforesaid lord duke granted this forest, or village, to the cloister, to be possessed forever. The account of this gift is fully written down in the foundation privilege of the cloister,[112] so enough said here about that.

[98] *That lord Duke Henry [II], killed by the pagans, confirmed Rudno for the cloister.* Now [we shall write] about Rudno, and by what reason this forest accrued to the cloister. In those days when Duke Henry the Bearded began to found the cloister of the nuns in Trzebnica,[113] Ilik, son of Lupus, had near Czerniawa a certain forest which is called Skępa. The lord duke received this forest from Ilik in exchange, in order that he might extend the boundaries [of the estate] of Trzebnica by that much more near Czerniawa, and [in exchange] granted to him for his forest of Skępa the aforesaid forest of Rudno and a certain village of Jaksonów, which is situated in the fields not far from Mount Ślęża. After the same Ilik possessed this forest of Rudno for a bit of time, he sold it to Count Mroczko, son of Przecław, for 28 silver marks. Afterwards, Count Mroczko in turn sold it to lord Conrad the notary for 34 silver marks. Of which silver, lord Conrad the notary paid the said Mroczko in the presence of the duke thirty marks before the pagans, while lord Bodo, abbot of this cloister, paid the same Count Mroczko four marks after the pagans.

[99] *About Notary Conrad, who he was.* But because at different times there were many notaries in this land by the name of Conrad, we wish to distinguish the names of some of the notaries of this land for our brothers who succeed us, so that they may know who this Conrad was who gave such alms to the monastery, and at what time he was notary; and so that they may endeavor to pray for him, as they are bound to do.

[100] *How many notaries there were who benefitted this cloister.* And thus the first notary of our times was lord Nicholas of blessed memory, through whom this cloister [was founded].[114] We have discussed some things about his pious acts in writing above,[115] and we decline to discuss anything more about him in this place. This Nicholas was succeeded in the notariate by a certain man Nasław, born of the most noble stock of this land, who in his times was also archdeacon in the [cathedral] church of Saint John of Wrocław. This Nasław was succeeded in the office of the notariate by Conrad, just mentioned, who aided this cloister

112. Budzów is indeed recorded, but without any additional details (and under the slightly different name, Budzyn), in Henry I's foundation charter for the monastery issued in 1228, and translated here as Supplementary Document no. 2.

113. See the introductory essay, nn. 116, 186, 301, 312, 317, 324, 328.

114. The words "was founded" are a gloss. There is a gap of about a dozen letters in the manuscript passage to which they are a gloss. See Grodecki, *Liber* (1991), after 225, fol. xix^r.

115. Chapters 2–14, 21–24.

with many favors, and who confirmed [these favors] by the authority of the dukes. These three aforesaid notaries reigned in this office, one after the other, before the pagans. About their followers we write nothing, because they arranged no favor for this cloister.

[101] *Here it is noted how lord Notary Conrad changed his vow.* In those days when the much mentioned Henry, the bearded lord duke, first entrusted the notariate to the said lord Conrad, the same Conrad held, not far from the cloister of Henryków, a certain village which was at that time called Jagielno among the Poles,[116] but [which is] now [called] Scribersdorf,[117] and which Conrad himself had granted to this cloister in eternal possession after his death, by the duke's will. After a few years passed, the Bearded Duke [Henry] entered upon the path of eternal life [in 1238]. When he died, and when his son, also Henry by name, began to reign in his father's stead, lord Conrad lived on for a little while. When he (that is to say, the same Notary Conrad) fell gravely ill, he was moved by the laments of Bogusław, his sister's son, so that just as he [Conrad] was on his last breath, he requested his lord the duke, and Master Peter of Bliż, and Master Gocwin the physician, to come to him, and he granted the village of Jagielno, which he had earlier given to the cloister, to the said Bogusław, his sister's son. As compensation for the same village of Jagielno, by the duke's will, on that same hour and before those same men, he granted to this cloister the forest of Rudno, already much mentioned, to be possessed forever. Also there at the time were the knights of the court, whose names are [mentioned] more expressly in the privilege concerning this gift issued by the lord duke himself. The tenor of that privilege is this, word for word.

[102] *The privilege of the killed Duke [Henry II] about Rudno.*[118]

In the name of the Lord, amen. The deeds of the mortals often disappear unless confirmed by the witness of worthy men. So it is that we, Henry, by the grace of God duke of Silesia, Kraków, and [Great] Poland, wishing to prevent such [results], make it known to all present and future [persons] that, in our presence and by our good will, lord Conrad our notary has granted to Saint Mary and to the house of Henryków the forest which is called Rudno, in the amount of fifty large hides (situated near the Czech Mountains, between the *przesieka*[119] and the path that leads to these

116. Chapter 34 above.

117. This is a good example of a "Germanization" of a place name between c. 1210 and 1268, reflecting German immigration and settlement in this region of Silesia; see Bartlett, *Making*, 162–64.

118. *S.U.*, 2:no. 196 (1240), 124.

119. The forested defense perimeter which had been reserved by the dukes as a limit of settlement until the second half of the thirteenth century; see the introductory essay above, nn. 16, 259–60.

mountains and that has the forest of this cloister [called] Budzyn[120] on one side), to be possessed forever by the brothers serving God in Henryków, for his sins and by our grace.

In order, then, that the reason for this gift may be noted more plainly, let it be known that our father, the celebrated Duke Henry [I] of venerated memory, had formerly given that forest of Rudno to Ilik, son of the late Lupus, by way of an exchange. Afterwards, Ilik sold it to Mroczko, son of Przecław. After that, Mroczko sold it to lord Conrad. But because this Conrad had previously, in our father's presence, and by his will and our own, promised his village of Jagielno to the cloister of Henryków – subject to the condition that the brothers were to possess the said village of Jagielno after his death – yet as the oft-mentioned Conrad was drawing nearer to the finger of death, in his last testament he granted his village of Jagielno to his sister's son, Bogusław, before ourselves, and Count Stephen of Wierzbno, and Theoderic of Szydłów, and Master Peter Bliż; and for it, with our good will and consent, right there he gave the forest of Rudno to the brothers of Henryków, in eternal possession. Hence, because the oft-mentioned brothers have, and ought to have, fifty large hides in Budzyn by our father's gift, it is [now] arranged by our order and will that, in the place where these forests meet, a German village may be established under the cloister's authority, so that on one side of the village he cloister of Henryków should possess Rudno, and on the other Budzów.

This was done in the year of the Incarnation of the Lord 1240, when the same Conrad confirmed his last testament in his village of Goła, before ourselves and the aforenamed men, with many knights and servants of our court also in attendance there. In order therefore that the brothers of Henryków may always in the future peacefully possess the said forests, Budzów and Rudno, [along] with the other goods justly granted to them by our father and by us, we caused this charter to be strengthened by the placement of our seal.

Here end the privileges issued by the dukes about Budzów and Rudno before the pagans.

[103] *Likewise, here begins the treatise about the amount of labor by which this village of Schönwald was retained after the pagans.* When the privilege recorded above was given to this cloister by Duke Henry [II], killed by the pagans, not quite a year later the cursed pagans entered this province, and, inasmuch as they did many things worthy of lament and tears, the cloister, too, was entirely reduced to ashes and embers in that general plague. Therefore Peter, son of the late Stosz, upon seeing that the cloister was nearly destroyed, usurped for himself these forests of Budzów

---

120. An alternative name for Budzów, here, in the later clause of this diploma, and in Duke Henry I's charter of 1228 (Supplementary Document no. 2).

and Rudno because they adjoined his village of Piotrowice,[121] and, in the place where the two forests meet, established a certain village which he called Schön-wald on the counsel of the village bailiff, for the reason that there was a most beautiful forest there at the time.[122] And by his shrewdness, Peter arranged it so that he possessed Budzów in one part of this village – or establishment – and Rudno in the other. The first bailiff of the village was someone named Sibodo, who possessed [the bailiwick] there by Peter's authority for two years.

[104] *In the following it is noted how after the pagans Abbot Bodo demanded this village.* At that time, when after the pagans' departure from this land lord Abbot Bodo returned with a few persons, he saw the cloister burned down and devastated and the cloister's manors almost lost in some places – among which evils, as was said, the village of Schönwald had just been removed. He was distressed with a great sadness and very disturbed, above all because in those days the land was ruled by Duke Bolesław [II], son of Duke Henry [II] killed by the pagans, which young Bolesław then occupied himself with nothing but foolish deeds. At length, continuously for five years, in every general assembly before Duke Bolesław himself and his barons, the abbot claimed that his house was exposed to violence from this Peter, son of Stosz. But the more often the abbot complained, the more the duke occupied himself with his juvenile pranks. So the abbot was disturbed within himself beyond measure.

[105] *About Notary Conrad, son of the late Berthold of Drzeniów.* In those days, while this and many similar things inconvenient for the cloister were occurring, Almighty God, Who never abandons those who place hope in Him,[123] elevated in the court of the said Duke Bolesław a certain notary by the name of Conrad of Drzeniów. In his boyhood, this same Conrad had been a school colleague of a certain monk of this cloister by the name of Peter.[124] This Peter quite often visited the courts of the princes together with the abbot. Hence it happened that one time Conrad said to Peter at court,

"I have seen you before, but I don't know where."

In return, Peter answered,

"And I hold a likeness of your person in my heart, but cannot at all bring back to memory where I've seen you."

As these things took place, and as these two men, that is to say Conrad and Peter, were recognizing one another, Notary Conrad said to Peter,

"From where is this abbot who complains before my lord so often?"

Peter answered,

---

121. Chapter 96 above.

122. The name means "beautiful forest" in German.

123. Jth. 13:17.

124. Almost certainly the future Abbot Peter and author of this portion of the *Henryków Book*.

"That is my abbot from Henryków. I am a monk there, and have taken vows from this abbot."

While the aforesaid Conrad and Peter were talking about this and many other similar things among themselves concerning their old friendship, the notary said again,

"Has something large been taken away from you?"

Peter said,

"There is a certain manor containing a hundred large hides, of which hides our house will be deprived forever unless someone discreet and God-fearing should talk to the duke on our behalf in our absence, suitably and repeatedly."

To which the same notary answered,

"I am near my lord in the evening and in the morning, and at every hour except for the time of sleep. So I will speak on your behalf. Let that help as it may! I do hope that, with God's help, in due course I may be of service. You therefore, together with your brothers, pray that God may enlighten my lord, so that he may lay aside his boyish pranks, and try to carry out just judgments as he is bound to do."

These things were done in Dziewin, beyond Głogów. And let it be known that lord Bolesław, the aforesaid duke, at that time always closed himself off [from his subjects], and did not admit to himself anyone at all beside the very important. He also then had secret entrances in his many living places, unknown to all men apart from those very familiar to him. Hence, after the acquaintance of Conrad the notary and Peter the monk described above became manifest, Notary Conrad led Abbot lord Bodo many times to the lord duke through the said hiding places, and did so until the cloister's business was brought to a good conclusion. Here, brothers, you see how an acquaintance of great men can sometimes be useful.

[106] *How and when this business of Schönwald was terminated.* After all these things written down [above] were effected, it happened that lord Duke Bolesław was celebrating a general and solemn assembly in a field near Wrocław. In this assembly also sat Władysław, duke of Opole, and the entire land gathered there, the rich and the poor. In the same assembly, Albert with Beard spoke for the cloister, and Stosz, son of Leonard, spoke for Peter of Piotrowice. As these two were wrangling among themselves, the duke summoned Paul of Słupowice, who, in the times of the old dukes[125] and at the time when this was going on, was a perambulator (*circuitor*) of many inheritances by the authority of the dukes. Publicly sitting in judgment, Duke Bolesław asked this same Paul,

"How much does Peter Stoszowic have, and according to what boundaries?"

Paul said,

"The oak forest [that extends] from the Czech path, *dąbrowa* in Polish."[126]

---

125. Bolesław I the Tall, Henry I the Bearded, and Henry II the Pious; see nn. 2 and 40 above.

126. Meaning "oak forest"; *S.Sp.*, 2:42–43, *s.v. dambrova*.

The duke said,

"To whom did my grandfather and father give the black forest?"

Paul answered,

"Lord, your grandfather and father gave the black forest between the Czech path and the *przesieka* to the cloister of Henryków."

Upon hearing this, the duke said,

"I command you, by virtue of your eyes, that you mark out the said forest with these boundaries for the abbot of Henryków and his cloister."[127]

After this was done, Duke Bolesław gave a privilege about this, written down in the following words.

[107] *Here begins the privilege concerning Rudno, issued by Duke Bolesław and by Mroczko after the pagans.*[128]

In the name of the Lord, amen. We, Bolesław, by the grace of God duke of Silesia and [Great] Poland, make it known to present and future [persons] that in the time of the illustrious Duke Henry [II], our father of happy memory, lord Conrad, our father's notary of blessed memory, bought from Count Mroczko fifty large hides in the forest which is called Rudno. This forest is situated between Czerniawa, our village, and the stream which is called Jadków. It has Piotrkowice[129] on one side, and, on the other, a village of the brothers of Henryków which is called Budzów – the one, that is to say, which our grandfather of pious memory [Henry I] formerly granted to the aforesaid house. And when Conrad, just mentioned, paid the aforesaid Count Mroczko for this village in full, for the remedy of his soul he granted it, before the aforenamed father of ours, to the house of the Holy Virgin of Henryków and the brothers who serve God there, to be possessed forever.

Therefore, in order that this gift, so solemnly made before such a duke – that is, our father – may remain firm and stable, we strengthen the present charter with the protection of our seal. This was done in the year of the Lord 1244, in the presence of these [persons]: lord Theoderic provost of Głogów, Count Bogusław castellan of Niemcza, Count Racław castellan

---

127. The expression is fully *Precipio tibi sub obtentu oculorum tuorum ut abbati de Heinrichow et suo claustro dictam silvam eisdem metis assignes*, which Grodecki translates, instead, as a command to Peter, threatening him (in the first phrase) with blinding, i.e., "on pain of loss of your eyes" – as I have also done in Górecki, "Politics of the Legal Process in Early Medieval Poland," *Oxford Slavonic Papers, New Series* 17 (1984), 22–44, at 43. However, I now think that, in view of the act to be performed – "assigning" boundaries – and of the range of meanings of *obtentus*, this command was addressed to Paul Słupowic in his capacity as a boundary perambulator; see Niermeyer, 733, *s.v.* 1. *obtentus*, 2. *obtentus*.

128. *S.U.*, 2:no. 270 (1244), 162.

129. This is another example of a slight variation of the versions of place names, both of which refer to Peter.

of Wrocław, Count Mroczko castellan of Ryczyn, who – because he [had] already [i.e., previously] sold the aforesaid village, and [later], before us and these witnesses, resigned it to the aforementioned house of Henryków in Notary Conrad's name – also affixed his seal to strengthen this charter. The witnesses of this deed are: Count Peter judge of the court, Count Nicholas .castellan of Bolesławiec, Zbyluch son of Przybysław (the late castellan of Lubusz), Gebhard castellan of Sądowel, and very many others.

Here ends the privilege.

[108] After all these things were thus accomplished, Peter Stoszowic still was so menacing that no one dared to live there under the cloister's authority. For which reason, on the counsel of Albert with Beard, Abbot Bodo ceded to this Peter fourteen hides of the cloister's forests, so that, within the borders of the cloister [that run] from the Czech path, he [i.e., Peter] would keep seven hides of the forest which is called Rudno on one side, and seven hides of the forest of Budzów on the other. Count Peter joined these fourteen hides to his village of Piotrowice. In this way, this Peter was reconciled with the cloister, and allowed a village to be established there in the cloister's name.

Upon hearing these things, perhaps our successors will wonder. To which we say that in the old days when this and similar things were taking place, the land over there nearby the mountains was very wooded, and almost completely deserted up to the village which is called Sadlno. Hence Peter's predecessors – that his to say his paternal uncle and his father[130] – were hiding in this wood as if they were some robbers, and very seldom or never appeared before the ancient dukes. They occupied themselves with violence against the neighboring poor at their pleasure, just as they wished. And let it be known that because of their violence the ancient duke by the nickname the Bearded was not able to establish any village in these forests during his days. Therefore, let no one wonder at the fact that Abbot Bodo ceded the aforesaid fourteen hides to Peter for the good of the peace.

[109] *Here it is necessary for our successors to know how, after Peter's friendship was secured, the village of Schönwald was established in the cloister's name.* Let it be known that when Peter was still an enemy of the cloister, he had placed in his name in Schönwald a certain village bailiff who was called Sibodo. When the village was already resigned to the cloister with Peter's good will, Abbot Bodo eliminated that same Sibodo with great effort. In order that it may be known how he was eliminated, we will truthfully write a bit about that here.

This same Sibodo, when he saw that he would be unable to live there under the authority of Count Peter, worked around the said Abbot Bodo in order to be able to live there under the authority of the cloister. But at that time the abbot was advised that, with all the effort he could muster, he should eliminate this Village Bailiff Sibodo – who had established a village in Peter's name – and

---

130. Chapter 96 above.

establish there a village bailiff under the cloister's authority who would always obey the cloister's command. Hence, lord Abbot Bodo gave the same Sibodo four silver marks, so that he would give up this settlement by his good will. All the things recorded above were done before worthy men, that is to say the citizens of Löwenstein, by whose counsel the lord abbot did and accomplished all the things that needed to be accomplished there. In this way, the said Sibodo, by his own spontaneous will, resigned this village bailiwick, for himself and for his heirs. Here let no one wonder at the fact that the aforesaid Village Bailiff Sibodo withdrew from that establishment (*locatio*)[131] by a spontaneous will for such a modest sum of money, because until that time this Village Bailiff Sibodo was possessing [land] in the goods of Count Peter – that is, at the edge of the village of Piotrowice – and did not as of then settle anyone at all in the cloister's forest of Schönwald.

[110] *About the first village bailiff placed in Schönwald in the cloister's name.* In those days when this and many other similar things were going on, some helpful and some harmful to the cloister, there was in Piotrowice a certain village bailiff by the name of Martin. This same Martin appeared, in sweet and cunning words, to be a friend to Abbot Bodo and to the cloister, but was in fact an enemy in every action he could. This same Martin measured out the cloister's forests from the aforesaid Czech path up to the *przesieka*, which is called "the hedge" (*hach*) in German.[132] In the old days, and also at the time when this was going on, the aforesaid *przesieka* encircled the entire land of Silesia. Hence the ancient dukes did not allow anyone at all to cut down anything in this *przesieka*, and this is the reason why at that time [land intended to be cleared for arable] was measured no further than to the boundaries of this *przesieka*. This measurement, and quantity of hides [measured out in it], remains in force there today. *About the first measurement [of land] in Schönwald, enough has been said here.*

[111] *Now let us turn back to those things which are more pressing.* When this aforesaid measurement of hides was completed (albeit falsely) by the said Martin in Schönwald, lord Abbot Bodo settled there a certain village bailiff by the name of John, son of a certain priest, who first began to assemble cultivators there, and to possess a village in the cloister's name. This same John had a uterine brother by the name of James, about which James we will write a bit more for the cloister's utility later.[133] And after cultivators and assarters multiplied there, John the village bailiff ordered these same peasants to raze the forests all through the hedge (*al durch den hach*),[134] and he did this by his own presumption, not by the

131. See nn. 46 and 106 above.
132. See n. 119 above, and the introductory essay above, nn. 16 and 259–60.
133. Abbot Peter says nothing more about John or James.
134. Abbot Peter expressed the words *all through the hedge* in German as *al durch den hach*, and did not translate them into Latin. Grodecki italicized these words, but in the fascimile their character appears identical to the text around them. See Grodecki, *Liber* (1991), after 225, fol. xxii[v].

abbot's order, because, as he said, the knights in the circuit are [already] cutting and destroying the *przesieka*. For this reason, the cloister later suffered great injuries from Duke Henry III. And when Village Bailiff John was rebuked by the abbot for this, he answered by saying,

"Lord, I have done what all the knights in the circuit who have inheritances near the *przesieka* are doing."

Let it be noted here that at the time when these things were going on – namely, after the pagans – everyone among the knights plundered what he wanted and how much he wanted. Hence, among others, a certain knight Przybek, son of a certain Dzierżko, by his presumption placed [a village][135] within the boundaries of the cloister – that is to say, between the mountain called Ziegenrücken, or in Polish Koziechrzebty,[136] and the stream of Budzów.[137] In those days when these things were going on, there were many assarters in Schönwald because of the freshness of the beautiful forest there, and they all gathered and said,

"How will we allow others to enter the inheritance of our lords, in order to live there and to deprive our heirs of their labors later?"

Having said this, they all gathered together with their foolish village bailiff, and forcibly ejected all the cultivators of the aforesaid knight Przybek from the cloister's boundaries. This deed would have exposed the cloister to great trouble at that time if God had not uplifted the spirit of a certain Albert by the nickname the Bearded, very powerful near the duke and throughout the land in those days. This same Albert had been a brother-in-law of the said knight Przybek.[138] This Albert took Przybek, and a certain Racław by the nickname of Drzemlik, and certain friends of each of them (that is of Przybek and of Racław), and ascended the mountain of Ziegenrücken just mentioned. With the aforesaid men there was also there a certain monk of Henryków by the name of Peter, at that time cellarer of the cloister. This Peter had arranged the gathering of these men with the said Albert. After these things were done, and those men were gathered at the peak of this mountain, Albert with Beard said,

"I know that my lord the duke does not wish Saint Mary's cloister of Henryków to suffer any harm within its boundaries in this place."

Having said this, Albert turned to the east, that is to say toward the Czech Mountains, and pointed to a certain pile of rocks at the peak of another mountain on the opposite side, saying,

---

135. The words "a village" are a gloss; see Grodecki, *Liber* (1991), after 225, fol. xxiii[r]. There is no gap in the relevant portion of the document, so in the translation Grodecki paraphrases the text to state that Przybek forced himself into the boundaries of the estate, without reference to a foundation of the village; but, oddly, in the Latin edition he supplies the gloss as translated here, a reading I much prefer.

136. The name means "goat's backs" in both languages.

137. Chapter 94.

138. Chapter 45.

"My friends and companions! If this seems right to you and pleases you, let us fix the boundaries of the cloister from this place through that hillock beyond the valley. In the sign of truth, let us send two men, who should make for us a richly smoking fire in the valley in between, so that by observing the smoke from this place – that is to say from where we now stand, namely Ziegenrücken – we may indirectly fix the cloister's boundaries through the valley, up to that hillock beyond the valley."

While this was being done, the same Albert ordered four peasant men, together with a ducal *camerarius*, that as they observed the fire and the smoke they should mark out the boundaries on trees by cutting through the forest and the valley. After these things were carried out and done, the cloister remained in this place in tranquillity and peace for a long time.

About Brukalice. The present writing truthfully demonstrates to all who read it by what reason – or, if you will, authority – the cloister possesses this manor.

[112] Because we fear that our lords and successors who battle for Almighty God in the cloister of Henryków long hence, may have to endure certain inconveniences from the kindred of the heirs of Brukalice, we wish truthfully to present in writing the origin of the heirs of this holding, in order that if afterwards anyone from among them should wish to raise a claim against the cloister, the lords and brothers may be able answer with reason based on the present writing.

[113] *About the first possessor of the same holding, and why it is called Brukalice.* Let it thus be known by all who view this book that in the old days, when the lord dukes of this province of Silesia were distributing inheritances and manors to the noble and the mediocre, there was a certain Czech by the name of Boguchwał. He served the old lord Duke Bolesław, that is to say the duke who founded the cloister of Lubiąż. In that same place which is now called Brukalice, this duke gave Boguchwał enough land for up to four oxen. But because at that time the land here in the circuit was wooded and completely empty of cultivators, this same Boguchwał the Czech usurped for himself in his circuit[139] fully enough forest for three large plows [of arable]. After he possessed [land] there for a time, he took as wife a daughter of a certain cleric, a fat and completely inept peasant woman. But let it be known that in those days here in the circuit water mills were extremely rare, so the wife of the said Boguchwał the Czech very often stood at the quern to grind. Her husband, the same Boguchwał, said to her in compassion,

"Let me grind too."

Which is in Polish,

139. By this reference to a *circuitus*, Abbot Peter suggests that Boguchwał had received a large area of forest in which to establish an estate, and, possibly, that the duke or someone else had perambulated its boundaries, which is a common meaning of the word "circuit" in the Polish documents.

"Daj ać ja pobrucze, a ty poczywaj."[140]

So that Czech ground in turn with the wife, that is, he turned the stone as often as the wife did. Seeing which, the neighbors – albeit few back then – called him Boguchwał Brukał,[141] and thus it is that his entire posterity is called Brukalice. Here, lords and brothers, present and future, we admonish and urge that in the subsequent record you may diligently inspect and note the names of the sons and the grandsons of this Boguchwał the Czech, in order that you may know how much you possess from each of them, and for what reason.

This Boguchwał the Czech begat three sons. He called the first-born Racław, the second[-born] James, the third[-born] Mścisław. When their father died, these three men divided this holding in Brukalice among themselves into three parts, exactly so that each of them would keep a third part of it. After these things were done this way, they took legitimate wives.[142] The first-born, Racław, begat by his wife two sons, Bogusza and Paul. From these two boys, the cloister possesses a third part of the inheritance of Brukalice. But by what reason and authority it accrued to the cloister from them, we wish to show truthfully in the following record, in order that, if it should be necessary, our successors may be able to answer the kinsmen of these youths without any error.

[114] *How things were first arranged with Bogusza and Paul.* When these two youths, Bogusza and Paul, were still in a youthful state,[143] their father Racław

---

140. Abbot Peter is paraphrasing. The full translation is, "Let me grind, and you rest." See Gerald Stone, "Honorific Pronominal Address in Polish before 1600," *Oxford Slavonic Papers, New Series* 17 (1984), 45–56, at 46; Józef Matuszewski, *Najstarsze polskie zdanie prozaiczne. Zdanie henrykowskie i jego tło historyczne* [The oldest Polish sentence in prose: the sentence of Henryków and its historical background] (Wrocław: Zakład Narodowy im. Ossolińskich, 1981).

141. Which may loosely be translated as "Boguchwał the Grind," from the old verb *bruczeć*, related to stonework, masonry, or pavement in modern Polish; Stone, "Pronominal Address," 46; Matuszewski, *Najstarsze*, 9.

142. The reference to "legitimate" wives suggests that about three generations after Boguchwał Brukał – and hence deep into the thirteenth century – sexual unions that were not considered full marriages (presumably in the eyes of the institutional Church and of all who were concerned with inheritance) were frequent. There are numerous references to "legitimate" wives in the second part of the *Book*. They suggest widespread concubinage in this society throughout the period documented by the *Book*. For the formal definition of a "legitimate" wife and her distinction from a concubine according to Roman law and practice, see James A. Brundage, *Law, Sex, and Christian Society in Medieval Europe* (Chicago: University of Chicago Press, 1987), 40–41.

143. *Iuventus*, in general medieval usage the age between 14 and 20 years; J. C. Russell, "Population in Europe, 500–1500," in *The Fontana Economic History of Europe*, ed. Carlo Cipolla, vol. 1: *The Middle Ages* (Glasgow: Collins/Fontana, 1972), 25–70, at 42.

died in the land of Opole.[144] After his death, those two, Bogusza and Paul, were foolish and thought nothing about their future welfare, but offered their holding for sale to various people for a long time. But here in those days, as was said, [people] cared little about any possession.[145] Hence, when no one wished to buy, they repeatedly said to Abbot Bodo and to Peter, cellarer of this cloister,

"Either you buy our holding, or we will give it to some knight who will be very onerous to your cloister."

After they repeatedly discussed this and many other similar things with the abbot, the lord abbot finally, for future security of the cloister, offered them an exchange in the province of Kraków, or of Opole, or of [Great] Poland. To which they said,

"Lord abbot, we will accept the exchange in [Great] Poland, but because we are poor, as you see, we need to receive some kind of assistance from you."

After these things were done, the aforesaid lord abbot gave them as much [land] as they had here [in Brukalice] in the inheritance of the cloister [called] Ochla, near Starogród, beyond Milicz, in the duchy of [Duke] Przemysł.[146] And he further provided for their assistance, as is written in the following privilege.

[115] *Here begins the first privilege about these deeds, issued by Duke Henry III to the cloister in Henryków.*[147]

In the name of the Lord, amen. We prudently escape many evils when we commend the affairs of our age to the memory of letters. For the things established by our predecessors come to our knowledge by the service of letters; for as long as the letter lives, so also lives the act committed to the letter, whose declaration sustains memory and perpetuates temporal acts.

Therefore we, Henry, by the grace of God duke of Silesia, wish it to be known by present and future [persons] that certain youths, Bogusza and Paul, sons of the late Racław of Brukalice, by a spontaneous will made an exchange with the brothers of Henryków of that part of their inheritance which belonged to them among their remaining brothers, receiving the same amount [of land] in the duchy of the illustrious Prince Przemysł, in a certain village which is situated near Starogród and is commonly called Ochla – with their brothers James and Peter offering their spontaneous assent to this exchange.

But because when this exchange was underway the aforesaid youths, that is to say Bogusza and Paul, were crushed by an extreme poverty, in order to get them to receive the holding in Ochla that much faster, the

---

144. That is, the Duchy of Opole, one of the duchies into which the province (initially duchy) of Silesia was divided in the course of the twelfth and thirteenth centuries.

145. Chapter 86 above.

146. This was the duchy of Great Poland. Duke Przemysł I was born in 1220 or 1221, succeeded Władysław Odonic to the rule of much of Great Poland in 1239, and died in 1257; Grodecki, *Liber* (1949), 144, n. 59; Krzysztof Ożóg, "Przemysł I," *Piastowie*, 138–41.

147. *S.U.*, 3:no. 97 (1253), 71–72.

abbot of Henryków gave them: two horses worth three marks; four oxen worth two and a half marks; two cows worth one mark; five pigs, each worth three fiertons;[148] five sheep worth eight *scoti*;[149] two tunics worth one mark; for their mother a mantle worth half a mark; likewise, for these youths eight measures (*modii*) of rye according to the measure of Wrocław, worth a mark; on their first journey (when they were going to Gniezno to receive the holding in this exchange from the duke of [Great] Poland) one mark for the expenses; later, in order to lead away their wives, with their children and things, to [Great] Poland, the abbot of Henryków hired out to them two carts with eight horses, worth two silver marks.

Therefore, in order that this exchange by the cloister of Henryków with those youths should always remain firm and fixed on both sides in the future, we caused the present charter to be strengthened by the placement of our seal. The witnesses of this exchange are: Count Mroczko castellan of Ryczyn, Count Jaksa castellan of Wrocław, Janusz Męka, John Osina, Dzierżysław son of Mojko, Arnold Kula, Paul Poduszka, Andrew of Grodziec, Bieńko son of Wojsław, Paul Słupowic, and very many others. Done in Münsterberg, in the year of the Lord 1253, on the day before the calends of August [July 31].

Here ends the privilege about the first matter with Bogusza and Paul of Brukalice.

[116] *Here begins the second matter with them.* When these things were done, and those two, Bogusza and Paul, lived in Ochla for three years, it happened that lord Abbot Bodo of this cloister went to Ochla to visit the cloister's inheritance and village there with his cellarer [Peter]. The aforesaid youths Bogusza and Paul came up to him (that is to say, to the abbot), and said,

"Lord, we fools can in no way live in this place for long, because we have already used up whatever we brought to this place, and have not met with any good fortune here."

The abbot said to them in response,

"I with my brothers have fulfilled your wishes in every way, beyond what I was obliged to do. I would be well disposed toward you if you were worth it."

After they discussed this and many other similar things there and then with the lord abbot, the lord abbot at last said to them,

"If you cannot live here, sell out to whomever you can."

Having said this, the abbot left and returned to the cloister. Later, after three weeks passed, the abbot sent Brother Peter his cellarer[150] to Dębnica and before the aforesaid duke of [Great] Poland, on the cloister's business. On his way there, he – that is to say Brother Peter – passed through Ochla. Hence, the said

---

148. A fierton (*ferto*) was one-quarter of a mark, and, as a unit of account, included 60 pence in the Polish duchies; Kiersnowski, *Wstęp*, 152–53; Spufford, *Money*, 212–13, n. 6.

149. See n. 47 above.

150. Almost certainly the future Abbot Peter, and the author of this portion of the *Book*.

youths, Bogusza and Paul, hearing that he was on his way to the duke, strenuously requested that he provide them, before the duke, with as much money as he may wish for their holding in Ochla. In addition they said,

"Because in this province no one cares to buy anything here, unless you redeem us, we will go away and leave it abandoned."

To which Brother Peter said in response,

"Come with me to the duke and we will do whatever he advises."

And let it be known that in his days the same Duke Przemysł was very well disposed to the cloister, and that he was somewhat lettered,[151] so Brother Peter, cellarer of this cloister, was always conversing with him in Latin. So the lord duke counseled by saying,

"You may buy it according to Polish custom for the cloister, because I shall decree and command before my barons that if anyone from their kindred should afterwards wish to redeem [his holding], he may redeem that which was bought here in my duchy in Ochla – but with respect to that which was given to the cloister in the duchy of Silesia in the exchange, [that] he shall have no power to redeem."

After the duke said this and some other similar things, Brother Peter the cellarer took counsel with certain canons of Poznań, and with other knights well disposed to this cloister, about what he should do, telling them the lord duke's words and counsel. What else? All advised by saying that this holding in Brukalice (which they had exchanged for the other [holding] in Ochla) will be strengthened for your cloister by this purchase. For which reason, the same Brother Peter bought from them, before the duke and his nobles, the holding which they had in Ochla, for twenty silver marks – which money Brother Peter the cellarer obtained as a loan from a certain canon of Poznań, and immediately paid out in full, right there before the duke and his barons named in the privilege written and issued about this.

[117] *Here begins the privilege issued by the aforesaid duke of [Great] Poland, Przemysł, concerning this deed.*[152]

In the name of the Lord, amen. We, Przemysł, by divine disposition duke of [Great] Poland, always prizing the truth from the depths of our soul, and by a spontaneous will contributing to the honor of the Holy Mother Church, wish it to be known to present and future [persons] that certain youths, Bogusza and Paul – Silesians from the kindred of lord Paul, late bishop of the church of Poznań[153] – made a certain exchange with the lord abbot of

---

151. *Litteratus*, which in medieval Latin meant not "literate" in today's sense of the word, but more specifically learned in the writings of classical and early Christian Antiquity, generally in Latin.

152. *S.U.*, 3:no. 179 (1256), 123.

153. This is an intriguing piece of information in the *Book*, indicating that Boguchwał the Czech and the bishop of Poznań who was most active in the foundation of the monastery were related.

Henryków, giving him a holding which they had near the cloister itself, and which is commonly called Brukalice, and receiving from him the same amount in Ochla, which the same cloister possesses by the gift of our father of happy memory [Władysław Odonic], and by our grace.[154]

Afterwards, the aforementioned youths sold to the cloister a holding which they had received in exchange in the land of our duchy, for twenty silver marks. We therefore declare by the present charter, strengthened by the placement of our seal, that these youths have sold the holding they had [held] in Ochla for the aforementioned money before ourselves and our barons. And if afterwards anyone from the kindred of the said youths wishes to redeem that which was bought before us, and which in the land of our duchy, that he may redeem; but they [*sic*] shall have no regard whatever to that which was given in exchange before the noble prince, lord Henry [III], duke of Silesia, our brother-in-law.

Done in Poznań, on the seventh [day before the] ides of May [May 9], in the year of the Incarnation of the Lord 1256. The witnesses of this matter are: Count Dzierżykraj palatine [of Great Poland], Boguchwał castellan of Poznań, lord John chancellor of our court, Świętosław castellan of Nakło, Peter and John, sons of Thomas, and very many others. I, Michael the notary was also in attendance there, and recorded these things by the mandate of the aforesaid duke.

Here ends the privilege concerning the purchase in Ochla issued by lord Przemysł, duke of [Great] Poland.

[118] *Here begins the confirmation of the same purchase, also issued to the cloister by our lord Duke Henry, the third [by that name] of this land.* After this purchase was effected and, as was said above, solemnly confirmed in [Great] Poland by the seal of the duke and of his aforenamed barons, we requested our duke, lord Henry III just noted above, that, just as this deed was confirmed in [Great] Poland before his brother-in-law, lord Duke Przemysł, so he himself may also deign to confirm it by his own privilege and by the witness of his barons. [In response] to this, lord Duke Henry himself favorably and very graciously granted his privilege as well to the cloister.

[119] *Here begins the second privilege of confirmation of Brukalice, granted to the cloister by our lord Duke Henry III.*[155]

In the name of the Lord, amen. Unless they are strengthened against the bold presumption of the moderns either by the voice of witnesses, or by the testimony of letters – whose declaration sustains memory – actions of the mortals will easily be voided or lost.

154. Compare this emphasis on the two Great Polish dukes with relation to the Henryków monastery with the other Great Polish charters, issued by Duke Władysław Odonic, Duke Przemysł, and Bishop Paul of Poznań, and translated here as Supplementary Documents no. 1, 3–4.

155. *S.U.*, 3:no. 251 (1257), 166–67.

Therefore we, Henry, by the grace of God duke of Silesia, declare to all who now exist and who shall succeed in the future, to whose hearing the present writing will be brought, that in our presence Bogusza and Paul, full brothers, sons of the late Racław of Brukalice, resigned to the lords and brothers in Henryków in Brukalice an inheritance containing the three small hides which had accrued to them in succession by the right of patrimony – to be possessed by the lords and brothers mentioned above forever, by hereditary right, barring any alteration which might come in the future, by [the action of] themselves or their children or any kinsmen whatever. And by way of this exchange and restoration of the inheritance in Brukalice, the aforesaid brothers assigned to Bogusza and Paul, noted above, the same number of hides in the village which is called Siera-kowo[156] in [Great] Poland, to be possessed by hereditary right.

After they held them for some time in legitimate possession, they sold them on their own initiative for 28 silver marks to the much mentioned brothers, their lords, to be possessed by hereditary right, subject to this condition: that if Bogusza and Paul should wish to redeem these goods, they will in the future be able to do so with respect to the hides possessed in [Great] Poland – but not, under any circumstances, their children or affines. While the goods in Brukalice, whatever circumstances arise, neither they, nor their heirs, or any kinsmen whatsoever will be able to redeem in the future – but the aforesaid house shall keep these goods by hereditary right, in eternal peace.

In order herefore that the arrangement fixed before us not be frivolously revoked in the future because of doubt among the ignorant, we caused the present writing to be strengthened by the corroboration of our seal. These things were done in Wrocław on the Sunday *Ad te levavi* [December 2], in the year of the Lord 1257, in the presence of these [persons]: Count John castellan of Ryczyn, Count Michael the judge, Master Gocwin, Count Sulisław Redzek, with Count Michael Daleboro-wic and Andrew Hugonic, who were the managers of this matter,[157] and from among the [court] servitors (*de servientibus*), Henzo son of Ilik, Simon, Guido, Jucha, Pakosław, Zdzieszyc, Stanisław the *subcamerarius*, and very many others. Given by the hand of lord Otto, writer of our court.
Here ends the privilege.

Here, lords and brothers, is shown to you the reason why you possess a third part of Brukalice from the oft-named men, Bogusza and Paul. We shall say a bit more about the deeds described above, so that our successors may be able to answer according to the order of reason anyone making a claim against them.

156. An alternative name for Ochla.

157. That is, representatives of the parties entrusted to arrange the transaction that culminated in the charter.

[120] *About a certain Peter, who was born of the mother of Bogusza and Paul, but not of their father.* Let it again be known to those who read this book that after the death of the father of Bogusza and Paul, their mother took [as husband] another man, also by the name of Racław, by whom she bore a son whom she called Peter. This Peter, because he is not a son of the Racław who was mentioned above, or from the stock of the first possessor Boguchwał the Czech, has no regard to the inheritance in Brukalice. Hence, lords and brothers, if he himself, or someone from among his descendants, wishes to disturb you, you can answer him according to the reason recorded here.

[121] *Likewise, you have a hide and a half there from Bogusza and Paul, the reason for which deed we will describe.* Observe carefully that we have described three sons of the aforesaid Boguchwał Brukał. The first was Racław – about whose (that is Racław's) sons, Bogusza and Paul, we have shown adequately the reason why you possess a third part there in Brukalice from them. Now we omit Boguchwał's second son, James by name, and will produce an account of Boguchwał's third son, Mścisław.

This Mścisław begat by his legitimate wife a son whom he called James. When this James was ten years old, his father Mścisław passed away. After he died, James's mother took [as husband] another man, a certain Czech by the name of Mirsław, which Mirsław the Czech brought up the stepson James, just mentioned, until the age of adolescence. In the meantime, he begat by his wife (that is to say, James's mother) four sons. This, lords and brothers, we wrote down for this reason: that you may know that because the sons of the aforesaid Mirsław were not born from the stock of Boguchwał the Czech, the first possessor of Brukalice, they have nothing by way of a claim to the inheritance there.

[122] *About the death of James, son of Mścisław.* Let it be known that the aforesaid James, son of Mścisław, passed away without ever having taken a wife and without heir, so his part of this inheritance accrued to his cousins, Bogusza and Paul, [and it comprised] half the holding of the aforesaid James.

[123] *Here we have just told about [Boguchwał's] third son Mścisław. Now we will tell about the second son of Boguchwał, whom we omitted above, by the name of James.* This James, just mentioned, was Boguchwał the Czech's second-born. After the father – Boguchwał – passed away, this same James took a wife and begat by her a son whom he called Peter. After his cousin's brother (that is to say James, son of Mścisław) passed away, this Peter, son of the said James, also received half of this James's holding. Here is the reason why the much mentioned brothers, Bogusza and Paul, since both were born [...].[158]

---

158. The text breaks off.

The *Henryków Book*: Book Two

Here begins the treatise introducing the second book about the foundation of this cloister.

[124] No one can set a foundation beyond the one that has been set, which is Christ Jesus.[1] Here is that proven and precious cornerstone placed at the foundation of the Church, upon which every built edifice grows into a holy temple in the Lord.[2] On this original stone, our first and foremost fathers, brought forth into this place of holy observance, cast all of their power and knowledge, and so – having placed the spring of this monastery in a lofty poverty upon the poor [body of] Christ – shining with faith, firm in hope, and aflame with love, they courageously erected the workshop of Christ for as long as it may endure.

[125] And thus in the year of the Lord 1227, on the fifth [day before the] ides of June [June 9], the men – revered in a sanctity of virtues, precocious in customs, serene in conversation, quick to run along the path of God's commands – that is to say, lord Henry, the first abbot of this cloister, and his remaining helpers in Christ, Bodo, Peter, Arnold, Burchard, Adelmann, Berthold the Jew,[3] Witigo, and Henry, departed from the Holy Eden of the monastery of Lubiąż for this place – then quite savage and covered with many forests – and not only did they furrow the earth here by hoe and plowshare, and sustain themselves by eating bread [they had baked] by the sweat of their brow,[4] but, because they were worthy of it that, thanks to them, the flower of the Cistercian Order (which, until the day of the Last Judgment, is the fragrance of [eternal] life in [temporal] life[5] for many thousands of souls) might be planted in this place, they also watered their cheeks with the tears of a joyous spirit – inasmuch as, according to the Prophet, their tears would be their spiritual bread and food, by day and by night.[6] And although the names of some of the original monks are unknown

---

1. 1 Cor. 3:11.

2. 1 Kings 5:17.

3. Although the force and meaning of a nickname like this is always difficult to identify, we seem to have an instance here of a convert, or a descendant of a convert to Christianity from Judaism. Like the few other fascinating glimpses into the presence and role of Jews in Poland before the 1260s, this detail (if indeed it refers to Judaism at all) is unique, and therefore cannot be situated in some broader context.

4. Gen. 3:19.

5. 2 Cor. 2:16.

6. Ps. 79:6.

because of oblivion and cannot be placed here, yet they should firmly be believed as correctly inscribed in the Book of Life.[7]

Oh, copious mercy of divine goodness, which has in the beginning taken care to bring hither such reverend fathers, powerful in virtue, happily speaking the Word of God, so as to sustain in this place a pediment of so famous an observance [as the Cistercian Order], and whom a humble and glad obedience in Christ propelled to this: that, with God's cooperation, signs and miracles have truly followed that obedience! About the holiness and the reverence of such and so distinguished men, I decline to write more, out of a humble fear that the indignity of the writer may not disfigure the dignity of the saints.

[126] How (that is, by what persons) this house was founded, or, if you please, in what way it was endowed, or augmented by purchase of tiny possessions, with the various circumstances that accompanied this, since its origin in the year of the Lord 1227 until the year of the Lord 1257, is explained splendidly in every detail in the preceding book, written by the venerable lord Peter, late abbot of this monastery, and one of the first builders of this place. But inasmuch as oblivion, or ignorance, is recognized as the mother of error, in order that the aforesaid may not cause our successors to err in some way regarding the circumstances and conditions of the possessions bought for this monastery by the abbots and elders of our house, or granted in alms by gifts of the faithful, after the year of the Lord 1257; and in order that long hence they may be able to answer those who make claims against them based on a fuller truth, I, the least of the brothers, the successor in vows – and also, I hope, in virtue! – of those first [monks] at this monastery, have, long after their death, accepted for the common good the solace of setting out this matter [in writing], so that as soon as the origins of the purchases or gifts are known, and the processes surrounding them described, these possessions can be preserved more quietly, and enhanced with a greater safety.

Therefore, in the name of the Lord, I undertake the treatise about the inheritances recorded below in this fashion: first, about Muszkowice; second, about the six and a half hides of the sons of Dzierżysław; third, about Nietowice; fourth, about Wiesenthal; fifth, about Raczyce; sixth, about the holding of Dalebór; seventh, about the holding of Ścibór and Przybysław his brother in Czesławice; eighth [...].[8]

Here begins the treatise about Muszkowice.

[127] First, about Muszkowice let it be known that this inheritance was [formerly] ducal, and belonged to the prince of the land since long ago. There was in those parts a certain knight John, by the nickname of Osina, who took this

---

7. Phil. 4:3; Apoc. 3:5, 13:8, 20:15, 21:27.
8. The text breaks off.

nickname from his village of Osina, situated near Münsterberg, which is commonly called Nossen;[9] and he was from the kindred of a certain knight by the name of Berold, at one time powerful and famous in this land. This Berold was killed in the great battle which took place near Siboto's village,[10] and is buried here in the monastery. After [the invasion of] the Tatars, who killed the founder of this house, the upright prince Duke Henry II, son of Saint Hedwig,[11] this John exceeded the other knights by a certain [degree of] power [in his standing] near the duke of Wrocław, Henry III, by the nickname the White,[12] son of the said founder of this monastery [Henry II]. And he performed for the same Duke Henry [III] such services that this duke granted to him for his services the inheritance of Muszkowice, to be possessed by proprietary right.

[128] *Under what circumstances Muszkowice accrued to Nikosz.* Afterwards, the same John gave his sole daughter in marriage to a certain noble man by the name of Nikosz, cousin of lords John and Andrew of Wierzbno, and promised him for the daughter's dowry 200 marks of the then-current coin and weight, for which [sum] he pawned his inheritance of Muszkowice to the said Nikosz until he might be able to redeem it from him for the said sum of money. In the course of time, the aforesaid Nikosz with that wife of his begat two sons, Burchard and Jeszko, and so his wife, that is to say the daughter of the said John Osina, paid the debt of human fate and died.[13]

During the intervening years, the aforesaid John bought out his inheritance of Muszkowice from his son-in-law Nikosz for the [sum of] money recalled above. But because he was now very old, and his son-in-law Nikosz was stronger than he in body and kindred, he [i.e., Nikosz] retained the same inheritance violently, and put it to his own uses for the rest of his life. And when Nikosz

9. This is another example of a "Germanization" of a place name (Chapter 101, nn. 116–17), this time by a change from a Polish word, *Osina*, to something that can be pronounced in German, *Nossen*.

10. This is another reference to the series of conflicts that ensued between the descendants of Duke Henry II after the mid-thirteenth century. The battle was fought in 1277 near a locality called Sieroszów, under lordship of a knight named Siboto. It pitted the supporters of Dukes Henry IV the Righteous against those of Bolesław II the Bald. Grodecki, *Liber* (1949), 156, n. 63.

11. As in the first section of the *Book*, Henry II the Pious is still remembered primarily for the manner in which he died. Now, however, he is also identified with the name of his mother, Duchess Hedwig of Bavaria, wife of Henry I the Bearded. She was instrumental in the endowment of several monastic communities in Silesia, especially the convent of the Cistercian nuns at Trzebnica. *Rodowód*, 1:76–77; Joseph Gottschalk, *St. Hedwig, Herzogin von Schlesien* (Cologne and Graz: Böhlau Verlag, 1964); Andrzej Marzec, "Henryk I Brodaty" [Henry I the Bearded], *Piastowie*, 375–86, at 375, 386.

12. Henry III the White, duke of Wrocław, was born between 1227 and 1230; he died in 1266; *Rodowód*, 1:109–11, 118–22; Tomasz Jurek, "Henryk III Biały" [Henry III the White], *Piastowie*, 415–17; Grodecki, *Liber* (1949), 98, n. 34.

13. As elsewhere in the *Book*, the author here suggests that she died in childbirth.

died, a certain knight, Stosz, who lived in Zarzyca (that is, in Rychów near Targowica), and who had [as wife] the aforesaid Nikosz's uterine sister, assumed for
himself the care of Nikosz's sons, Burchard and Jeszko, at the instance of his
wife (who was the said boys' aunt), with their other friends also eagerly requesting this. And when the aforesaid boys reached legitimate age, one of them, namely
Jeszko, took a legitimate wife, daughter of the honest knight, Vincent of Kus-
maltz, while Burchard, his brother, remained without a legitimate [wife].

[129] *How Muszkowice returned to John Osina.* While these things were going on,
already during the reign of the renowned Duke Henry IV (who is called the
Righteous because of the many things that he virtuously effected),[14] the oft-mentioned John Osina, discerning a suitable time, lodged a claim before the same
Duke Henry against his two grandsons, the aforesaid Burchard and Jeszko, [and
alleged] that they were in possession of his inheritance of Muszkowice violently,
and he demanded a judgment to be made for him about this at once. Thus, after
Burchard and Jeszko were summoned to judgment, the case was argued until the
sentence was rendered for John Osina, who was then also fully restored into
possession of the aforesaid inheritance by the duke's *camerarii*.[15] After these
[proceedings] were concluded, the aforesaid Burchard and Jeszko, scarcely able
to bear the sentence pronounced against them, acted unwisely, and, removing
themselves to Duke Bernard (who at that time reigned in Löwenberg, and was a
cousin of Duke [Henry IV] the Righteous),[16] burned down the said inheritance
of Muszkowice, and left it completely desolate for fully five years. Since they also
committed other spoils, robberies, and thefts in the land, their faults grew
famous, they were outlawed, and, in the course of their outlawry, one of them,
that is to say Burchard, was caught and beheaded.

[130] *That John Osina sold Muszkowice to the duke.* The aforesaid John Osina,
grieving over his inheritance of Muszkowice, so desolate, began to think diligently about how he might extract something of use from it. And, remembering
bygone events (that is to say that the same Duke [Henry IV] the Righteous had
taken away the village of Szydłów, situated on the other side of the Odra, one
mile from Brzeg, from him – about which village the same duke claimed that John
had unduly usurped it for himself during his boyhood), he offered the inheritance of Muszkowice to the same duke for sale. The duke bought it for 120

14. Henry IV the Righteous, the only son Henry III the White, was born in 1257 or
1258, and died in 1290; *Rodowód*, 1:161–63; Anna Waśko, "Henryk IV Prawy (Probus)"
[Henry IV the Righeous], *Piastowie*, 427–431.

15. The *camerarii* were local ducal officials with assorted police duties; Chapter 111
above, and Piotr Górecki, "*Viator* to *ascriptitius*: Rural Economy, Lordship, and the
Origins of Serfdom in Medieval Poland," *Slavic Review* 42 (1983), 14–35, at 28.

16. Duke Bernard the Agile was a son of Duke Bolesław II the Bald. He was born
between 1252 and 1258, assumed the title of duke of Löwenberg in 1281, and died in
1285. *Rodowód*, 1:151–53; Anna Waśko, "Bernard Zwinny" [Bernard the Agile], *Piastowie*,
425; Grodecki, *Liber* (1949), 158, n. 64.

marks of black silver in Wrocław weight,[17] and furthermore he restored to this John the village of Szydłów – not, however, by reason of purchase, or exchange made for Muszkowice, but in the name of grace – in order that Jeszko, John's grandson, would not in any way disturb John about this village, [which was] given to John as if by exchange.

[131] *About the purchase of Muszkowice, made by the abbot with the duke.* After the aforenoted inheritance of Muszkowice rightfully accrued to this prince by this purchase, Merciful God, Who saw that this convent was expanding for His glory, also affectionately arranged for the enhancement of His servants' happiness. While inspiring the prince to offer this inheritance to the abbot for purchase, He also inspired the lord [abbot] to buy it, toward much future comfort of the convent.

Discerning this, Satan, envious of the salvation of all good [persons], prompted some among the citizens of Münsterberg – may they not be disciples of eternal perdition! – to incite an honest man, a brother and a special friend of this house, Conrad, hereditary judge there [in Münsterberg],[18] to deprive this convent of 200 marks in the purchase of the aforesaid inheritance. Because, just as the abbot was finally about to buy this inheritance for 500 marks in current coin and weight, the said Conrad came up to the prince, and resolutely offered 600 marks for it. Hearing which, the lord abbot, although considerably disturbed, yet, as a magnanimous man, believing in God, returned to the prince, and, aware that the matter could not be closed in any other way, promised the prince 700 marks, and thus securely consummated the purchase.

[132] *About the liberty, and the definition of the boundaries, of the inheritance of Muszkowice.* After the purchase was completed, the lord duke himself resigned the aforesaid inheritance, forever free from all services, to the abbot, and, after an interval of a few days, with a pleased countenance, he enclosed it within boundaries by performing a circuit around it in person, to enhance a firm possession by this convent – something, however, that he had never done before, nor did afterwards. The entire aforesaid purchase, resignation, and gift of liberty, and also John Osina's renunciation and annulment of his [written] instruments, if he had any, are attested by the aforesaid duke's solemn privilege, whose tenor is noted here below, word for word, in the witness of truth.

17. This meant low-grade silver, presumably measured out in the old, "thin" pence (*denarii*), after several generations of debasement; Grodecki, *Liber* (1949), 159, n. 65.

18. A hereditary judge of a town at the outset of the fourteenth century was the chief official of a town established according to German law, who inherited and bequeathed his judicial office along with several other formal capacities. This position was one of the adaptations of the multiple roles of the German settlement entrepreneurs – village bailiffs and advocates – who were rewarded for their functions with a wide seigneurial, governmental, and economic authority over the units of settlement which they headed. Plezia, 5:1089–94, *s.v. iudex*, especially cols. 1090–91.

[133] *The privilege concerning Muszkowice.*[19]

In the name of the Lord, amen. Prudent antiquity has decreed that, lest they slip away from the memory of men through the flow of time, those things which are accomplished temporally by men should be made eternal by authentic writings.

For this reason we, Henry [IV], by the grace of God duke of Silesia and lord of Wrocław, wish it to be known to [all persons] present as well as future, that, in the presence of our barons, Count John called Osina, our knight, has willingly and in good health sold us his goods commonly called Muszkowice, situated near Münsterberg, with their appurtenances – that is to say, mills, meadows, forests, and pastures, as they are marked around the circumference of their limits and boundaries – for 120 marks in our weight and of black silver,[20] freely renouncing every right which he had or could have in these goods, for himself and for his heirs. There, he also cheerfully accepted the above sum of money, [which had been] promised to him by us, and we assigned it to be paid out to him by the venerable abbot of Henryków at specified times.

But later, as we heard, the same knight changed his wish, and said that he had not sold the said goods willingly at all. And because it is not fitting that someone who has clearly made a declaration in his [live] voice should weaken in the same matter, after we, wishing to investigate the truth, summoned this John into our presence, he again, asked about these matters, answered as before: that he had sold us the said goods willingly, and that, by his free will, he [now] withdraws, and has [formerly] withdrawn, for himself and for his heirs, from every right and action which appeared to pertain to him in these goods – so that we may put this inheritance to our own or anyone else's uses, without any difficulty. The aforesaid John also promised us that before the nearest Christmas he would faithfully present letters or [written] instruments concerning this inheritance which he had received from our father of good memory or from ourselves. But if he should be unable to gather them in any way, he has [in that eventuality] utterly renounced every right he had, or could have, in these goods, and every action which seemed from the said letters to belong to him and his heirs, by expressing with his hand his faith about the matters set out above.[21]

---

19. *S.U.*, 5:no. 13 (1282), 12–13; with a variant added in Irgang's edition.

20. Here and elsewhere, marks assessed "in our weight," or "accoding to our weight," mean according to the weight (or quantity of silver pence) that defines a mark in a particular duchy, in this case the part of Silesia governed by Henry IV. Similarly, marks could be assessed according to the "weight of" some central locality (Wrocław, for example), that is, according to the weight or quantity of pence customary in that locality and its region.

21. That is, by swearing an oath.

After a passage of time, when many [persons] requested us many times to let the said inheritance be sold and bought, we – observing that it adjoined the aforementioned cloister of Henryków, and not so much concerned with their future good as fearing the insolence of evil [persons at present] – out of that sincere depth of the love by which we have always most kindly worshipped them above all others, have sold this inheritance to the venerable lord Frederick, abbot of the cloister described above, and to his convent, in order that the cult of divine service may be enhanced there for the glory of God's holiness, for 700 silver marks in current coin – transferring [it] to them, to be possessed forever by the same right, lordship, and liberty as they possess and retain their remaining goods in our land, according to the form [defined] at the foundation of their church.

Done in Wrocław, in the year of the Lord 1282, in the presence of these [persons]: lord Hartlieb abbot of Lubiąż, Counts Michael castellan of Wrocław, Racław of Ryczyn called Drzemlik, Budziwój castellan of Sądowel, Andrew of Wierzbno our marshal, Henry called Spiegel, and very many other trustworthy [persons]. Given by the hand of lord Bernard, provost of the church of Meißen, our chancellor, on the fourth [day before the] calends of May [April 28].

[134] *About the renunciation made by Jeszko, Burchard's brother, regarding Muszkowice.* Jeszko (brother of Burchard whom we have mentioned above, and grandson of the said John Osina), upon hearing how rightfully the duke had bought the aforesaid inheritance, and in addition sold it to the abbot and convent of Henryków, began to solicit him [i.e., the duke] through friends and noted [persons] that he might deign to receive him back into his grace. Finally, overcome by the barons' prayers, the duke restored his grace upon the same Jeszko.

Having regained grace, he [i.e., Jeszko] came into the lord duke's presence, gave thanks, willingly resigned to the duke the aforesaid inheritance of Muszkowice, and renounced, for himself and for all his descendants, the benefit of every action and right which he may have had or could have in the same. And the same Jeszko saw to it that the instrument of this renunciation, made in his name, was subscribed with the seals of the many nobles and honorable persons who then attended. Jeszko offered this renunciation, recorded and sealed in this way, to the duke, and earnestly requested that it be authenticated under the aforesaid duke's seal – which, inclined by Jeszko's prayers, the duke did. That renunciation is briefly noted here below, in these words.[22]

[135] *The privilege concerning Jeszko's renunciation of Muszkowice.*[23]

In the name of the Lord, amen. I, Jeszko, son of Nikosz, brother of Burchard of Muszkowice, desire that all present and future [persons] who

---

22. The author implies here that the subsequent text is an abbreviation of Jeszko's privilege, not the privilege itself.

23. *S.U.*, 5:no. 14 (1282), 14–15.

have notice of the present [writings] know that, in return for the grace restored upon me in answer to his barons' prayers by my lord Henry [IV], illustrious duke of Silesia and lord of Wrocław – which I had forfeited forever because of my sundry and manifest offenses, and because of the outlawry to which I had been condemned for my well-ascertained faults, and [because] I had, forever and for just cause, by reason of judgment and law, and by the requirement of the custom of the whole land, lost [the right to remain in] this land – I transfer, freely give, and resign to the same lord of mine the inheritance commonly called Muszkowice, with all the uses and revenues pertaining to it, as it had been marked around the circumference of its limits and boundaries, not compelled, not constrained, but by my spontaneous will, forever renouncing for myself and for all my descendants every right and action regarding the same inheritance.

In fuller evidence and eternal strength of this matter, I strengthened the present letter with the seals of the lords recorded below, who were also present at this gift and renunciation, and who, inclined by my prayers, affixed their seals. The witnesses are the following lords: Michael of Sośnica castellan of Wrocław, Peter of Groznowe, James doctor of the laws,[24] Conrad advocate of Münsterberg, Henry Spiegel, Baldwin notary of the court of my illustrious lord the duke of Silesia, and very many trustworthy others. Done and given in Wrocław, in the year of the Lord 1282, on the sixth [day before the] ides of May [May 10].

[136] *About the aforesaid Jeszko's death.* When all the aforesaid things were arranged in this way, the oft-mentioned Jeszko kept the the lord duke's grace that was restored upon him for a short time, but, after again persisting in pillage and robbery, he was captured, put on trial, and struck by a capital sentence.

[137] *About the fire set in Muszkowice by the aforesaid Jeszko's son.* The aforesaid Jeszko left four sons, that is to say, Burchard, Nicholas, Przecław, and Jeszko, and two daughters, namely Catherine and Hanka. In the year of the Lord 1302, during the Lord's Advent, one of these four brothers, namely Burchard, secretly burned down one sheep-fold with 313 choice sheep that belonged to the convent in Muszkowice. But, by God's judgment, barely a month later he was suddenly and miserably killed by Arnold of Owe in Strzelce beyond Opole, on account of a horse which he had stolen from the same Arnold. I have discussed the blaze inflicted upon the house by this Burchard for the following reason. If his brothers should ever attempt anything against the convent, this fire shall be used as a defense against them, inasmuch as it is quite probable that Burchard had burned down this sheep-fold with his brothers' counsel and assent – because a claim by many about one matter proves their counsel and assent.

---

24. A *doctor legum* was an expert in canon and Roman law, according both to general medieval and Polish usage; Plezia, 3:811, *s.v. doctor.*

[138] *About the death of John Osina's sons.* Nor did I think that I should pass over the fact that the aforesaid knight John Osina had two sons, Andrew and Jeszko, who, while their father was alive, inflicted grave threats upon this house because of Muszkowice, nor did their father compel them to stop. But God, the abyss of Whose judgments[25] no one can penetrate, silenced the aforesaid two brothers when He wished, in this way. Because of the homicides they had perpetrated one time on Easter Day – by killing three citizens of Münsterberg in their grove near Little Nossen[26] – He caught up with them at a certain hour, and He hastened the judgment (as though with the sons of Babylon) in such a way that, by the rigor of justice, their heads were cut off, under a single judge, the most Christian prince Duke Bolko,[27] by a single executioner, on a single day, and in a single place, Reichenbach.[28]

[139] *About the new clearings* (novalia)[29] *in Muszkowice.* Let it also be known that, although the tithe in Muszkowice belongs to the custodian of the [episcopal] church of Saint John in Wrocław, yet there are also newly cleared goods (*bona novalia*) there from which the convent is not obliged to pay tithe – that is to say, from the fields which have been created out of the meadow and thicket [situated] toward Krzelków, and from the field situated between the hops and the hamlet in which the gardeners live, and similarly from the gardens – because there the convent has cut down the beautiful forest extending up to the farmstead, and created new clearings. Within these new clearings are equally encompassed the gardens and the hamlet with the remaining field, up to the hops [situated] near the road from the left as one goes toward the cloister from the farmstead. These things said about Muszkowice suffice. *Here ends [the account] of Muszkowice.*

25. Perhaps a paraphrase of Ps. 35:7.

26. See n. 9 above.

27. Bolko I, a son of Bolesław II the Bald, was born between 1252 and 1256, and died in 1301; *Rodowód*, 1:148–51; Lidia Korczak, "Bolko I," *Piastowie*, 575–77; Grodecki, *Liber* (1949), 165, n. 66.

28. The appearance of a specialized executioner in a town at the turn of the thirteenth and fourteenth centuries is one of several traces of the proliferation of judicial and enforcement institutions documented in this period, largely centered in towns, and patterned on German law. See the introductory essay above, nn. 213, 217, 273, 276–78; Hanna Zaremska, *Niegodne rzemiosło. Kat w społeczeństwie Polski XIV–XVI w.* [The unworthy craft: the executioner in Polish society between the fourteenth and the sixteenth centuries] (Warsaw: Państwowe Wydawnictwo Naukowe, 1986), 15; see also Zaremska, *Banici w średniowiecznej Europie* [Outlaws in medieval Europe] (Warsaw: Semper, 1993), 136–42.

29. The word *novalia* means either the tithes owed from newly cleared arable, or that newly cleared arable itself, that is, new clearings. Following Grodecki, I translate it here according to the second possibility, because that option greatly simplifies what this paragraph says: namely, that the monastery is exempted from the payment of tithe, otherwise due to the bishops of Wrocław, in the areas of arable which it has recently created, and which are identified here.

Here begins the treatise about the six and a half hides of Jeszko and Mojko, sons of Dzierżysław.

[140] Second, this treatise moves onto the six and a half hides of Jeszko and Mojko, sons of Dzierżysław of Byczeń. About this Dzierżysław it should briefly be noted that he originated from Bohemia, and took a wife from the land of Bautzen, sister of the most illustrious man lord Bernard of Kamenz, later bishop of Meißen.[30] This Dzierżysław with his aforesaid wife begat three sons, Dzierżko, Jeszko, and Mojko. While the aforesaid Dzierżysław was establishing his village of Czerńczyce (which is commonly called Frowin's Village) according to German law,[31] he retained for himself six and a half large hides outside the [land] measure[d out as the arable] of the said village, in its farther portion, in the fields and forests. And in the aforesaid village, by [permission of] the lord bishop, he secured the payment to his parish priest of one fierton[32] from each hide annually on the feast of Saint Martin in Krzelków as tithe.

[141] *How the aforesaid hides accrued to the cloister.* After the aforesaid Dzierżysław was killed, when his sons Dzierżko, Jeszko, and Mojko divided their possessions among themselves, the aforesaid six and a half hides were allotted into the holdings of Jeszko and Mojko, who both, after a passage of time, cut down the entire forest which had stood until then in one part of the aforesaid hides, leaving only the tree stumps. After they did this, by equal counsel – and also with the consent of their brother Dzierżko – they sold the said hides to the lord abbot and the convent of this monastery. That is to say, Jeszko sold his portion, which was larger, for a hundred marks, and Mojko sold his for fifty marks, in current coin and weight, adding that the lord abbot ought to pay the aforesaid parish priest the fiertons due as tithe from each hide which had just been cleared, annually, just as the peasants of Frowin's Village have paid by custom.

When all these [agreements] were made known before the righteous Duke Henry IV, the duke himself ratified each and all, resigning those hides to the lord abbot and the convent, to be possessed freely, and also confirming the aforesaid sale and purchase with all its circumstances by letters patent, in these words.

30. Bernard was bishop of Meißen between 1293 and 1296; Pius Bonifacius Gams, *Series episcoporum ecclesiae catholicae* (1886, repr. Graz: Akademische Druck- u. Verlagsanstalt, 1957), 291. Meißen was a principality in one of the regions of intensive German colonization between the Elbe and the Odra, just west of Silesia, during the twelfth and thirteenth centuries, and Kamenz was one of the towns of that principality (Map 1).

31. Here is another example of a "Germanization" of the place name, and presumably of the population living in the locality it designates; nn. 9, 26 above.

32. A fierton (*ferto*) was one-quarter of a mark, and, as a unit of account, included 60 pence in the Polish duchies; Ryszard Kiersnowski, *Wstęp do numizmatyki polskiej wieków średnich* [Introduction to Polish medieval numismatics] (Warsaw: Państwowe Wydawnictwo Naukowe, 1964), 152–53, and Peter Spufford, *Money and Its Use in Medieval Europe* (Cambridge: Cambridge University Press, 1988), 212–13 (n. 6).

[142] *The privilege about Jeszko's part.*[33]
In the name of the Lord, amen. It pleases us to be inclined by our subjects' just desires, and to be so well-disposed in confirming matters agreed upon by them that while we vigilantly attend to their conveniences, we may also observe them to be ever watchful for the enhancement of our honor.

Therefore we, Henry [IV], by the grace of God duke of Silesia and lord of Wrocław, publicly declare to those present that Jeszko, son of the late Dzierżysław of Byczeń, standing in our presence, declared that he has sold four large hides situated near the village of Muszkowice which belonged to him by a true title of property, to the religious man lord Frederick abbot in Henryków and to his monastery, with the consent of his brothers, namely Dzierżko and Mojko, for a hundred marks of common weight and coin. The same Jeszko gave and conveyed to this abbot and monastery the value of the said hides that exceeds the aforesaid [sum of] money, for the remedy of his father's soul and for his own sins, with the good will and consent of his brother. Jeszko also added that, by reason of tithe, the said lord abbot and convent are obliged to give the rector of the church in Krzelków a fierton of silver annually from each cleared hide.[34] Each party requested our kindness to confirm this sale and conveyance.

We also, inclined by the prayers of the seller as well as the buyers, by our usual benevolence confirm the aforesaid sale, abdication, and resignation, duly and rightfully made public before us, by means of the present [writings], declaring it fixed and joyful. In witness and fuller evidence of this matter, we ordered that the present letters, strengthened by our seal, be written. Done in Wrocław, in the year of the Lord 1288, in the presence of these witnesses, summoned to this [occasion]: Peter provost of the church of the Holy Cross, James custodian there, Simon the Gaul, Pakosław the marshal, Hermann of Eichelburn, Henry Blesow. Given by the hand of Master Louis notary of our court, on the sixteenth [day before the] calends of April [March 17].

[143] *The privilege about the holding of Mojko, son of Dzierżysław.*[35]
In the name of the Lord, amen. It pleases us to be inclined by our subjects' just desires, and to be so well-disposed in confirming matters agreed upon by

---

33. *S.U.*, 5:no. 370 (1288), 292–93.

34. That is, the rights of a parish church to receive tithes from an area granted to the monastic estate. As a result of the grant, the tithe revenues were either appropriated by the monastery (usually with compensation to parish priests and other prior possessors), or were not appropriated, and continued to support the prior possessor. The provision for the parish priest of Muszkowice is the latter case. For a story of a monastic appropriation of a parish priest's tithe revenue, see the segment of Abbot Peter's account of Skalice in Chapters 65–68.

35. *S.U.*, 5:no. 371 (1288), 293.

them that while we vigilantly attend to their conveniences, we may also observe them to be ever watchful for the enhancement of our honor.

Therefore we, Henry [IV], by the grace of God duke of Silesia and lord of Wrocław, publicly declare to those present that Mojko, son of the late Dzierżysław of Byczeń, standing in our presence, has declared that he sold two and a half large hides situated near Muszkowice, which belonged to him by a true title of property, to the religious man Frederick, abbot in Henryków, and to his monastery, with the consent of his brothers, namely Dzierżko and Mojko, for fifty marks of the weight and [amount of] coin of Wrocław. The same Mojko gave and conveyed to this abbot and monastery just aforesaid the value of the said hides that exceeds the aforesaid [sum of] money, for the remedy of his father's soul and for his own sins, with his brothers' good will and consent – with this reservation: that from each of the aforesaid cleared hides a fierton of silver shall be paid as tithe each year to the rector of the church in Krzelków, by the said abbot or by his convent. Each party requested our kindness to confirm this sale.

And we, inclined by the prayers of the seller as well as the buyers, by our usual benevolence confirm the aforesaid sale, abdication, and resignation, duly and righfully made public before us, deeming it fixed and joyful. In witness of this matter, we strengthened the present writing with our seal. Done in Wrocław, in the year of the Lord 1288, in the presence of these [persons]: Peter provost of the church of the Holy Cross, James custodian there, Simon the Gaul, Pakosław the marshal, Hermann of Eichelburn, Henry Blesow. Given by the hand of Master Louis notary of our court, on the sixteenth [day before the] calends of April [March 17].

[144] *About the tithe from the same hides.* About these aforesaid hides let it be known that, out of them, three – in which the forest had been newly cut down, and the stumps left standing – were preserved, so that the forest might grow back on them. And from the other three and a half [hides] – which were cultivated, and which, by God's grace, are cultivated today, to which also belongs the field called the Garden of the Beasts – one common mark shall be paid to the parish priest of Krzelków in tithe annually, on the feast of Saint Martin. And while only four and a quarter fiertons may accrue to the same parish priest from four and a quarter hides, yet he shall also receive an additional half a fierton on the profits which he might get from the peasants, if they possessed the aforesaid hides. Concerning the payment of the aforesaid mark, a privilege of the lord bishop óf Wrocław, John Romka,[36] is kept [by the monastery], whose content is noted here as a precaution for posterity.

[145] *The tithe privilege concerning the three and a half hides in Muszkowice.*[37]

---

36. John was bishop of Wrocław between 1292 and 1301; Jerzy Kłoczowski, "Jan zwany Romką" [John, nicknamed Romka], *P.S.B.*, 10:432–33.

37. *S.U.*, 6:no. 368 (1298), 290.

In the name of the Lord, amen. In order that the truth of an accomplished deed may be known among present [persons] and that it also may enjoy certainty among future [persons], for that reason we, John, by the grace of God bishop of Wrocław, wish all who have notice of the present [writings] to know that lord Henry, rector of the church of Krzelków, standing in our presence, has declared that he has accepted for himself one silver mark, in the weight and coin of Wrocław, as adequate reparation for the tithe [due] from three and a half hides that belong to the the village of Czerńczyce – which [hides] the lord abbot and his convent of Henryków have bought from Jeszko the knight (son of Count Dzierżysław, late heir of Krzelków of happy memory), and from which [village, i.e., Czerńczyce] he [i.e., Rector Henry] used to receive single fiertons from single hides as tithe. The abbot and the convent of the said monastery of Henryków promised before us to give and pay the same lord Henry and his successors this mark forever and without hindrance, always on the feast of Saint Martin each year, on account of the aforesaid church of Krzelków.

In order that no uncertainty about this may arise in the future, and no difficulty may be inflicted (that is to say, in order that the parish priest may not demand more, and the abbot and convent attempt to give less) we – declaring his arrangement, lawfully made public before us, secure and joyful, and confirming it with the eternal protection of the present writing – have, in response to the same parties' request, caused the present charter to be issued in evidence of the same matter, and to be strengthened by the protection of our seal. Done and given in Otmuchów, on the eighteenth [day before the] calends of January [December 15], in the year of the Lord 1298, in the presence of the lords: Walter the chancellor and John the notary, canons of Wrocław; James of Lubusz and Koźmian of Opole, canons; Henry of Paczków, John the parish priest of Kryniczno, and many others.

[146] Because these aforesaid hides were situated near Muszkowice, immediately after the sale they were joined to the aforesaid inheritance by the lord abbot, and are [now] cultivated with it, in the same way. *Here ends [the account] of the seven and a half hides of Dzierżysław's sons.*

Here begins the treatise about Nietowice.

[147] Third, we should touch upon Nietowice. About this inheritance let it be known that it has seven small hides. There was an heir of the said inheritance by the name of Stephen of Kobylagłowa[38] and by the nickname of Kotka. He was

---

38. Perhaps a son, and surely a successor, of the heir of Kobylagłowa with the same name whom Abbot Peter documented as an adult in 1234, in his account of Głębowice (Chapter 85 above). For the two men, see Marek Cetwiński, *Rycerstwo śląskie do końca XIII*

called Kotka for the reason that, just as a cat roams about at nighttime and hunts her prey,[39] so he hunted what belonged to others in nocturnal roamings.

In the year of the Lord 1278, this Kotka sold two hides of the aforesaid inheritance to two citizens of Münsterberg, that is to say, Tammo of Wide and John of Paczków, for thirty common marks, on this condition: that the same citizens or their successors should from the aforesaid hides pay the aforesaid Stephen or his successors five fiertons of current coin and two pairs of leather high boots annually, on the feast of Saint Martin, in rent; and that in this way they would possess these hides free from all [other] payments and services, and Stephen himself or his successors should present to the prince of the land[40] full services [due] from these two hides together with the remaining five [hides]. And although the privilege which Stephen himself issued to the aforesaid citizens concerning the sale of these hides may contain [a record of] two and a half hides, nevertheless a measurement conducted through the same hides later revealed that there were two hides there, and nothing more. I took care to note the content of this privilege here, for the memory of our successors.

[148] *Stephen's privilege, issued to Tammo of Wide and John of Paczków, concerning the two hides in Nietowice.*[41]

Stephen of Kobylagłowa to Tammo of Wide, John of Paczków, and their heirs, [grants] the present writing, to be effective forever. Because, like a river, agreements of the mortals pass away and perish, it is useful that they be confirmed by writings and witnesses, so they may not pass away.

I therefore make it known to all who inspect this letter that, with the favor and counsel of my friends,[42] I sold to the aforesaid two men two and a half hides in Nietowice for thirty silver marks, to be settled according to German law, and to be possessed freely, without any [obligation of] service; provided, however, that every year they should pay me and my boys five fiertons of the common weight and silver from the said fields on the feast of Saint Martin. Furthermore, if by chance my villagers (*villani*) initiate a claim with their settlers (*coloni*), the said Tammo and John, or their heirs, shall judge [the litigants] according to their law, whatever kind of case it may be; and if [a claim is raised] the other way around, I shall subject [the dispute] to my laws. For this, each year they shall honor me with two pairs of leather high boots.

Therefore, in order that there may be no doubt among our successors concerning these [provisions], I issued the present writing – confirmed by the placement of the seal of my paternal uncle Strzeżywój and of my own

w. Biogramy i rodowody [Silesian knighthood through the end of the thirteenth century: biograms and genealogies] (Wrocław: Zakład Narodowy im. Ossolińskich, 1982), 183.

39. The nickname means a female cat; *S.Sp.*, 3:364, *s.v. kotka.*

40. A common expression for the duke.

41. *S.U.*, 4:no. 348 (1278), 230–31.

42. The word here is, again, *amici*; Chapter 86, n. 98.

seal – to the aforesaid men and their successors. The witnesses of this sale are: Count John of Osina, Count Baldwin, lord Conrad advocate in Münsterberg, Martin his brother, Henry advocate of Frankenberg, Henry of Jawor, and very many others. Given in Münsterberg by the hand of Lawrence, writer in Münsterberg, in the year of the Lord 1278, on the day of Saint Nicholas [December 6].

[149] *How the said hides accrued to the cloister.* After a passage of time, Tammo and John, the aforesaid citizens, sold the same hides to the Hospitallers in Münsterberg, who later sold them to a certain citizen there by the name of Mencelin, who took [as wife] a daughter of a certain fellow citizen of his by the name of Arnold of Frankenberg, and begat by her a son by the name of Tammo, and a daughter by the name of Clara. After Mencelin died, and his wife likewise, Arnold assumed for himself his small grandchildren with the aforesaid two hides, and was made their guardian.[43] And when the same Arnold's grandchildren attained lawful years, Arnold himself bought these hides from them, and later sold them to a certain fellow citizen of his by the name of Hermann Rume, for 24 common marks. This Hermann, having held onto the same hides for a short time, sold them to the lord abbot and the convent of this monastery, in the year of the Lord 1300, on the day of Saint George the Martyr [April 24], for the sum of 24 marks, as was expressed above.

[150] *How the grant of the aforesaid hides accrued to Peter of Lubnów.*[44] In the meantime, as in the course of time one [person] succeeded another in [the possesion of] the said hides, the aforementioned Stephen, the first heir, was beheaded in Lower Głogów because of the plunder which he had committed there.[45] However, he left survivors: one son, Paul by the nickname of Kotka, and one daughter by the name of Paulina, whom a certain youth from Frankenstein named Peter took [as his wife]. He [i.e., Paulina's husband] was allotted the nickname of his father-in-law and of his brother-in-law, so that he was called Peter Kotka.

This Peter lawfully gained for himself the hereditary portion in Nietowice by reason of [marriage to] his wife. And by the consent of Paul, his wife's brother, he gave the lordship and the rent of the aforesaid two hides, [in exchange] for one war-horse, to a certain Peter, called "from Lubnów," then a Polish judge[46] in

---

43. The words, *tutor eorum effectus fuit*, suggests a more active degree of appointment by someone than the more neutral "became," which is how Grodecki translates it.

44. Although the word translated here as "grant," *collatio*, has several rather technical meanings in medieval Latin, one of its meanings is quite straightforward, as grant, gift, or conveyance; Niermeyer, 198, *s.v. collatio*. This rubric is therefore a wordy expression of the simple fact that Peter of Lubnów received the hides.

45. Chapter 147 above.

46. The *iudex polonicalis* was in the early fourteenth century a judge who settled conflicts according to Polish law, a body of rules explicitly different from the rural and urban legal régimes that made up German law; Plezia, 5:1090, *s.v. iudex*.

this frontier region (*confinium*),[47] and a son of the late bailiff of the village of Lubnów – adding this condition: that the same Peter of Lubnów should from now on perform the customary services from the aforesaid two hides to the prince of the land, at suitable times.

[151] *How the remaining five hides of Nietowice accrued to the cloister.* Paul Kotka, who is named above, together with his brother-in-law Peter, sold their remaining five hides in Nietowice to a certain knight, Cieszybór of Czesławice, for 110 marks of common coin and weight. After a few years passed, this Cieszybór sold the same five hides to this convent for the same sum for which he himself had bought them; and he promised that if any demand for ducal service from the aforesaid two hides should arise against the house, for the duration of the time over which he held the remaining five hides, he himself would satisfy the demand, through his own labors and expenditures, without damage to the convent.

[152] *About the claim [made] regarding these two hides by reason of ducal service.* After these things were accomplished, Peter of Lubnów, who had bought the lordship and the rent of the aforesaid two hides for one war-horse, as was said above, gave this lordship [as payment] for [his] debts of fifteen marks, to Nicholas of Watzenrode, then a citizen in Münsterberg. When this was done, two men from Frankenstein [...][48] came up, whose inheritances [together] with Nietowice furnished the duke with a service of one war-horse, and who said that for as long as the aforesaid Cieszybór had possessed Nietowice, they performed full service from Nietowice to the lord duke, seeking no relief [from that service] by reason of the aforesaid two hides. But the lord abbot, accused by them about this, did not give Nicholas of Watzenrode the rent from the aforesaid two hides, unless he [i.e., Nicholas] should satisfy the service [owed the duke]. He also requested Cieszybór to relieve him and the convent from the demand for service from the said two hides, as he [i.e., Cieszybór] had promised.

Finally, by mediation of discrete men, this compromise was arranged: that the lord abbot gave Nicholas eight marks in current pence, and Cieszybór [gave him] five marks, and that Nicholas, from then on and into the future, withdrew in favor of the lord abbot from the lordship and the payment of the said two hides, for himself and for all his successors; and, with the two men from Frankenstein described above, this Nicholas agreed amicably concerning the past service from these hides, giving them three marks – provided, however, that in the future the abbot would unite this service with the remaining inheritance.

[153] *About the resignation from Nietowice, made before lord Hermann of Barboy.* The same Cieszybór, together with his two sons Jeszko and Albert, and with his two

---

47. In translating *in isto confinio* in this way, I follow Grodecki, though the phrase could more simply mean "within this boundary."

48. Grodecki left a space for the names here in the 1949 edition of the text; it was reissued in 1991. The manuscript indeed has a space here of a length of half a line, corresponding to about two dozen characters. See Grodecki, *Liber* (1991), after 225, fol. xxxiv[r].

daughters Obiecka and Bogudarka, thus resigned his inheritance of Nietowice to the abbot and the convent, here at the doors of the cloister, before the noble man lord Hermann of Barboy (then captain of the land on behalf of the illustrious Prince Hermann margrave of Brandenburg),[49] who was at that time guardian of his sister's sons, the princes of this land Bernard, Henry, and Bolko.[50] Because the margrave was then outside the boundaries [of Silesia], and the princes of the land were below age, a privilege concerning the aforesaid inheritance could not be obtained at the time. Many knights were present at the aforesaid resignation, that is to say: lord Albert of Hakeburne, Reinsko of Schwengfeld, Peter his son, Kunmann of Siedlec, Gunther of Kuesburg, Henry of Schildberg, Boruta and his son Nicholas, Henry the Thuringian, and many others. The aforesaid five hides were bought in the year of the Lord 1303, on the Annunciation of the Lord [March 25]. The lord abbot joined these hides with Muszkowice, in order to be spared special labors and outlays in this [part of the estate] as well. *Here ends [the account] of Nietowice.*

Here begins the treatise about Wiesenthal.

[154] Fourth, about Wiesenthal let it be known that this village consists of two inheritances, of which the larger was [formerly] called Wadochowice, the smaller Nieciepła Izba. Ever since they were joined into a single village, this village is commonly called Wiesenthal.[51] This village [formerly] belonged to a certain rather famous knight, Jaksa by name, and for this reason certain Poles still call the village

49. Hermann of Barboy was a governor of the new type, a *starosta*, of Silesia, on behalf of the principality of Brandenburg; this is rendered in Latin as *capitaneus*, and hence my translation, "captain." The *starostowie* were first instituted in Bohemia; they were transferred to the Polish duchies during the rule over most of them by the Czech king, Václav II. See Paul W. Knoll, *The Rise of the Polish Monarchy: Piast Poland in East Central Europe, 1320–1370* (Chicago: University of Chicago Press, 1972), 26–27; Jerzy Wyrozumski, *Kazimierz Wielki* [Casimir the Great] (Wrocław: Zakład Narodowy im. Ossolińskich, 1982), 38–44, 178–81. For an instance of this governor's competence, see Piotr Górecki, "Assimilation, Resistance, and Ethnic Group Formation in Medieval Poland: A European Paradigm?" in *Das Reich und Polen: Parallelen, Interaktionen und Formen der Akkulturation im hohen und späten Mittelalter*, ed. Thomas Wünsch and Alexander Patschovsky, Vorträge und Forschungen 59 (Ostfildern: Jan Thorbecke Verlag, 2003), 447–76, at 447–48, 452–55.

50. Hermann was a governor on behalf of Margrave Hermann of Brandenburg, son of Margrave Otto V the Long, and brother of Beatrice, who was married to Duke Bolko I. After Bolko's death in 1301, Hermann ruled Silesia on behalf of Beatrice and the three minor sons of Bolko and Beatrice; Grodecki, *Liber* (1949), 176, n. 68; Lidia Korczak, "Bernard," *Piastowie*, 579–81; Korczak, "Henryk," *Piastowie*, 582–84.

51. Another example of "Germanization" of place names (above, nn. 9, 26, 31), this time after the consolidation of two earlier localities with Polish place names into one larger village. The ethnic significance of this particular place-name change is further noted in Chapter 159.

itself Jaksice, mimicking the name of the aforesaid knight. This Jaksa had two sons, of whom the older, Zbrosław by name, was a cleric, while the younger was a knight who was called Poltko of Schnellenwalde. But the same Jaksa sold his village of Wiesenthal to the famous man lord William of happy memory, bishop of Lubusz, who is buried here.[52] This William, while he was alive, gave the aforesaid village to the convent here, but because during his life he did not bring the convent into possession of the village, Duke Henry IV, in whose times the same bishop died – Jaksa, however, having died earlier – took away the aforesaid village from the house, and returned it to Poltko, whose father had sold it, and he also violently seized the church treasure[53] which the same bishop had placed here. Because of which, this convent was very much disturbed.

[155] *That John Zeruch built a mill near Wiesenthal by grace, not by right.*[54] There was at that time a certain knight John, son of Zeruch, living near Wiesenthal in Jonsdorf. This one obtained from the aforesaid lord bishop permission to build one mill in the fields of the village of Wiesenthal, from which [mill] the same knight was paying the lord bishop one common mark annually in rent. But the peasants of the village complained in the strongest terms about the damage to their sown fields and meadows because of this mill. When Poltko regained the village after the lord bishop's death, as was said, he refused to maintain the aforesaid mill within his inheritance, saying that he wished to rid himself of the said rent [obligation]. And he arranged to have the mill burned down to the ground, and did not allow another to be built there anew.

[156] *That Poltko sold Wiesenthal to the duke by his good will.* After the death of Duke Henry IV [1290], already during the reign in these parts of the illustrious Duke Bolko [I], the aforesaid Poltko was refusing to serve this prince at [the prince's] pleasure, and, at one time, he neglected to perform the service of three war-horses, by which he was nevertheless obligated. For this neglect – according to the statute which the duke had promulgated, and which is in force today – the duke made him give ten current marks of coin for each war-horse as pawn, and so took from him thirty marks for the three war-horses, and did not relax anything [of this debt]. Assuming this pawn reluctantly, Poltko came up to the prince by his own willing impulse, and offered him for sale all his villages, which he [i.e., Poltko] held under him [i.e., Duke Henry], that is to say, Wiesenthal, Służejów, and Berenwalde.

52. Presumably meaning the monastery itself (by analogy with Chapter 11), not Wiesenthal.

53. *Depositum*, here translated following Niermeyer, 321, *s.v. depositum*; Grodecki translates it simply as "things" (*rzeczy*), or, to put it a bit colloquially, stuff.

54. This title is rather puzzling in light of the story narrated under it. It is not clear who was the legitimate source of "right," and of mere "grace," with respect to the construction of a mill. John clearly had the bishop's permission to build the mill; perhaps in addition he needed the duke's permission, or perhaps the author is telescoping the controversies surrounding its construction into a blanket assertion of dubious legitimacy.

From among them, the duke bought only Wiesenthal for 550 marks, with all its uses and appurtenances, excepting absolutely nothing, but [to be possessed on the same terms] as Poltko had held it, and as, by God's grace, the convent holds it today, just as the privileges also demonstrate. Służejów, on the other hand, he [i.e., Poltko] sold to John, advocate of Münsterberg, and Berenwalde to those [who lived in, or were advocates] of Puszewice, and to Kusching. The duke neither coerced him toward this sale, nor impeded the buyers [in their purchases], but, in response to the said Poltko's petition, the lord duke resigned these villages to them with a pleased countenance.

These things are written down for future precaution, so they may be known to successors – because Poltko's two sons Jaksa and Theoderic say that their father was compelled to sell Wiesenthal, and today they demand the household gardens of the village[55] – which (according to the information from their father), they say are [situated] outside of the measurement of the hides,[56] and for that reason they assert that they have a right to them. In fact, however, the duke bought absolutely everything [in the village from Poltko], and these household gardens are encompassed by the measurement of the hides, and have belonged to the peasants since long ago.

[157] *About the exchange which the duke made with this convent.* Not a long time before the aforesaid [transactions] were effected, the Lord Sabaoth, Who does not cease to extend the vine of the Holy Church, had inspired the said prince, Duke Bolko [I], to plant a noble vine-branch in the field of the Lord, that is to say a monastery of the Cistercian Order. Which he did, and he chose for this monastery to be named Saint Mary's Grace.[57] After the convent was sent to this monastery, in the year of the Lord 1293, on the seventh [day before the] ides of August [August 7], and the lord duke strove to endow the same convent toward [its] future necessities and conveniences, he observed that two villages of the convent here [i.e., of the monastery of Henryków], Richenow and Quolsdorf, more suitably adjoined his [new] foundation [i.e., the monastery of Saint Mary's Grace], while Wiesenthal was best situated for future comfort of the convent here [i.e., Henryków]. He made an exchange with the abbot and the convent of this house [i.e., Henryków], and gave his [new] foundation [i.e., Saint Mary's

55. The Latin phrase is *ortos ville*, literally "the gardens of the village," meaning the intensely cultivated, household kitchen gardens of particular peasants, as Grodecki translates it (*zagrody wiejskie*), and Niermeyer, 499–50, *s.v. hortifer, hortilis, hortivus, hortulanus, hortus.*

56. The Latin phrase is *extra mensuram mansorum*, which means a space outside of the arable measured out within the village into a specified number of hides. Plans to establish settlement according to German law frequently anticipated that actual clearing might exceed the strictly planned size of the arable, and provided for this eventuality; this is what Jaksa and Theoderic claimed had actually happened in Wiesenthal.

57. Bolko I established this Cistercian monastery at Krzeszów (later Grüssau) in 1292, replacing a community of hermits that had been established there since the 1240s; Grodecki, *Liber* (1949), 180, n. 72; Korczak, "Bolko I," 577.

Grace] Richenow and Quolsdorf, and this monastery here [i.e., Henryków] Wiesenthal, with all its appurtenances and with the liberty of the court,[58] as is clearly recorded in the privilege.[59]

[158] *A note about the mill in Wiesenthal.* The mill which is in Wiesenthal was [formerly] held by a certain citizen of Münsterberg who was called Siegfried the Butcher, from whom Poltko removed the same mill violently, asserting that the said Siegfried did not perform the services he owed him from this mill. After he held the mill in this way for a certain time, he pawned it to a certain knight by the name of Alsik, for thirty marks of common weight and silver, from whom the lord abbot [of Henryków] redeemed the said mill for the same sum for which it had been pawned. And when Siegfried died, his daughter Hildegund – who remained as a survivor[60] and was married to a certain citizen of Nysa by the name of Siegfried the Tanner – raised a claim against Poltko regarding the aforesaid mill. He made an amicable composition with her, and persuaded her to renounce her right [to the mill], and completely to cease all action [to regain it].

The lord abbot also gave the prince himself twenty marks for one free hide in Wiesenthal. And whatever utility there was in Wiesenthal beyond that which was there in Richenow and Quolsdorf, all of that the duke generously gave to the convent here,[61] for the glory of God and for the remission of his sins. The tenor of the privilege about this exchange is inserted here for the memory of our successors.

[159] *The privilege concerning Wiesenthal.*[62]

In the name of the Lord, amen. In order that the succession of deeds not be cast under a cloud of oblivion because the haste of time, the skilled diligence of the elders has decreed that the deeds of the mortals be made eternal by witnesses and by the testimony of letters.

Therefore we, Bolko [I], by the grace of God duke of Silesia and lord of Fürstenberg, by letters patent make it known to present and future [persons] that, with our barons present, Poltko, called "from Schnellenwalde," our knight, standing in good health of body as well as of mind, has willingly sold us his village, formerly called Wadochowice in the Polish mode, and now commonly called Wiesenthal according to German law,

---

58. *Cum libertate iudicii,* which presumably meant freedom for the monastery to exercise jurisdiction in the village, without interference from ducal judges and other officials, or an exemption of the inhabitants of the village from summons before ducal courts, or any courts other than the monastery's seigneurial court.

59. It is not clear which privilege the author had in mind; here as elsewhere he refers to a charter without citing it. The document should have been an immunity charter, and contained, among other terms, a description of "liberty of the court" explained in the preceding note.

60. *Superstes,* generally a surviving heir, or more specifically a family member entitled to a reversion stipulated by a will after the death of another family member.

61. This passage presumably refers to Henryków, but that is not clear.

62. *S.U.,* 6:no. 91 (1293), 77–79.

situated in the frontier regions of our principality[63] near the cloister of Henryków, for 550 silver marks of the weight and [amount of] coin then current in our duchy, pure to about one *lotto* of silver [per mark],[64] publicly renonucing all property and right which he and his heirs or any descendants, sons, grandsons, and friends seemed to enjoy in the aforesaid village, so that we may freely put it to any uses of ours, free from all hindrance and doubt.

This same village, which we procured by such a fitting purchase from our said knight Poltko as property belonging to us by law, and [for which] we paid him in full, contains twenty-seven and a half rent-paying hides, of which hides each pays one silver mark of common coin and weight, and one large measure of triple grain – wheat, rye, and oats – every year on the feast of Saint Martin.[65] Concerning this rent, the peasants of the said village have made homage to us, and each of them has vowed to give it by the said term.[66] Furthermore, the aforementioned village of Wiesenthal has a bailiff[67] with [an estate consisting of] three hides, a tavern, a third penny from [each] trial, a butcher and a baker, free from every service; [and the village also includes] one hide, a fish-pond and a mill in the village itself, a field of hops and a household garden[68] belonging to the hop grower, and a meadow adjoining the

63. As earlier, the phrase used here, *in nostri principatus confiniis*, can mean either a frontier region, as translated here, or, more simply, "in the frontiers of our principality;" see also Chapter 150, n. 47.

64. This difficult passage states that the sale was effected *pro quingentis et L marcis argenti tunc in nostro dominio currentis ponderis et monete circa unum lottonem puri*. The *lotto* is an ambiguous term; it refers to a weight of silver, and ordinarily meant 1/16 of a mark, or 1/4 of a quarter-mark. (Kiersnowski, *Wstęp.*) In translating the *lotto* as a measure of purity of the silver in which this substantial transaction was effected, I follow Grodecki's translation into Polish, at *Liber* (1991), 181–82.

65. These are standard obligations placed on each hide (*mansus*) possessed by German settlers, and held according to "German law." An annual payment of one mark and the large measure of several grains (twelve small measures of three grains) had been a recurrent charge on German hides since at least the 1220s. Nothing in this schedule explains the exorbitant price the duke paid for Wiesenthal.

66. This is the only reference to peasant homage from the Piast duchies of which I am aware. It is therefore impossible to situate this fascinating glimpse into the definition of dependent peasant status within a broader context, apart from that provided by the other kinds of ties of dependence richly documented by Abbot Peter and his continuator.

67. *Scultetus*, always translated as "village bailiff" or "bailiff" in Book Two. For translations of the official titles of German village headmen, see Chapter 94, n. 107.

68. *Ortum*, n. 55 above.

village – all free [of customary obligations], and belonging to the lord of the said village.[69]

Our purchase encompassed all of these [goods and revenues], exactly as they have been marked around the circumference of its boundaries at the beginnings of the settlement of this village; and as they were now, every one of them, equally confirmed by us. Yet after this purchase – so rightfully and duly carried out between ourselves and our knight Poltko – we observed that our aforesaid village of Wiesenthal more conveniently adjoined [the estate of] the religious men of the Cistercian Order, the brothers of the house of Henryków. [Thus], moved by a pious disposition toward them, and concerned with their advancement and convenience, we gave them, in a mutual exchange, our aforesaid village of Wiesenthal for two villages of theirs, that is to say Richenow and Quolsdorf.[70]

Provided, however, that whatever may be there in our village in addition to the said price and value, all of that we carefully add to the eternal alms of the house of Henryków and of the brothers, for the glory of Almighty God and of His Mother the Glorious Virgin, in order to cleanse the sins of ourselves, of our beloved wife Beatrice,[71] and of our children who now exist or who might arrive in the future. We wish, therefore, that in the aforesaid village of Wiesenthal the brothers of Henryków may rejoice in every use, right, and liberty, just as [we rejoiced in them when] we bought it, because we have granted them this village with all its appurtenances indicated above, to be freely possessed forever. And we confirm [this] by the present [letters] – except that the rent-paying

---

69. The final words of this phrase, *cuncta libera dominum dicte ville contingencia*, may mean adjacent to the lord in a physical sense, or abtractly pertaining – belonging – to him; Grodecki opts for the second translation, and I follow him here. The most plausible reading of this long list of goods and revenues, punctuated in the middle by the words *ab omni liberum servicio* (and amplified by my glosses in brackets) is that it describes two reserved farms, or demesnes, within the village of Wiesenthal: one belonging to the village bailiff; the other to the lord of the village. This type of arrangement was, by the end of the thirteenth century, a standardized mode of allocating resources in villages established "according to German law." On the reserved portions of land and other lucrative goods in German-law estates, see the introductory essay above, pp. 49–50 and nn. 194, 196, 201–02; Richard C. Hoffmann, *Land, Liberties, and Lordship in a Late Medieval Countryside: Agrarian Structures and Change in the Duchy of Wrocław* (Philadelphia: University of Pennsylvania Press, 1989), 94–113; Piotr Górecki, *Economy, Society, and Lordship in Medieval Poland, 1100–1250* (New York: Holmes and Meier, 1992), 213, 216, 219, 239–42.

70. Chapters 21–22 above and 207 below.

71. Beatrice, daughter of Margrave Otto V of Brandenburg, was born in 1270, was married to Duke Bolko I in 1279, became regent after Bolko's death in 1301, and died between 1312 and 1316; *Rodowód*, 1:149; Grodecki, *Liber* (1949), 176, n. 68; Korczak, "Bolko I," 575–76; Korczak, "Henryk," 582.

hides in the same place shall be of service to us, exactly like the other goods of the religious[72] situated in our duchy.

Finally, because the oft-mentioned knight Poltko maintained that he had no valid document whatsoever concerning the village of Wiesenthal, by the tenor of the present [letters] we completely annul and cancel all [prior] letters or instruments issued by anyone in confirmation of the said village, in order that they may at no time be of help to Poltko,.or to any of his descendants, in support [of a possible claim] made in prejudice to the present valid document and to the brothers of Henryków. Whereas it is indecent and unjust that anyone should assert his will about the possession of another against the [rightful] possessor, we so confirm the aforenoted village of Wiesenthal upon the house of Henryków and the brothers therein, that – save by their good pleasure – no one at all from among men, of whatever condition, nobility, or sex, may have the power to build mills, graze any animals in the meadows or in the fields, catch fish in the rivers, or inflict injury in any way whatsoever, within the entire boundaries and borders of the said village. Whoever does the contrary should know that for such boldness he shall be struck with a severe punishment by us or by our successors.

In order, then, that this aforenoted purchase and exchange of ours, effected with the brothers, may perennially remain inviolable and firm, we caused the present letters, strengthened with our seal, to be written. Done in Strzegom, in the year of the Lord 1293, in the presence of the witnesses recorded below, summoned to this [occasion]: lord Louis of Hakeburne our brother-in-law, lord Witigo of Kiteliz, Count Jarosław of Habirsdorf, Count Ulric of Lubin, Count Henry Samborowic, Gosko advocate of Münsterberg, and many faithful others. Given by the hand of Siegfried protonotary of our court,[73] on the fifth [day before the] calends of March [February 25].

[160] *The account of the liberty of trial of Wiesenthal.*[74] Let it be known that our original ancestors first established the aforesaid villages, Richenow and Quolsdorf, when there were still forests there;[75] and that this house had its village bailiwicks in these villages completely free and absolved from ducal services. There

---

72. That is, monastic estates; for the meanings of "the religious," see the introductory essay above, n. 292, and Chapter 5, n. 12.

73. The protonotary was a chief notary in the Silesian chanceries in the later twelfth and thirteenth centuries; Karol Maleczyński, Maria Bielińska, and Antoni Gąsiorowski, *Dyplomatyka wieków średnich* [Diplomatics of the Middle Ages] (Warsaw: Państwowe Wydawnictwo Naukowe, 1971), 176–82.

74. That is, an explanation of seigneurial jurisdiction over the peasants of the village.

75. Chapters 21–22; Supplementary Documents no. 6–7.

was once in Richenow a certain village bailiff who was called Siegfried Rindfleisch,[76] and who was foolishly striving to raise himself up against the lord abbot and over the peasants of this village. In order to do this more easily, he offered himself in obedience to the knights of the land, and, in addition, moved by his own will, began to serve Duke Bolesław [II] himself with one war-horse.

He persisted in his arrogance until the lord abbot could no longer ignore it, but – albeit with difficulty – bought him out of the village bailiwick. He [i.e., the abbot] did not hold it for long, but, with the help of counsel from the elder monks of the house, sold it to a certain peaceful man [...].[77] But because the aforesaid Siegfried had made the village bailiwick subject to a service with one war-horse, it behooved the abbot to buy out that war-horse for forty marks, before the prince. In this way, he [i.e., the abbot] restored the aforesaid village bailiwick to [its] original liberty [from service]. After many years passed – when, after the death of Duke Bolesław [II, in 1278], his son Duke Bolko [I] was making the exchange described above with this convent – [in return] for the liberty which the lord abbot had formerly bought for the village bailiwick in Richenow [from Siegfried], Duke [Bolko I] gave this convent the liberty of the village bailiwick in Wiesenthal,[78] to be possessed forever.

[161] *About Nenker's claim regarding the building of a mill.* At the same time as the convent was put in possession of the said village of Wiesenthal, there was a certain knight, Nenker by name, living near the cloister in Jonsdorf, who had [as wife] a daughter of the aforesaid John Zeruch. This John, as was said above, had, by grace of the bishop of Lubusz, built in the fields of the village of Wiesenthal that mill which Poltko later refused to tolerate.[79] Before Duke Bolko [I] in the castle of Świdnica, this Nenker resolutely raised a claim against the lord abbot [of Henryków] regarding the construction of the aforenoted mill, and asked to be given judges about it.

However, the lord abbot humbly requested the duke not to allow anyone at all to build a mill within the boundaries of the said village, with prejudice to the cloister's utility – especially since the aforesaid John Zeruch had not possessed the aforesaid mill by hereditary right or by a right of purchase, but only by grace, throughout the course of his life. Upon hearing these words, the duke imposed an eternal silence on the aforementioned Nenker concerning the claim about the aforesaid mill, and ordered the inclusion of a prohibition against strangers build-

76. The nickname means "beef" in German, and so we have here one of three (presumably different) Siegfrieds with nicknames concerning, more or less directly, carcasses of large animals: Siegfried the Butcher, Siegfried the Tanner, and now Siegfried the Beef (Chapter 158).

77. A space is missing here, corresponding to about twelve letters in the manuscript. See Grodecki, *Liber* (1991), after 225, fol. xxxvi[v].

78. That is, presumably, both a right to establish the village bailiwick and an exemption of the bailiff's estate from common obligations.

79. Chapters 154–55, 158.

ing any mill within the boundaries of the aforesaid village, in the privilege whose tenor is expressed above.[80]

[162] *About Peter Gisele's claim concerning one free hide.* After these events, when a short time passed, a certain peasant who was called Peter Gisele, and who had formerly dwelled under [the lordship of] Poltko in Wiesenthal, demanded the one free hide which Poltko had sold to the duke there, and which the lord abbot had bought from the duke for twenty marks, just as is set out above. Concerning the aforesaid claim, the duke established as judge a certain knight, Jarosław of Habirsdorf, who set the term and the day of the trial in Münsterberg – on which term the lord abbot and the aforesaid Peter appeared, and on which Poltko, who was obliged to answer in the dispute about the said hide, was summoned [to appear] by the duke's letters. Therefore, while the aforesaid judge sat in the judgment seat in the presence of lords Gosko and John (then hereditary judges in Münsterberg) and of Henry of Schildberg, the said Peter lodged the complaint. Poltko answered him so fully that, by the counsel of the wise, sentence was pronounced against Peter, and an eternal silence concerning his accusation about the aforesaid hide was imposed by the rigor of justice on him and on all his sons, daughters, and any descendants whatsoever.

[163] *That the lord abbot bought out the village bailiwick in Wiesenthal.* At the time when the convent [of Henryków] was able to make the said village of Wiesenthal suitable for its uses, in all of its small portions, there was a certain youth in Münsterberg, Gobelo of Watzenrode, who held the bailiwick of the aforesaid village by paternal succession. But upon taking a wife in Wrocław, and permanently moving to her there, he publicly sold the aforesaid village bailiwick to the lord abbot, with every utility and right, just as he had held it, for 300 marks of coin – of which, however, he relaxed a hundred marks for [the love of] God, and as a favor to his uterine brother and co-heir who was a monk of this monastery, by the name of John. And [the remaining] 200 marks the lord abbot paid out to this Gobelo in Wrocław, at a suitable place, time, and term. And whereas the aforesaid village bailiwick, as was touched upon above, was given to the convent in a free exchange, after the purchase of the same bailiwick the lord abbot obtained from Duke Bernard (son of Duke Bolko [I]) a privilege stating that this convent can freely put the hides of the aforesaid bailiwick to whatever uses it wishes. A formal copy[81] of this privilege is noted here below, in exact words.

[164] *The privilege concerning the liberty of the village bailiwick in Wiesenthal.*
In the name of the Lord, amen. Whereas a pious mind does not suffer those who give themselves over to divine services to be bound in temporal matters by the laws of servitude – because God wished those who

---

80. Chapter 159.

81. The Latin word is *rescriptum*, meaning a formal copy of an original charter; Niermeyer, 912, *s.v. rescriptio, rescriptum*; Olivier Guyotjeannin, Jacques Pycke, and Benoît-Michel Tock, *La diplomatique médiévale* (Turnhout: Brepols, 1993), 271.

have committed themselves to God's service to have liberty – for that reason we, Bernard and Henry, dukes of Silesia and lords of Fürstenberg, by the tenor of the present privilege – may it be strong forever! – make it known to the memory of future [persons], and publicly declare, that the lord abbot and convent of Henryków hold in their village of Wiesenthal – which had accrued to them as an inheritance by a rightful exchange with our father of happy memory, the celebrated prince Duke Bolko [I] – four free hides that belong to the village bailiwick, which [hides] the said lord abbot and convent have duly and rightfully bought out from their village bailiff together with the bailiwick [itself].

With this purchase effected, the aforesaid lords [i.e., the abbot and monks of Henryków], approaching us, humbly requested that out of our kindness and [good] will they may be able to put these hides, subject to the same liberty, to their own uses. Truly, discerning no danger to ourselves in this request, and inclined by the lord abbot's prayers and by the merits of the holy observance in his convent, we [hereby] undergird the aforenamed hides with a legal title of the following liberty, to remain in force perennially, by eternal law: that they [i.e., the hides] may be completely absolved from all payments and exactions, and from ducal services of any kind, just as they have been until now. No less, we give the lord abbot and his convent the full authority and freedom to sell the same hides (protected by the same liberty) [to someone else, in return] for an annual rent,[82] or to exchange them for something better; or to treat them in any way whatsoever, just as appears best to them for enhancing their monastery's utility.

In order that oblivion may not erase, nor an evil-doer's shrewd desire infringe upon, this present grant of liberty of ours, we took care, in the witness of truth, to strengthen this writing with our seal. These things were done in Henryków, in the year of the Lord 1310, on the Sunday when the *Invocavit* is sung [March 8], in the presence of the witnesses noted below: lord Kilian of Hugowice, lord Hermann of Reichenbach, lord Gosko of Münsterberg and his brother lord Nikuszko, lord Henry of Mugelin, lord Heinmann of Adelungesbach, lord Hermann Hake, and very many other trustworthy [persons]. Given by the hand of Conrad our protonotary.

Here ends [the account] of Wiesenthal.

82. This rather cryptic passage appears to mean that if the monks wish to sell or lease the hides, the hides remain exempt from common obligations according to the present immunity. The "annual payment" suggests that the contemplated alienation is not an outright sale but some kind of lease, for which the lessee should pay an initial price and the annual rent thereafter.

Here begins a treatise about Raczyce.

[165] Fifth, we should discuss Raczyce. About this inheritance let it be known that formerly there were four uterine brothers who possessed it, of whom one was called Żupczy, another Gniewko Woda, the third John Rzeźnik, the fourth Cieszko. They were Poles, and held office in the prince's court – that is, they were *camerarii*[83] – and they frequently distressed the poor by their evil deeds.

[166] *In what way three portions of the inheritance accrued to Gniewko Woda.* Żupczy, wishing to have a dwelling by himself, separated himself from his brothers, and received a fourth part of the inheritance for himself, the other three brothers remaining together in one dwelling and on one bread. Of those three, one, that is to say Cieszko, became a leper and died without children. Another, that is to say John Rzeźnik, while at one time guarding his horse in a pasture behind his farmstead, lay down in the grass and likewise passed away by a sudden death, leaving no offspring. And so the portions of the inheritance which belonged to those two, accrued to Gniewko Woda alone, because the aforesaid three brothers had dwelled jointly, and had never intended to separate themselves from one another. This is the reason why the same Gniewko Woda took possession of three portions of the aforesaid inheritance, and Żupczy only of a fourth part.

This Żupczy took a wife, and begat five sons by her, that is to say, Theoderic, Eberhard, Czesław, Jasiek, and Krzyżan. Also leaving them as survivors, one day, as he stood before judgment in Niemcza, he died.[84] After he died, his son Eberhard successively bought out his remaining brothers, and, solely by himself, took possession of the fourth part of the aforesaid inheritance, which his father Żupczy had possessed [before his death], peacefully and quietly. Similarly, when Gniewko Woda took a wife, he begat by her three sons, namely Sułko, Więcław, and Nicholas. After his wife thus died,[85] the same Gniewko took another, and by her begat two sons, namely Stanko and Jeszko. Afterwards, one day he came here to the cloister, and, as he was sitting at the table in the old kitchen and eating, was seized by a sudden death. And his sons, named above, took possession of the three portions of the aforesaid inheritance – that is to say, of Raczyce, which he himself had possessed [before his death].

[167] *How Raczyce came [to be subjected] to a service with a war-horse.* As the princes were succeeding one another in this land, and that portion of the land [where Henryków is situated] accrued by succession to the famous prince Duke Bolko [I], the same inheritance, Raczyce, was ascribed to the prince's table by the senior

---

83. For the meaning of ducal *camerarii*, see above, Chapters 81, 111, 129.

84. The text is not clear about whether Żupczy left his five sons as *superstes* by the simple act of dying, or whether he first established them as *superstes* by some formal act and then died.

85. The phrase *et sic uxore defuncta* suggests that she died as a result of the begetting, that is, in childbirth.

knights who were dividing up the land, just as it had belonged to it since long ago. Hence, Duke Bolko wished to eliminate [from this holding] all of those named above, who were calling themselves the heirs of Raczyce. But many knights intervened on their behalf, and the final result was that they obligated themselves to serve the duke with one war-horse from the aforesaid inheritance, and so received the inheritance from the prince's hand in fief.

[168] *How the fief and the service from Raczyce accrued to those [i.e., the possessors or the heirs] of Hugowice.* Before Duke Bolko [I] attained [the rule of] this land, there was a war among the margraves of Brandenburg, that is to say Otto the Long and Otto with Spear, and Duke Bolko was supporting Margrave Otto the Long.[86] Margrave Otto with Spear was present in a certain city of the bishop of Brandenburg which is called Ziesar, and Duke Bolko's men lingered before the city, and right there Margrave Otto with Spear waged battle against them and triumphed, and, capturing many of them, snatched away their booty.

Among those captured was also the worthy knight Otto, son of Rudeger of Hugowice. In addition to other horses and various supplies, he lost there one war-horse – for which Duke Bolko himself had [earlier] offered Rudeger of Hugowice eighty marks here in those parts,[87] and yet was unable to obtain it. The said Rudeger demanded this war-horse, and [compensation for] the other damages which he had suffered there on account of his son Otto, for so long that at last, when the duke came into possession of this land [within Silesia where Henryków is situated], he gave the same Rudeger and all his successors the fief and the service of a war-horse [due] from Raczyce, by proprietary right, [as compensation] for the aforesaid damages. And so he repaired for the aforesaid Rugeder the damages which he had suffered.

[169] *About the purchase [effected by] the abbot [of Henryków] with those [heirs] of Raczyce.* After these events transpired in this way, it pleased the Father of Peace to remove the robbers from the boundaries of Israel,[88] and it seemed useful to the heirs of Raczyce to sell the inheritance to the lord abbot and convent [of Henryków]. The lord abbot bought it quickly by the convent's counsel, for 212 marks of common weight and coin. The heirs of Raczyce who sold the said village to the lord abbot were these: Żupczy's sons Eberhard and Theoderic, and Eberhard's son Nicholas; Gniewko Woda's sons by his first wife, Sułko, Więcław, and Nicholas, and by his second wife, Stanko and Jeszko; Sułko's sons

86. By the turn of the thirteenth and fourteenth centuries, Silesian dukes supported factions for political dominance among various margraves in Brandenburg; one such episode pitted Margrave Otto V the Long against Margrave Otto "with Spear" shortly before 1290. Duke Bolko I supported Otto V, father of his wife Beatrice. Grodecki, *Liber* (1949), 204, n. 80; Korczak, "Bolko I"; Korczak, "Henryk."

87. The phrase is *hic in partibus*, by which the author means within the duchy of Silesia and the region of Henryków, both before and far away from the military campaign described here.

88. Isa. 42:22–24.

Raszko, Nicholas, Henry, Vincent, and Heidenrich, and Nicholas's son Michael; and a certain butcher from Münsterberg called Henning of Oława.[89] Before the aforesaid Rudeger of Hugowice, all of them voluntarily resigned the said inheritance to the lord abbot of the said house, for themselves and for their remaining brothers who were unable to resign it because of the tenderness of years, on the day, at the place, and in the presence of witnesses, just as the instrument compiled about this demonstrates. Its copy is clearly appended here.

[170] *The privilege concerning Raczyce.*

In the name of the Lord, amen. Whereas by the fluidity of the times the acts of men are wont to undergo change, so that they may never remain in the same state, prudent antiquity has provided that deeds worthy of memory be secured with the support of letters and witnesses.

For which reason I, Rudeger of Hugowice, publicly declare to all whom the present writing will reach that, after the fief of the village of Raczyce accrued to me and to my legitimate descendants from my lord the beloved prince and duke of pious memory, Bolko [I], by a right of purchase, the hereditary possessors of the aforesaid village of Raczyce – Sułko, Nicholas, and Więcław, uterine brothers, and their cousins Eberhard and his brother Theoderic, and also Stanko with his brother Jeszko, and a certain butcher, Henning by name – unimpaired in strength and perception, standing in my presence, willingly and publicly acknowledged that they have sold the said village of theirs, Raczyce, to lord Abbot Peter and the convent of Henryków, for 212 marks of common coin, in eternal possession, with full right and all utility which they themselves and their children had or could have there, in arable fields, meadows, gardens, fisheries, thickets, and any other things whatever which were originally included within the boundaries of the said village since the outset of its establishment.[90]

Each party requested that this purchase and sale be confirmed by my goodness. And I, moved by the parties' requests, in the presence and with the voluntary consent of my sons, Kilian, Otto, Schade, Rudeger, and Gelferat, resigned the aforenamed village of Raczyce – [which had been] offered into my hands by the heirs described above in a good spirit – to the aforesaid lord abbot and convent of Henryków, to be possessed by proprietary right, renouncing cleanly and simply for God's sake all service

89. It is not certain whether all of the people in this last rather long list were Sułko's sons. The punctuation in both Grodecki's edition and my translation has to be somewhat arbitrary.

90. The "establishment" here is called *locatio*, and the meaning of both words is the same as at Chapter 94, n. 106. The qualification of parts of the estate as having been included "fundamentally" (*radicaliter*) since the *locatio* suggests that the elements granted on this occasion had been spelled out in a plan during the *locatio* itself, and perhaps recorded in an earlier charter.

and feudal right which I had, or which I could at any time soever have, in the said village, for myself and for all my descendants. All of the aforesaid sons of mine were at hand at this renunciation, and, with me, also offered their willing consent to it.

In order that the path to future evils may be closed more completely, the aforesaid heirs of the aforesaid village placed before me all their children whom they could bring along because of the tenderness of [their] years – so that Sułko placed his five sons, that is to say, Raszko, Nicholas, Henry, Vincent, and Heidenrich, and Nicholas brought his son by the name of Michael, while Eberhard brought his son, Nicholas by name.[91] All of them, together with their aforesaid fathers, and with Wenceslas, Theoderic, Stanko, and Jeszko, the[ir] cousins, and with Henning the butcher, without coercion and happily, resigned the aforementioned village of Raczyce to the said lord abbot and convent of Henryków, through my hands, expressly renouncing, for themselves and for all their heirs, sons, daughters, brothers, sisters, near relations, and friends, and for all [their] descendants whatsoever, recourse to any action or law which might support any [claim to] power, their own or their heirs' or successors', over the aforenoted village – with prejudice to quiet possession by the lord abbot and convent of Henryków.

But in order that after this public and willing affirmation no one may bring forward a denial regarding this event, all those named above, the old as well as the young, who are the former heirs of the aforenoted village of Raczyce, have acknowledged before me and my aforesaid sons, plainly and with their seals, that the lord abbot and convent of Henryków have paid them the moneys owed them, according to the extent of their holdings, so virtuously, beneficially, and fully that the lord abbot and convent ought at no time to suffer demands or disturbances about these holdings from anyone among men. They added that they removed their buildings (which they had excluded [from the transaction] during the sale) without any hindrance, and freed them for their own uses, with effective assistance by the lord abbot and the convent.

In order that oblivion may not abolish, nor an evil-doer's malice infringe upon, this purchase, resignation, declaration of payment, and removal of buildings, and this renunciation of my service and right for

---

91. The text at this point contains the following additional note in what Grodecki calls "a slightly later hand," situated, in his words, "under the text." The note is in fact situated on the bottom margin of the text, in strongly cursive Gothic; see Grodecki, *Liber* (1991), after 225, fol. xxxix[r]:

Let it be known that Wenceslas had four sons, Peter, Wenceslas, Martin, and James, who have not been placed in this privilege, and who had not been present at the resignation, because the older two were serving [the duke] outside the boundaries [of the duchy] at that time, and [the younger] two were so tender [in years] that their age excused them.

myself and for my descendants, I wished that the present letters be writ-ten – which I also, in the witness of truth, signed with seals – that is to say my own, and my oldest son Kilian's – my other sons not having seals yet. These things were done in Henryków, in the year of the Lord 1305, on the Day of Saint Margaret the Virgin and Martyr [July 12], in the presence of the aforesaid sons of mine, and also of the virtuous knights who were brought there for witness: lord Dzierżko of Byczeń, lord Cieszybór of Czesławice, lord Gosko castellan of Münsterberg, lord Nicholas his brother, lord John his uncle and advocate of Münsterberg, lord John of Peterswald, likewise John by the nickname of Sapek and James Smok his relative, and very many trustworthy others.

[171] *About the holdings of [which] the aforesaid inheritance [consists], and [about] what was given to each single [possessor] for his holding. First about Eberhard's holding.* Here it should be noted that Eberhard, Żupczy's son, held a fourth part of the inheritance of Raczyce by himself. Because the inheritance itself was bought for 212 marks, forty marks were given to the same Eberhard for his part. And to Michael, Kózka by nickname, who held three parts of one hide in Eberhard's holding, thirteen marks were given on Eberhard's order, which were deducted from Eberhard's compensation. Thus, the overall sum which accrued to Eberhard for his entire holding, and to Michael Kózka in Eberhard's name, reached the level of 53 marks.

[172] *About Sułko's holding.* The remaining three parts of the aforesaid inheritance of Raczyce belonged to Sułko, Więcław, Nicholas, Stanko, and Jeszko – sons of Gniewko Woda. The reason why they had accrued to them was explained above. Those three parts were [later] divided equally into four [new] parts. Of which four parts, Sułko held one, and, when he himself made a division with his sons (named above), he retained only a fourth part of one hide for himself. For that [part], four marks were given to him by the lord abbot. To Sułko's sons – that is to say, Raszko with his remaining brothers – 27 marks were given for the residual part that belonged to them. Thus, in total father and sons received 31 marks.

A certain butcher in Münsterberg called Henning of Oława bought one hide in Sułko's holding from Raszko, his son, to whom he gave [in exchange] for the same hide his town lot[92] in Münsterberg, situated near the castle. Beyond that, he [i.e., Henning] promised him [i.e., Raszko] to add six marks, which he paid out to

---

92. The word for "town lot" is *curia*, that polyvalent term meaning a substantial farm (sometimes used interchangeably with the term *grangia*), household, or court (especially the place where there ruler was present or resided), depending on the context. In addition to these meanings, the *curia* was the unit into which the land area situated within towns established according to "German law" was divided for tax, rent, and tithe purposes. In that sense, it was the urban equivalent of the hide (*mansus*); Plezia, 2:1502–09, *s.v. curia*; Górecki, *Economy*, 217–18.

the same Raszko in part in measures of cloth, deducting the remainder to cover the expenses which he had incurred with Raszko earlier. It behooved the lord abbot to buy this hide from the same Henning specially for eighteen marks. For that reason, the lord abbot was there deprived of nine marks and one fierton, because, as a result of the special purchase of this hide, [the price of] Sułko's part cost the lord abbot 49 marks, when, however, according to the earlier and approved purchase it should have cost no more than forty marks, less one fierton – which, nevertheless, the lord abbot calmly disregarded, lest a major gain be sacrificed for a trifle.

[173] *About Wenceslas's*[93] *holding.* Wenceslas held the other part, for which the lord abbot gave the same Wenceslas forty marks less one fierton. Nothing more belonged to the same Wenceslas.

[174] *About Nicholas Woda's holding.* The third part was held by Nicholas, who personally took from the lord abbot thirty marks and three fiertons for it. And Thomas, Sułko's son-in-law, who held half a hide in the holding of the aforesaid Nicholas, specially took for himself nine marks from the lord abbot by reason of this half a hide – however, [he did so] by the command, and with the consent, of the same Nicholas. Thus forty marks less one fierton were totally and fully ceded to Nicholas for his holding, as well as to Wenceslas.

[175] *About Stanko and Jeszko's holding.* The fourth part was held by Stanko and Jeszko, who made this arrangement among themselves: that the lord abbot gave Stanko fourteen and a half marks for his portion, while Jeszko reserved for himself (and directed that they be given out of his portion to a certain peasant of the cloister [who] then [lived] in Wiesenthal by the name of Nicholas Druscherf) three marks, which the lord abbot also gave to the same Nicholas.

In addition, the same Jeszko assigned to lord Kilian of Hugowice, on behalf of (*pro*) John of Peterswald,[94] six marks of the sum that had accrued to him, which [six marks] the lord abbot paid out to the same Kilian, while Jeszko himself personally took from the lord abbot nine fiertons, and fourteen marks besides. And so the entire sum paid out to Stanko and Jeszko (and on Jeszko's behalf to Nicholas Druscherf and Kilian) by the lord abbot reached forty marks less one fierton. Nor is the lord abbot obligated by anything more, to them or to their other brothers.

Although that Jeszko – along with his other brothers and cousins who resigned from Raczyce – might be placed by name in the privilege of lord Rudeger of Hugowice, nevertheless [it should be known that] he himself, specially and as the last among [them] all, willingly resigned his inheritance before

---

93. This is another, latinized way of writing Więcław; following the original written text, I retain both forms.

94. That is, John of Peterswald was, for some unexplained reason, in debt to Kilian of Hugowice; Jeszko assumed at least part of John's debt, and paid out six marks of it to Kilian.

Kilian in Jawór, and acknowledged at a solemn trial[95] in Münsterberg that the abbot had fully paid [him] for it. The reason why the said Jeszko ought to be placed [by name] in the privilege of lord Rudeger of Hugowice – even though he had not been present at the original resignation effected before lord Rudeger of Hugowice – is because when, on the day set for the resignation, all his brothers and cousins came together and resigned [the inheritance], and declared all [these acts] to be firm, the same Jeszko was expected to come [later], and Rudeger ordered that a privilege be compiled in full, and he said,

"Afterwards, when Jeszko comes, we will accept his resignation, and show him a copy of the privilege."

Because after lord Rudeger's death the same Jeszko delayed the resignation, the money was also not paid out to him, until he resigned [his inheritance] before Kilian, as was said. [The monastery] keeps the original documents[96] about this resignation and payment. From them, small notes are recorded here[97] for the memory of our successors.

[176] *Kilian's privilege concerning Jeszko's resignation.*

In the name of the Lord, amen. I, Kilian of Hugowice, publicly declare and attest to all who behold this writing that in the year of the Lord 1309, on the nearest Tuesday after the octaves of Epiphany [January 14], Jeszko of Raczyce came up to me in Jawór, and, before many, resigned to me a holding out of his inheritance, [which had earlier been] sold to the lords [i.e., the monks] of Henryków, and I, in turn, because of the absence of the brothers of Henryków, warranted [this holding] for him with a declaration of faith by [my] hand for twenty marks, which he had asserted that they [i.e., the monks] owed him.

From this sum, the same Jeszko there and then deducted six marks, [due] to me because of the debt of John of Peterswald to me; and the remaining fourteen marks the lord abbot paid out to Jeszko, just as the said Jeszko later declared before me. Furthermore, later, on the Sunday of

95. The *bannitum iudicium* was a trial that was opened formally and ceremonially, in a manner customary under German law; in this respect, it differed from trials held according to Polish law, which were opened with considerably less formality. The venue of this trial were also specific to German law; in this case, the court that held the *iudicium bannitum* was a town court; Plezia, 1:1035–36, *s.v. bannitus*. For the Polish counterparts of that word under direct influence of German law, see *S.Sp.*, 2:377–78, 380–81, *s.v. gaić, gajać, gajenie, gajony.*

96. The Latin word here is *autentica* [*sic*], plural, or perhaps feminine form, of *authenticum*, which in medieval Latin means a source that is both valid and original, in the sense of serving as prototype of all kinds of copies – full, excerpted, or summarized; Niermeyer, 73–74, *s.v. authenticus, authenticum;* Guyotjeannin, Pycke, and Tock, *Diplomatique*, 271.

97. In other words, the charters that follow are presented as an abbreviation, or a compilation ("small notes") from a series of charters. The full phrase introducing the charters is *quorum hic notule sunt ad memoriam posteris annotate.*

Invocavit [February 16], Jeszko himself, together with [two] lords of Henryków, that is to say Brother Winand master of the works,[98] and Brother John the cellarer, came up to me in Kąty, and once again resigned the entire portion of his inheritance into my hands, and I [in turn] resigned it to the brothers. In addition, he [i.e., Jeszko] solemnly declared in their presence the bestowal of the six marks which he had [earlier] deducted from [his obligation to] me because of John.

In order, therefore, that the oft-mentioned Jeszko, since he is fickle and unstable, from now on may not dare disturb the aforenamed brothers by raising some claim regarding the same six marks which I have received, or regarding the remaining fourteen marks which the lord abbot has paid out to him, I wished the present letter, under my seal, to be written, with the [presence of] witnesses who appeared on both sides at different times. In Jawór, there were: Hermann of Reichenbach, Timo of Ronow, Peter Capra, Hanmann the provincial advocate in Jawór, likewise in Kąty lord Henry the protonotary, likewise Henry the Jew, likewise Frederick and Rudeger of Maruch, and very many others.

[177] *The declaration of John, advocate of Münsterberg, concerning Jeszko's payment.* In the name of the Lord, amen. In order that after a public affirmation no one may be able to make a denial in the same case, prudent antiquity has devised that deeds of the faithful should be made eternal through witnesses, and by letters of witness. Here is what I, John (sub-advocate of lord John hereditary judge in Münsterberg) make it known to all whom the present writing will reach, that, standing in the presence of myself and of the witnesses recorded below, Jeszko, formerly heir of the hamlet of Raczyce, has publicly declared at a solemn trial that he has been fully, entirely, and totally paid for the holding which he had formerly held in the aforesaid village of Raczyce, by the lord abbot and the convent of Henryków. In witness of this matter, I delivered the present letter, strengthened with the seal of my aforenamed lord, Advocate John. Given in Münsterberg, in the year of the Lord 1309, on the ides of June [June 13], in the presence of the witnesses recorded below: Siedelmann of Grodków, Berthold the writer, Henry the Rich, Henry of Wigand's Village, Arnold of Brunow, Meynher, and Krystan of Wiesenthal – then magistrates,[99] sitting at trial.

98. *Magister operis*, the person in charge of major construction and structural repair of the abbey.

99. Because of the uncertainty of divisions within witness lists, it is not clear what proportion of the witnesses were magistrates (*scabini*). Because of the plural, I would assume that at least the two persons mentioned in the witness lists held this office. In general medieval ususage, the *scabini* were judges who jointly sat on a court, or assessors, that is, judicial officials who assisted the judge who presided over a court in reaching the decision. Niermeyer, 941, *s.v. scabinus*; Jacques Boussard, *The Civilization of Charlemagne*, trans. Frances

[178] *About the declaration of the citizens in Münsterberg concerning payment to the remaining heirs of Raczyce.* Let it also be known that all those remaining who had been heirs of Raczyce, and who had sold the said inheritance to the lord abbot, came to Münsterberg and, in the aforesaid city, together with the lord abbot, selected four citizens standing beyond all reproach – that is to say, Hermann Rume, Nicholas of Watzenrode, Berthold the writer, and Henry Gralok – [to serve] as mediators and witnesses of the payment to be made to them [i.e., the remaining heirs] by the lord abbot. Approving the requests of both parties, they took on the matter, and attended to the compilation of letters patent concerning each and every one of the abbot's full payments to the heirs, under the seal of the city of Münsterberg, in these words.

[179] *The privilege confirming the declaration concerning the common payment*[100] *for Raczyce.*

In the name of the Lord, amen. Whereas by the generic debt [of mankind][101] witnesses to human action, just like the actors [themselves], surrender to the slaughter of death, it is fitting that deeds worthy of memory be so strengthened by ever living letters that, when the witnesses die, trusty evidence may not equally be undermined.

Therefore we, citizens of Münsterberg, that is to say Hermann Rume, Nicholas of Watzenrode, Berthold the writer, and Henry Gralok, wish it to be known to all whom the present writing will reach, that after lord Peter, abbot of Henryków, justly and rightfully bought the hamlet of Raczyce, and agreed with those who had been heirs of this hamlet about specified times for payment, both parties, by their own decision and at the good pleasure of their will, have amicably elected us as witnesses and mediators of the payment for the aforesaid village, and moved us with their prayers that the payment by the lord abbot or by his brothers, and the acknowledgment of the payment by those who had been heirs of the aforesaid village, may be effected before us. And so, whatever we acknowledge the lord abbot as having paid, by himself or through his brothers, shall be deemed as paid; and whatever we acknowledge him or his [monks] as not having paid, that he shall pay at an opportune time.

We, taking on the said business with a view to peace and justice, faithfully wrote down every payment made by the abbot or by his brothers on every term, and every acknowledgment [of payment] by those to whom these payments were owed and paid. And finally, having taken diligent account of every [transaction], we find that the abbot has paid the said former heirs for the aforesaid hamlet in full. In these writings, therefore,

Partridge (New York: McGraw Hill, 1976), 26, 34; Rosamond McKitterick, *The Frankish Kingdoms Under the Carolingians* (London: Longman, 1983), 91–93.

100. *Communis solutio*, presumably meaning the overall payment, "common" in the sense of being directed to and shared by the entire kindred of Raczyce.

101. *Debitum generale*, an interesting allusion to original sin.

we declare in the name of the Lord, and say in the word of truth, that the aforesaid lord abbot of Henryków has fully and completely paid Sułko, Wenceslas, Nicholas, Eberhard, Stanko, Jeszko, Raszko with his brothers (of whom Raszko was then guardian), and Henning the butcher – former heirs of the said hamlet – for the aforesaid hamlet of Raczyce, to everyone according to the extent of his holdings. And they acknowledged the same thing before us, where also, giving thanks to the lord abbot, they forever left him and his convent free of all debt.

To strengthen, and in binding memory of, all [transactions] described above, we issued letters patent, certified by the seal of our city of Münsterberg, in the year of the Lord 1309, on the ides of June [June 13].

[180] *Summary of the full amount given for Raczyce.* In order that the full sum which was given for Raczyce – and which is described [above] in a scattered manner, one holding after another – may be considered globally, let it be known that for the fourth part of the entire inheritance, which he had held, Eberhard received 53 marks.

The remaining three parts of the aforesaid inheritance, as was said above, had been divided into four parts, of which one was held by Sułko and his sons, who received for themselves 31 marks [for it], while Henning the butcher received eighteen marks for the one hide which he had bought out of the holding of Sułko and his sons.

Another part was held by Wenceslas, who took forty marks less one fierton for it.

The third part was held by Nicholas, who received forty marks less one fierton for it.

The fourth part was held by Stanko and Jeszko, to whom were also given forty marks less one fierton for it.

And so the full sum reaches beyond 220 marks and five fiertons. And although the principal purchase had been for 212 marks, nevertheless this [sum] exceeds it by nine marks and one fierton, because of the special purchase which it was fitting to effect with the abovementioned Henning the butcher.

[181] *About additions.* In order that all [matters] among the convent and the said former heirs of Raczyce may be amicably put to rest, when the heirs were departing from the aforesaid inheritance, the lord abbot added for them, beyond the principal sum mentioned above, voluntarily and as a courtesy, four marks for Eberhard, three marks for Wenceslas, and nine marks for Nicholas – of which he gave him two in ready cash, and, concerning the remaining seven, he placed the chamberlain of the cloister, to whom they were owed, at his disposal.[102]

For Raszko, Sułko's son, he also added one and a half mark, and for Stanko five fiertons.

102. That is, he paid off Nicholas's debt of seven marks to the chamberlain of the monastery.

And so the sum of the additions reached nineteen marks less a fierton. May these additions forever quell all [claims] about Raczyce.

[182] *About the liberty of Raczyce.*[103] When the lord abbot completed the purchase of the aforesaid inheritance with the said heirs, he began to have discussions with lord Rudeger and his son Kilian of Hugowice about the liberty of Raczyce. Showing themselves well-disposed to this, they sold the liberty of the aforesaid inheritance to the convent for a hundred marks of Prague groats.[104] After the lord abbot paid them fifty marks, they absolved the convent of the remaining fifty in their last will. In the course of time, when lord Rudeger was already dead, his son lord Kilian procured for this house a confirmation of the aforesaid liberty from Dukes Bernard and Henry. The content of this confirmation is placed here in these words.

[183] *The ducal privilege concerning the liberty in Raczyce.*

In the name of the Lord, amen. One generation passes, another arrives, and nothing is permanent under the Sun, for which reason the ingenuity of the ancients has decreed that efforts made by mortals should be made eternal by worthy witnesses and by the inscription of letters.

Therefore we, Bernard and Henry, by the grace of God dukes of Silesia and lords of Fürstenberg, wish it to be known by all whom the present writing will reach, the present as well as the future, that Kilian, called "from Hugowice," our knight, standing in our presence, has made it public in a live voice and demonstrated by trustworthy witnesses that a former ducal service due from Raczyce, situated near Wiesenthal, was given and sold to his father Rudeger (called "from Hugowice") and to himself and his brothers, by our father of happy memory the illustrious Duke Bolko [I], for a hundred marks, in compensation for the damages they had sustained [in combat] at his side on [military] expeditions directed toward Saxony – to be freely put to their use forever, as their long-term possession [of the village from which they owe the service] also indicates.

When, therefore, the aforesaid [men] from Hugowice were in possession of the aforenamed service, peacefully and without any contradiction, as its true hereditary owners,[105] by inspiration of divine grace they sold the same service [due] from Raczyce to the monastery of Henryków – already after this monastery acquired the inheritance of Raczyce by a title of purchase – for fifty marks. Provided, however, that whatever more there

103. In this context, liberty (*libertas*) refers to immunity, that is, an exemption of a region, area of settlement, or category of persons from a range of customary obligations to the duke.

104. The diverse units and systems of coinage become especially bewildering here and elsewhere in the second portion of the *Book*; for help, see the introductory essay above, n. 248.

105. The expression is *hereditarii patroni*; the term *patronus* had several meanings, but in this context it apperently refers to absolute possessory right. Grodecki, however, translates *patroni* as "lords."

may be by way of price or of value in the said service [beyond fifty marks], all that they gave by testament in eternal alms to the brothers assiduously serving God there – for the praise of Almighty God and the glory of His Mother the Chaste Virgin, as well as for the cleansing of their sins.

Therefore, our oft-mentioned knight Kilian of Hugowice, and some from among the brothers of Henryków, came up to us, and humbly and earnestly requested that the aforesaid sale and gift made to the cloister be confirmed by our good will. We, in view of the pleasing services of both – the brothers of Henryków and lord Kilian of Hugowice – rendered to us at suitable places and times, and to be rendered in the future, [now] confirm the sale and gift of the said service as definite and final – notwithstanding certain registers of ours, from which, whether by deformity of the books or by neglect, it [i.e., the record of service due to the duke from Raczyce] has not yet been removed. And we render the said brothers free and absolved of the same service forever.

For a greater force and in fuller evidence of this liberty, we caused letters patent, strengthened by the protection of our seal, to be written. Done and given in Reichenbach, by the hand of our protonotary, Conrad, in the year of the Lord 1309, on Saint Michael's Day [September 29], in the presence of the witnesses recorded below: lord John Wsthube, lord Hermann of Reichenbach, Heinmann of Adelungisbach, lord Dobiesz of Domanice, Tyszko of Muszów, John of Łagów, Pezold of Piława, and very many trustworthy others.

[184] *About the claim [raised] by Wenceslas of Raczyce.* After this convent possessed the aforesaid inheritance of Raczyce for five years, one of the aforesaid heirs, by the name of Wenceslas, brought a claim against the lord abbot, saying that he [the abbot] was until then under a hereditary obligation to pay him three marks, because of which [marks] he saw to it that the lord abbot himself was summoned – albeit illegitimately – before lord Nicholas of Münsterberg, then judge of the court.[106] When the lord abbot sent two from among the brothers in his stead to Münsterberg on the prescribed term, the case was conducted so that the proof of the payment – by witnesses or by letters of witness, within eight days from that day – was imposed upon the lord abbot.

Oh, how truly terrible and exceedingly fearsome is the depth of God's judgment! For as the aforesaid brothers and Wenceslas were leaving the place of trial, and as the same Wenceslas came before the house of his host,[107] the time was at hand when God wished to humiliate the slanderer – and, by God's judg-

---

106. *Iudex curiae*, one of several categories of ducal judges. Persons with this title frequently occur in the witness lists of charters.

107. The Latin states *domus sui hospitii*, meaning a house of some unspecified person who presumably put him up during his stay in Münsterberg where court was situated and the trial was held.

ment, he [i.e., Wenceslas] did not enter the house, but, struck by a sudden death before the doors, expired. Still, this formidable judgment of divine vengeance did not deter Wenceslas's wife and his son Peter from wrongful action. On the eighth day after her husband's death, she, together with her son Peter, hearing the abbot's rightful proofs before the aforesaid judge in Münsterberg, failed in the case, and, by a just sentence, was struck with a fine. Concerning the aforesaid proofs, and the absolution of the lord abbot, the letter testimony by the aforesaid Nicholas judge of the court is recorded below.

[185] *The letter of the judge of the court concerning the quashing of the aforesaid claim.*

I, Nicholas of Münsterberg, judge of the court of Świdnica, make it known to all who behold this letter that the widow of Wenceslas of Raczyce and his son Peter raised a claim against the lord abbot of Henryków and the convent for three marks by reason of hereditary payment. Brother Winand, the prior there, having come into my presence, demonstrated publicly by testimonial letters and by live witnesses that the lord abbot and the convent have fully paid Wenceslas and his heirs for the hereditary holding in Raczyce that belonged to them. In order, therefore, that in the future no claim may be instigated [about this], I ordered the present little page to be written, under my seal, corroborated by the witnesses noted below, that is to say: lord Burchard Stoszowic, lord Frederick Spiegel, Henry of Landesberch, Hermann Rume, Südelmann then provincial advocate, and very many others. Given in Münsterberg in the year of the Lord 1310, on the fourth [day before the] nones of December [December 2].

Here ends [the account] of Raczyce.

Here begins [the account] of Dalebór's holding.

[186] In the sixth place, we move onto Dalebór's holding. For clarification of those things that concern this holding, let it be remembered that there was a certain knight, Michael by name, who formerly resided between the city of Münsterberg and this cloister. This Michael was discussed above, in the first book about the foundation.[108] Michael left two sons, also knights, of whom one was called Alsik, the other Dalebór. Over a long time, these two brothers inflicted many violent distresses upon the convent, in the cloister's forests near the new farmstead,[109] and in the alderwood behind the cloister.

However, since the Lord wished to relieve this convent from the aforesaid two brothers, one of them, that is to say Alsik, having attached himself [in service] to the duke of Opole, sold his holding – containing nine small hides – to

---

108. Of the monastery, meaning Abbot Peter's portion of the *Henryków Book*; Chapters 27, 76, 80–81.

109. *Nova curia*, a monastic unit of exploitation, presumably a grange, which has been newly established in a forested area.

the citizens of Münsterberg for 260 marks of public coin. The other [brother], namely Dalebór, was banished [from the province] for the robberies he had committed, but, by the intercession of the lord abbot on his behalf, was finally restored into the fullness of grace, under Hermann of Barboy, then captain of this land[110] – subject to the agreement [that he must pay] two gold marks. When Dalebór was reconciled in this way, the lord abbot bought from him his holding, which in its entirety contained four and a half small hides, for 130 marks of Prague groats, as the privilege [issued about this] declares; but the aforesaid holding surely costs the convent much more,[111] just as the following [accounts] truthfully show.

[187] *About the sum which was given for Dalebór's holding to him and to others in his stead.* When, therefore, the purchase by the lord abbot with Dalebór was rightfully effected, by the order of lord Hermann of Barboy, then captain in this land, the lord abbot gave Hermann, advocate of Reichenbach, and also then judge of the court, thirty marks of pence [called] "quarters,"[112] on Dalebór's prayers, and toward his reconciliation in [fulfillment of] the agreement concerning the two gold marks mentioned above. In addition, the same Dalebór pledged the said holding to a certain citizen of Münsterberg by the name of Pilgrim.

On the feast of the Rogations, here in the house, in the presence of the lord abbot and of the senior monks of the house, of Dalebór, and of many other worthy men summoned to this [event], this Pilgrim reflected carefully, and assessed Dalebór's debts at 102 marks. For this entire [sum], the lord abbot thereupon – by the order and in the name of Dalebór himself, and in the presence of those who are mentioned above – reached an agreement with the same Pilgrim for seventy marks of "quarters," which he [i.e., the abbot] paid out to him [i.e., Pilgrim].

And he added for him the first blades of grass of the current year [i.e., the first hay harvest] in the meadows of the aforesaid holding, which were appraised at over ten marks. And so eighty marks of "quarters," with the meadow and in ready cash, were paid to the same Pilgrim by the lord abbot on Dalebór's behalf.

Likewise, the lord abbot gave Michael, who was Dalebór's legitimate son, 33 marks of Prague groats by reason of patrimony. This Michael, together with his

110. See n. 49 above.

111. The switch to present tense just here (from "bought" [*emit*] to "costs" [*constat*]) is not an error, either mine in translation, or Grodecki's in his edition of the original manuscript (for which see Grodecki, *Liber* [1991], after 225, fol. xliiiᵛ). However, in contast to Grodecki in his Polish translation, I retain it here, despite the grammatical problem of tense inconsistency – guessing, on my part, that the expenses described here are so close to the present at which the second portion of the *Henryków Book* was written as to still constitute an exprense in the present, from the author's perspective.

112. The *denarii quartenses*, or *kwartniki* in Polish, were fractions of the regional variant of the "fat" pence introduced throughout Europe after the mid-thirteenth century. See the introductory essay, n. 248; Chapter 182; Spufford, *Money*, 233.

father Dalebór, resigned the aforesaid holding to this convent, by a good and free will, before lord Hermann of Barboy.

Likewise, to Nicholas of Watzenrode the lord abbot gave four marks of "quarters" for Dalebór.

Likewise, for the same [Dalebór], the lord abbot gave Tilo of Freiberg four marks of "quarters" less one fierton.

Likewise, to Hermann Rume the lord abbot gave nine fiertons for him.

Likewise, to Helwig, former notary of Heidenrich of Mühlheim near Wrocław, [the abbot gave] for the same Dalebór five marks and nine *scoti* of [pence called] "royals."[113]

Likewise, to Dalebór himself the lord abbot personally gave half a mark of "quarters," while he [i.e., Dalebór] was going to his son Michael in order to persuade him to [accept] the resignation.

Likewise, he later gave the same Dalebór two marks of "quarters," for the purpose of enabling him to pay off, by himself, totally, and in full, the minor debts which he had incurred here and there.

When, therefore, everything that the lord abbot paid out to Dalebór (that is, to himself in person, and to others in his stead but by his order) is summed up, the sum reaches 38 marks and nine *scoti* of Prague groats, and 122 and a half marks of pence [called] "quarters."[114] In addition, for the resignation from the aforesaid holding, the lord abbot specially gave lord Hermann of Barboy half a mark of gold, which is not to be counted as part of the payment and sum indicated above.

[188] *About Dalebór's second resignation, which he made before Duke Bernard.* After a passage of time, when the princes of this land grew up and Duke Bernard, as the oldest, held primacy among his brothers, the same Dalebór appeared here in the house, before Duke Bernard, and, with a good will, resigned to the lord abbot a second time the aforesaid holding which he had sold him [earlier] – on behalf of himself, of Michael his legitimate son, and of all his descendants The deed of his resignation is recorded here, in its exact words.

[189] *The ducal privilege concerning Dalebór's resignation.*

In the name of the Lord, amen. Whereas because of transient human memory those things which are done among men fall into oblivion unless they are strengthened by the witness of writings, for this reason we, Bernard and Henry, by the grace of God dukes of Silesia and lords of Fürstenberg,

---

113. The same currency as the "Prague groats"; that is, the "thick" pence issued by the king of Bohemia, the only crowned ruler who sought to assert control over Silesia and the other Piast duchies between 1295 and 1320; see Spufford, *Money*, 233.

114. In view of the large number of payments summed up just here, it is not clear (at least to me) whether this is a sum of the two totals, separated by the words *groats, and*, and consisting of two kinds of coins, both circulating at the same time; or whether these are two alternative expressions of one total in each kind of coin.

wish it to be known from these writings to [persons] present and future that Dalebór, formerly our knight, standing before us in a good health of mind and body, asserted that by the consent of his son Michael he has sold the holding out of his inheritance, situated near the cloister of Henryków, which [had earlier] accrued to him by paternal succession, to the lord abbot and convent of Henryków for 130 marks of [pence called] "royals." He also acknowledged that [the holding] was fully paid for, to himself and his aforesaid son Michael – who received for his portion 33 marks, so that he would cede all right [to it]. For which reason, the said Dalebór has forever, by his good will and by our assent, resigned the same holding to the lord abbot and the convent, to be possessed by hereditary right. Each side requested that this purchase and resignation be confirmed by our favor.

We, moved by the prayers of both parties – and declaring this purchase and resignation, solemnly made public before us, fixed and firm – confirm it with our usual kindness. In clearer evidence of this, we gave the lord abbot and his convent letters patent, strengthened by the protection of our seal. These things were done in Henryków, in the year of the Lord 1310, on the nones of March [March 7], before the witnesses recorded below: lord Matthew of Nieszeniów, lord John advocate of Münsterberg, lord Hermann Hake, lord Nicholas of Münsterberg, likewise Titzko of Muszów, Nikuszko of Wiadrów, Pezold Runge, and very many other trustworthy [persons]. Given by the hand of Conrad our protonotary.

[190] *About the purchase of the liberty of the aforesaid holding.* Those aforesaid holdings of Alsik and of Dalebór contain thirteen and a half small hides, and were subject to service to the prince of the land with half a war-horse, whenever the prince demanded his service. Of these hides, as was said, the citizens of Münsterberg held nine, and this convent four and a half. But because one of those four and a half hides closely adjoined [the holdings of] the citizens, the lord abbot sold the same [hide] to them, and so only three and a half hides remained for the convent – from which, together with the hides of the citizens, it [i.e., the monastery] was obliged to serve the prince.

But because the servitude of the sons of Hagar forever clashes with the freedmen of Christ,[115] the lord abbot, having come up together with the aforesaid citizens of Münsterberg to the prince, bought out[116] from him the aforesaid service of half a war-horse, for 55 marks of Prague groats – which 55 marks, by order of the prince, the lord abbot and the aforesaid citizens fully and entirely paid according to the extent of their holdings to Nicholas of Münster-

---

115. Gal. 4:22–26.

116. The word here is *exemit*, in the second person. Thus, the author describes the abbot as the actual purchaser.

berg, then judge of the court. A privilege is kept [by the monastery] about that removal [of the service obligation] and payment.[117] Its tenor is now placed here.

[191] *The ducal privilege concerning the liberty of Dalebór's holding.*

In the name of the Lord, amen. Human actions would lapse from the memory of men in all kinds of ways unless confirmed by the support of letters and by the aid of witnesses.

Hence it is that we, Bernard, Henry, and Bolko, by the grace of God dukes of Silesia and lords of Fürstenberg, desire it to be known to all – those living as well as those who will live – that, by the title of a just purchase, we have sold to the religious men, brothers of Henryków, and to our faithful citizens of Münsterberg, the service of half a war-horse belonging to us by reason of lordship from the goods of the late lord Dalebór and Alsik, situated between the city of Münsterberg and the cloister of Henryków, for 55 marks of common coin and weight.

Which money the aforesaid monks of Henryków, together with our citizens of Münsterberg, paid fully, in our stead and name, to the bold knight lord Nicholas of Münsterberg, our judge of the court at that time. After the purchase – celebrated mutually, duly, and rightfully among ourselves, the aforesaid monks, and the citizens – we [now] leave the oft-mentioned monks of Henryków and our citizens of Münsterberg, with their successors to whom these goods may accrue, forever free of the aforesaid service of half a war-horse, and unfettered. We wish that if [the record of] this service of half a war-horse has not been laid aside or removed from our register, that fact should not be prejudicial or harmful to those who have this [unexpunged record in our registers], and who possess the oft-mentioned goods situated between Henryków and Münsterberg.

In stronger witness and memory of this matter, we caused the present page, prepared concerning this sale, to be strengthened by the protection of our seal. Done and given in Strzelin, in the year of the Lord 1310, on the Day of Saint Lucy the Virgin [December 12], in the presence of these [persons]: lord Nicholas of Münsterberg our judge of the court, lord Peter the Goat, lord Mirror,[118] Ripert Unvogil, Nicholas son of lord Gosko of Münsterberg, Conrad our protonotary, and very many trustworthy others.

Here ends [the account] of Dalebór's holding.

---

117. The full phrase in Latin is *[h]uius autem exempcionis et solucionis privilegium habetur.* The word used here, *exemptio*, means, at the same time (and surely with a deliberate ambiguity), a purchase, an exemption – that is, a type of liberty – and a removal, or a cancellation of something that existed before.

118. The original states *domino Speculo*; this should be a translation into Latin of the German word for *Spiegel*, a frequent surname or nickname in the witness lists ot these documents.

Here begins the treatise about Czesławice, and first about Ścibór's holding.

[192] In the seventh place we should look at Czesławice. This inheritance is situated between the old fish enclosure and the cloister's great forest. Two knights, uterine brothers, of whom one was named Sulisław and the other Cieszybór, indeed possessed this inheritance by paternal succession. This inheritance, although it may contain a little bit more, was nonetheless since long ago recorded in the account[s] of ducal service at twelve small hides. The aforesaid two brothers divided this inheritance among themselves, so that Sulisław retained the lower portion of the inheritance situated very near to the fish enclosure, while Cieszybór retained the higher part toward the forest by patrimonial right. After Sulisław died, his three sons, Jeszko, Ścibór, and Przybysław, and their uterine sister by the name of Trzeszka, took possession of their father Sulisław's said holding by hereditary right.

But the Pious Lord, Who does not cease to weed out the Amorite from amongst His children[119] until today, upon observing with the eye of divine mercy the His humble convent was repeatedly molested in its forests, crops, rivers, and meadows by the aforesaid heirs, by a secret and terrible judgment brough it about that when Jeszko, the oldest and foremost of the three aforesaid brothers, was riding a horse, he and the horse fell, and he broke his neck and died. The remaining [siblings], Ścibór that is to say, and Przybysław, and their sister Trzeszka, divided the aforesaid holding among themselves, so that Ścibór specially acquired for himself the third part belonging to him, and separated himself from his brother and sister. Przybysław held his part jointly with his sister's part, until, by equal counsel, they sold the said two parts at the same time. After this division, a sudden devastation afflicted the heirs. And Ścibór – who had first separated himself from his brother and sister, and had lived foolishly and carelessly – accepted money at interest from a certain Jew, Merkelin by name, then residing in Münsterberg.

When, at the appropriate time, the same Jew counted up [the debt] with the said Ścibór, the principal and interest rose to 66 marks of public coin. But Ścibór, having no way to pay, gave the aforesaid Jew the entire holding of his ineritance by proprietary right, for fifty marks. And because he had nothing more from which he could pay the Jew the remaining sixteen marks, he obtained from the aforesaid Jew the favor of relief [from that part of the debt], through the requests of many worthy men.

[193] *About the purchase which the lord abbot effected with the aforesaid Merkelin the Jew.* After Ścibór gave the aforesaid Jew the entire holding of his inheritance by a just purchase in [satisfaction of the] debts, as was said, the same Jew sold the aforesaid holding to the lord abbot for fifty common marks. The same Ścibór came up to Duke Bolko [I] in Legnica, with the lord abbot and the aforenamed

---

119. A tribe of enemies of the Jews, frequently mentioned in the Old Testament.

Jew, and, before the duke, resigned his aforesaid holding – in its entirety, and with every use that belonged to it – to the Jew, to be possessed by hereditary right. And because the lord abbot refused to receive the much mentioned holding from the hand of the Jew, the Jew resigned the same [holding] into the hand of the aforesaid duke, and the duke resigned it to the abbot and this convent in eternal possession.

The sequence of every purchase and resignation effected between Ścibór and the Jew, and subsequently between the Jew and the lord abbot, was compiled in writing. The deed of its compilation is noted here.

[194] *The ducal privilege concerning Ścibór's holding of Czesławice.*[120]

In the name of the Lord, amen. Whereas man's memory is transient – since he is formed from a vile and corruptible matter, and since nothing is more certain than death and nothing less certain than the hour of death – this is the reason why the remedy of holy writing[121] was invented, in order that the deeds which have been arranged by the disposition of men in the present may clearly be confirmed for eternal memory.

For which reason we, Bolko [I], by the grace of God duke of Silesia, lord of Fürstenberg, and warden of Wrocław,[122] make it known to all present and future [persons] that, standing in our presence, Merkelin the Jew certified that he has sold and forever abandoned to the religious men, brothers of Henryków the entire portion of Ścibór's goods situated in Czesławice which belonged to him by reason of patrimony as his third part [of the total holding], for fifty marks of common coin, to be possessed by that same right as the aforesaid Ścibór [had] possessed it, and subject to the same services [due] from it which Ścibór – from whom the Jew procured the aforesaid goods by the title of a just purchase, just as Ścibór has declared in our presence – used to perform.

He [i.e., Ścibór] promised, together with John Sieczka, that in the future he may not come forth, by himself or through another, against the aforesaid sale, because of hereditary right or in any other way whatever; and that, by means of every use and custom of the land, he will warrant and liberate – that is, defend – the aforesaid goods on behalf of the aforesaid brothers against anyone who may demand the goods from them. And the aforesaid Jew resigned as [his] proprietary goods that portion of the said goods, which the oft-mentioned brothers received from our hand as a true and legitimate property.

---

120. *S.U.*, 6:no. 291 (1297), 233–34.

121. *Remedium sacre scripture*, surely a pun referring simultaneously to the Old and New Testament and to writing in general.

122. Duke Bolko I exercised wardship over the Duchy of Wrocław in the name of the minor sons of Duke Henry V between 1296 and 1301; Grodecki, *Liber* (1949), 216, n. 90.

In witness of this matter, we caused the present page, strengthened by the placement of our seal, to be granted. Given in the castle of Legnica, by the hand of Master Henry Berner notary of our court, in the year of the Lord 1297, the day before the calends of February [January 31], in the presence of lord Louis of Hakeborne our brother-in-law, Ivan of Provin, Richard Schaff, Otto of Kamenz, Siegfried our protonotary, Peter of Lubnów, and very many others.

[195] *About the holding of Przybysław, Ścibór's brother, and of his sister Trzeszka, in Czesławice.* A moderate amount of time after the aforesaid purchase, Przybysław, brother of the aforesaid Ścibór, and his sister Trzeszka fully sold the holdings which they possessed in Czesławice – plainly and with every use which there was, or which could be had, in the said holdings – to the lord abbot and this convent for 175 common marks, with the expression of consent to this by Ścibór, brother of the aforesaid [sellers], and by Herbord of Meynhousen, Trzeszka's husband. Przybysław first made the resignation in Kąty, before Duke Bolko [I], while Ścibór, together with his sister Trzeszka and her husband Herbord, resigned the aforesaid holdings later, before the same prince, here at the doors of the cloister. A privilege from this duke about their purchase and resignation, faithfully sealed, is kept [by the monastery], in the following words.

[196] *Duke Bolko's privilege concerning Przybysław's holding in Czesławice.*
In the name of the Lord, amen. Whereas the continuous flow of temporal matters may [only] become known to the future [persons], and be resurrected in their recollection, by the witness of writing, for this reason we, Bolko [I], by the grace of God duke of Silesia, lord of Fürstenberg, and warden of Wrocław, make it known to all [persons], the present as well as those who succeed in the future, that Przybysław, brother of Ścibór of Czesławice, standing before us in good health in Kąty, has freely and publicly declared that he sold to the lord abbot and the convent of Henryków – with, to be sure, the consent of his sister Trzeszka and his brother Ścibór – the entire hereditary portion that belonged to him and to his sister Trzeszka patrimonially in Czesławice, with the forests, fields, meadows, rivers, mills, gardens, the tavern, and with all other uses encompassed inside the boundaries of the said inheritance, for 175 marks of common coin and weight, to be possessed by eternal proprietary right – subject to the performance to ourselves or to our successors of the same services from this inheritance as those which Przybysław himself had been obliged to perform.

No less, the said Przybysław added that the aforesaid 175 marks were fully paid out to him and to his sister, and he promised to defend the aforesaid inheritance totally, against anyone, according to the custom of our land, and that in the future he may never raise anything by way of objection or opposition against the aforesaid sale, by himself or through anyone else whatsoever, on the basis of hereditary right or in any other way at all – expressly renouncing for himself, and for his sister and brother, and for all the descendants, relatives, and any friends whatsoever, theirs and his own, any action and recourse to the law which might ever support any power at all for him and for his [relatives and friends just mentioned] with respect to the aforesaid inheritance.

Each party requested that we confirm this sale and purchase by our favor. We, kindly showing approval to both parties, received the aforesaid inheritance from the hand of the said Przybysław, and resigned it to the aforesaid lord abbot and his convent, to be possessed forever, in order that each and every [act] recorded above may remain unchanged for them, that is to say for the abbot and his convent. In this way, we generously confirmed [the sale and purchase] by the authority of our rule. Later the same Przybysław, at another time, placed before us at the doors of the cloister of Henryków his brother Ścibór, his sister Trzeszka, and her legitimate husband Herbord of Meinhousen, who all willingly resigned the said inheritance to the aforesaid lord abbot and convent, with our favor, faithfully renouncing, for themselves and for all their descendants, relatives, and friends, [all claims] to the aforesaid inheritance according to all the terms set out above.

In order that the strength of this sale, purchase, payment, resignation, and renunciation may remain in force perpetually, we ordered that our present instrument be strengthened with our seal. Done in Kąty, in the castle, in the year of the Lord 1301, in the presence of our knights who came up to us all at once [as witnesses] during the second resignation which was effected at the doors of the cloister of Henryków. They were these [men], that is to say, lords Wojciech Rinbabe, Boguszko of Michałów, Budko his uncle, Dzierżko of Byczeń, Rudeger of Hugowice, Gunther of Kuesburg, Kunmann of Siedlice, and very many others. Given by the hand of Siegfried, our protonotary, on the calends of September [September 1] of the year aforesaid.

Here ends the treatise about the holding of Ścibór and Przybysław of Czesławice.

Here begins the treatise [...]. [123]

---

123. The text breaks off. Note that this is the "eighth" holding the author also omitted from the initial list of holdings he intended to describe in Chapter 126.

The *Henryków Book*: The Bishops of Wrocław

The beginning of the ordination of the bishops of Wrocław, whose names are recorded by the present booklet.

[197] Because the cloister of Henryków is situated and endowed in the diocese of Wrocław, and most gloriously raised up by the gifts of certain fathers, that is to say the bishops of that diocese, it is fitting that we, the first monks of the said cloister,[1] should commit the memory of our benefactors to our successors in written form. Therefore, in order that the glory of divine praise may multiply in this place everyday forevermore in honor of Almighty God and of Saint John the Baptist, and that honorable enrichments may always accrue to our Revered Mother the Church of Wrocław, we wish to set out the names of the venerable father bishops of this diocese in written form, for this purpose: that our successors, aware of the names of their benefactors from this writing, may forever strive to pray for them with a most ardent devotion.

The first bishop of Wrocław, at the beginning of the conversion [of Poland] into the faith of Christ. Thus, the first bishop of this diocese of Wrocław was Jerome. He was ordained in the year of the Lord 1046. He died in the year of the Lord 1063.

The second bishop. John was ordained in the year of the Lord 1066. He died in the year of the Lord 1072.

The third bishop. Peter was ordained in the year of the Lord 1074. He died in the year of the Lord 1101. At that time, Saint Stanisław passed away, in the year of the Lord 1079.[2]

The fourth bishop. Żyrosław I was ordained in the year of the Lord 1112. He died in the year of the Lord 1120.

The fifth bishop. Haymo was ordained in the year of the Lord 1120. He died in the year of the Lord 1126.

---

1. This self-description of the authors of the bishops' list (in conjunction with the references to Abbot Peter in the third person below, at Chapters 203–04, 206–08) is the circumstantial grounds for identifying Abbot Peter himself as its author, on which see the introductory essay, pp. 16–19 with nn. 47–59, and Chapters 69, 105, 111, 114, 116, 125–26, 205, 208.

2. Stanisław, bishop of Kraków, executed by King Bolesław II the Bold under very sparsely documented circumstances. Daniel Buczek, "Saint Stanisław, Bishop and Martyr: Fact and Legend," in *Saint Stanisław, Bishop of Kraków* (Santa Barbara: Polish Historical Association, 1979), 15–36; Tadeusz Grudziński, *Bolesław Śmiały/Szczodry i biskup Stanisław* [Bolesław the Bold (or the Generous) and Bishop Stanisław] (Warsaw: Interpress, 1982).

The sixth bishop. Robert was ordained in the year of the Lord 1127. He was transferred to the episcopate of Kraków, and is also said to have consecrated the church of Saint Wenceslas in Kraków.[3] He died in the year of the Lord 1140.

The seventh bishop. John II, who was called Janik, was ordained in the year of the Lord 1141. After a little time spent in the church of Wrocław, he was transferred to the archiepiscopate of Gniezno, where he honorably ended his days.

The eighth bishop. Walter was ordained in the year of the Lord 1146. He died in the year of the Lord 1159.

The ninth bishop. Żyrosław II was ordained in the year of the Lord 1171. He died in the year of the Lord 1198.

The tenth bishop. Jarosław the duke[4] was ordained in the year of the Lord 1199. He died in the year of the Lord 1201.

The eleventh bishop. Cyprian was received [in Wrocław] from the episcopate of Lubusz,[5] in the year of the Lord 1201. He died in the year of the Lord 1207.

[198] *The twelfth bishop.* Lawrence was ordained in the year of the Lord 1207. He died in the year of the Lord 1232. During the time of this Bishop Lawrence, our cloister of Henryków was founded, in the year of the Lord 1227, under the pious Duke Henry nicknamed the Bearded. That same year, on the fifth [day before the] calends of June [May 28], the convent entered here into Henryków.[6] And let it be known that the same lord Bishop Lawrence of venerated memory gave this cloister certain tithes out of his piety, but not with the same eagerness or generosity as did his successor, whose good deeds we shall describe in their place.[7]

[199] *The noble man Master Thomas of holy memory succeeded the aforesaid Lord Lawrence in the episcopate. He was ordained in the year of the Lord 1232. He died in the year of the Lord 1268, on the night of the Cantianorum*[8] *[May 30].* This same Master Thomas was born of the noblest stock in this province, so fully adorned with learning and integrity that in his days the fame of his virtues shone brightly among great men at the Roman court[9] and in many other places. Concerning the favors effected by that glorious father for this cloister we ought to inform our successors in written form in a proper place. But first we also ought to disclose to our brothers the favor effected for this cloister by lord Peter, provost of Wrocław.

---

3. The cathedral church in the Kraków castle.

4. Bishop Jarosław of Wrocław had also been duke of Opole. He was born between 1143 and 1160, became duke of Opole after 1177, and was bishop of Wrocław in or shortly before 1198 and 1201; Andrzej Marzec, "Jarosław," *Piastowie*, 372.

5. *Assumptus est de episcopatu lubucensi*, that is, had been bishop of Lubusz and became bishop of Wrocław. For contacts of the clerical circles in Wrocław and Lubusz, see Chapter 2.

6. Chapters 2, 6, 11.

7. Chapters 37, 68, 201, 207.

8. This is a Latin name for three saints whose feast day, May 30, was a part of the monks' liturgy; Grodecki, *Liber* (1949), 223, n. 93.

9. *Curia romana*, the court of the pope with its clergy and administration.

[200] *About the disposition and gift by lord Peter, provost of Wrocław.* Let it be known that in those days when the same Master Thomas was first ordained bishop, there was in the church of Saint John a certain man and provost, lord Peter, most noble in name, birth, and habits. He was an uncle of lord Thomas, the bishop just mentioned. This same Peter – because he was a wise man, much adorned by the virtue of habit – reigned over the episcopate in temporal matters for a few years after the beginnings of Bishop Thomas's ordination. While he was holding this power, Provost Peter came here to the cloister one time, to enjoy a quiet night office.[10] And let it be known that at the time when this was going on, this cloister was burdened by such poverty that, on that day when the lord provost, came to enjoy the night office together with his entourage, there were only four loaves of bread in the cloister. For which reason, lord Abbot Bodo immediately sent out to the farmsteads and to the enclosure, and collected so many loaves of bread as to be able to take care of the same provost and his entourage most worthily, that night and at breakfast the next day. After these things were done, lord Provost Peter said,

"Lord abbot, because you did well for me and mine, I will do you and yours a favor, if I live [to do it]. See and consider carefully whether my lord the bishop might possess any tithes adjoining you around your cloister, and in return for this night office I will request them for your house."

Having said this, the lord provost left. After this, the following week, lord Abbot Bodo went to Wrocław to the same provost, saying that he had found the tithes. The same provost at once requested them from the bishop for the cloister, and the lord bishop confirmed them right there by his own seal and by the seal of his chapter. At that time a privilege concerning this deed was issued to the cloister by the bishop and his chapter. Its content is as follows, word for word.

[201] *The privilege concerning those tithes.*[11]

In the name of the Lord, amen. We, Thomas, by the grace of God bishop of Wrocław, make it known to all that, in view of the observance and the poverty of the brothers of Henryków of the Cistercian Order, and because of piety, with the consent of our brothers, canons of our church, we have conceded to them and their house forever the tithes from that entire part of the circuit of Henryków from which lord Lawrence, custodian of our church, and his predecessors, used to receive the tithe by reason of his custodianship. The value of the same tithe is appraised at eight silver marks.

[In exchange] for this tithe, we assigned for the same custodian, by virtue of his custodianship, tithes from three villages, that is to say from

10. *Nocturna* generally meant prayers held at night, a part of monastic liturgy; Niermeyer, 719, *s.v. nocturnus*. However, it could also mean night rest, which is how Grodecki translates it.

11. *S.U.*, 2:no. 138 (1237), 90.

Muszkowice, Głębowice, and the village of Czesławice – with the said lord custodian accepting and in all respects approving this. We also granted to the brothers and their house tithe from two villages, that is to say Wadochowice and Nieciepła Izba, which their chaplain Nicholas had possessed by our predecessor's grace.[12] We also added for them tithe from the holding of Thomas Okrzesic, which is [collected] next to their fields, and likewise from Bukowina, as they possess a part of it [by a gift] from the lord duke, and another [part] by a purchase from Stephen of Kobylagłowa.[13] Confirming thus for them all the aforesaid [tithes] conceded to them by the assent of our chapter, in the witness of truth we caused this charter to be strengthened, by the seal[s] of ourselves, and of our church, and of the aforesaid custodian. Given in the year of the Incarnation of the Lord 1237.

Here ends the privilege.

[202] *Let it be known that lord Thomas was the thirteenth bishop in the church of Saint John, but the first by this name, Thomas.* Here, lords and brothers, you see how hospitality leads to good – because by a single night of hospitality, your cloister acquired the aforesaid goods.

[203] *Likewise, we should say more in writing about the kindness of the aforesaid lord bishop.* In those days, when lord Duke Henry the Bearded was already embarked upon the path of the eternal life [in 1238], and his son, also Henry, was confirmed in the reign [as the replacement] for his father, by the incitement of the Wicked One[14] a grave quarrel arose between the lord bishop and the duke, and it was so serious that the lord bishop did not dare to send out any messenger at all from his entourage anywhere concerning his business. While this and many similar evils were going on in the land, the lord bishop was [based] in Głogów, and resided beyond Przychowa at the time. Since, while this quarrel lasted, this lord bishop was staying in Głogów with his entourage, by a certain courier he sent to the abbot of this cloister letters saying,

"Send me some monk from among your brothers through whom I may be able to fulfill my needs safely. But this monk should come to me as if here were sent out by you on your cloister's business."

At that time there was here in the cloister a certain monk whose name should be inscribed in the Book of Life.[15] This same monk was in those days cellarer of this cloister. Lord Bodo, at the time abbot, sent this same monk to Głogów, to

---

12. Abbot Peter narrates the deprivation of this particular "chaplain" of his tithe revenue from Bishop Thomas in 1234, in his account of Skalicc (Chapters 65, 68).

13. Here, Thomas is adding a detail of the history of the forest called Bukowina, subsequent to the events narrated by Abbot Peter in his account of Głębowice, up to the year 1234; Chapters 82, 84–89; Supplementary Document no. 24.

14. The devil.

15. Chapter 125, n. 7.

the bishop. At that time, this bishop caused the same monk to travel on horseback between Otmuchów and Głogów five times without a break, as if to pursue this cloister's business. When the business was completed, and the lord bishop was already reconciled with the duke, the bishop said to the same monk,

"If I live [to do it], I will repay you and your house at the right time for the service you have provided me."[16]

To which the monk answered the bishop,

"Lord, I ask for no reward from you, but humbly request that you may extend something by way of aid to my house, at a suitable time and according to your grace."

[204] *This is the reason why lord Bishop Thomas first bound himself by great promises that he would favor this cloister.* After these things were done, and after the passage of many years, it happened that the aforesaid monk was made abbot in this cloister. As the lord bishop consecrated him as abbot, he admonished and requested, by himself and through certain others who were familiar with the bishop, that the lord bishop might fulfill his vow regarding the cloister of Henryków in whatever way he wished.

[205] *We will now write about lord Eckhard and his kindness toward our cloister.* Let it be known to our current and succeeding lords and brothers that while this was going on, there was in the church of Saint John a certain canon by the name of Eckhard, a man shining with the adornment of great virtues. Truly, he was very circumspect and earnestly eager for the welfare of the poor. Because of his great discretion, this same lord Eckhard was the highest counselor in all matters to lord Bishop Thomas after lord Peter, the provost mentioned above.[17] So, when the same lord Canon Eckhard heard that the lord bishop was bound by such pious promises regarding our cloister, at the right moments he admonished and urged with all the diligence he could muster that the lord bishop might deign to bring this deed – that is to say, his promise regarding this cloister – to fruition during his days [i.e., in his lifetime]. And he did this for as long as it took to incline the lord bishop's spontaneous will to it.

When this was done, lord Eckhard sent for this cloister's abbot, saying that the lord bishop's will regarding this closter was fully turned to the good. He, that is to say lord Eckhard, then kept the abbot together with his entourage near himself in Otmuchów for three days at his own expense; and he worked with an effort beyond what can be believed to distract the lord abbot from other

---

16. Abbot Peter is obviously reticent about the mission of the abbot's messenger. He does make it is clear that the monastery of Henryków was crucial in smoothing the conflict between Duke Henry II the Pious and Bishop Thomas, that Thomas had wanted to keep his mission secret, and that Peter continued to be very discreet as to the conduct of the mission (though not as to its real purpose and the initial deception about it) twenty years later.

17. Chapters 199–200.

business, and sought to bring our business to fruition. Finally, on the third day after breakfast, lord Eckhard, having excluded all guests from the castle, ordered the castle of Otmuchów to be closed, and asked the lord bishop to sit down quietly in his garden. And when Peter, abbot this place [i.e., Henryków] was called, the lord bishop began to write down the privilege about tithes which follows in this booklet.

In this privilege, there are certain villages and manors indicated by name. The lord bishop received the names of these villages from the mouth of Peter, at the time abbot of the cloister; and he expressed them in written form by means of a privilege of confirmation of the tithes.

[206] *Here, brothers, you see how carefully lord Eckhard worked to bring it about that the bishop and chapter of Wrocław might grant this cloister a confirmation of the tithes in his days.* Lords and brothers, current and future, you should endeavor to pray assiduously for Thomas, the glorious bishop, and for his chapter. We will try to commend this bishop to the brothers' prayers more fully in the proper place.

[207] *Now follows the record of the privilege, gathered in writing in the following fashion.*[18] In the name of the Lord, amen. We, Thomas, by the grace of God bishop of Wrocław, make it known to the memory of our successors that when, among other religious houses, the house of the brothers of Henryków of the Cistercian Order arose by divine grace during the times of our predecessor Bishop Lawrence of happy memory, for the salvation of the souls serving God there, and in order to offer an example of integrity to others, and, planted in a severe poverty, fully required support for its sustenance and advancement from the mercy of prelates who might irrigate it with favors and advance the observance dear to God – it was, just exactly as this is known to us, furnished with some support, that is to say, with tithes belonging to the episcopal table, by our said predecessor [Bishop Lawrence], a man of great piety, and to a degree by ourselves, after our canons expressed consent to this.

And although the gifts made to them may have been offered at various times, nevertheless we, on the petition of the brothers of the aforesaid house, have specially caused them to be recorded together in the present writing, from valid documents which we saw, legitimately prepared, with our own eyes. They are these. From the beginning, by our predecessor's gift, they have the tithes from Kołaczów – under which name are included these villages: Jaworowice, Skalice, Raczyce, and Witostowice[19] –

---

18. *S.U.*, 3:no. 448 (1263), 294–95. In general, this charter incorporates, and supplements, Bishop Thomas's charter of 1237 (Chapter 201 above).

19. Abbot Peter notes the story of Kołaczów, the settlements subsequently established in it, and the tithe revenue from it, in his account of Henryków (Chapters 36–37).

which, although it[20] may formerly have been given to the parish church, yet, by our rightful arrangement, was added to the uses of the aforesaid brothers.

In addition, they should have, and do have, tithes from a certain village of Richnow, containing a hundred large hides; and right there, we added for them tithe from another village situated near that one, which is called New Richnow. They also have there their village of Quolsdorf, containing fifty large hides, with the tithe.[21]

Likewise, in another place around Bardo they have a hundred large hides in the village of Schönwald, within which are included the small hamlets of Budzów, Rudno, and Notary's Village,[22] with the tithe confirmed for them.

Likewise the tithes from the circuit of all of Henryków, a certain part of which [formerly] belonged to the *custodia*[23] of the church of Wrocław – in compensation for which, we gave to this *custodia* in the times of Custodian Lawrence tithes from the villages of Mieszkowice, Głębowice, and Czesławice, of a value estimated at eight silver marks – with the custodian himself freely accepting this.[24]

We also gave the aforesaid brothers and their house tithe from two villages, namely Wadochowice and Nieciepła Izba,[25] which their chaplain Nicholas had possessed by the grace of our predecessor and by our grace.

Likewise belongs to them the tithe from a certain village which was called Brukalice, in which they have now established their grange.[26]

Likewise, the tithe from the holding of Thomas Okrzesic, which is now within their borders.

Likewise from Bukowina with the meadow, just as they have it from lord Duke Henry the Old,[27] and a part of it bought from Stephen Kobylagłowa. If this forest is ever cleared, the tithe from it shall belong to this cloister.[28]

---

20. The "it" here refers to the village of Kołaczów, not the tithes from it; in the original Latin, "the tithes" are unambiguously in the plural, while this pronoun is clearly in the singular.

21. Chapters 21–22; Supplementary Document no. 2.

22. Chapters 94–111.

23. One of the offices of the cathedral chapter; its holder was the custodian.

24. Chapter 201.

25. Chapter 154.

26. Chapters 112–17, 119–21. In this case "grange" is a translation of *grangia*, which is why on this occasion I do not translate the name for this unit of monastic exploitation as "farmstead."

27. One of Abbot Peter's alternative designations for Henry I the Bearded.

28. Chapters 82–84, 89–90.

All these aforesaid [tithes] we declare the aforesaid house of Henryków legitimately to possess by the gift of our predecessor, and by our gift. And by consent of our chapter we forever confirm them for the aforesaid cloister – lovingly requesting the brothers that in their prayers they may hold our memory in a good state, for the aid of our soul and the enhancement of their love.

Given in Wrocław, in the chapel of Saint Guido, the year of the Incarnation of the Lord 1263, the second [day before the] calends of September [August 31], in the presence of these [persons]: lord Nicholas dean of Wrocław, Gerlach provost of Lubusz, Gregory provost of Opole, Martin, Eckhard, Volker, Bogusław, Leonard, Hartwig, Valentinus, Leonard, Thomas, Master Frank, Master Peter, Piotrko the chancellor, Wierzchosław, and Nicholas [son] of Dmitrii, canons of Wrocław. For firmness and in memory of this matter, we strengthened the present charter with the seals of ourselves and of our chapter. Written by the hand of Andrew our writer.

Here ends the tithe privilege of the bishop and the canons.

[208] *A decree that you should pray for the canons.* Now everyone, present and future, who serves God in this cloister under rigor of the Order, ought to know that the three abbots who succeeded one another here in turn, that is to say Peter, Geoffrey, and Roland,[29] arranged and decreed that there should forever be commemoration of the lord Bishop Thomas and his chapter – that is to say, of the persons named in the privilege written above[30] – with masses for the dead, holy vigils, and other prayers, in order that Almighty God may repay them for their good deeds for us with eternal life. Amen.

[209] *Likewise, [the abbots decreed] that lord Thomas, the oft-mentioned bishop, together with lord Eckhard, should forever be mentioned by name in the canon of the mass*[31] *by each priest.* Likewise, because lord Bishop Thomas and lord Eckhard did great things for this cloister, the aforesaid abbots decreed that each priest, present and future, should always make a remembrance by name of lord Bishop Thomas and of lord Eckhard in the canon of the mass.

[210] *In order that this decree may not be oppressive or unwelcome to anyone at a future time, we will write something a bit more for our successors about the kind piety of these men.* In order, therefore, that you may know in what year and at what time every single one of those who benefitted this cloister departed from this life, let it be known that lord Peter, the aforesaid provost of Wrocław, fell asleep in Christ in the year

29. Two abbots who followed Peter in that office after 1268, the latter until 1276; Chapter 1, n. 1; Grodecki, *Liber* (1991), 105, n. 95.

30. The reference here is to the list of the canons of Wrocław in the final paragraph of Chapter 207.

31. The canon (*canon missae*) is the central part of the liturgy of the mass; Niermeyer, 126, *s.v. canon.*

of the Lord 1240. From that year onward, let his death anniversary be celebrated for him in the cloister with vigils, masses, and other funeral ceremonies, every year, on any day and at any time. Lord Thomas, the thirteenth bishop of Wrocław (and the first in this church by that name, Thomas), died in the year of the Lord 1268, on the night of the *Cantianorum* [May 30]. Because by his generosity he strengthened the divine office in this cloister, we urge and request our present and future lords and brothers that they endeavor to celebrate his [death] anniversary with vigils and solemn masses on the day recorded above forever.

[211] *On what day and at what time lords Eckhard and Leonard, canons of the church of Wrocław, died.* Let it thus be known that lord Eckhard of Kalków migrated from this world in the year of the Lord 1273, on the tenth [day before the] calends of April [March 23]. Lord Leonard, canon of Wrocław, died in the same year, on the fourth [day before the] nones of April [April 2].

Supplementary Documents
Relating to the Henryków Monastery

I *Politics of the monastic foundation: Alternative views*

The documents in this, the first of three sections, represent a variety of views concerning the relationship between the foundation of the Henryków monastery and, on the one hand, several Piast dukes, and on the other Nicholas, notary of one of those dukes, Henry I the Bearded of Silesia, but also an individual with contacts in two other provinces, Great Poland and Little Poland. That relationship – especially those aspects of it that linked Nicholas and Henry the Bearded – is a central subject of Abbot Peter's portion of the *Henryków Book*. However, even Peter conveys glimpses of several alternative interpretations (or memories) concerning that relationship and its implications for the question of the "true" agency behind the monastery's foundation.

The seven charters in Section I reflect both the common elements of, and the divergences between, those interpretations.[1] Abbot Peter's reconstruction is broadly consistent with the diplomas issued by Duke Henry I the Bearded in 1228 (no. 2), and by his grandson, Bolesław II the Bald in 1263 (no. 6), but Duke Władysław Odonic and his son Przemysł I, Bishop Paul of Poznań, and Duchess Grzymisława of Kraków and Little Poland (no. 1, 3–5), all interpret the specific role and status of Notary Nicholas, and the identity of the dukes who ought to receive credit for the Henryków foundation, quite differently – from each other, and from Abbot Peter. The letter from Pope Clement IV, issued in 1268 (no. 7), frames these subjects, yet again, rather distinctly.

Duke Henry I's diploma of 1228 (no. 2) is the foundation charter of the monastery, presumably issued at the consecration ceremony Abbot Peter describes in Chapter 21. The 1263 diploma by Bolesław II (no. 6) is strongly conciliatory toward the monastery, expresses regret for his past behavior, and mentions Abbot Peter by name – suggesting that as of that year, the monastery's political grievances toward that duke were resolved, and that this fact was an important element of the context of the writing of the *Book* itself.

1 In the name of our Lord Jesus Christ, amen. I, Władysław, the younger son of Duke Odo of happy memory, by divine mercy duke of [Great] Poland,[2] have decided that the wise arrangements made to strengthen my lordship should be

1. On this subject, see Piotr Górecki, "An Interpreter of Law and Power in a Region of Medieval Poland: Abbot Peter of Henryków and his *Book*," in *Building Legitimacy: Political Discourses and Forms of Legitimation in Medieval Societies*, ed. Isabel Alfonso, Hugh Kennedy, and Julio Escalona (Leiden: Brill, 2004), 263–89.

2. Władysław Odonic, duke of portions or all of the province of Great Poland between 1194 and 1239; *Poczet królów i książąt polskich* [The roll of the Polish kings and dukes], ed. Andrzej Garlicki (Warsaw: Czytelnik, 1980), 460; Krzysztof Ożóg, "Władysław Odonic Plwacz" [Władysław Odonic the Spitter], *Piastowie*, 131–41.

entrusted to the present writing. Therefore, let present and future [persons] know that, after deliberation, I have firmly decreed that Germans, or other guests, shall be settled in the territory of Nakło.[3] The boundaries of this territory are: Koniawy to the south, Bruchownica to the north, the road that runs from Tonin through Kamień to the east, and the large road that runs to Sławno to the west. I have granted this territory to Saint Mary in Lubiąż, of the diocese of Wrocław, and to the daughter of that monastery[4] which is to be constructed within the patrimony of lord Nicholas, notary of the duke of Silesia.

I establish the following arrangement for the said monasteries. The house of Lubiąż shall have full first right to the lake called the Lesser Pezachne, and below it [to the territory extending] toward Nakło through Koniawy, so that a city[5] may be constructed within the portion of [the planned estate that belongs to the monks] of Lubiąż. To this city shall belong not only the villages [of the monks] of Lubiąż, but also villages of their said daughter, except for the tithes. The first boundary of the villages [of the daughter monastery] runs along the Pezachne, and the last is a stream called Bruchowniki, near which the localities called Białowieża touch the boundary. The new shoot[6] shall have this territory with all rights, just as the house of Lubiąż has its [portion], with the three lakes [called] Sikory which are situated within it, and with the lands, meadows, and other uses. When the house of Lubiąż begins to settle (*locare*)[7] its portion, the said daughter shall similarly undertake to settle its portion. If it refuses to do this, all of the said territory shall belong to the house of Lubiąż.

I forever establish German law, which is to be kept in full and undiminished, in the city itself, and in all the villages belonging to it.[8] They [i.e., the city,

---

3. Nakło is a locality in far northern Great Poland (Map 2), and one of the bases of the power of Władysław Odonic early in his struggles with his most important competitor, Henry I the Bearded of Silesia. It became one of the early centers of ambitious, large-scale plans by Władysław to recruit groups of Germans into Great Poland; see on this Piotr Górecki, *Economy, Society, and Lordship in Medieval Poland, 1100–1250* (New York: Holmes and Meier, 1992), 262–75.

4. See the introductory essay, "The *Henryków Book* and Its Contexts" above, nn. 117, 301.

5. Here and elsewhere, "city" always translates the word *civitas*, which means community or central place as well as more strictly speaking an urban center. What is being planned here is a central locality, to be established according to German law, with a large number of outlying settlements. See Górecki, *Economy*, 203–08, 263–64, 266, 269, 271–72; and the introductory essay above, nn. 215–17.

6. "The shoot," or "new shoot" – *plantatio* or *novella plantatio* – is a recurrent metaphor for new Cistercian monasteries; Abbot Peter, Władysław Odonic, Przemysł I, and others apply it frequently specifically to the Henryków monastery, in the *Henryków Book*, and in several documents translated here.

7. This is a verb form of *locatio*; Chapter 49, n. 46.

8. "German law" is the set of terms on which German immigrants – and, since the mid-thirteenth century, other settlers, including Polish peasants – were settled in the Po-

villages, and their inhabitants] shall not be oppressed by any services or obligations, by the *podwody*, or by other Polish customs which are foreign to German
law, such as tracking fugitives, the *przewód*, and such.[9] I also wish all the present
and future [persons] to know that I forever confirm the place on the Odra and
the hides near Lubusz, which Henry [I], duke of Silesia, gave to the house of
Lubiąż for the construction of a farmstead (*curia*),[10] and I pronounce the said duke's
grant fixed. In the Year of Grace 1225, on the sixth [day before the] nones of
October [October 2], in the presence of the monks, Peter of Sittichenbach,[11] and
Guido and Alexander of Lubiąż; of Arnold our chaplain, the knight Conrad, and
the knight Alexander. Done in our castle, Nakło.

S.U., 1:no. 252 (1225), 184

2 In the name of the Lord, amen. We, Henry [I], by the grace of God duke of
Silesia, yearning to exalt the Venerable Mother Church in our time, and seeking to
augment the salvation of the souls of the faithful, which the Lord shall give, for the
increase of our merit wish present and future [persons] to note that once upon a
time lord Nicholas, our late notary of blessed memory, resigned the possessions he
had in our land, into the hands of ourselves and of our son Henry [II], in the
following fashion: that, for the honor of God, the Holy Virgin, and Saint John the
Baptist, the flower of the Cistercian Order shall be planted in Henryków by the
authority of ourselves and of our son; and that a cloister shall be built there for the
servants of Christ, serving God according to the rigor of this Order. So as not to
impede the works of piety, but to allow Nicholas's requests in a happy spirit, we, at
the instance of Bishops Lawrence of Wrocław and Paul of Poznań, confirm all the
inheritances which he possessed in our duchy by our grace while he was alive
(whether by reason of purchase, or though some kind of gift), as eternal
possessions of the said Cistercian Order, for our own and for our son's salvation;
and we grant to the cloister, and to the inheritances recorded below, eternal liberty
from all exactions [customarily levied] by ourselves and by our barons.

In order that the confirmation of this gift be more fully known, the possessions which Nicholas held while he was alive, and which he granted to the grey

---

lish duchies and elsewhere in East Central Europe; the introductory essay above, nn. 175–
78, 193–96, 200–03, 210–15; Chapters 49, 94–96.

9. This element of "German law" is an immunity, that is, an exemption for the beneficiaries (the peasants and the regions they were to inhabit) from a number of obligations
otherwise common to the inhabitants of the Piast duchies, some of which are expressed
in the vernacular. For a brief discussion of immunity, see the introductory essay above, n.
214; for "German law" in the specific context of immunity, see Górecki, *Economy*, 193–203.

10. See the introductory essay above, nn. 323–24; Chapter 36, n. 36.

11. Sittichenbach was the location of a Cistercian monastery in east-central Germany,
about 200 kilometers to the west of Lubiąż (Map 1). Like Lubiąż, it was a daughter house
of Pforta; see *Cystersi w Polsce* [The Cistercians in Poland], ed. Daniel Olszewski (Kielce:
Wydawnictwo Jedność w Kielcach, 1990), pocket supplement, figure 6.

monks by our authority, are these: Henryków with its ambit in which the cloister was founded, a forest near Morzyna, Nikłowice near Ręków, Osiek near Żmigród, and a hundred large hides in the forest near the game park called Richnow. We declare that the cloister of Henryków and the brothers who serve God there possess these aforenamed inheritances legitimately, by the gift of the said Nicholas, and by the confirmation and authority of ourselves and of our son Henry. In order that the brothers of Henryków may in the future implore [God] for our soul with that much more zeal, on the same day we granted to the said cloister a hundred large hides of forest (fifty of which are in Budzyn[12] near our village of Ternav, between the *przesieka*[13] and the Czech Path, and fifty in Chwaliszów between Richnow, a forest of the said cloister, and [the holding of] Bogumił Męka), to be possessed by that cloister forever, for [remission of] our sins.

The confirmation of this gift was made in the Year of the Lord's Incarnation 1228, the second after Nicholas's death, in Henryków itself, at the time when the monastery was founded there, under our authority, by the venerated fathers, Lawrence bishop of Wrocław and Paul bishop of Poznań, and when two altars were most solemnly consecrated by these fathers in that place.[14] Many of our barons, the noble and the mediocre, were also there, and they all appeared as witnesses of this confirmation. The most important among them were: the aforenamed fathers lord Bishops Lawrence and Paul, lord Nasław our notary, our lords and barons Emmeram of Strzegom, Stephen of Wierzbno, Przecław, Jarosław, Bogusław, Conrad of Krosno, Mojko, Jaskotel, Jawór, and Racław, and all the knights and servitors of our court, and many others. In order that this most solemn gift and confirmation of ours in favor of the said Order and the house of Henryków may always stand firm in the future, we have caused this charter to be confirmed by the placement of our seal, and by witness of the aforenamed men and of many faithful.

S.U., 1:no. 290 (1228), 213–14

3 In the name of the Lord, amen. Let it be known to [persons] present and future that I, Grzymisława, by the grace of God duchess of Kraków,[15] [am

---

12. An alternative name for Budzów, discussed by Abbot Peter in the early portion of his account of Schönwald (Chapters 94–96).

13. See the introductory essay above, nn. 16, 259–60.

14. Chapter 21.

15. Duchess of Little Poland, and widow of the recently deceased Duke Leszek the White (see the next footnote), whom she married in or soon after 1206, survived in 1227, and outlived until her own death in 1258 – an active and powerful ducal widow, especially during the minority of her son, Bolesław the Chaste; Andrzej Marzec, "Leszek Biały" [Leszek the White], *Piastowie*, 181–88, at 183, 188; Marzec, "Bolesław Wstydliwy" [Bolesław the Chaste], *Piastowie*, 191–97, at 191–92, 196–97; Dariusz Karczewski, "Nieznany dokument księżnej krakowskiej Grzymisławy z roku 1228. Przyczynek do najwcześniejszego uposażenia klasztoru Cystersów w Henrykowie" [An unknown document issued by

confirming] the same village which my husband Leszek, late duke of Poland,[16] granted to Nicholas, notary of Henry [I the Bearded], duke of Silesia. This same Nicholas gave this village, called Milejewice,[17] to be possessed by hereditary right (*hereditario iure possidendam*) to his monastery (*suo claustro*) which is called Henryków, for the remedy of his soul and of the souls of his predecessors. In order that this gift not be subject to attempted violation by the snares of the wicked, I strengthened this present page with the protection of my seal, together with the seal[s] of lord Ivo bishop of Kraków and of Christian bishop of Prussia. These things were done in the year 1228 after the Incarnation of the Lord, on the first indiction of the month of March, in the assembly celebrated at Skaryszew,[18] with the following witnesses present: lord Theodoric abbot of Jędrzejów,[19] John provost of Miechów, Gregory dean of Saint Florian's, Pakosław the palatine, Mark the palatine, Mszczuj castellan of Wiślica.[20]

Karczewski, "Nieznany dokument," p. 98;
S.U., 1:no. 286 (1228), 210 [register only]

---

the duchess of Kraków, Grzymisława, in 1228: A contribution to the earliest endowment of the Cistercian monastery in Henryków], in *Venerabiles, nobiles et honesti. Studia z dziejów społeczeństwa Polski średniowiecznej* [*Venerabiles, nobiles et honesti*: Studies in the history of medieval Polish society], ed. Andrzej Radzimiński, Anna Supruniuk, and Jan Wroniszewski (Toruń: Wydawnictwo Uniwersytetu Mikołaja Kopernika, 1997), 89–99, at 98, n. 1.

16. Leszek the White, duke of Little Poland with its main cities Kraków and Sandomierz, born around 1186, assumed ducal office in 1202, and died in 1227. He married the Russian duchess, Grzymisława of Lutsk, in or soon after 1206; Marzec, "Leszek Biały;" Karczewski, "Nieznany dokument," 98, n. 2.

17. Neither Abbot Peter nor his continuator mention this holding; Peter's record of Nicholas's "inheritances" in Little Poland is limited to the brief note in Chapter 24. The locality called Milejewice appears in the context of the difficult relationship between the monastery and the inhabitants of Brukalice (a relationship Peter describes at length, in Chapters 112, 114–19), in Supplementary Documents no. 21–23, 27. On the most likely placement of this locality during Nicholas's lifetime, see Karczewski, "Nieznany dokument," 95–97.

18. An assembly presided over by Duchess Grzymisława shortly after the death of her husband; for the significance of that assembly, and of Skaryszew as its venue, see Karczewski, "Nieznany dokument," 91–93, and Piotr Górecki, "Communities of Legal Memory in Medieval Poland, c. 1200–1240," *Journal of Medieval History* 24 (1998), 127–54, at 130–31, 137–40, 152.

19. This monastery, situated about thirty kilometers to the northeast of Kraków, was, along with the Great Polish community of Łekno, the earliest Cistercian monastery in Poland. In contrast to Łekno, it was affiliated directly with Morimond, one of the original five Cistercian houses; the introductory essay above, nn. 307, 317.

20. For the significance of the canons regular of the Holy Sepulchre in Miechów, and the list of Little Polish secular and ecclesiastical figures noted here, see Jerzy Kłoczowski, "Zakony na ziemiach polskich w wiekach średnich" [Monastic orders in the Polish lands during the Middle Ages], in *Kościół w Polsce* [The Church in Poland], ed. J. Kłoczowski, 4 vols. (Kraków: Znak, 1966), 1:375–494, at 436–37; Karczewski, "Nieznany dokument," 98 (n. 7), 99 (nn. 11–15); Górecki, "Communities," 133–36.

4 In the name of the Holy and Indivisible Trinity, amen. We, Paul, by the grace of God bishop of the church of Poznań,[21] make it known to those present and future that once upon a time we have received from the illustrious Władysław [Odonic], duke of [Great] Poland of blessed memory, a village called Dębnica (which is situated next to [the holding of] Peter Hoyerowic, and which has on the other side a village of the archbishop, also called Dębnica), in its entirety, to be possessed forever. Afterwards, truly noting the poverty of the house of the Holy Virgin at Henryków of the Cistercian Order, situated in the diocese of Wrocław, and founded by our brother of happy memory, Nicholas, notary of Henry [I] duke of Silesia, we granted to this house – for the remission of our sins, and for the remedy of the soul of the said Władysław duke of [Great] Poland – this village with its appurtenances, that is, with 38 cattle, under the same right by which we had [it], to be forever possessed by the brothers who serve God there; provided, however, that as long as we are alive, we shall receive the young males of this cattle.

In order, therefore, that this gift of ours may remain firm and stable, the illustrious Władysław, by the grace of God current duke of [Great] Poland, son of Odo, former duke of [Great] Poland, has tendered his devoted acceptance of our request, and strengthened the present charter with the protection of his seal, together with our seal. The witnesses of this gift are: our venerable brother lord Michael, by divine grace bishop of Cuiavia, who also affixed his seal to strengthen this charter at our request; lord Baldwin dean of Gniezno, Bozo the provost, and the full chapter of that church, whose seal is also appended in witness of this gift; Witosław dean of Poznań, Peter the archdeacon, Master Polonus, Theophilus, and the full chapter of that church, whose seal has also been appended in witness, by unanimous consent. This was done in the Year of the Lord 1236, the sixth indiction, in the presence of these [men]: Dzierżykraj the palatine, Bogumił castellan of Gniezno, Cieczyrad castellan of Poznań, Albert the judge, Domerad, and many other nobles of [Great] Poland.

S.U., 2:no. 124 (1236), 81–82

5 In the name of the Holy Trinity, amen. We, Przemysł [I], by the grace of God duke of [Great] Poland, make it known to those present and future, that the beloved Duke Władysław [Odonic], our father of blessed memory, had once upon a time had four holdings near Starygród which adjoined one another within a single district (*ambitus*), of which one was called Sierakowo, another Świętnice, the third Przewodowo, and the fourth Konarskie – all of which this father of ours gathered into a single inheritance, and, for the honor of God and the Holy Virgin and the remedy of his soul, granted to the cloister at Henryków of the Cistercian Order situated in the diocese of Wrocław and the brothers who serve

21. The bishop of Poznań whom Abbot Peter identifies as an important agent in the foundation of the Henryków monastery in 1222, 1227, and 1228 (Chapters 6, 21).

God there, in eternal possession, so that the said inheritance would remain entirely free from every right of his castellans and officials. He also gave the brothers the liberty in this holding to settle Germans if they wished, according to whatever law might be pleasing to the brothers.[22]

Later, after the brothers possessed their inheritance for a few years in peace and without opposition, war arose between Duke Henry [I] and our father,[23] and the brothers suffered damage in Sierakowo by those who endlessly went to and fro.[24] For this reason – albeit against their wish – they abandoned this holding, and afterwards, because of a sequence of many obstacles, this inheritance re-mained alienated from the house of Henryków for a long time. But after the convent of the ladies entered Owińska,[25] the abbot of Henryków began to labor diligently for a revindication of the said inheritance of Sierakowo. Therefore, we, having heard the causes of this gift and this loss from the beginning, forever confirm this village of Sierakowo with the holdings named together with it, for the cloister of Henryków and its servants, to be possessed freely and according to the same law and liberty on which our father first gave it [to them].

In order to make this stronger, we have caused the present charter, strengthened with the witness of our seal, to be issued to the said monastery. The renewal of this gift was made in Owińska, in the Year of the Lord 1252, on All Souls' Day [November 2], with these [persons] present: the venerable lady Gertrude abbess of Trzebnica, lady Agnes daughter of Duke Henry, Herkenbold castellan of Kalisz (who, at our direction, removed his brother from the said village of Sierakowo), Pakosław the hunter, Bożęta the *dapifer*, Andrew the butler, Bogusza the *subcamerarius*, Henry the proctor, and many others.

S.U., 3:no. 46 (1252), 41

22. This is an interesting example of a choice in the future disposal of an estate by the ecclesiastical lord to whom it was granted. Duke Przemysł was anticipating recruitment of further settlers into the "circuit" where these four Polish localities were situated – by Germans, or by someone else; and by a "law" to be chosen accordingly. For the choice of "laws" (of which "German law" was one, by far the most important, variant), see Górecki, *Economy*, 275–81.

23. This is a reference to several periods of warfare between Henry the Bearded and Władysław Odonic, specifically concerning control over the region near the common boundary of Silesia and Great Poland.

24. That is, presumably, by armed men who passed by while supporting either side in the course of the conflict.

25. Location of a convent of Cistercian nuns, which Duke Władysław Odonic estab-lished early in the second decade of the thirteenth century, and which was closely con-nected with the Silesian Piasts. See Gerard Kucharski, "Początki klasztoru cysterek w Ołoboku" [Beginning of the monastery of the Cistercian nuns in Ołobok], in *Cystersi w społeczeństwie Europy Środkowej* [Cistercians in the society of Central Europe], ed. Andrzej Marek Wyrwa and Józef Dobosz (Poznań: Wydawnictwo Poznańskie, 2000), 314–38.

6 In the name of the Lord, amen. What has been bestowed by the dignity of a leader ought to be cherished by the care of the follower. Therefore, we, Bolesław [II], by the grace of God duke of Silesia, together with our son Henry [V],[26] forever declare to those present that, after the perusal of the privileges granted by the illustrious princes and dukes of Silesia, [Great] Poland, and Kraków, Henry [I], our grandfather, and our dearest father, also Henry [II] of happy memory to the brothers and convent of Henryków, of the Cistercian Order, concerning the villages situated within our lordship [i.e., duchy] which they had granted to the said house by everlasting testament for the remission of their sins – by our benign favor, we [now] continue their rightful deeds, and have directed that they deserve to be confirmed.

That is, [we confirm] in the village of Quolsdorf fifty hides, according to the layout and arrangement described in their privileges; and in Richnow a hundred hides, of the quantity and measure which lord Nicholas, at one time the said dukes' notary, is known to have granted to the said brothers with their [i.e., the dukes'] favor and consent, for the remedy of his soul. And because our ancestors' privileges about these hundred hides are lacking, we wish to introduce [information that comes] from them as if it were our own. Urged and moved by the devoted prayers of lord Peter, at that time abbot of the house,[27] and of its other brothers, we granted to this house (toward the dismissal of our debt of 52 silver marks, by which we had been obligated to them; and toward the[ir] full resignation to us of 25 hides, which they had held in the village of Baumgarten, next to the village of Richnow; and for the remission of our sins) a hundred hides in Richnow, to be possessed forever, [thereby] terminating our action against them [in this matter].[28]

And because, as devoted men, they have, by a kind disposition, unanimously forgiven us for disturbing them in any way (if indeed we have done so), we in turn compensate them by extending over their goods, [situated] in our land, a liberty from the burden of all exactions for six years from the Feast of Easter most recently past. Done in Jawór, on the Saturday after the octaves of Easter [April 14], in the Year of the Lord 1263, in the presence of our faithful [men]: Count Stoigniew castellan of Legnica, Count Jacko the great *camerarius* there, lord Henry of

26. Bolesław II's son, Henry V the Fat, was subsequently (between 1290 and 1296) duke of one of the duchies into which Silesia had been subdivided in the course of the thirteenth century; Roman Grodecki, Stanisław Zachorowski, and Jan Dąbrowski, *Dzieje Polski średniowiecznej* [A history of medieval Poland], 2 vols. (2nd ed., Kraków: Universitas, and Kryspinów: Platan, 1995), 1:352, 359; Tomasz Jurek, "Henryk V Gruby (Brzuchaty)" [Henry V the Fat (the Pot-Bellied)], *Piastowie*, 421–23.

27. The author of the first portion of the *Henryków Book*.

28. This promise suggests that, like his brother, Henry III, Bolesław II offended the brothers of Henryków by – among other things – confiscating from them parts of the estate that Henry I had granted in 1228 (Supplementary Document no. 2), and that on the present occasion he was returning the revindicated holdings.

Provin, Przybko our *subdapifer*, Ripert the sub-marshal, Henry of Borowe, Siedelmann of Saalburg. Given by the hand of Master Louis, our notary.

S.U., 3:no. 437 (1263), 288

7 Clement, bishop, servant of the servants of God,[29] to the beloved sons [———],[30] abbot and convent of the monastery of Saint Mary and Saint John the Baptist in Henryków, of the Cistercian Order, and of the diocese of Wrocław, greeting and apostolic benediction. Whereas something which is just and honorable has been requested from us, the force of equity as well as the order of reason compel us that it may be brought to a deserved fruition through the solicitude of our office. Indeed, a request from you placed before us contained [the information] that while the late Nicholas, notary of Henry [I], duke of Silesia of bright memory, was alive, he resigned certain possessions that belonged to him, which he held in fief from that duke, into the hands of the duke, on this condition: that, for the honor of God, and of Saint Mary the Virgin, and of Saint John the Baptist, he [i.e., the duke] might bring it about that a monastery of your Order be newly founded with a part of the possessions of this kind, in the place called Henryków, where you are bound by divine service until the present; and that it be endowed with the remaining part of these possessions[31] [as well, or at a later date].

Indeed, the said duke founded and endowed this monastery with those possessions, according to Nicholas's pious disposition, with the consent of the bishops of good memory, [Lawrence] of Wrocław, and our brother [Paul] of Poznań,[32] in whose dioceses these possessions are situated,[33] and with the assent

29. Pope Clement IV (1265–68).

30. A gap in the text; evidently a space to be filled out with the name of the abbot, who at this time was Abbot Peter.

31. The reader will likely be puzzled by this classification, as of 1268 (and undoubtedly on the basis of some information provided to the papal chancery by Abbot Peter himself) of Nicholas's accumulated holdings, described early in the *Henryków Book*, into two "parts." According to this recollection, the original endowment of the monastery – that is, presumably the "territory of Henryków" and all that went into it (described in Chapters 3–4, 22, 27–39) was only one of these two "parts"; we simply do not know what the other "part" was. Whatever the answer, both parts were "possessions of this kind" – *de parte possessionum huiusmodi*, referring, surely, to the immediately preceding description of Nicholas's holdings as an estate held "in fief from the duke" – yet another classification of the relationship between Notary Nicholas, Duke Henry the Bearded, and the estate granted to the monks between 1222 and 1228, on which see Górecki, "Interpreter," 277–78.

32. Two gaps in the text, to be filled in with the name of Bishops Lawrence and Paul, the author of the charter here presented as Supplementary Document no. 4.

33. Indicating here – again, with no internal or external explanation – that some of the holdings granted to the monastery in Great Poland (that is, the province encompassed by the diocese of Poznań, of which Paul was bishop) were also interpreted as having once been Nicholas's "fiefs."

of the noble man Henry [II], the said duke's son, as is more fully stated in the letters compiled about this and sealed with the said duke's seal.[34]

Hence, moved by your supplications, by apostolic authority we pronounce everything that has piously and carefully been done concerning these [matters] fixed and firm, and we strengthen it with the protection of the present writing. No one therefore among men may infringe upon, or by a bold act contradict, this letter of our confirmation. If anyone presumes to attempt this, let him know that he shall be cursed by the indignation of Almighty God and of his blessed Apostles Peter and Paul. Given at Viterbo, the sixth [day before the] calends of November [October 27], the fifth year of our pontificate [1268].

S.U., 4:no. 78 (1268), 65–66

II *Powerful neighbors of the Henryków monastery: Coexistence, conflict, alliance*

The documents in this section supplement the histories of some of the more important individual landholders who held estates in, or near, the "territory of Henryków," and in Schönwald, at different times in the history narrated by Abbot Peter and by his continuator. One topic of both portions of the *Henryków Book* are the relationships of those individuals (and others like them) to the monastery. The documents in this section shed further light on those relationships.

In contrast to the documents in Section I, the charters here are not presented chronologically, by the date of their issuance. Instead, the order follows the sequence of the first appearances of the relevant individuals within the text of the *Henryków Book*. For instance, the individual called (with some variation) Albert Łyka, Albert with Beard, Albert the Beard, and Albert the Bearded – the same person – appears in that text relatively early, and so the charters concerning him and his descendants make up the first group below. Similarly, in sequence, concerning Duke Henry III, Peter Stoszowic, and Poltko of Schnellenwalde.

Except for Poltko, who is represented by only one document, each individual is reflected in a small dossier of documents. Within each dossier, the order of presentation is chronological. The rationale of this arrangement is to facilitate access by the reader to the long-term fates of particular persons (including their successors), in a sequence that matches the structure of our principal source, the *Henryków Book* itself.

All three documents relating to Albert the Bearded (no. 8–10) concern, in a direct sense, his descendants – two sons, and one grandson – although two of them mention him. (The particulars of the genealogical identifications appear in the footnotes.)[35] Confusingly, one of the sons, and the grandson, share the first name and the nickname with the protagonist of Abbot Peter's history; the Albert "the Beard" noted in no. 8 is the

34. Presumably the diploma here presented as Supplementary Document no. 2.

35. For a full prosopographical study of Albert's kindred, including the sons and the grandson reflected by these three documents, see Tomasz Jurek, *Obce rycerstwo na Śląsku do połowy XIV wieku* [Foreign knighthood in Silesia until the mid-fourteenth century] (2nd ed., Poznań: Wydawnictwo Poznańskiego Towarzystwa Przyjaciół Nauk, 1998), 194–96, supplementing and correcting the earlier reconstruction by Marek Cetwiński, *Rycerstwo śląskie do końca XIII w.: biogramy i rodowody* [Silesian knighthood through the end of the thirteenth century: biograms and genealogies] (Wrocław: Zakład Narodowy im. Ossolińskich, 1982), 63–66 (nn. 4, 6, 12), 105–06 (n. 216).

protagonist's son, and the man with the same name and nickname in no. 9–10 is his grandson. The latter two charters clearly refer to the original Albert, and identify them as the ego's grandfather; in addition, one of these (no. 16) identifies, as the ego's father, Grabisza, the second son of of the first Albert.

Either of these two sons might be the bad, "tyrannical" first-born son of the first Albert whom Abbot Peter identifies in Chapter 52 as an oppressor of his monastery until his deathbed reconciliation. The offenses noted in no. 8 by the papal legate Philip match, in detail, the offenses Peter attributed to that unnamed first-born – namely, unauthorized confiscations of tithe revenues from the Henryków monastery – except that, according to no. 8, the victim monastery was the community at Kamieniec, not Henryków, and that this offender had died unreconciled, until the posthumous reconciliation recorded in no. 8.

We know, from no. 10, much less about the other son, Grabisza, except that his son, the third Albert, recorded in this document his own promise to the abbot of Henryków not to contest his grandfather's transfer of Cienkowice to the monastery – a transaction which Abbot Peter describes in Chapter 49, and does not himself present as subsequently problematic. Although, therefore, these three documents do not fully answer the questions raised by Abbot Peter's terse narration about the difficulties posed by Albert's descendants, they certainly show us the nature and the duration of those difficulties, and the elements of their resolution over time.

Similarly with the two documents concerning Peter Stoszowic (no. 13–14), which show the aftermath of the property conflict between him and the Henryków monastery described by Abbot Peter in Chapters 103–09. One of the charters concerns Peter himself (no. 13), the second was issued by his son Paszko (no. 14).[36] Document no. 13 records a gift by Peter to the monastery, right within the region over which the conflict had raged, and so perhaps reflects a part of the reconciliation between him and the monks after Abbot Peter ended that story. And no. 14 records a property seizure by Paszko which, in its particulars, is very similar to what his father had done, thus triggering the conflicts described by Abbot Peter – followed, in turn, by Paszko's own reconciliation. In contrast with Albert, we know nothing about Paszko, or about any other descendants of Peter Stoszowic, from the *Henryków Book*. Yet, as with Albert the Bearded, we also have a story of difficulties raised by two generations of powerful neighbors of the monastery, and the resolution of these difficulties, all of them spanning a considerable period.

The two remaining documents issued by Duke Henry III (no. 11–12), each record a resale to the Henryków monastery of a property that had been formerly given to it, but that that duke subsequently confiscated, for reasons Abbot Peter obliquely explains in Chapter 78. Document no. 11 is fully a part of the abbot's story of one holding, Jaworowice; it is an expanded and detailed version of Henry III's charter recording that same resale, issued a few days earlier, and actually incorporated by Abbot Peter into Chapter 79.

In contrast, no. 12 concerns a resale of Głębowice, a holding whose history Abbot Peter ends much earlier. Therefore, we know nothing from the *Henryków Book* itself about that particular ducal confiscation, and thus have yet another glimpse at an aftermath of Abbot Peter's story. Henry III's confiscation of Głębowice is certainly consistent with Abbot Peter's characterization of the widespread nature of confiscations of properties by this duke, from the Henryków monastery and from other landholders, in Chapter 78. This gives us insight into a rather different kind of property difficulty, and its resolution.

---

36. On the genealogy, see Cetwiński, *Rycerstwo*, 136 (nn. 629–30), 164 (n. 637), 185–86 (n. 785). This is not reassessed by Jurek, *Obce*, because Peter Stoszowic and his family were indigenous, Polish lords, and therefore outside the scope of Jurek's book.

Finally, the last document, no. 15, sheds further light on the property conflict between the monastery and another troublesome neighbor, Poltko of Schnellenwalde, which culminated in the final decade of the thirteenth century, and which is a prominent subject of the second portion of the *Book*, especially Chapter 162. In this case, the estate under contestation was relatively modest, but, in conjunction with the text of the *Book*, we have an unusually vivid record of a trial, and of its principally urban and German setting, around the turn of the thirteenth and the fourteenth centuries.

8   To all who inspect the present letters, Philip, by divine mercy bishop of Fermo, legate of the Apostolic See,[37] greetings in the Savior of all. May your entire community know that the religious men, the abbot and the convent of the monastery at Kamieniec[38] of the Cistercian Order in the diocese of Wrocław, came up and urged us by their petition that, when he was alive, a certain noble man, Albert called the Beard,[39] from Więcemierzyce in the diocese of Wrocław, had unduly and violently occupied, seized, and removed from them certain tithes [due] from the said place, Więcemierzyce, which belonged to their monastery by full right.

For which reason – and because he [also] invaded, seized, and with a damnable presumption occupied and removed, certain other tithes, goods, and rights of churches and of ecclesiastical persons – he was, without a doubt, struck by [ecclesiastical] judgment, by the tenor of a decision of Guido, cardinal of good memory, formerly legate of the Apostolic See in the province of Poland,[40] as well

---

37. A legate was a high cleric and a pope's representative, typically with a very broad mandate to carry out reform, or settle a major conflict, within a very large administrative unit of the Church – in this case, the archdiocese of Gniezno and its constitutent bishoprics, which included Wrocław. This particular legate, Philip of Fermo, was a papal legate for all of Poland and Hungary in the late 1270s, and, in a mission that brought him to Silesia in 1282, resolved a wide array of diplomatic and ecclesiastical issues affecting the dukes and bishops in Silesia and Little Poland; Paweł Żmudzki, *Studium podzielonego królestwa. Książę Leszek Czarny* [A study in a divided kingdom: Duke Leszek the Black] (Warsaw: Wydawnictwo NERITON, 2000), 285, 302, 304, 311, 314, 319–20, 322–23, 332; Kazimierz Gołąb, "Filip z Fermo i jego statuty legackie z 1279 r." [Philip of Fermo and his legatine statutes of 1279], *Roczniki Historyczne* 26 (1960), 255–64. The transactions concerning the deceased Albert the Bearded (n. 39 below) were a small part of that much larger agenda.

38. Chapter 68, n. 67.

39. This was a son, and a namesake, of the first Albert the Bearded (a very important actor of Abbot Peter's portion of the *Henryków Book*), quite possibly the "tyrant" who had illicitly retained the tithe revenues due to the Henryków monastery from a holding granted by his father until shortly before his death (Chapter 52); Jurek, *Obce*, 195.

40. Guido was a papal legate with a mission to Silesia in 1267; Tadeusz Silnicki, "Kardynał legat Gwido, jego synod wrocławski w roku 1267 i statuty tego synodu" [Cardinal Legate Guido, his Wrocław synod of 1267, and the statutes of this synod], in Silnicki, *Z dziejów kościoła w Polsce. Studia i szkice historyczne* [Fragments of the history of the Church in Poland: studies and historical sketches] (Warsaw: Państwowe Wydawnictwo Naukowe, 1960), 321–80; Piotr Górecki, *Parishes, Tithes, and Society in Earlier Medieval Poland, ca. 1100–*

as by a synodal decision made by the late venerable father Pełka (by the grace of God archbishop of Gniezno),[41] and also by the sentences [based upon the letter] of various other canons.[42] While thus bound by those sentences, he embarked on the path of all flesh [i.e., died]. And although his body was buried in the ecclesiastical cemetery, yet we, in response to the request by the abbot and convent, pressed by justice, have mandated that he be exhumed and cast off far away from ecclesiastical burial.

Then the noble man Nicholas, brother of the deceased, appeared and stood in our presence, and, touching the Holy Gospels, offered an oath on the deceased's behalf to comply with the sentences of excommunication mandated by the Church and by ourselves which he [i.e., the deceased] had incurred in any way whatsoever. [He also promised] that, while he was alive, he would adequately compensate the abbot and convent for that [deceased brother]. He expressly obligated himself and all his goods to be restored to us, on behalf of all whom it concerns or may concern: that he would freely and absolutely satisfy, according to our will and mandate, all the damages, injuries, and offenses which the deceased had inflicted on churches or on ecclesiastical persons, and for which he had been bound by the chains of excommunication. He also promised the abbot and the convent, and specially obligated himself and all his goods to them, that he will bring it about and take care that the heirs of the said deceased will not in the future by any means, acting by themselves or through others, disturb the aforesaid abbot and convent or their monastery about those tithes, or [otherwise] molest them at any time whatever.

Then, after the noble man Pakosław the knight, son of the late Zdzieszyc from the diocese of Wrocław, likewise obligated himself and his goods in this matter, warranting that Nicholas will observe the aforesaid [terms], we have allowed the body of the aforesaid deceased – after the debts of his absolution were satisfied – to be buried anew in the ecclesiastical cemetery, according to the form of the Church observed in such matters. Given in Wrocław, the twelfth [day before the] calends of April [March 21], in the Year of the Lord 1282, tenth indiction, the second year of the pontificate of lord Pope Martin IV.

S.U., 5:no. 8 (1282), 8–9

1250, Transactions of the American Philosopical Society 83.2 (Philadelphia: American Philosophical Society, 1993), 18, 52, 62–64, 107–19.

41. Pełka was archbishop of Gniezno between 1232 and 1258; Jerzy Kłoczowski, *Dzieje chrześcijaństwa polskiego* [A history of Polish Christianity], vol. 1 (Paris: Nasza Rodzina, 1987), 54.

42. That last phrase, *necnon et alias diversas canonum sentencias*, seems to refer to sentences imposed according to rules of canon law, and, in contrast to the preceding two phrases, not to the ecclesiastical officials who imposed the sentences. However, in a grammatical sense, it could also mean sentences that were imposed by canons, that is, cathedral clergy (presumably from Wrocław or from Gniezno), as yet another source of sanction against Albert.

9 In the name of the Lord, amen. It behooves the sons to so favor the faithful testaments of the fathers, that that which the labor of salvation has approved by a well-disposed mind may benefit from [further] increases, infused by the Grantor of the saving virtues of grace. Therefore I, Albert, called the Beard,[43] noting, in view of my need of salvation, that my ancestors have very sorely lacked salvation and grace, and that they have, for that reason, not without merit, sweated with salvific labors to compensate for that fact – make it known to the [persons] present and future that when my grandfather, by the name of Albert with Beard[44] (who had once upon a time resided in his village of Ciepłowoda) observed that the cloister of the Holy Forever Virgin Mary in Henryków of the Cistercian Order was beset by a great poverty, and that the brothers dwelling there were serving God most uprightly, he affectionately wished to alleviate their poverty to the best of his ability, and granted to them his inheritance of Cienkowice (which the brothers of the said cloister possess until the present)[45] for his sins, so that, just as he had offered them support in temporal matters at the outset of the foundation, [now], aided by their prayers, he may enjoy eternal rest.

In the course of time, after I passed the years of boyhood, and, as a true heir, by reason of legitimate patrimony, was in possession of the aforementioned village Ciepłowoda (which had belonged to the said Albert, my grandfather, and to my father, Grabisza),[46] one day when I was visiting the cloister of Henryków in order to gaze upon the divine offices, the lord abbot kindly spoke to me after the solemnities of the prayers, and made a speech about the said inheritance of Cienkowice, and exhorted me never to be tempted by a sting of vexation to deprive [the monastery] of it, but to rejoice in these things in approval of my grandfather's affectionate gift.

Therefore, considering it wrong for wholesome promptings to be resisted, I publicly declare by open writings my father's and my own full consent regarding my grandfather's gift to the cloister of Henryków, so that no one from among men whatsoever may be able, or ought, to disturb the brothers of Henryków with respect to the inheritance of Cienkowice just mentioned. In eternal memory of this matter, I strengthened the present letters with my seal, during the Year of the Lord 1287, on the Day of the Purification of Saint Mary [February 2], in the presence of the witnesses: Count John Osina, Count Dobiesław of Targowica, Count Bartholomew of Stachów, Count Zdziśko, Count Frisko of Bischofsheim, and Jeszko son of [Count John of] Osina, and many others.

S.U., 5:no. 317 (1287), 250–51

---

43. Also a namesake of the first Albert the Bearded, this particular Albert was his grandson (as he clearly states below); Jurek, *Obce*, 195.

44. Chapters 45–57, 74, 108, 111.

45. Chapter 49.

46. This is another son of the original Albert the Bearded, and, like Albert II, quite possibly the person whom Abbot Peter remembered as a "tyrant" afflicting the monastery after Albert's death; Chapter 52; Jurek, *Obce*, 195.

10 In the name of the Lord, amen. In order that deeds effected in the present by the effort of devotion may always flourish undiminished among the successors, it is absolutely necessary to make them eternal through letters and witnesses. Therefore I, Albert, called the Beard[47] – affirming that nothing is more excellent in life than to do well and to glory in the Lord thanks to a good conscience, which is no better obtained and possessed than [by performance of] works of mercy – through the present writings bring this to the knowledge of all [persons], present and future: that, for the splendor and glory of the Merciful God and of His Inviolate Mother, and for the remedy of the sins of myself, of my father, and of my mother, I gave in alms to the brothers of the said house a single holding out of my forest containing two small hides and three rods, and closely adjoining the forest of the brothers of the house of Henryków; and, by the favor of lord Duke Bolko [I] and in the presence of his *camerarius* Bartosz, I delimited the holding itself with manifest boundaries.[48] I resigned and transferred the aforesaid holding to the brothers of the house, by a title of property so eternal that I have utterly cut off all jurisdiction in it from myself and all my successors.

To strengthen, and in perennial memory of, this spontaneous gift of mine, I enlivened the present writing by the placement of the seals of myself and of the noble men, Sambor my brother-in-law, and Henry of Schildberg his brother. These things were done in Henryków, in the Year of the Lord 1296, on the twelfth [day before the] calends of December [November 20], with the witness of the nobles: Sambor my brother-in-law; Henry of Schildberg, his brother; Gunther of Smelow; likewise Gunther of Wojnicz and Peter, his brother; likewise Heinmann of Talwiz, and many others.

S.U., 6:no. 282 (1296), 226–27

11 In the name of the Lord, amen. We, Henry [III], by the grace of God duke of Silesia, wish it to be known to those present and future, that, with the consent of our brothers, Bolesław [II] and Conrad,[49] we sold our village of Jaworowice[50] – which is situated between the cloister of Henryków and Kunzendorf (a property of the house of Trzebnica), contains sixteen small hides, and was measured out on our command by Paul Słupowic and by the village bailiff (*villicus*) of Heidenrichsdorf – to the same house of Henryków and the brothers serving God in it, for eighty silver marks, to be

47. Presumably the same person as the author of the preceding document, that is, grandson of the original Albert the Bearded, now in old age.

48. Another example of a perambulation of a boundary; see the introductory essay above, nn. 263, 284–85.

49. Henry III and Bolesław II, as above; and Conrad I, duke of the region of Silesia centered in Głogów, who died in 1273 or 1274 (Tomasz Jurek, "Konrad I," *Piastowie*, 613–15). Henry issued the present charter a few days after an earlier, shorter charter concerning the same transaction, transcribed as Chapter 79.

50. Chapters 27, 36, 57, 74–79.

possessed freely by these brothers forever.[51] In order that the said house and its servants may forever peacefully possess this particular village of Jaworowice without opposition, we cause this charter to be strengthened by the placement of five seals, that is to say our own, and our mother's, and those of our aforenamed brothers, and of the venerable father Thomas, bishop of Wrocław, who has also placed his seal on this charter upon our request, in the witness of truth.

Thus, we have directed that this letter, strengthened by such seals, be granted to the oft-mentioned monastery, so that none of our successors may presume to infringe upon this deed, mandated and established by ourselves and by our brothers, for any cause, or to weaken it in any way. The witnesses of this deed are: Count Jaksa castellan of Wrocław, Count John of Wierzbno castellan of Ryczyn, Count Michael judge of the court, Conrad the butler, Master Gocwin, Paul Słupowic, Stanisław, Lawrence key-keeper of Wrocław. Given by the hand of Walter, writer of the court, in the Year of the Incarnation of the Lord 1255, on the morrow of the calends of July [June 30].

S.U., 3:no. 151 (1255), 106–07

12   In the name of the Lord, amen. It is the custom to commit all transactions that need to remain in a sound and unfailing condition to the presence of worthy witnesses and to the signs of letters. We, Henry [III], by the grace of God duke of Silesia, wish it to be known by, and publicly to avow to each and all who inspect this letter, that the lord abbot and the entire convent of the monastery of Saint Mary in Henryków, of the Cistercian Order, in the diocese of Wrocław, have bought from us the inheritance called Głębowice,[52] situated on the stream [called] Morzyna, adjoining the cloister itself, and containing eleven small hides, for 110 silver marks (that is, ten silver marks for each hide), to be possessed by the said cloister forever.[53] On our mandate, the aforenoted abbot and his brothers have presented this money, in its entirety, to these men, that is to say: to David the Russian fifty marks, to Conrad the Westphalian twenty, to Simon Papa thirty, to John the goldsmith ten.

In order that in the future this deed may not be revoked, or frivolously disturbed in any way, by our brothers, or sons, or any affines whatever, we took care to give to this convent the present writing, strengthened with the protection of our seal, and also with the record of the witnesses who were present at this transaction, and whose names are: William, the venerable bishop of Lubusz,

---

51. This is one of several examples of a ducal resale of a formerly granted holding to the Henryków monastery after a revindication, a practice of which Abbot Peter accused Henry III in particular; Chapters 77–79; the introductory essay above, nn. 261–62.

52. Chapters 27, 82–91, 93; Supplementary Document no. 19.

53. This is another example of a resale, by Duke Henry III, of a holding that had been earlier granted to the monastery; Chapters 86–90.

John of Wierzbno castellan of Ryczyn, [and] Racław the judge, who were the arrangers (*ordinatores*) of this agreement,[54] John the castellan in Uraz, Master Gocwin, Dziersław, Ulric the *subdapifer*, Dzietko the sub-butler, Grabisza the marshal, Eberhard and Simon, brothers, and very many others. Given in Wrocław, by the hand of Otto, notary of the court. Done in the same place, in the Year of the Lord, 1263, the fifteenth [day before the] calends of October [September 17].

S.U., 3:no. 452 (1263), 298–99

13 In the name of the Lord, amen. We, Henry [III], by the grace of God duke of Silesia, make it known to those present and future, that, for the salvation of his soul and of the souls of his ancestors, Count Peter Stoszowic has, in our presence, and by his good, spontaneous, and free will, ceded to the lord abbot of Henryków and to his house [a gift] of a certain mill and ten hides, located between Piotrowice and Schönwald,[55] granting them the aforesaid hides and mill with all uses which might arise from them, now or in the future, to be possessed happily and quietly, and also renouncing every right which is believed to belong to him or to his descendants in the goods just aforesaid. In witness of this matter, he has requested that the present letter be strengthened by the placement of our seal. These things were done in Wrocław, in the Year of the Lord's Incarnation 1254, in the presence of our venerable fathers lord Thomas bishop of Wrocław and lord William bishop of Lubusz, and Master Gocwin canon of Wrocław, and Count John of Wierzbno, and Count Zbylut, and Count Dzierżysław.

S.U., 3:no. 141 (1254), 99–100

14 In the name of the Lord, amen. I, Count Paszko, son of Peter Stoszowic, desire it to be known to all that I have long experienced a certain excitement in my soul against the house and brothers of Henryków because of certain goods possessed by them which I have [long] believed to belong to me. On the counsel of my friends, who were of the opinion[56] that I did [in fact] have some [kind of] right to them, during the captivity of the illustrious prince, my lord Henry [III]

54. Witness lists of the Polish documents frequently include names of participants who facilitated the recorded transactions, and refer to them with a wide variety of names – mediators, friends, worthy persons, "arrangers" – suggesting that their roles in the legal process were perhaps informal in an institutional sense, yet important; see Górecki, "Communities," 28–29, 136–37, 147–48. The best description of mediation preparatory for legal transactions in the Polish sources is Abbot Peter's account of the role of the bishops of Wrocław, Poznań, and Lubusz on behalf of Notary Nicholas, in Chapters 6–10, 21.

55. Chapter 103.

56. The phrase here is *amicorum meum arbitrantium*, and the last word refers both to having an opinion (as here translated), and to a mediating capacity – an ambiguity that is surely intentional in the Latin original, and lost in English.

duke of Silesia,[57] I usurped these goods (ten hides in Schönwald, the village of the brothers) by a bold act for myself, and I fixed a boundary around them as my own.[58] Later, after the lord duke was by God's will already freed from captivity, these brothers brought a quarrel [against me before the duke], and he assigned judges to adjudicate the case between them and myself,[59] and the brothers obtained these hides by a just judgment and [testimony of] witnesses.

And although until now I may have persevered in my obstinacy and aggravated the men of the aforesaid village with frequent injuries and disturbances, [now] at last, pulled away from my error by men who favor justice, and at the same time moved by repentance, in the presence of this duke and his barons, and by my good will, I completely withdrew from the goods which I had unjustly demanded, gave up every right and jurisdiction which I appeared to have in the said goods, and further strengthened the present charter by the placement of my seal, so that no one among my successors may be snared by this error. These things were done in Wrocław, in the Year of the Lord 1278, in the presence of these [men]: lord Peter the protonotary, Count Siegfried of Baruth, Count Nicholas Grzymisławic, Count Simon, Count Racław Drzemlik, Count Conrad son of the butler, lord John son of Master Gocwin, and very many trustworthy others.

S.U., 4:no. 350 (1278), 232

15 In the name of the Lord, amen. Because trust may not be placed in words unless they receive the support of the witness of truth, we, Gosko and John, hereditary judges, and all the consuls, assessors, and other citizens of Münsterberg, make it known to those whom the present writing may reach, present and future, that when the village of Wiesenthal[60] (which the illustrious Prince Bolko [I], duke of Silesia, had [earlier] bought from his knight Poltko)[61] [later] accrued, by a worthy exchange, to the religious men, brothers of Henryków, a certain Peter by the nickname of Gisele asserted that, although Poltko might have [licitly] held the village at the time, yet a single hide in it had been taken away from him

---

57. Capture by his younger brother, Conrad, in 1250 – not to be confused with the earlier captivity of his older brother, Bolesław II (Chapter 77), but part of the same political context; see Tomasz Jurek, "Henryk III Biały" [Henry III the White], *Piastowie*, 415–17, at 415.

58. Compare the transgressions by Peter Stoszowic himself, narrated in Chapters 93–111, especially 103.

59. From around the mid-thirteenth century onward, dukes frequently assigned judges in this way, presumably in those cases when, for whatever reason, they did not wish to act as judges themselves. Assignment of judges to try specific cases emerges as an important judicial role of the dukes; compare Duke Bolesław II's decision to preside over the trial of Peter Stoszowic himself (Chapter 106), with his decision to delegate the trial of the heirs of Bobolice to a "noble man," so that he could represent the monastery in person (Chapter 61).

60. Chapters 126, 154–64, 177, 183.

61. Chapter 156.

through the said Poltko's violence; and he occupied himself with demanding the said hide back from the brothers.[62]

A term concerning this demand was assigned for the said Peter in our city of Münsterberg, and the aforesaid Poltko (who had promised to defend the said village from every [legal] claim)[63] was summoned to the same [assigned term] by the said Duke Bolko. Duke Bolko gave Count Jarosław to Poltko and Peter as judge concerning the said hide. Sitting as a court in our presence, the assessors heard the cases of each party, and pronounced a just sentence against the said Peter, duly and rightfully depriving him of the said hide, and granting Poltko the protection of the law.[64] These things were effected in the year 1293, on the Day of Saint Gregory [March 12], in the attendance of Counts Henry of Schildberg and Mojko, son of the late Dzierżysław, who were summoned to this matter in the witness of truth.

After the said Peter embarked on the path of all flesh [i.e., died], his two sons Conrad and Peter, moved by foolish counsel, unworthily demanded the hide recorded above, of which Peter, their father identified above, had been deprived, and they repeatedly went to the trouble of exhorting the said brothers about it. Yet, after a more healthy counsel led them to an understanding of the truth, appearing before us by a free and spontaneous will, they publicly declared that they had no right whatsoever to the said hide. And they made a solemn and certain renunciation of the said hide, for themselves and their heirs, sons and daughters, and all future descendants whatever, relatives, and friends – and they warranted the above [transactions] by touching [the relics of] the saints, beyond the [usual?] security confirmed by oath.[65] Therefore, to strengthen, and in eternal memory of, this common [i.e., public] and spontaneous renunciation, we have signed [these] letters patent with the stamp of our seals. This renunciation was made in our presence, and by our witness, in Münsterberg, in the Year of the Lord 1296, on the Day of Saints Philip and James, Apostles [May 1].

S.U., 6:no. 257 (1296), 208

---

62. Chapter 162.

63. That is, at an earlier occasion Peter had promised to act as warrantor of the holding for the monastery (n. 74 below), which was a recurrent relationship between persons who gave away, sold, or exchaged estates and their ecclesiastical recipients in fourteenth-century Poland.

64. This sentence describes several formal steps of early-fourteenth-century court procedure, including the duke's grant of a fixed term for trial, and the duke's assignment of one or more judges to try the case.

65. This is a rather ornate description of an oath, which in the Middle Ages involved direct contact with relics.

III *Family histories, property divisions, alienations, and disputes*

This final, rather long section is similar in arrangement to the preceding section. However, instead of using particular individuals as the main organizing criterion, it uses particular localities making up (at different points in the big story) parts of the monastery's estate. As in Section II, the sequence of presentation follows the order in which the two authors of the *Book* present the selected localities. Like Section II, this section also does not claim to present an exhaustive compendium of the resonances in the charters of every single important locality mentioned in the *Henryków Book*; instead, it offers a range of additional material that gives the principal source greater depth.

The reader will not fail to observe that there is an overlap in the principal subject of Section II and III, in as much as they both illustrate, in additional depth, relationships between the monastery and particular persons. For instance, the first three documents here (no. 16–18) identify, as an important actor, John – an heir of Skalice who, until he was bought off, threatened the monastery with property conflict over that locality, for reasons explained by Abbot Peter in Chapters 71–72. They also supplement Peter's narrative considerably, no. 17 by means of a full charter which the abbot seriously abbreviated, for some reason, in Chapter 72. Similarly, the remaining documents are also, from one perspective, about people who appear important in the two portions of the *Book*: Michael Daleborowic and his sons, the second Stephen Kobylagłowa, and, perhaps above all, the very troublesome two grandsons of Boguchwał Brukał, Bogusza and Paul. From that perspective, some or all of these documents could easily have been included in the preceding section. Yet these documents are not, pricipally, about particular people who mattered. From document no. 16 onward, we see other social configurations: above all, larger groups of kindred and property holding. This kind of collective actor becomes especially important in the documents concerning the successors of Boguchwał Brukał (no. 20–23), but matters in every single portion of this section. This, put simply, is the reason it is more convenient to adopt a criterion keyed to particular localities, not individuals, in this section.

The documents concerning Skalice, then, tell us much about the original Nicholas and Stephen, and, in the next generation, John, but they also, in no. 16, point us to kinship and property – reinforcing Abbot Peter's insight into the same subjects, especially in Chapters 65, 69–70. The sole document concerning Głębowice (no. 19) describes, many generations after its eponym Głąb, a familial property claim to what had been his original holding – a type of difficulty that, quite conspicuously, was *not* one of Abbot Peter's, or his continuator's worries about that holding! The remaining documents illustrate what William North has recently called the fragmentation and redemption of particular monastic properties[66] – again, best viewed from the perspective of place, at least as a point of departure. This is the common theme of the increasingly detailed and what from a reader's perspective may be occasionally tedious charters of the second half of this section.

Perhaps the best example of this response to fragmentation are no. 20–23, concerning Brukalice. These four documents fill in the details of the troublesome relationship between the Henryków monastery and the two grandsons of Boguchwał Brukał, Bogusza

66. William North, "The Fragmentation and Redemption of a Medieval Cathedral: Property, Conflict, and Public Piety in Eleventh-Century Arezzo," in *Conflict in Medieval Europe: Changing Perspectives on Society and Culture*, ed. Warren C. Brown and Piotr Górecki (Aldershot: Ashgate, 2003), 109–130.

and Paul, whom Peter describes in Chapters 113–19. In addition, these four documents shed light on the other descendants of Boguchwał to whom Abbot Peter devoted the final, unfinished, chapter of his portion of the *Book* (Chapter 123).

16 In the name of the Lord, amen. We, Henry [III], by the grace of God duke of Silesia and [Great] Poland, make it known to those present and future that the heirs of Skalice, John,[67] Peter, Paul, Robert, Zdzisław, Andrew, Szczę-stowój, Benik, and Janik, have, in the presence of ourselves and of our barons, resigned in favor of the cloister of Henryków of the Cistercian Order from every right and jurisdiction which they had or may have in the said territory of Skalice, for themselves and for their heirs and relatives – by whatever title, whether by gift or by sale, the mentioned inheritance will have devolved on the aforenamed cloister. We, therefore, in approval of their resignation, have freely granted the oft-mentioned manor to the aforenoted monastery, and we confirm by the present page that it is to be possessed forever, entirely free from any claim by the oft-mentioned kindred – which, in order that it be more strongly bolstered, we caused to be strengthened by the placement of our seal and by the witness of our barons. This was done in Nysa, in the year of the Incarnation of the Lord 1250, on the tenth [day before the] calends of May [April 22], in the presence of these [men]: Count Jaksa castellan of Niemcza, Count Mroczko castellan of Ryczyn, Count Albert castellan of Wrocław, Count Janusz son of Jarosław, Count Janusz son of Bogumił, by the nickname of Męka, and many others.

S.U., 2:no. 392 (1250), 249

17 In the name of the Lord, amen. We, Henry [III], by the grace of God duke of Silesia, yearning for the advancement of the Venerable Mother Church in our time, and in every way approving our predecessors' just deeds, forever confirm the privileges, gifts, and confirmations granted to the house of Henry-ków by our grandfather and father, [Dukes Henry I and Henry II], and we wish them to remain firm and fixed forever, in our own time and the times of our successors, undisturbed by the succession of times and persons.

We especially confirm a certain privilege issued to the cloister of Henryków by the illustrious Duke [Henry II], our father of happy memory.[68] We declare everything in it fixed, and we wish our succeessors to agree. Fearing the possibility of danger, we renew the tenor of that charter, word for word, in this way:

We, Henry [II], by the grace of God duke of Silesia, Kraków, and [Great] Poland, make it known by our full declaration of witness to present and future [persons] that, in the presence of the illustrious Duke Henry [I], our father, certain uterine brothers of Skalice, Nicholas and Stephen, granted two of the three parts of the inheritance which belonged to them among

67. Chapters 70–72; Supplementary Documents no. 17–18.
68. Chapter 70.

their remaining brothers, to Saint Mary and to the brothers of Henryków who serve God there, to be possessed forever, for the remedy of the souls of their father and mother, and of their own [souls]. After his brother accepted the habit, and entered into [monastic] observance, Stephen sold the third part to the said house for 27 silver marks, to be possessed by hereditary right, so that, by the direction and decree of our remembered father, and with our [own] agreement, from now on neither Stephen nor his successors shall have any ability to redeem [Skalice].[69]

But at the time when this was going on, there was a little son of the aforesaid Stephen, John by name. This John, after he reached the years of full discretion and took a wife, resigned before ourselves and our barons from every right and every jurisdiction which he had or may have had in the said inheritance of Skalice, for himself and for his heirs and relatives.[70] Hence, for the good of the peace and by his good will, the abbot of Henryków bought two small hides from the goods of the cloister in this land of Silesia for the same John,[71] to be possessed by hereditary right forever.

In order therefore that the house of God in Henryków and the brothers serving God there may in the future always possess this holding of Skalice – which accrued to the same cloister in the manner noted above in the times of our grandfather and father – in peace from all demands by the aforesaid kindred, we strengthen the present charter by the placement of our seal and by witness of our barons. These things were done in Wrocław, in the year of the Lord 1259, the tenth [day before the] calends of March [February 20], in the presence of these [persons]: Count John of Wierzbno, Master Gocwin, Count Michael the judge, Count Sulisław Irdzek, lord Henry our chaplain of Reichenbach, Heinzo our scholar,[72] and, from among the servitors, Henry Ilkowic, Ingram his brother, Simon and Pakosław, and many others. Given by the hand of lord Otto.

S.U., 3:no. 281 (1259), 186–87

18 In the name of the Lord, amen. All things that take place in time easily waver unless strengthened by writing and by the support of witnesses. We, Henry [IV], by the grace of God duke of Silesia, wish this to reach the knowledge of all [persons], present as well as future: that John, son of the late Stephen, standing bodily in our presence, has publicly resigned before us all

---

69. Chapters 65–67, 69–70.

70. Abbot Peter transcribed a portion of a charter issued on the same date as the present charter – but apparently not of the present charter itself – on this subject, in Chapter 72.

71. As noted in the next document (no. 18), these hides were situated in Schönwald, one of the localities described by Abbot Peter (Chapters 94–111).

72. *Scholasticus* meant a learned person in general, or specifically a person learned in the law, or instructor of a school. In all these capacities, he could be attached to a court, abbey, or cathedral; Niermeyer, 945–46, *s.v. schola, scholaris, scholasticus*.

jurisdiction in the inheritance commonly called Skalice, which inheritance the same Stephen, his father, and Nicholas, his uncle, generously granted and gave to the house in Henryków for the remedy of their souls; and he promised and vowed to the said house that if in the course of time the aforesaid inheritance should be disturbed in whatever manner, or by whatever person, he would render it entirely free from every harm and disturbance.

Furthermore, in order that John may love and cherish the house of Henryków, the lord abbot and his convent in return granted to him and his heirs two small hides in Schönwald, immune from every exaction and all services and payments, to be possessed freely in the future, according to German and hereditary law,[73] adding and promising that if anyone should attempt to disturb John in [his possession of] these hides, he would free [John] from all [such] disturbance.[74] In witness of which matter, we have caused the present page to be strengthened with the protection of our seal, with the witnesses noted below, that is to say, Counts Janusz, Stosz, Racław, John called Zerucha, Despryn, Bogusław Jaworowic, and many trustworthy others. Done in Wrocław, in the Year of the Lord 1272, [on the day] following the Day of Saint Martin [November 12].

S.U., 4:no. 190 (1272), 135

19 In the name of the Lord, amen. Let all who inspect this letter know that a certain Nicholas, son of Michael, incessantly afflicted the cloister of Henryków with cruel threats because of a certain inheritance of the same cloister which is called Głębowice.[75] That is, the same Nicholas was saying that this inheritance, Głębowice, belonged to him by hereditary right through the death of his great-grandfather called Głąb, and of his grandfather called Concodron, and of his father called Michael.[76] When lord Gierko, proctor[77] of the illustrious duke of

---

73. This is either a full description, or an additional element, of the gift made by the abbot of Henryków to John "for the good of the peace," to prevent the danger of a property claim by him, which Abbot Peter describes in Chapter 72, and which the preceding document also notes.

74. This is an early example of the use in Polish property transactions of warranty, that is, a promise by some interested party – usually the donor or seller of a holding – to aid the recipient in future disputes concerning its possession.

75. Supplementary Document no. 12.

76. Abbot Peter describes Głąb, and his grandson Kwiecik, in Chapters 82–84; and in Chapter 86 notes that Głąb had a brother, Pirosz, who had descendants known by Pirosz's patronymic (*Piroszowice*) in 1234. However, he says nothing about Głąb's son – or sons – and the name of a son is identified here. The name *Concodron* sounds extremely odd, and I assume it is garbled. Either Concodron was the father of Michael and Kwiecik; or he was Kwiecik's uncle. Whether they were brothers or cousins, Michael and Kwiecik lived in the same generation. Since Kwiecik died in 1245, at an old age, Nicholas, as an offspring of his generation, must himself have been very old at this conclusion of his quarrel with the monastery.

77. This is one of the medieval terms for an agent in court, a person with full authority to act on behalf of, and bind, the party whom he represents – that is, a principal.

Opole,[78] took on this [matter], he intervened, moved by devotion, and – especially because of the brotherhood with the cloister which he had[79] – made peace between the same Nicholas and the brothers of Henryków according to this form: that [the monastery] shall give the aforesaid Nicholas two marks of ready silver,[80] in order that in the future the same Nicholas or his successors may not presume to demand the inheritance of this cloister which is called Głębowice, in the same way as they value the health of the body.

This the aforesaid Nicholas has just promised, having given faith [i.e., sworn an oath] to the brothers of Henryków in Upper Głogów, before Advocate Conrad[81] and lord Gierko, judge of the court of Opole, and the assessors,[82] in an established court,[83] in the presence of the duke and his knights, lord Eckeric of Wallenstein, lord Theodric called Stange, and Count Hermann called Kłaj, whose authentic [names][84] are placed on this charter. The assessors of the city of

---

In this context, the proctor was someone designated by a duke to settle disputes, apparently not by an imposition of a formal sentence – that is, not as a judge or arbitrator – but through mediation. Note, however, that later in this document Gierko is explicitly called the "judge of the court of Opole."

78. Bolesław, duke of Opole, was born between 1254 and 1258, succeeded to the rule of the duchy after the death of his father Władysław in 1281 or 1282, and died in 1313. *Rodowód*, 3:38–40; Stanisław A. Sroka, "Władysław," *Piastowie*, 722–23; Sroka, "Bolesław I," *Piastowie*, 726–78.

79. The *fraternitas* with a monastery meant several kinds of possible relationships, ranging from friendship and informal close association – of the kind amply documented by Abbot Peter, especially in his stories of Albert the Bearded, as noted earlier – through a confraternity or a group of laymen associated with a monastery in several possible ways, to the inclusion of the "brother" in a group that merited a monastery's prayers, especially after death. Among other things, Abbot Peter's section of the *Book* is an annotated list of those persons who were to enjoy the monks' "brotherhood" in the latter sense. See Niermeyer, 452, *s.v. fraternitas*.

80. The Latin states *parati argenti*, a phrase similar to what I elsewhere translate as "ready cash" – meaning a payment actually delivered in coin, not expressed as debt.

81. In this context, an advocate was the chief official of the town, and of the town council.

82. The *iudex curiae* was one of several kinds of ducal judges, based variously in ducal entourages during their travels, or in specified important towns. "Assessors" here and elsewhere always translates *scabini*, formal assistants to the judge, who appear in the course of the thirteenth century specifically as functionaries of German-law urban courts – as in the reference to the assessors of Głogów, with German names, immediately below in this document – and in the course of that century are gradually – though not very systematically – included in other types of courts, including the ducal courts.

83. The Latin states *in iudicio confirmato*, meaning a formally held court session, differentiated from some other kind of assembly before the town council, judges, and assessors.

84. *Authentica*, a word that usually means documents in fact issued by the authors (Niermeyer, 73–74, *s.v. authenticus, authenticum*), a meaning unlikely in this context. I assume here it means a signature, monogram, or seal, whence my somewhat vague translation here and elsewhere.

Głogów are a certain H. [son] of Iliana, P. son of Krystan, Siedelmann the coultersmith, Hermann son of Albus, Borzyk of Milwan, Jano the carpenter, Werner the tailor. And very many other trustworthy citizens were also present. These things were done and effected in the Year of the Incarnation of the Lord 1296, the eighth [day before the] calends of June [May 25].

S.U., 6:no. 260 (1296), 209–10

20 In the name of the Lord, amen. And thus we, Henry [III], by the grace of God duke of Silesia, wish it to be known to those present and future whose hearing this letter will reach that Paul and Bogusza, uterine brothers, sons of the late Racław of Brukalice,[85] made in our presence an exchange of the parcel which accrued to them by a right of patrimony from their paternal uncle James, son of Mścisław,[86] with the abbot and convent of the brothers of Henryków,[87] assigning to them[88] [in exchange] for the part [i.e., the inherited parcel] just noted [a piece of land] in their village called Milejewice[89] ([situated] in the land of Opole) – so that the same brothers, Paul and Bogusza, would receive twice as much [land] in the village of Milejewice as they possessed in Brukalice, while fully resigning that part of theirs which they held in Brukalice.

Furthermore, the lord abbot and the brothers gave in aid to each of the same, much-noted, Paul and Bogusza, a horse worth a mark and a half, and a cow with a bull calf, two oxen, five sheep, five pigs, a tunic worth half a mark, and for their mother a cloak worth a fierton. But because Paul, by a certain grace of the cloister, had specially possessed two arable fields, subject to planting with fifteen measures of seed, the aforementioned abbot and brothers redeemed this from him with five silver marks, paying out the money to him at once. Therefore, the cloister in Henryków shall forever retain all the things conceded to the brothers [i.e., the monks] in this exchange, without possibility of any change to come in the future.

85. For Abbot Peter's story of Brukalice, of which this charter and the subsequent three documents (no. 21–23) are, jointly, both an aspect and a continuation, see Chapters 27, 93, 112–23.

86. Abbot Peter describes this father and son, and their implications for succession to portions of Brukalice, in Chapters 113, 121–22.

87. This document, issued by Duke Henry III, records a second phase of reconciliation between the Henryków monastery and these two difficult brothers before this duke; the first phase, in 1257, is marked by Henry III's charter concerning another exchange, and incorporated in Abbot Peter's portion of the *Book* as Chapter 119.

88. There is something wrong with the syntax of the document; the pronoun in the phrase *assignantes eisdem* appears gramatically to say that the two brothers were giving Milejewice to the monks – but of course, just the opposite, the two brothers were instead giving up a portion of their holding, Brukalice, and receiving twice as much land in Milejewice, situated far to the east, in the region of Opole.

89. Supplementary Document no. 3, n. 17.

In witness of this matter, we directed that this page be strengthened with our seal. These things were done in Wrocław, in the Year of the Lord's Incarnation 1259, on the morrow of the calends of August [July 31], in the presence of these [men]: Count John of Wierzbno, Count Michael the judge, Count Despryn the sub-judge, Count Sulisław Rezek, Count Dzietko the sub-butler, Count Michael son of Dalebór,[90] Boruta our servitor, and very many others. Given by the hand of Otto, writer of our court.

S.U., 3:no. 298 (1259), 197

21 In the name of Our Lord Jesus Christ, amen. Because the deeds of the times pass as the times do, unless strengthened by writing and by the voice of witnesses, let it be known to all those present as well as future who view the present page that, before ourselves, Władysław, by the grace of God duke of Opole,[91] and before our barons, lord Peter abbot of Henryków,[92] together with his brothers, has by mediation of [our] judgment reclaimed the land [which the monastery had] acquired in their village of Milejewice, through an exchange with the knight Paul and with his brother Bogusza (in return for their inheritance which is commonly called Brukalice, and situated near Henryków), from Pucław the knight, to whom the said Paul and Bogusza had [later] sold the exchange[d holding] just described in Milejewice by hereditary right,[93] and [for which they] had received an assessed sum of money. Pucław fully regained from the aforenamed Peter the lord abbot, and from his brothers, the sum of money which he had given for the aforesaid land, and, in our audience, he ceded possession of the said land upon them.

In order that those deeds which were transacted before us may remain firm and stable, we have caused the present page to be strengthened with the protection of our seal. These things were done in Czeladź, during [the Day of] the Translation of Saint Stanisław [September 27], before these witnesses: Count Dzietko castellan of Racibórz, Dobiesz castellan of Bytom, John the highest judge of the court, Sułka castellan of Chrzanów, Dzierżko the *subcamerarius*, Stephen the chaplain, and very many others. Given in the Year of the Lord's Grace 1262, the ninth [day before the] ides of October [October 5].[94]

S.U., 3:no. 418 (1262), 277

90. Chapters 27, 76, 80–81, 186–91; Supplementary Documents no. 26–27.

91. Władysław, son of Casimir of Opole and Duchess Viola, was born around 1225, succeeded to rule in the duchy in 1229 or 1240, and died in 1281 or 1282; *Rodowód*, 3:17, 27–28; Sroka, "Władysław."

92. The author of the first section of the *Henryków Book*.

93. Abbot Peter tells us nothing about this transaction, or about Pucław himself; yet, clearly, this charter continues the story of Brukalice in an interesting direction, showing as it does the abbot's own revindication of the monastery's former holding, Milejewice, some years after its loss to James Brukalic. The next charter (no. 22) is an expanded redaction of this one, describing Pucław, the transaction, and the background, in more detail.

94. The editor of this document, Winfried Irgang, is baffled by the discrepancy of the two dates offered in the document; see his remarks at *S.U.*, 3: 277. Perhaps the actions

22   In the name of Our Lord Jesus Christ, amen. Because the deeds of the times pass as the times do unless they are strenghtened by writing and the voice of witnesses, we, Władysław, by the grace of God duke of Opole,[95] make in known to all those present as well as future who view the present page that certain youths, Bogusza and Paul, Silesians, uterine brothers, and sons of the late Racław Brukalic,[96] have effected with the abbot and the brothers of Henryków an exchange of the portion of their inheritance which belonged to them among their remaining brothers, by giving that portion of their inheritance of Brukalice to the cloister, and receiving from the brothers of Henryków, out of our land[holding called] Milejewice,[97] a portion and a quantity of [land] of the same inheritance of Milejewice, just as was agreed upon by the abbot of Henryków and the said youths Bogusza and Paul among each other.

After the aforesaid youths possessed their holdings in Milejewice for some time, they sold it for eight silver marks to a certain Pucław, brother of Jarosław castellan of Oświęcim. After the same Pucław fully paid this [sum of] money to Bogusza and Paul, and possessed the aforesaid holding in Milejewice for a long time, the brothers of Henryków bought the oft-mentioned holding in Milejewice from the same Pucław, before ourselves, with the same Pucław's good will and consent, for eight silver marks, which money the aforesaid brothers of Henryków fully paid out to Pucław, before ourselves – where the same Pucław, in the presence of ourselves and of our barons, resigned the same portion of Milejewice to the cloister of Henryków, for himself and for his heirs, in eternal possession.

In order therefore that all the things which have so solemnly been done and established before us and our barons may remain firm and stable in the future, we have caused the present page to be strengthened with the protection of our seal. These things were done in Czeladź, in the Year of the Lord 1262, [on] the ninth [day before the] ides of October [October 5], during [the Day of] the Translation of Saint Stanisław [September 27],[98] before these witnesses: Count Dzietko castellan of Racibórz, Dobiesz castellan of Bytom, John the highest judge of the court, Sułka castellan of Chrzanów, Dzierżko the *subcamerarius*, Stephen rector of the church of Czeladź, and many others.

S.U., 3:no. 419 (1262), 278

---

recorded in the document (*acta sunt hec*) were carried out on the earlier date, and the document itself was issued (*dat[um]*) on the latter.

95. This document is an infinitely clearer restatement of the immediately preceding one, except that it lacks some of the information conveyed by it.

96. A patronymic of *Brukał*, and singular of *Brukalice*; Chapter 112.

97. The Latin original states here in *terra nostra Mileueuich*, which is interesting for two reasons: as an unusual designation of an estate or landholding as *terra*; and because of Władysław's identification of that holding as his own, *nostra*. Perhaps we have here another instance of the ambiguity of property rights over lands held by the Henryków monastery, which is so nicely reflected in Section I above.

98. Now the discrepancy in dates is really quite baffling.

23 In the name of the Lord, amen. We, Henry [III], by the grace of God duke of Silesia, in approval of just deeds wish it to be known to all [persons] present and future who view this letter that Benek, son of the late Wojsław of Dębiszyn, made an exchange with Peter, son of the late James of Brukalice,[99] of a holding [which was a portion] of the inheritance that belonged to Peter himself by right of patrimony among his cousins (*fratres patrueles*) in Brukalice – by giving the same Peter a part of the inheritance which belonged to the same Benek by right of patrimony among his brothers in Dębiszyn. Afterwards, while Benek possessed this holding in Brukalice by hereditary right, and Peter was justly keeping his holding in Dębiszyn in possession, the same Benek sold this holding in Brukalice to the brothers of Henryków and to the cloister itself for fifty silver marks, to be possessed forever by hereditary right.

These things were done in the Year of the Lord 1262, on the octave [of the Day] of Saint Martin [November 18], in the assembly which was held in Wrocław, at the time of the discussions between ourselves and Bishop [Thomas] about the arrangements for the tithes,[100] in the presence of these [men]: Count John castellan of Ryczyn, called "from Wierzbno," Count Racław judge of our court, Count Janusz castellan of Niemcza, Count Przecław his brother, Count Stosz son of Leonard, Count Despryn our sub-judge, Count Bogusław castellan of Bardo, Count Michael the palatine, Count Berthold of Kobylagłowa, and very many others.

Also before us and our aforesaid barons were all the relatives of each, that is to say of Benek and Peter: Henry, the aforesaid Benek's uterine brother; Sławibór, son of Racibór Benek's uncle; Żyrosław, son of Włościbór also his uncle; his brother Nicholas; Bogusza, son of the late Racław of Brukalice (that is to say, of the aforsaid Peter's uncle); and Paul, brother of the same Bogusza.[101] All of them resigned every right and jurisdiction which they had in the holding of Brukalice, for themselves and for all their heirs or successors, by a spontaneous will, before ourselves and our barons. We therefore confirm for this cloister the same holding of Brukalice, which the brothers of Henryków have so solemnly bought from Benek – subject, that is to say, to this condition: that neither Benek, nor Peter, or anyone from among their successors may ever have the power to redeem [it from the monastery]. In order that these things remain firm in the future, we took care to strengthen the present page more firmly and more diligently by the placement of our seal.

S.U., 3:no. 424 (1262), 280–81

99. Abbot Peter mentions this father and son in Chapter 123, which is incomplete, and which concludes his portion of the *Book*. Thus, the present charter fills in a part of Peter's story. As for the other actors named here, either Benek or Wojsław, and the sale and purchase, Abbot Peter says nothing about them.

100. These "arrangements" are presumably the substance of the long charter issued by Bishop Thomas of Wrocław in 1263, and transcribed as Chapter 207.

101. In this list of persons it is difficult to sort out the members of each of these two kin groups, except that Bogusza and Paul are the same persons who appear in the preceding three charters, and in the passages of the *Book* annotated there, and thus are members of the Brukalice kindred.

24 In the name of the Lord, amen. In order that the contrivance of fraud may have no power to weaken duly effected arrangements, it is fitting to strengthen their bounty through the witness of the Patron of Truth, and through ever living letters. For which reason I, Peter, called "from Lubnów,"[102] make it known to all [persons] present and future who hear the succession of letters patent that the two small hides situated in Nietowice – the grant of which belongs to me, and which Stephen of Kobylagłowa[103] had formerly sold to Tammo of Wide and John of Paczków[104] – accrued in the course of time to Hermann Rume, citizen of Münsterberg,[105] by a rightful sale, and [later] he, standing before me in good health, declared spontaneously that he sold them to lord John, abbot of Henryków, and to his convent, to be possessed forever, subject to such rights as are described below, for 24 marks of pure silver, which he declared to have been paid out to him in full; and he promised never to come against the said sale in the future, by himself or through others, for reason of hereditary right or in any other way, by word or by deed.

Each party requested that this sale be confirmed by my goodness. Therefore I, approving the parties' requests, resigned these hides, which the said Hermann had willingly transferred into my hand, to the abbot and his convent, to be freely possessed in eternal possession by proprietary right, with this exception: that each year, on the Feast of Saint Martin, the abbot or his vicar shall pay me or my heirs five fiertons of common pennies, and two leather high boots, as rent from the said hides. And so he shall hold the same hides entirely free from all services, exactions, and payments, ducal as well as civil, German or Polish, under whatsoever names they are assessed, and from all other burdens – because I am obligated by service for all the said obligations to my lord the duke for as long as I am alive, and my heirs and successors shall also perform them in the future.

The aforenamed Stephen left a surviving son, namely Paul, and a daughter by the name of Paulina. Before the abbot effected the said purchase, they had made a claim to the said hides, in the presence of my lord Duke Bolko [I], and they both, in equal degree, entrusted the action concerning this claim to Peter, Kotkowic by nickname,[106] the same Paulina's husband, both completely and forever removing themselves from it. Within a year after the said sale, this Peter was summoned by the lord abbot and Hermann Rume to Münsterberg before

102. The anonymous continuator of Abbot Peter indentifies Peter of Lubnów as a "Polish judge," and provides other details about him, in Chapters 150 and 152. He narrates the complicated succession of rights to Nietowice in Chapters 147–54.

103. Chapter 147, n. 38.

104. Chapters 147–48.

105. Judge Peter here considerably simplifies the interesting history of the succession to that holding narrated in Chapter 149. However, later in this document, the judge amplifies that history in other interesting detail.

106. A patronymic version of Kotka, the nickname by which Abbot Peter's continuator remembered the same Peter; Chapters 147, 150.

me – who then, by the mandate of my lord Duke Bolko, held [the right to administer] Polish justice in the whole land[107] – concerning the aforesaid claim, in order either to proceed with the action of his claim according to law, or to cease, equally in the claim and in the action. Mature reflection having been taken, by a good and free will he ceased from the demand as well as from the action, renouncing the support of any right whereby the said Paul and Paulina, or he, or they, or any successors whatever of theirs or of his, might ever be strengthened concerning the said hides, or disturb the abbot, or his convent, or anyone else, if perhaps the abbot should at some time sell these hides to anyone at all.

Therefore, to strengthen, and in eternal memory of, this purchase, sale, and spontaneous renunciation of the said Peter, I strengthened my present writing with the stamp of my seal. Done and given in Münsterberg, in the Year of the Lord 1300, on the Day of Saint Lawrence the Martyr [August 10], in the presence of the witnesses recorded below: lord Gosko castellan in Münsterberg, John the advocate there, and Nicholas Gosko's brother, Gerung, Tilo of Freiburg, Siedelmann, and Nicholas of Watzenrode, citizens there, and many others.

S.U., 6:no. 444 (1300), 345–46

25   I, John, hereditary judge in Münsterberg,[108] wish it to be known by public declaration to all who behold the present writing that the distinguished man Peter, called Kotka,[109] standing before me and the citizens in Münsterberg, has declared in a live voice that he had had a certain claim for the return of two hides in Nietowice on behalf of lady Paulina, his spouse,[110] but that, since a friendly composition was reached and achieved between the religious men Brother Conrad (then chamberlain) and his companion Brother Rudolf on the one hand,[111] and the said Peter on the other, concerning the said claim which he asserted to have toward these hides, Peter has utterly renounced any claim for return, or demand, or right, which he has until now appeared to have toward these hides; and promised from now on never to disturb the monastery about this deed. In addition, he obligated himself, under [penalty of] loss of his things, that if any-

---

107. That is, he was the chief judge of Polish law, appointed by Duke Bolko I, and thus had a capacity similar to Judge Peter's, though perhaps at a higher level in the judicial hierarchy.

108. Chapter 131, n. 18.

109. Mentioned in the preceding document, where see the cross-references.

110. "On behalf of [the] spouse" translates *ex parte coniugis*, meaning that the husband formally brought the case before the court as the agent of his wife, whose own standing to act on her own before courts was limited; see Bogdan Lesiński, *Stanowisko kobiety w polskim prawie ziemskim do połowy XV wieku* [The position of the woman in Polish common law until the mid-fifteenth century] (Wrocław: Zakład Narodowy im. Ossolińskich, 1956), 176–87.

111. Here "religious men" translates *viri religiosi*, that is, monks (the introductory essay above, n. 292), one of whom, Conrad, was also an official of the monastery.

one should ever make a claim against the said hides or their possessors, he was willing to defend [them] in every way, and to ward off all obstacles.[112]

In everlasting memory of this matter, inclined by the prayers of the brothers recorded above,[113] I desired that this page be written down, strengthened with the protection of my own and the city's seals. These things were done in Münsterberg, in the Year of the Lord 1303, on the day before the nones of October [October 6], before the witnesses noted below: Frederick the smith, proconsul at the time, Tilo of Freiburg, Siedelmann of Grodków, Nicholas of Watzenrode, Hermann Rume, Petzold Schenk, and Berthold the writer.

Stenzel, no. 51 (1303), 202

26 In the name of the Lord, amen. We, Władysław, by the grace of God and the divine calling archbishop of the Holy Church of Salzburg, duke of Silesia,[114] make it known to [persons] present and future that, after the market was established in Ziębice (that is, Münsterberg),[115] Michael, son of the late Dalebór,[116] allowed certain citizens of Münsterberg to build a certain mill within his inheritance, subject to this right: that Michael and his successors would receive from

---

112. Garbled though it is in Latin, this sentence appears to assign to the alienor (Peter Kotka) the role of a guarantor of the alienation against any future threat – not just by heirs dispossessed by the alienation, but apparently by anyone – against the security of the monastery's possession of the holding in question. This form of warranty becomes a standard source of security of alienation in medieval Poland in course of the fourteenth century; note its recurrence in some of the other sources translated here.

113. That is, Conrad and Rudolf; the two monks who mediated the settlement of the dispute also requested the judge to produce the present document.

114. Duke Władysław, son of Henry II, was born in 1237, succeeded to the rule of the Duchy of Wrocław upon Henry III's death in 1266, and died in 1270. His brief rule was preceded by a longer tenure as archbishop of Salzburg. Chapters 74, 77 above; *Rodowód*, 1:129–32; Grodecki, *Liber* (1949), 123, n. 50; Tomasz Jurek, "Władysław," *Piastowie*, 418–19.

115. This is the only reference, anywhere in the record, to a Slavic name that had been used for Münsterberg sometime before its expansion as a German town; and a trace of an establishment of a market before, or early on during, the migrations of Germans, which resulted in the change of place name, formal *locatio* of the town, and so forth. The two place names suggest an earlier Polish settlement. A clearly documented transition from a Polish settlement, through foundation of a market under ducal authority, to the establishment of a town and its district "according to German law," was Środa, later Neumarkt, perhaps the most important regional center of "German law" in the Polish duchies during the thirteenth and early fourteenth centuries. See Górecki, *Economy*, 216–17, 256, 260–61; and Zbigniew Zdrójkowski, "Miasta na prawie średzkim (materiały)" [Towns established according to the law of Neumarkt – the sources], *Sobótka* 41 (1986), 343–51.

116. The story of Michael Daleborowic begins with one of the later accounts by Abbot Peter (Chapters 27, 76, 80–81), and resumes with the continuator's story about the *sors Daleborii* beginning with Chapter 186.

this mill one and a half silver marks each year in eternal payment, and the milling requirements of his farmstead. After these events, the abbot [—][117] and convent of the Henryków monastery bought this mill from those citizens for their cloister for thirty silver marks, to be possessed forever – provided, however, that they would render the aforesaid rights of the mill to Michael and his heirs.[118]

After the passage of a few years, Michael was touched by the finger of considerable poverty, and he sold to the Henryków monastery the fields in which the said mill stood (from the course of the Oława [river] up to the great road that divides [the holdings of] Dziersław and the same Michael on the side, and also from the place in which a trench had been dug from the Oława [river] to the said mill, up to the boundaries of the cloister, lengthwise), the payment [due] from this mill, and the liberty to grind grain there, for ninety silver marks, to be possessed by the cloister forever.

After all these things were done and confirmed by worthy witnesses before our brother, Duke Henry [III] of happy memory, a certain January by the nickname of Daleboryc, Michael's cousin,[119] came up, returned the money to the abbot and convent of the Henryków monastery, and by a just judgment received the said fields. After this, Dalebór, Michael's son,[120] restored his money to January, and by a just judgment received his patrimony, as he should have. After Dalebór held that patrimony of his for some time, he effected an exchange of the said fields and the mill payment with the abbot and convent of the Henryków monastery, and received from the abbot, in Milejewice in the land of Opole, twelve small hides and a farmstead of the cloister and a mill that stands there; and, before ourselves and our barons, he resigned the said fields and the right to grind grain to the cloister of Henryków in eternal possession, for himself and for his heirs. Because the fields in Milejewice had appeared to be barren,[121] the abbot and the convent of the Henryków monastery added 150 silver marks for Dalebór in this exchange, and Dalebór acknowledged before ourselves and our barons that he had fully received this sum of money from the cloister.

In order therefore that this exchange between both sides, the cloister and Dalebór, may at no time be violated, but that it may forever stand strong and firm in the future, we caused this charter to be strengthened by the placement of our seal. And although all the aforesaid things had been done at diverse times, this final exchange was effected in the Year of the Lord 1268, in the presence of the venerable father lord Thomas bishop of Wrocław, lord Janusz of Michałowo, Stosz,

117. A gap in the text, presumably to be filled in by the name of Abbot Bodo.

118. Neither author of the *Book* says anything about this transaction, involving a mill, between the monastery, the town, and Michael. Abbot Peter incorporates a charter issued by Henry III (Chapter 81), recording a grant of another mill to Michael by the monks of Henryków.

119. Not otherwise documented by either author.

120. He, in contrast, is extensively noted by Abbot Peter's continuator, Chapters 186–91.

121. *Steriles*, that is, infertile or impossible to cultivate.

Thimo judge of our court, John Zerucha, who perambulated this inheritance, and lord Peter our notary, lord Elias our chaplain, and many others.

S.U., 4:no. 67 (1268), 58–59

27 In the name of the Lord, amen. We, Władysław, by the grace of God duke of Silesia and archbishop of Salzburg,[122] make it known to all [persons] present and future that, within our presence, and by the grant of our favor, Michael, son of the late Dalebór, equally with his two sons, Alsik and Dobiesław, consented and assented to the exchange made by his son Dalebór with the venerable abbot of Henryków and the convent, of the inheritance situated between the cloister of Henryków and [the holding of] Goblin's sons lengthwise, and the boundaries [of the holding] of Dziersław on the side, up to the river called the Oława, according to the terms which are more clearly contained in our privilege concerning this exchange and the additional grant of money.[123] The said Michael, along with his sons, shall forever consider this exchange firm and fixed, and shall not at any time violate it in any way, by himself or through anyone from among his friends.

He has also promised that he would in no way assent to the making of an exchange of the remainder of his own and his aforesaid sons' inheritance in favor of any person other than the abbot and the brothers of Henryków – which sons had, at the time of the consent to the said exchange, not been separated from their father Michael in any way.[124] We confirm all of this with the protection of the present writing. In witness of this matter, we have ordered the making of the present charter, and strengthening it with the protection of our seal. These things were done in the Year of the Lord 1269, the sixteenth [day before the] calends of August [July 17], in the presence of lord Peter our notary, Racław Drzemlik, John Zaja, Simon the Gaul, Paul Słupowic, Jarosław son of Mroczko, and many others. Given in Wrocław by the hand of James, notary of our court.

S.U., 4:no. 96 (1269), 76

28 I, Gosko, castellan in Münsterberg, declare to all who behold the present writing that Ścibór of Czesławice has appeared in my presence, and publicly avowed that he had offered half a hide to Brother Wolfram of Henryków for six marks, [to be possessed] from the Feast of Saint Michael the Archangel in the Year

---

122. See n. 114 above.

123. Taken together, the documentation is not clear on whether this transaction is the same as the one described in the preceding document; in view of the identity of most of the parties, I would assume it is. The *Book*'s manuscript is not helpful on that question.

124. This expression may mean that the father and sons were a joint group in the legal sense, that is, that they were a collective agent for the purpose of disposal of property; or that – perhaps in addition – they held the property as a physically undivided holding, that is, cultivated it as one farmstead. Familial holdings undivided in one or both of these senses occasionally occur in the Polish sources; compare the account of Raczyce, especially Chapter 166.

of the Incarnate Word 1301, until the Year of the Lord 1307, within the term just noted, subject to this agreement: that, by reason and in the name of rent, Brother Wolfram shall give Ścibór one fierton each year, with six marks remaining [to be paid] in their entirety. And if after the years have passed Ścibór does not redeem his half-hide, from then on this half-hide shall remain in Brother Wolfram's possession according to the said agreement, until the entire modest sum is paid.

In order that no claim may arise against this arrangement because of the absence of Przybek, Ścibór's brother Jeszko (son of the noble man Cieszybór, also from Czesławice) came together with Ścibór to Münsterberg, and promised before me to incline Przybek's assent to this [transaction] immediately after [Przybek] comes [back to the locality]; and if the said Przybek refuses to agree, then Jeszko himself shall remain under the obligation, [jointly] with Ścibór.

In memory of this matter, inclined by the prayers of both parties, I have ordered the present page to be strengthened by the stamp of my seal, with the witnesses noted below, that is, Gerung of Bolesławiec, provincial advocate at the time, Tilo of Freiburg, proconsul, and Nicholas of Watzenrode, Hermann Rume, and Berthold the writer, consuls of the city. Done in Münsterberg, in the castle, in the Year of the Lord 1301, on the Friday next after [the Day of] the Glorious Ascension of the Lord [May 12].

Stenzel, no. 48 (1301), 199–200

29 I, John, hereditary judge in Münsterberg, publicly declare to the knowledge of all persons by the tenor of the present [letters] that the noble man Przybisz of Czesławice, standing in my presence in Münsterberg, has declared with his mouth that he sold the entire holding of his inheritance which belonged to him and his sister Trzeszka by paternal succession within Czesławice, to Bezelin, then chamberlain in [the monastery of] Henryków, and to his companion Wolfram, for 175 marks in current coin; and that he received this money in full from the said brothers and their successors, that is, Henry the chamberlain and his companion Rudolf. Therefore, inclined by the prayers of both parties, in clearer evidence of this duly effected sale and rightful payment, I have caused the present page to be written down, and I gave it to the said Henry, then chamberlain, and to Brother Rudolf, eternally strengthened with the seal of myself and of the city.

Given there in Münsterberg, in the Year of the Lord 1302, on the Day of the Holy Martyrs Dennis and His Companions [October 9], in the presence of: Nicholas, brother of Gosko, Cieszybór of Czesławice, Frederick the Mirror, the consuls of the city, that is, Tilo of Freiburg, Frederick the smith, Siedelmann the baker, Hermann Rume, Nicholas of Watzenrode, Berthold the writer, and likewise Hermann of Rosenberg and Peter of Dolen, then assessors, and many other trustworthy [persons].

Stenzel, no. 50 (1302), 201–02

30 In the name of the Lord, amen. Since those things which are settled by agreement or judgment ought to be fixed upon the tablet of writing so that they may remain unafflicted by an anxiety of recurrent challenge in the course of time, therefore we, the brother called Peter, abbot of Henryków,[125] make it known to all who hear the series of the present [letters] that, after various quarrels and questions which arose repeatedly between ourselves on one side, and the noble man Cieszybór of Czesławice, and also Nicholas of Watzenrode, on the other, by reason of the service of two hides in Nietowice, which they are obliged to perform among [i.e., along with] us according to the common custom of the land – about which at last, by mature counsel of wise men and by mediation of arbiters selected by each of us for this [purpose],[126] we have spontaneously arrived at an eternal and friendly union of agreement.

That is, [we agreed] that the said noble, Cieszybór, shall give Nicholas of Watzenrode five marks in current coin; and likewise we [now] give him an equal amount of the same coin, for [his] renunciation of the rent which the possessor of the said hides shall pay at specified times to us, or to whomever we shall assign [the right to receive it]. And we wish these hides, along with the remaining five hides adjoining [them] under the same name, to perform service from now on – subject, however, to this agreement: that whatever [level] of service from the said hides has been neglected up to the date of the present [transactions], the said men, Cieszybór and Nicholas, are obligated to defend this [missed service] faithfully in every way.[127]

In memory of this matter, we have directed that the present page be written down, and requested that it be strengthened with the seal of the city of Münsterberg. These things were done in Münsterberg, in the Year of the Lord 1304, seventh [day before the] ides of June [June 7], in the presence of the witnesses noted below, that is: Gerung, provincial advocate, James called "from Colina" and Pilgrim the Citizen, Cieszybór's arbiters; lord John castellan of Münsterberg and Gerung, Nicholas of Watzenrode's arbiters; Tilo of Freiburg and Hermann of Rume, our arbiters; James Koszobór; and many others. Given in Münsterberg, in the Year of the Lord 1304, on the Day of Saints Gervasius and Protasius the Martyrs [June 19].[128]

Stenzel, no. 53 (1304), 204–05

125. This is not Abbot Peter the author of the first portion of the *Henryków Book*.

126. Arbiters (*arbitri*) were yet another type of agents through whom the parties to a legal event reached an amicable decision; note the names and the positions of the arbiters in this case who are also recorded among the witnesses below.

127. This phrase appears to mean that Cieszybór and Nicholas are responsible for making up those service obligations attached to the land which have been due in the past but have not been performed. Here and elsewhere (in the body of the *Book* and in the documents) it is clear that obligations of military service are clearly attached to tenures – that is, that a variant of a fief was very important and routine in Silesia in the early fourteenth century.

128. Here as earlier, I assume that the events recorded in the disposition of the document took place on the earlier date, while the document itself was issued twelve days later.

31 I, Jeszko of Czesławice, make it known to all who hear the series of the present [letters] that, on the direction of my father, Cieszybór, and by the will and the assent of my brother Albert, I have offered a hide and a half in Czesławice, my own and my aforementioned brother's inheritance, to lords Nicholas the chamberlain and Brother Rudolf, for twelve marks in current coin, [as a lease, to run] for three years from the date of the present [transactions], subject to this form and condition: that the said men, or whoever becomes chamberlain in their stead, shall give me or my father nine fiertons as rent each year, and shall possess the said arable fields free from all ducal services and also other Polish exactions, under whatever names they are assessed.

In addition, if, because of my own or my father's needs these fields are pawned, I and my father [hereby] bind ourselves to defend this [arrangement], by means of our expenses and efforts. After the passage of three years, if I shall have paid the said brothers the sum of twelve marks, the said arable fields shall revert to me as their heir without obstacle of any objection; while if I lack the money with which to pay, then the said arable fields shall remain obligated as has been described above, with this addition: that every year I or my father are unable or unwilling to pay, we ought to notify the chamberlain at the appropriate time, so as to enable him to furnish himself from the arable, and with summer and winter seeds.

In memory of this matter, I wished that the present little page be written down and strengthened with the protection of my seal, with the witnesses noted below: John [——],[129] my brother Albert, Henry the village bailiff (*scultetus*) of Wiesenthal, [——][130] of Ciepielowice, Krystan, Henning, and Albert, peasants of Wiesenthal.[131] Given in Henryków, in the Year of the Lord 1304, the sixteenth [day before the] calends of December [November 16].

Stenzel, no. 55 (1304), 206–07

32 In the name of the Lord, amen. In order completely to curtail every anxiety of doubt about matters that ought to be certain, it is useful to set down the measure of accomplished deeds in letters and among witnesses. Therefore I, Cieszybór of Czesławice, and my two sons Jeszko and Albert, willingly acknowledge to all whom the present writing may reach that we gave two hides of arable fields within our inheritance of Czesławice to Abbot Peter and the convent of Henryków in pawn, for fifty marks in current coin, [which we shall receive] each year, from [the Day of] the Annunciation of Saint Mary the Virgin, subject to the conditions noted down below.

---

129. A gap in the text.

130. A gap in the text.

131. "Peasants" translates *rustici* here, as above. The presence of a *scultetus* clearly indicates that there was a settlement of Germans, established according to German law, in Wiesenthal, which is unsurprising in view of the German place name and of the German names of the inhabitants.

First, and indeed above everything else, during the period of the said obligation, the abbot and his convent shall have every right and capacity within the said hides which I and my sons had there, and he shall freely apply them for his uses in whatever way is profitable to him. Furthermore, if during the said period the abbot or his convent should in any way experience any damages within, or for reason of, the said hides, from anyone [acting] on behalf of myself, the said sons of mine, or anyone who belongs to me, I and the said sons of mine shall make the abbot and his convent whole in every way. Throughout the entire period of the said obligation, the abbot himself and his convent shall perform the customary services from the said hides to the prince of the land at suitable times. And if after some time it should please the abbot to purchase the aforesaid hides, and of he should request the lord of the land for a [charter confirming our] resignation – whenever he bids me and my sons to do so, we shall sell and resign the said hides to him and his convent, and in the purchase shall deduct for him the said fifty marks, which we also acknowledge to have been fully paid out to us to our satisfaction for the obligation of the said hides.

All the [matter] that arose above, and all others which I and my sons have negotiated with the lord abbot through the mediation of worthy men, we shall guard as fixed and whole, after a display of faith by our hand [i.e., an oath given] to the abbot, by me and my said sons. To provide a solid and stable pillar for everything aforesaid, I and my sons caused the present letter to be written, and, on our petition, to be prudently strengthened with the seal of the city of Münsterberg, and of my son Jeszko, since I lack my own. These things were done in Henryków, in the Year of the Lord 1306, on the Day of the Annunciation of Saint Mary the Virgin [March 25], in the presence of the witnesses lord Henry of Lubawia, lord John of Peterswald, his grandson Henry the master, Siedelmann, Nicholas of Watzenrode, Berthold the scribe, Nicholas his relative, Nicholas, Rumo's brother-in-law, the citizens of Münsterberg, and many other trustworthy [persons].

Stenzel, no. 57 (1306), 208–0

33 I, Cieszybór of Czesławice, make it known to all who hear the series of the present [letters] that, by the will and assent of my sons, Albert, who is present, and Jeszko, who is absent (and for whom I vouch that he shall uphold whatever I promise in these writings), I offered a hide and a half of my own and my sons' inheritance in Czesławice to lord Winand the chamberlain and to Brother Hermann, for 22 marks of [pence called] "royals,"[132] [as a lease, to run] for three years from the Day of Saint Martin in the Year of the Lord 1310,

132. The "marks of 'royals'" (*marcae regalium*) is an unavoidably awkward translation of marks – that is, standardized units of weight and of quantity of coin – consisting of a "thick" pence called the *regalis*, so named after the king of Bohemia who ruled Silesia and (briefly) the rest of Poland in the early fourteenth century; the introductory essay above, n. 248; Chapter 48, n. 44.

subject to this condition: that the said men, or whoever becomes chamberlain in their stead, shall give me and my son Albert nine *scoti* each year as rent, and shall possess the aforenamed arable fields free from all ducal services, and also from other exactions, under whatever names they are assessed.

Furthermore, if, because of my own or my sons' needs, someone should pawn these fields, I and my sons [hereby] bind ourselves to defend this [arrangement], by means of our expenses and efforts. After the passage of three years, if I shall have paid the said brothers the said sum of 22 marks, the said arable fields shall be returned to me and my sons without obstacle of any objection; while if I lack the money to pay, then the said arable fields shall remain obligated as has been described above, with this addition: that every year I or my sons are unable or unwilling to pay, we ought to notify the chamberlain at the appropriate time, so as to enable him to furnish himself from the arable, and with summer and winter seeds.

In witness of this matter, I wished that the present page be written down, and strengthened with the protection of the seals of Nikuszko, judge of the court, and of myself. These things were done in Münsterberg, on the eve [of the Day] of Saint Bartholomew the Apostle [August 23], in the Year of the Lord 1310, before the witnesses noted below: lord Apezko, called "the Sheep," lord Frederick the Mirror, Tilo of Freiburg, Hermann Rume, Wigand of Służejów, James Gralok, and many other trustworthy [persons].

Stenzel, no. 60 (1310), 211–12

Bibliography

Abrams, Philip, and E. A. Wrigley, ed. *Towns in Societies: Essays in Economic History and Historical Sociology*. Cambridge: Cambridge University Press, 1978.

Abulafia, David, and Nora Berend, ed. *Medieval Frontiers: Concepts and Practices*. Aldershot: Ashgate, 2002.

Adamska, Anna. "Dieu, le Christ et l'Église dans les préambules des documents polonais au Moyen Âge." *Bibliothèque de l'École des chartes* 155 (1997), 543–73.

—. *Arengi w dokumentach Władysława Łokietka. Formy i funkcje* [Preambles in the charters of Władysław the Short: forms and functions]. Kraków: Towarzystwo Naukowe Societas Vistulana, 1999.

—. " 'From Memory to Written Record' in the Periphery of Medieval Latinitas: The Case of Poland in the Eleventh and Twelfth Centuries." In *Charters and the Use of the Written Word in Medieval Society*, ed. Karl Heidecker, 83–100. Turnhout: Brepols, 2000.

Alfonso, Isabel. "Presentación." *Historia Agraria* 31 (2003), 11–12; 33 (2004), 13–14.

Appelt, Heinrich, ed. *Schlesisches Urkundenbuch* Vol. 1. Vienna, Cologne, and Graz: Hermann Böhlhaus, 1963–71.

Astill, Grenville, and Annie Grant, ed. *The Countryside of Medieval England*. Oxford: Basil Blackwell, 1988.

Austin, John L. *How to Do Things with Words*. Oxford: Oxford University Press, 1962.

Baker, Derek. "The Genesis of English Cistercian Chronicles: The Foundation History of Foutains Abbey." *Analecta Cisterciensia* 25 (1969), 14–41, and 31 (1975), 179–212.

Banaszkiewicz, Jacek. *Kronika Dzierzwy. XIV-wieczne kompendium historii ojczystej* [Dzierzwa's Chronicle: a fourteenth-century compendium of native history]. Wrocław: Zakład Narodowy im. Ossolińskich, 1979.

—. "Czarna i biała legenda Bolesława Śmiałego" [The black and the white legend of Bolesław the Bald]. *Kwartalnik Historyczny* 88 (1981), 353–90.

—. *Podanie o Piaście i Popielu. Studium porównawcze nad wczesnośredniowiecznymi tradycjami dynastycznymi* [The tale of Piast and Popiel: a comparative study of early-medieval dynastic traditions]. Warsaw: Państwowe Wydawnictwo Naukowe, 1986.

—. *Polskie dzieje bajeczne mistrza Wincentego Kadłubka* [Polish fable history by Master Vincent Kadłubek]. Wrocław: Monografie FNP/Leopoldinum, 1998.

Barber, Malcolm. *The Two Cities: Medieval Europe, 1050–1320*. 2nd ed. London: Routledge, 2004.

Bardach, Juliusz. *Historia państwa i prawa Polski* [History of the state and law in Poland]. Vol. 1. Warsaw: Państwowe Wydawnictwo Naukowe, 1964.

Barthélemy, Dominique. *La société dans le comté de Vendôme de l'an mil au XIVe siècle.* Paris: Fayard, 1993.

Bartlett, Frederick C. *Remembering: A Study in Experimental and Social Psychology.* Cambridge: Cambridge University Press, 1932. Repr. 1995.

Bartlett, Robert. *Gerald of Wales, 1146–1223.* Oxford: Oxford University Press, 1982.

–. "Technique militaire et pouvoir politique, 900–1300." *Annales: Économies, Sociétés, Civilisations* 41 (1986), 1135–59.

–. *The Making of Europe: Conquest, Colonization and Cultural Change, 950–1350.* Princeton: Princeton University Press, 1993.

–, and Angus MacKay, ed. *Medieval Frontier Societies.* Oxford: Oxford University Press, 1989.

Berend, Nora. *At the Gate of Christendom: Jews, Muslims and "Pagans" in Medieval Hungary, c. 1000–c. 1300.* Cambridge: Cambridge University Press, 2001.

–. "Défense de la Chrétienté et naissance d'une identité: Hongrie, Pologne et péninsule Ibérique au Moyen Age." *Annales: Histoire, Sciences Sociales* 58 (2003), 1009–27.

Berman, Constance Hoffman. *Medieval Agriculture, the Southern French Countryside, and the Early Cistercians: A Study of Forty-three Monasteries.* Transactions of the American Philosopical Society 76.5. Philadelphia: American Philosophical Society, 1986.

Biddick, Kathleen. *The Other Economy: Pastoral Husbandry on a Medieval Estate.* Berkeley and Los Angeles: University of California Press, 1989.

–. *The Shock of Medievalism.* Durham, NC: Duke University Press, 1998.

Bieniak, Janusz. "Clans de chevallerie en Pologne du XIIIe au XVe siècle." In *Famille et parenté dans l'Occident médiéval,* ed. Georges Duby and Jacques Le Goff, 321–33. Rome: École française de Rome, 1977.

–. "Knightly Clans in Medieval Poland." In *The Polish Nobility in the Middle Ages,* ed. Antoni Gąsiorowski, 123–76. Wrocław: Zakład Narodowy im. Ossolińskich, 1984.

Biskup, Marian, and Gerard Labuda. *Dzieje Zakonu Krzyżackiego w Prusach. Gospodarka – społeczeństwo – państwo – ideologia* [History of the Teutonic Order in Prussia: economy, society, state, ideology]. Gdańsk: Wydawnictwo Morskie, 1986.

Bisson, Thomas N. "On Not Eating Polish Bread in Vain: Resonance and Conjuncture in the *Deeds of the Princes of Poland* (1109–1113)." *Viator* 29 (1998), 275–89.

–. *Tormented Voices: Power, Crisis, and Humanity in Rural Catalonia, 1140–1200.* Cambridge, MA: Harvard University Press, 1998.

–. "Princely Nobility in an Age of Ambition (c. 1050–1150)." In Duggan, *Nobles and Nobility,* 101–13.

–. "*La terre et les hommes*: A Programme Fulfilled?" *French History* 14 (2000), 322–45.

Bjork, Elizabeth Ligon, and Robert A. Bjork, ed. *Memory*. San Diego: Academic Press, 1996.

Bloch, Marc. *Feudal Society*. Trans. L. A. Manyon. Chicago: University of Chicago Press, 1961.

—. *French Rural History: An Essay on Its Basic Characteristics*. Trans. Janet Sondheimer. Berkeley and Los Angeles: University of California Press, 1966.

Bogucka, Maria. "The Towns of East-Central Europe from the Fourteenth to the Seventeenth Century." In Mączak, Samsonowicz, and Burke, *East-Central Europe*, 97–108.

Borgolte, Michael. *Europa entdeckt seine Vielfalt, 1050–1250*. Stuttgart: Verlag Eugen Ulmer, 2002.

Boussard, Jacques. *The Civilization of Charlemagne*. Trans. Frances Partridge. New York: McGraw Hill, 1976.

Brown, Warren. *Unjust Seizure: Conflict, Interest, and Authority in an Early Medieval Society*. Ithaca: Cornell University Press, 2001.

—. "Charters as Weapons: On the Role Played by Early Medieval Dispute Records in the Disputes They Record." *Journal of Medieval History* 28 (2002), 227–48.

—. "When Documents are Destroyed or Lost: Lay People and Archives in the Early Middle Ages." *Early Medieval Europe* 11 (2002), 337–66.

—, and Piotr Górecki. "What Conflict Means: The Making of Medieval Conflict Studies in the United States, 1970–2000." In Brown and Górecki, *Conflict*, 1–35.

—, and —, ed. *Conflict in Medieval Europe: Changing Perspectives on Society and Culture*. Aldershot: Ashgate, 2003.

Bruder, Artur. *Najstarszy kopiarz henrykowski* [The earliest Henryków cartulary]. Wrocław: Wydawnictwo Uniwersytetu Wrocławskiego, 1992.

Brundage, James A. *Law, Sex, and Christian Society in Medieval Europe*. Chicago: University of Chicago Press, 1987.

Brunel, Ghislain and Benoît Cursente. "Tendencias recientes de la historia rural en Francia." *Historia Agraria* 31 (2003), 35–56.

Buc, Philippe. *Dangers of Ritual: Between Early Medieval Texts and Social Scientific Theory*. Princeton: Princeton University Press, 2001.

Buczek, Daniel. "Saint Stanisław, Bishop and Martyr: Fact and Legend." In *Saint Stanisław, Bishop of Kraków*, 15–35. Santa Barbara: Polish Historical Association, 1979.

Buczek, Karol. "Powołowe – poradlne – podymne." *Przegląd Historyczny* 63 (1972), 6–9.

Burns, Robert I. "The Significance of the Frontier in the Middle Ages." In Bartlett and MacKay, *Medieval Frontier Societies*, 307–30.

Carruthers, Mary. *The Book of Memory: A Study of Memory in Medieval Culture*. Cambridge: Cambridge University Press, 1990.

Carter, F. W. *Trade and Urban Development in Poland: An Economic Geography of Cracow, from Its Origins to 1795*. Cambridge: Cambridge University Press, 1994.

Cetwiński, Marek. *Rycerstwo śląskie do końca XIII w.: Biogramy i rodowody* [Silesian knighthood through the end of the thirteenth century: biograms and genealogies]. Wrocław: Zakład Narodowy im. Ossolińskich, 1982.

—. " 'Nowy Izrael.' Księga henrykowska i kształtowanie poczucia wspólnoty mnichów z Henrykowa" ["New Israel": The *Henryków Book* and the formation of a sense of community among the monks of Henryków]. In Radzimiński, Supruniuk, and Wroniszewski, *Venerabiles,* 71–6.

Christiansen, Eric. *The Northern Crusades: The Baltic and the Catholic Frontier, 1100–1525.* Minneapolis: University of Minnesota Press, 1980.

Cipolla, Carlo, ed. *The Fontana Economic History of Europe.* Vol. 1: *The Middle Ages.* Glasgow: Collins/Fontana, 1972.

Clanchy, Michael. *From Memory to Written Record: England 1066–1307.* 2nd ed. Oxford: Blackwell, 1993.

Coleman, Janet. *Ancient and Medieval Memories: Studies in the Reconstruction of the Past.* Cambridge: Cambridge University Press, 1992.

Connerton, Paul. *How Societies Remember.* Cambridge: Cambridge University Press, 1989.

Crouch, David. *The Image of Aristocracy in Britain, 1000–1300.* London: Routledge, 1992.

Davies, Norman. *God's Playground: A History of Poland.* 2 vols. New York: Columbia University Press, 1982.

—. *Europe: A History.* Oxford: Oxford University Press, 1996.

Davies, Wendy. *Small Worlds: The Village Community in Early Medieval Brittany.* Berkeley and Los Angeles: University of California Press, 1988.

Davis, G. R. C. *Medieval Cartularies of Great Britain: A Short Catalogue.* London: Longman, 1958.

Dekański, Dariusz Aleksander. "Cystersi i dominikanie w Prusach – działania misyjne zakonów w latach trzydziestych XIII wieku. Rywalizacja czy współpraca?" [Cistercians and Dominicans in Prussia – missionary activities in the 1230s: competition or collaboration?]. In Wyrwa and Dobosz, *Cystersi,* 227–50.

Demade, Julien. "El mundo rural medieval en la historiografía alemán desde 1930." *Historia Agraria* 33 (2004), 31–79.

Derwich, Marek. *Monastycyzm benedyktyński w średniowiecznej Europie i Polsce. Wybrane problemy* [Benedictine monasticism in medieval Europe and Poland: selected problems]. Wrocław: Wydawnictwo Uniwersytetu Wrocławskiego, 1998.

Dockès, Pierre. *Medieval Slavery and Liberation.* Trans. Arthur Goldhammer. Chicago: University of Chicago Press, 1979.

Duby, Georges. *La société aux XIe et XIIe siècles dans la région mâconnaise.* 2nd ed. Paris: S.E.V.P.E.N., 1971.

—. *Rural Economy and Country Life in the Medieval West.* Trans. Cynthia Postan. Columbia, SC: University of South Carolina Press, 1968.

—. *The Early Growth of the European Economy: Warriors and Peasants from the Seventh to the Twelfth Century.* Trans. Howard B. Clarke. Ithaca: Cornell University Press, 1974.

Duggan, Anne, ed. *Nobles and Nobility in Medieval Europe: Concepts, Origins, Transformations.* London: Boydell and Brewer, 2000.

–. "Introduction: Concepts, Origins, Transformations." In Duggan, *Nobles and Nobility,* 1–14.

Dyer, Christopher. *Making a Living in the Middle Ages: The People of Britain, 850–1520.* New Haven: Yale University Press, 2002.

–, and Philipp R. Schofield. "Estudios recientes sobre la historia agraria y rural medieval británica." *Historia Agraria* 31 (2003), 13–33.

Everard, Judith. "Sworn Testimony and Memory of the Past in Brittany, c. 1100–1250." In van Houts, *Medieval Memories,* 72–91.

Fennell, John. *The Crisis of Medieval Russia, 1200–1304.* London: Longman, 1983.

Fentress, James, and Chris Wickham. *Social Memory.* Oxford: Blackwell, 1992.

Fossier, Robert. *Enfance de l'Europe, Xe–XIIe siècles: Aspects économiques et sociaux.* 2 vols. Paris: Presses Universitaires de France, 1982.

–. "L'Économie cistercienne dans les plaines du nord-ouest de l'Europe." *Flaran* 3 (1983), 53–74.

Freedman, Paul. *The Origins of Peasant Servitude in Medieval Catalonia.* Cambridge: Cambridge University Press, 1991.

–. *Images of the Medieval Peasant.* Stanford: Stanford University Press, 1999.

Freeman, Elizabeth. *Narratives of a New Order: Cistercian Historical Writing in England, 1150–1220.* Turnhout: Brepols, 2002.

Gams, Pius Bonifacius. *Series episcoporum ecclesiae catholicae.* 1886, repr. Graz: Akademische Druck- u. Verlagsanstalt, 1957.

García de Cortázar, José Ángel, and Pascual Martínez Sopena. "Los estudios sobre historia rural de la sociedad hispanocristiana." *Historia Agraria* 31 (2003), 57–83.

Garlicki, Andrzej, ed. *Poczet królów i książąt polskich* [The roll of the Polish kings and dukes]. Warsaw: Czytelnik, 1980.

Garton Ash, Timothy. "Does Central Europe Exist?" *New York Review of Books* 33, no. 15 (October 9, 1986), 45–53.

Gawlas, Sławomir. *O kształt zjednoczonego królestwa. Niemieckie władztwo terytorialne a geneza społecznoustrojowej odrębności Polski* [Toward the shape of the united kingdom: German territorial lordship and the origins of the socio-political distinctness of Poland]. Warsaw: Wydawnictwo DiG, 1996.

Geary, Patrick J. *Phantoms of Remembrance: Memory and Oblivion at the End of the First Millennium.* Princeton: Princeton University Press, 1995.

–. "*Auctor* et *auctoritas* dans les cartulaires du haut Moyen Âge." In Zimmermann, *Auctor,* 61–72.

–. *The Myth of Nations: The Medieval Origins of Europe.* Princeton: Princeton University Press, 2002.

Genet, Philippe. "Cartulaires, registres et histoire: l'exemple anglais." In *Le métier d'historien au moyen âge: Études sur l'historiographie médiévale,* ed. Bernard Guenée, 95–138. Paris: Publications de la Sorbonne, 1977.

Gieysztor, Aleksander, and Sławomir Gawlas, ed. *Państwo, naród, stany w świadomości wieków średnich. Pamięci Benedykta Zientary, 1929–1983* [State, nation, estates in medieval consciousness: in memory of Benedykt Zientara, 1929–1983]. Warsaw: Państwowe Wydawnictwo Naukowe, 1990.

Gołąb, Kazimierz. "Filip z Fermo i jego statuty legackie z 1279 r." [Philip of Fermo and his legatine statutes of 1279]. *Roczniki Historyczne* 26 (1960), 255–64.

Gottschalk, Joseph. *St. Hedwig, Herzogin von Schlesien*. Cologne and Graz: Böhlau Verlag, 1964.

Górecki, Piotr. "*Viator* to *ascriptitius*: Rural Economy, Lordship, and the Origins of Serfdom in Medieval Poland." *Slavic Review* 42 (1983), 14–35.

—. "Politics of the Legal Process in Early Medieval Poland." *Oxford Slavonic Papers, New Series* 17 (1984), 22–44.

—. *Economy, Society, and Lordship in Medieval Poland, 1100–1250*. New York: Holmes and Meier, 1992.

—. *Parishes, Tithes, and Society in Earlier Medieval Poland, ca. 1100–1250*. Transactions of the American Philosopical Society 83.2. Philadelphia: American Philosophical Society, 1993.

—. "*Ad Controversiam Reprimendam*: Family Groups and Dispute Prevention in Medieval Poland, c. 1200." *Law and History Review* 14 (1996), 213–43.

—. "Rhetoric, Memory and Use of the Past: Abbot Peter of Henryków as Historian and Advocate." *Cîteaux* 48 (1997), 261–93.

—. "Communities of Legal Memory in Medieval Poland, c. 1200–1240." *Journal of Medieval History* 24 (1998), 127–54.

—. "Local Society and Legal Knowledge: A Case Study from the Henryków Region." In *Christianitas et cultura Europae. Księga Jubileuszowa Profesora Jerzego Kłoczowskiego* [*Christianitas et cultura Europae*: A Jubilee Book for Professor Jerzy Kłoczowski], ed. Henryk Gapski, 1:544–50. 2 vols. Lublin: Instytut Europy Środkowo-Wschodniej, 1998.

—. "Poland: To the 18th Century." In the *Encyclopedia of Historians and Historical Writing*, 929–34. London: Fitzroy Dearborn, 1999.

—. "Violence and the Social Order in a Medieval Society: The Evidence from the Henryków Region, ca. 1150–ca. 1300." In *The Man of Many Devices, Who Wandered Full Many Ways: Festschrift in Honor of János M. Bak*, ed. Balázs Nagy and Marcell Sebők, 91–104. Budapest: Central European University Press, 1999.

—. "Words, Concepts, and Phenomena: Knighthood, Lordship, and the Early Polish Nobility, c. 1100–c. 1350." In Duggan, *Nobles and Nobility*, 115–55.

—. "A Historian as a Source of Law: Abbot Peter of Henryków and the Invocation of Norms in Medieval Poland, c. 1200–1270." *Law and History Review* 18 (2000), 479–523.

—. "Medieval East Colonization in Post-War North American and British Historiography." In *Historiographical Approaches to Medieval Colonization of East Central Europe: A Comparative Analysis against the Background of Other European Interethnic Colonization Processes in the Middle Ages*, ed. Jan M. Piskorski, 25–61.

Boulder and New York: East European Monographs/Columbia University Press, 2002.

—. Review of Myśliwski, *Człowiek*. *Speculum* 77 (2002), 1368–72.

—. "A View from a Distance." *Law and History Review* 21 (2003), 367–76.

—. " 'Tworzenie Europy' Roberta Bartletta w kontekście anglosaskich badań historycznych nad początkami i kształtowaniem się Europy" [Robert Bartlett's *The Making of Europe* in the context of English-language scholarship on the origins and formation of Europe]. In Robert Bartlett, *Tworzenie Europy. Podbój, kolonizacja i przemiany kulturowe, 950–1350*. Trans. Grażyna Waluga, ed. Jan M. Piskorski, 505–15. Poznań: Wydawnictwo Poznańskiego Towarzystwa Przyjaciół Nauk, 2003.

—. "Assimilation, Resistance, and Ethnic Group Formation in Medieval Poland: A European Paradigm?" In Wünsch and Patschovsky, *Das Reich und Polen*, 447–76.

—. "An Interpreter of Law and Power in a Region of Medieval Poland: Abbot Peter of Henryków and his *Book*." In *Building Legitimacy: Political Discourses and Forms of Legitimation in Medieval Societies*, ed. Isabel Alfonso, Hugh Kennedy, and Julio Escalona, 263–89. Leiden: Brill, 2004.

—. "Los campesinos medievales y su mundo en la historiografía polaca." *Historia Agraria* 33 (2004), 81–103.

Górski, Karol. *L'Ordine teutonico alle origini dello stato prussiano*. Turin: Einaudi, 1971.

Griffiths, Fiona. "Nuns' Memories or Missing History in Alsace (c. 1200): Herrad of Hohenbourg's Garden of Delights." In van Houts, *Medieval Memories*, 132–49.

Grodecki, Roman, ed. and trans. *Księga henrykowska. Liber Fundationis claustri sancte Marie Virginis in Heinrichow* [The *Henryków Book*/the *Liber Fundationis claustri sancte Marie Virginis in Heinrichow*]. Poznań and Wrocław: Instytut Zachodni, 1949.

—. *Liber Fundationis claustri sancte Marie Virginis in Heinrichow, czyli Księga henrykowska* [The *Liber Fundationis claustri sancte Marie Virginis in Heinrichow*, or the *Henryków Book*], with a new introduction by Józef and Jacek Matuszewski. Wrocław: Muzeum Archidiecezjalne we Wrocławiu, 1991.

—, Stanisław Zachorowski, and Jan Dąbrowski. *Dzieje Polski średniowiecznej* [A history of medieval Poland]. 2 vols. 2nd ed. Kraków: Universitas, and Kryspinów: Platan, 1995.

Grudziński, Tadeusz. *Bolesław Śmiały/Szczodry i biskup Stanisław* [Bolesław the Bold (or the Generous) and Bishop Stanisław]. Warsaw: Interpress, 1982.

Grüger, Heinrich. "Das Patronatsrecht von Heinrichau." *Cîteaux* 28 (1977), 26–47.

—. "Das Volkstum der Bevölkerung in den Dörfern des Zisterzienserklosters Heinrichau im mittelschlesischen Vorgebirgslande vom 13.–15. Jahrhundert." *Zeitschrift für Ostforschung* 27 (1978), 241–61.

—. *Heinrichau: Geschichte eines schlesischen Zisterzienserklosters, 1227–1977*. Cologne and Vienna: Böhlau, 1978.

Guenée, Bernard. *Histoire et culture historique dans l'Occident médiéval*. Paris: Aubier Montaigne, 1980.

Guyotjeannin, Olivier, Jacques Pycke, and Benoît-Michel Tock. *La diplomatique médiévale*. Turnhout: Brepols, 1993.

–, Laurent Morelle, and Michel Parisse, ed. *Les cartulaires. Actes de la Table Ronde organisée par l'Ecole nationale des chartes et le G.D.R. 121 du C.N.R.S. (Paris, 5–7 décembre 1991)*. Paris: École des Chartes, 1993.

Hägermann, Dieter, and Andreas Hedwig. "Hufe." *Lexikon des Mittelalters* 5:154–56.

Halbwachs, Maurice. *On Collective Memory*. Ed. and trans. Lewis A. Coser. Chicago: University of Chicago Press, 1992.

Havighurst, Alfred A., ed. *The Pirenne Thesis: Analysis, Criticism, and Revision*. 3rd ed. Lexington, MA: D. C. Heath and Company, 1976.

Heck, Roman. "The Main Lines of Development of Silesian Medieval Historiography." *Quaestiones Medii Aevi* 2 (1981), 63–87.

–, ed. *Dawna świadomość historyczna w Polsce, Czechach i Słowacji* [Former historical consciousness in Poland, Bohemia, and Slovakia]. Wrocław: Zakład Narodowy im. Ossolińskich, 1978.

Hensel, Witold. *U źródeł Polski średniowiecznej* [At the sources of medieval Poland]. Wrocław: Zakład Narodowy im. Ossolińskich, 1974.

–. *Słowiańszczyzna wczesnośredniowieczna. Zarys kultury materialnej* [Early-medieval Slavic peoples: outline of the material culture]. 4th ed. Warsaw: Państwowe Wydawnictwo Naukowe, 1987.

Hilton, Rodney H. "Introduction." In *The Stoneleigh Leger Book*, ed. R. Hilton, ix–lvii. Oxford: Dugdale Society/Oxford University Press, 1960.

Hodges, Richard. *Dark Age Economics: The Origins of Towns and Trade, AD 600–1000*. New York: St. Martin's, 1982.

Hoffmann, Richard C. *Land, Liberties, and Lordship in a Late Medieval Countryside: Agrarian Structures and Change in the Duchy of Wrocław*. Philadelphia: University of Pennsylvania Press, 1989.

Innes, Matthew. *State and Society in the Early Middle Ages: The Middle Rhine Valley 400–1000*. Cambridge: Cambridge University Press, 2000.

–. "Keeping It in the Family: Women and Aristocratic Memory, 700–1200." In van Houts, *Medieval Memories*, 17–35.

Irgang, Winfried. "Das Urkundenwesen Herzog Heinrichs III. von Schlesien (1248–1266)." *Zeitschrift für Ostforschung* 31 (1982), 1–47.

–, ed. *Schlesisches Urkundenbuch*. Vols. 2–5. Vienna, etc: Hermann Böhlhaus/Böhlau Verlag, 1978–93.

–, and Daphne Schadenwaldt, ed. *Schlesisches Urkundenbuch*. Vol. 6. Cologne, Weimar, and Vienna: Böhlau Verlag, 1998.

Jasiński, Kazimierz. *Rodowód Piastów śląskich* [The genealogy of Silesian Piasts]. Vol. 1: *Piastowie wrocławscy i legnicko-brzescy* [The Piasts of Wrocław and Legnica–Brzeg]. Vol. 3: *Piastowie opolscy, cieszyńscy i oświęcimscy* [The Piasts of Opole, Cieszyn, and Oświęcim]. Wrocław: Zakład Narodowy im. Ossolińskich, 1973, 1977.

Jasiński, Tomasz. *Przerwany hejnał* [The interrupted bugle call]. Kraków: Krajowa Agencja Wydawnicza, 1988.

Jordan, William C. *From Servitude to Freedom: Manumission in the Sénonais in the Thirteenth Century*. Philadelphia: University of Pennsylvania Press, 1986.

Jurek, Tomasz. *Dziedzic Królestwa Polskiego Książę głogowski Henryk (1279–1309)* [The heir of the Polish Kingdom, the duke of Głogów, Henry (1279–1309)]. Poznań: Wydawnictwo Poznańskiego Towarzystwa Przyjaciół Nauk, 1993.

—. *Obce rycerstwo na Śląsku do połowy XIV wieku* [Foreign knighthood in Silesia until the mid-fourteenth century]. 2nd ed. Poznań: Wydawnictwo Poznańskiego Towarzystwa Przyjaciół Nauk, 1998.

—. "Bolesław II Rogatka (Łysy)" [Bolesław II Rogatka (the Bald)]. In *Piastowie*, 408–12.

—. "Henryk III Biały" [Henry III the White]. In *Piastowie*, 415–17.

—. "Władysław." In *Piastowie*, 418–19.

—. "Henryk V Gruby (Brzuchaty)" [Henry V the Fat (the Pot-Bellied)]. In *Piastowie*, 421–23.

—. "Konrad I." In *Piastowie*, 613–15.

Kaczmarek, Krzysztof. "Nieudana fundacja cysterska księcia Władysława Odonica z 1210 roku" [A failed Cistercian foundation by Duke Władysław Odonic in 1210]. In Wyrwa and Dobosz, *Cystersi*, 273–89.

Kałużyński, Stanisław. *Dawni Mongołowie* [The former Mongols]. Warsaw: Państwowy Instytut Wydawniczy, 1983.

Kanior, Marian. "Zakon cysterek i jego rozwój w Europie Środkowej w XII–XVI wieku" [The Order of women Cistercians and its development in Central Europe between the twelfth and the sixteenth centuries]. In Wyrwa and Dobosz, *Cystersi*, 109–22.

Karczewski, Dariusz. "Nieznany dokument księżnej krakowskiej Grzymisławy z roku 1228. Przyczynek do najwcześniejszego uposażenia klasztoru Cystersów w Henrykowie" [An unknown document issued by the duchess of Kraków, Grzymisława, in 1228: a contribution to the earliest endowment of the Cistercian monastery in Henryków]. In Radzimiński, Supruniuk, and Wroniszewski, *Venerabiles*, 89–99.

Kiersnowski, Ryszard. "Kwartniki śląskie i czeskie grosze" [The Silesian *quartenses* and the Czech groats]. *Wiadomości Numizmatyczne* 6 (1962), 225–44.

—. *Wstęp do numizmatyki polskiej wieków średnich* [Introduction to Polish medieval numismatics]. Warsaw: Państwowe Wydawnictwo Naukowe, 1964.

—. "W sprawie genezy kwartników śląskich" [Concerning the origins of the Silesian *quartenses*]. *Wiadomości Numizmatyczne* 10 (1966), 197–220.

—. "Złoto na rynku polskim w XIII–XIV w." [Gold in the Polish market in the thirteenth and fourteenth centuries]. *Wiadomości Numizmatyczne* 16 (1972), 129–56.

Kiss, István. "Agricultural and Livestock Production: Wine and Oxen. The Case of Hungary." In Mączak, Samsonowicz, and Burke, *East-Central Europe*, 84–96.

Kłoczowski, Jerzy. *Dominikanie polscy na Śląsku w XIII–XIV wieku* [Polish Dominicans in Silesia in the thirteenth and fourteenth centuries]. Lublin: Wydawnictwo Katolickiego Uniwersytetu Lubelskiego, 1956.

—. "Jan zwany Romką" [John, nicknamed Romka]. In *P.S.B.*, 10: 432–33.

—. "Zakony na ziemiach polskich w wiekach średnich" [Monastic orders in the Polish lands during the Middle Ages]. In Kłoczowski, *Kościół*, 1:375–494.

—. "Les Cisterciens en Pologne, du XIIe au XIIIe siècle." *Cîteaux* 28 (1977): 111–34.

—. "Dominicans of the Polish Province in the Middle Ages." In Kłoczowski, *Christian Community*, 73–118.

—. *Europa słowiańska w XIV–XV wieku* [Slavic Europe in the fourteenth and fifteenth centuries]. Warsaw: Państwowy Instytut Wydawniczy, 1984.

—. *Dzieje chrześcijaństwa polskiego* [A history of Polish Christianity]. Vol. 1. Paris: Nasza Rodzina, 1987.

—. *Młodsza Europa. Europa Środkowo–Wschodnia w kręgu cywilizacji chrześcijańskiej średniowiecza* [The younger Europe: East Central Europe in the ambit of medieval Christian civilization]. Warsaw: Państwowy Instytut Wydawniczy, 1998.

—. *A History of Polish Christianity*. Cambridge: Cambridge University Press, 2000.

—. "Cystersi w Europie Środkowowschodniej wieków średnich" [The Cistercians in East Central Europe during the Middle Ages]. In Wyrwa and Dobosz, *Cystersi*, 27–53.

—, ed. *Kościół w Polsce* [The Church in Poland]. 4 vols. Kraków: Znak, 1966.

—, ed. *The Christian Community of Medieval Poland: Anthologies*. Wrocław: Zakład Narodowy im. Ossolińskich, 1981.

Knoll, Paul. *The Rise of the Polish Monarchy: Piast Poland in East Central Europe, 1320–1370*. Chicago: University of Chicago Press, 1972.

—. "The Urban Development if Medieval Poland, with Particular Reference to Kraków." In *The Urban Society of Eastern Europe in Premodern Times*, ed. Bariša Krekić, 63–136. Berkeley and Los Angeles: University of California Press, 1987.

—. "Economic and Political Institutions on the Polish–German Frontier in the Middle Ages: Action, Reaction, Interaction." In Bartlett and MacKay, *Frontier Societies*, 151–74.

—, and Frank Schaer, trans. and ed. *Gesta Principum Polonorum: The Deeds of the Princes of the Poles*. Budapest: Central European University Press, 2003.

Kondracki, Jerzy. *Geografia regionalna Polski* [The regional geography of Poland]. Warsaw: Wydawnictwo Naukowe PWN, 1998.

Korczak, Lidia. "Bolko I." In *Piastowie*, 575–77.

—. "Bernard." In *Piastowie*, 579–81.

—. "Henryk." In *Piastowie*, 582–84.

Kozak, Stanisław, Agata Taras-Tomczyk, and Marek L. Wójcik. "Henryków." In Wyrwa, Strzelczyk, and Kaczmarek, *Monasticon*, 2:64–78.

Koziol, Geoffrey. "The Dangers of Polemic: Is Ritual Still an Interesting Subject of Scholarly Inquiry?" *Early Medieval Europe* 11 (2002), 367–88.

Kucharski, Gerard. "Początki klasztoru cysterek w Ołoboku" [Beginning of the monastery of the Cistercian nuns in Ołobok]. In Wyrwa and Dobosz, *Cystersi*, 314–38.

Kuhn, Walter. "Der Löwenberger Hag und die Besiedlung der schlesichen Grenzwälder." In W. Kuhn, *Beiträge zur schlesischen Siedlungsgeschichte*, 32–66. Munich: Delp, 1971.

—. *Vergleichende Untersuchungen zur mittelalterlichen Ostsiedlung*. Cologne and Vienna: Böhlau, 1973.

Kula, Witold. "Miary i wagi" [Measures and weights]. In *Encyklopedia historii gospodarczej Polski do 1945 r.* [Encyclopedia of the economic history of Poland until 1945], ed. Antoni Mączak et al., 1:510–18. Warsaw: Państwowe Wydawnictwo Naukowe, 1981.

—. *Measures and Men*. Trans. Richard Szreter. Princeton: Princeton University Press, 1986.

Kürbis, Brygida. "Cystersi w kulturze polskiego średniowiecza: trzy świadectwa z XII wieku" [Cistercians in the culture of the Polish Middle Ages: Three twelfth-century sources]. In Strzelczyk, *Historia*, 321–42.

Kurtyka, Janusz. "Hofämter, Landesämter, Staatsämter und ihre Hierarchien in Polen im mittleleuropäischen Vergleich (11.–15. Jh.)." In Wünsch and Patschovsky, *Das Reich und Polen*, 129–213.

—. *Odrodzone Królestwo: Monarchia Władysława Łokietka i Kazimierza Wielkiego w świetle nowszych badań* [A restored kingdom: The monarchy of Władysław the Short and Casimir the Great in light of recent research]. Kraków: Towarzystwo Naukowe Societas Vistulana, 2001.

Labuda, Gerard. "Paweł, biskup poznański" [Paul, bishop of Poznań]. In *P.S.B.*, 25:363–5.

Lawrence, C. H. *The Friars: The Impact of the Early Mendicant Movement on Western Society*. London: Longman, 1994.

—. *Medieval Monasticism: Forms of Religious Life in Western Europe in the Middle Ages*. 3rd ed. Harlow: Longman/Pearson Education, 2001.

Leciejewicz, Lech. "Early-Medieval Sociotopographical Transformations in West Slavonic Urban Settlements in the Light of Archaeology." *Acta Poloniae Historica* 34 (1976), 29–56.

—, ed. *Miasto zachodniosłowiańskie w XI–XII wieku. Społeczeństwo–kultura* [The Western Slavic town in the eleventh and twelfth centuries: society and culture]. Wrocław: Zakład Narodowy im. Ossolińskich, 1991.

Lesiński, Bogdan. *Stanowisko kobiety w polskim prawie ziemskim do połowy XV wieku* [The position of the woman in Polish common law until the mid-fifteenth century]. Wrocław: Zakład Narodowy im. Ossolińskich, 1956.

Lewis, Archibald. "The Closing of the Medieval Frontier, 1250–1350." *Speculum* 33 (1958), 475–83.

Lexikon des Mittelalters. 10 vols. Munich and Zurich: Artemis Verlag, 1977–99.

Lifshitz, Felice. "Beyond Positivism and Genre: 'Hagiographical' Texts as Historical Narratives." *Viator* 25 (1994), 95–113.

Lilley, Keith D. *Urban Life in the Middle Ages, 1000–1450.* Houndmills: Palgrave, 2002.

Litak, Stanisław. "Rise and Spatial Growth of the Parish Organization in the Area of Łuków District in the Twelfth to Sixteenth Centuries." In Kłoczowski, *Christian Community*, 149–81.

Little, Lester K., and Barbara H. Rosenwein, ed. *Debating the Middle Ages: Issues and Readings.* Oxford: Blackwell, 1998.

Lodowski, Jerzy. *Dolny Śląsk na początku średniowiecza (VI–X w.): podstawy osadnicze i gospodarcze* [Lower Silesia at the beginning of the Middle Ages (the sixth through the tenth centuries): the settlement and economic base]. Wrocław: Zakład Narodowy im. Ossolińskich, 1980.

Lotter, Friedrich. "The Crusading Idea and the Conquest of the Region East of the Elbe." In Bartlett and MacKay, *Frontier Societies*, 267–306.

Łowmiański, Henryk. *Początki Polski* [The origins of Poland]. 6 vols. Warsaw: Państwowe Wydawnictwo Naukowe, 1963–85.

—. "Rozdrobnienie feudalne Polski w historiografii naukowej" [The feudal fragmentation of Poland in the historiography]. In *Polska w okresie rozdrobnienia feudalnego* [Poland during the period of feudal fragmentation], ed. H. Łowmiański, 7–34. Wrocław: Zakład Narodowy im. Ossolińskich, 1973.

Lukowski, Jerzy, and Hubert Zawadzki. *A Concise History of Poland.* Cambridge: Cambridge University Press, 2001.

Mączak, Antoni, Henryk Samsonowicz, and Peter Burke, ed. *East-Central Europe in Transition: From the Fourteenth to the Seventeenth Century.* Cambridge: Cambridge University Press, and Paris: Éditions de la Maison des Sciences de l'Homme, 1985.

Maitland, Frederic William. *The History of English Law before the Time of Edward I.* 2 vols. 2nd ed. Cambridge: Cambridge University Press, 1968.

—. *Domesday Book and Beyond: Three Essays in the Early History of England.* 2nd ed. Cambridge: Cambridge University Press, 1987.

—. "Introduction." In *Liber Memorandorum Ecclesie de Bernewelle*, ed. John W. Clark, xliii–lxiii. Cambridge: Cambridge University Press, 1907.

Makkai, Laszlo. "Economic Landscapes: Historical Hungary from the Fourteenth to the seventeenth Century." In Mączak, Samsonowicz, and Burke, *East-Central Europe*, 24–35.

Maleczyńska, Ewa, and Karol Maleczyński. *Dzieje Śląska* [The history of Silesia]. Warsaw: Wiedza Powszechna, 1955.

Maleczyński, Karol. "Uwagi nad dokumentem legata Idziego biskupa tuskulańskiego dla klasztoru w Tyńcu rzekomo z roku 1105" [Remarks on the document of Legate Guido, bishop of Tusculum, for the monastery in Tyniec, supposedly of 1105]. *Collectanea Theologica* 17 (1936), 339–65. Repr. in K. Maleczyński, *Studia nad dokumentem polskim* [Studies in the Polish document], 150–69. Wrocław: Zakład Narodowy im. Ossolińskich, 1971.

–, Maria Bielińska, and Antoni Gąsiorowski. *Dyplomatyka wieków średnich* [Diplomatics of the Middle Ages]. Warsaw: Państwowe Wydawnictwo Naukowe, 1971.

Markgraf, Hermann, and J. W. Schulte, ed. *Liber fundationis episcopatus Wratislaviensis. Codex Diplomaticus Silesiae.* Vol. 14. Breslau: Max, 1889.

Marzec, Andrzej. "Bolesław Wstydliwy" [Bolesław the Chaste]. In *Piastowie*, 191–97.

–. "Bolesław I Wysoki" [Bolesław I the Tall]. In *Piastowie*, 363–68.

–. "Henryk I Brodaty" [Henry I the Bearded]. In *Piastowie*, 375–86.

–. "Jarosław." In *Piastowie*, 372.

–. "Leszek Biały" [Leszek the White]. In *Piastowie*, 181–88.

Matuszewski, Jacek. *Vicinia id est ... . W poszukiwaniu alternatywnej koncepcji staropolskiego opola* [*Vicinia id est*: in search of an alternative conception of the Old Polish neighborhood]. Łódź: Wydawnictwo Uniwersytetu Łódzkiego, 1991.

Matuszewski, Józef. *Najstarsze polskie zdanie prozaiczne. Zdanie henrykowskie i jego tło historyczne* [The oldest Polish sentence in prose: the sentence of Henryków and its historical background]. Wrocław: Zakład Narodowy im. Ossolińskich, 1981.

–, and Jacek Matuszewski: *see also* Grodecki, Roman, ed. and trans.

McKitterick, Rosamond. *The Frankish Kingdoms Under the Carolingians.* London: Longman, 1983.

–. *The Carolingians and the Written Word.* Cambridge: Cambridge University Press, 1989.

–. *History and Memory in the Carolingian World.* Cambridge: Cambridge University Press, 2004.

Michałowski, Roman. *Princeps fundator. Studium z dziejów kultury politycznej w Polsce X–XIII wieku* [*Princeps fundator*: a study in the history of political culture in Poland between the tenth and the thirteenth centuries]. Warsaw: Arx Regia, 1993.

Miller, Edward. *The Abbey and Bishopric of Ely.* Cambridge: Cambridge University Press, 1951.

–, and John Hatcher. *Medieval England: Rural Society and Economic Change, 1086–1348.* London: Longman, 1978.

– and –. *Medieval England: Towns, Commerce and Crafts, 1086–1348.* London: Longman, 1995.

Minnis, Alastair J. *Medieval Theory of Authorship: Scholastic Literary Attitudes in the Later Middle Ages.* London: Scholars Press, 1984.

Młynarska-Kaletynowa, Marta. *Wrocław w XII–XIII wieku. Przemiany społeczne i osadnicze* [Wrocław in the twelfth and thirteenth centuries: social and settlement changes]. Wrocław: Zakład Narodowy im. Ossolińskich, 1986.

Modzelewski, Karol. "The System of the Ius Ducale and the Idea of Feudalism: Comments on the Earliest Class Society in Medieval Poland." *Quaestiones Medii Aevi* 1 (1977), 71–99.

–. *Chłopi w monarchii wczesnopiastowskiej* [The peasants in the early Piast monarchy]. Wrocław: Zakład Narodowy im. Ossolińskich, 1987.

–. *Organizacja gospodarcza państwa piastowskiego, X–XIII wiek* [The economic organization of the Piast state from the tenth to the thirteenth century]. 2nd ed. Poznań: Wydawnictwo Poznańskiego Towarzystwa Przyjaciół Nauk, 2000.

Morris, Colin. *The Papal Monarchy: The Western Church from 1050 to 1250.* Oxford: Clarendon Press, 1989.

Mularczyk, Jerzy. *Władza książęca na Śląsku w XIII wieku* [Ducal power in Silesia in the thirteenth century]. Wrocław: Zakład Narodowy im. Ossolińskich, 1984.

Murray, Alan V., ed. *Crusade and Conversion on the Baltic Frontier, 1150–1500.* Aldershot: Ashgate, 2001.

Myśliwski, Grzegorz. "Boundary Delimitation in Medieval Poland." In *Perspectives on Central-European History and Politics (Selected Papers from the Fifth World Congress of Central and East European Studies, Warsaw, 1995),* ed. Stanislav Kirschbaum, 27–36. Houndmills: Macmillan, 1999.

—. *Człowiek średniowiecza wobec czasu i przestrzeni. Mazowsze od XII do poł. XVI wieku* [Medieval man with regard to time and space: Masovia from the twelfth to the mid-sixteenth century]. Warsaw: Wydawnictwo Krupski i S-ka, 1999.

—. "Boundaries and Men in Poland from the Twelfth to the Sixteenth Century: The Case of Masovia." In Abulafia and Berend, *Medieval Frontiers,* 217–37.

—. "Old Age and Longevity in Medieval Poland against a Comparative Background." *Acta Poloniae Historica* 86 (2002), 5–45.

—. "Utilisation of Water in Central Europe (12th–16th Cents.)." In *Economia e energia secc. XIII–XVIII: Atti della "Trentaquattresima Settimana di Studi" 15–19 aprile 2002,* Serie II. Atti delle "Settimane di Studi" e altri Convegni 34, ed. Simonetta Cavaciocchi, 321–333. Florence: Le Monnier, 2003.

Nelson, Janet. Review of Berend, *At the Gate. American Historical Review* 107 (2002), 1279–80.

Nicholas, Barry. *An Introduction to Roman Law.* Oxford: Clarendon Press, 1962.

Niermeyer, J. F. *Mediae Latinitatis Lexicon Minus.* Leiden: Brill, 1976. Repr. 1984.

Nip, Renée. "Gendered Memories from Flanders." In van Houts, *Medieval Memories,* 113–31.

North, William. "The Fragmentation and Redemption of a Medieval Cathedral: Property, Conflict, and Public Piety in Eleventh-Century Arezzo." In Brown and Górecki, *Conflict,* 109–130.

Nowakowski, Tomasz. *Idee areng dokumentów książąt polskich do połowy XIII wieku* [Ideas in the preambles of the documents issued by Polish dukes through the mid-thirteenth century]. Bydgoszcz: Wydawnictwo Uczelniane Wyższej Szkoły Pedagogicznej w Bydgoszczy, 1999.

Olszewski, Daniel, ed. *Cystersi w Polsce* [The Cistercians in Poland]. Kielce: Wydawnictwo Jedność w Kielcach, 1990.

Ożóg, Krzysztof. "Władysław Odonic Plwacz" [Władysław Odonic the Spitter]. In *Piastowie,* 131–41.

—. "Przemysł I." In *Piastowie,* 138–41.

Partner, Nancy. "The New Cornificius: Medieval History and the Artifice of Words." In *Classical Rhetoric and Medieval Historiography,* ed. Ernst Breisach, 5–59. Kalamazoo: Medieval Institute Publications, 1985.

Piskorski, Jan M. *Kolonizacja wiejska Pomorza Zachodniego w XIII i w początkach XIV wieku na tle procesów osadniczych w średniowiecznej Europie* [Rural colonization of Western Pomerania in the thirteenth and the early fourteenth centuries in the context of settlement processes in medieval Europe]. Poznań: Wydawnictwo Poznańskiego Towarzystwa Przyjaciół Nauk, 1991.

Plezia, Marian, ed. *Słownik łaciny średniowiecznej w Polsce. Lexicon mediae et infimae latinitatis Polonorum* [A dictionary of medieval Latin in Poland]. 7 vols. to date. Wrocław: Zakład Narodowy im. Ossolińskich, 1953– .

Pohl, Walter, Ian Wood, and Helmut Reimitz, ed. *The Transformation of Frontiers: From Late Antiquity to the the Carolingians*. Leiden: Brill, 2000.

Polski Słownik Biograficzny. 39 vols. to date. Kraków: Polska Akademia Umiejętności, 1935–1939; Wrocław: Zakład Narodowy im. Ossolińskich, 1947– .

Pomian, Krzysztof. *Europa i jej narody* [Europe and its nations]. Trans. Małgorzata Szpakowska. Rev. ed. Gdańsk: Wydawnictwo słowo/obraz terytoria, 2004.

Postan, Michael M. "The Famulus: The Estate Labourer in the XIIth and XIIIth Centuries." *Economic History Review* Supplement 2 (1954).

–. *The Medieval Economy and Society*. Harmondsworth: Penguin, 1975.

Pounds, Norman J. G. *An Economic History of Medieval Europe*. London: Longman, 1974.

–. *An Historical Geography of Europe, 450 BC–AD 1330*. Cambridge: Cambridge University Press, 1973.

–. *Hearth and Home: A Study of Material Culture*. Bloomington: Indiana University Press, 1993.

Powierski, Jan. "Aspekty terytorialne cysterskiej misji w Prusach" [Territorial aspects of the Cistercian mission in Prussia]. In Wyrwa and Dobosz, *Cystersi*, 251–70.

Provero, Luigi. "Cuarenta años de historia rural del medioevo italiano." *Historia Agraria* 33 (2004), 15–29.

Quirk, Kathleen. "Men, Women and Miracles in Normandy, 1050–1150." In van Houts, *Medieval Memories*, 53–71.

Rabiej, Piotr. "Henryk II Pobożny" [Henry II the Pious]. In *Piastowie*, 393–400.

Rady, Martyn. "The Medieval Hungarian and Other Frontiers." *Slavonic and East European Review* 81 (2003), 698–709.

Raftis, J. Ambrose. *The Estates of Ramsey Abbey: A Study in Economic Growth and Organization*. Toronto: Pontifical Institute of Mediaeval Studies, 1957.

–. *Tenure and Mobility: Studies in the Social History of the Medieval Village*. Toronto: Pontifical Institute of Mediaeval Studies, 1957.

Radzimiński, Andrzej, Anna Supruniuk, and Jan Wroniszewski, ed. *Venerabiles, nobiles et honesti. Studia z dziejów społeczeństwa Polski średniowiecznej* [*Venerabiles, nobiles et honesti*: studies in the history of medieval Polish society]. Toruń: Wydawnictwo Uniwersytetu Mikołaja Kopernika, 1997.

Remensnyder, Amy G. *Remembering Kings Past: Monastic Foundation Legends in Medieval Southern France*. Ithaca: Cornell University Press, 1995.

Rosenwein, Barbara, ed. *Anger's Past: The Social Uses of an Emotion in the Middle Ages.* Ithaca: Cornell University Press, 1998.

Reynolds, Susan. *An Introduction to the History of English Medieval Towns.* Oxford: Clarendon Press, 1977.

—. "Medieval *Origines Gentium* and the Community of the Realm." *History* 68 (1983), 375–90.

—. *Kingdoms and Communities in Western Europe, 900–1300.* 2nd ed. Oxford: Clarendon Press, 1997.

—. "The Historiography of the Medieval State." In *Companion to Historiography,* ed. Michael Bentley, 117–38. London: Routledge, 1997.

—. "The Emergence of Professional Law in the Long Twelfth Century." *Law and History Review* 21 (2003), 347–66.

Rosłanowski, Tadeusz. "Comparative Sociotopography on the Example of Early-Medieval Towns in Central Europe." *Acta Poloniae Historica* 34 (1976), 7–27.

Russell, J. C. "Population in Europe, 500–1500." In Cipolla, *Economic History,* 25–70.

Schmid, Heinrich Felix. *Die rechtlichen Grundlagen der Pfarrorganisation auf westslavischen Boden und ihre Entwicklung während des Mittelalters.* Weimar: Böhlhaus, 1938.

Searle, Eleanor. *Lordship and Community: Battle Abbey and Its Banlieu.* Toronto: Pontifical Institute of Mediaeval Studies, 1974.

Silnicki, Tadeusz. "Kardynał legat Gwido, jego synod wrocławski w roku 1267 i statuty tego synodu" [Cardinal Legate Guido, his Wrocław synod of 1267, and the statutes of this synod]. In Silnicki, *Z dziejów kościoła w Polsce. Studia i szkice historyczne* [Fragments of the history of the Church in Poland: studies and historical sketches], 321–80. Warsaw: Państwowe Wydawnictwo Naukowe, 1960.

Słownik Staropolski. 11 vols. Warsaw: Polska Akademia Nauk, 1953–1955; Wrocław: Zakład Narodowy im. Ossolińskich, 1956–1987; Kraków: Zakład Narodowy im. Ossolińskich, 1988–1995; Kraków: Polska Akademia Nauk, 1995–2002.

Smoliński, Marek. *Polityka zachodnia księcia gdańsko-pomorskiego Świętopełka* [The western policy of the duke of Gdańsk Pomerania, Świętopełk]. Gdańsk: Wydawnictwo Uniwersytetu Gdańskiego/Officina Ferberiana, 2000.

Smolka, Stanisław. *Mieszko Stary i jego wiek* [Mieszko the Old and his age]. Warsaw: Gebethner i Wolff, 1881, repr. Warsaw: Państwowe Wydawnictwo Naukowe, 1959.

Sonnlechner, Christoph. "The Establishment of New Units of Production in Carolingian Times: Making Early Medieval Sources Relevant for Environmental History." *Viator* 35 (2004), 21–37.

Southern, Richard W. *Western Society and the Church in the Middle Ages.* Harmondsworth: Penguin, 1970.

—. *Scholastic Humanism and the Unification of Europe.* Vol. 1: *Foundations.* Oxford: Blackwell, 1995.

Spufford, Peter. *Money and Its Use in Medieval Europe*. Cambridge: Cambridge University Press, 1988.

Sroka, Stanisław A. "Władysław." In *Piastowie*, 722–23.

—. "Bolesław I." In *Piastowie*, 726–78.

Stanford, Michael. *An Introduction to the Philosophy of History*. Oxford: Blackwell, 1998.

Stein, Peter. *Legal Institutions: The Develoment of Dispute Settlement*. London: Butterworths, 1984.

Stenzel, Gustav A., ed. *Liber Fundationis Claustri Sanctae Mariae Virginis in Heinrichow*. Breslau: Josef Max & Komp., 1854.

Strzelczyk, Jerzy, ed. *Historia i kultura Cystersów w dawnej Polsce i ich europejskie związki* [History and culture of the Cistercians in old Poland and their European connections]. Poznań: Wydawnictwo Naukowe UAM, 1987.

Świechowski, Zygmunt. "Architektura polskich cystersów w kontekście europejskim" [The architecture of Polish Cistercians in a European context]. In Strzelczyk, *Historia*, 137–47.

—. "Architektura cystersów w Polsce, Czechach i na Węgrzech" [Cistercian architecture in Poland, Bohemia, and Hungary]. In Wyrwa and Dobosz, *Cystersi*, 54–77.

Szczur, Stanisław. *Historia Polski – Średniowiecze* [A history of Poland: the Middle Ages]. Kraków: Wydawnictwo Literackie, 2002.

—, and Krzysztof Ożóg, ed. *Piastowie. Leksykon biograficzny* [The Piasts: a biographical lexicon]. Kraków: Wydawnictwo Literackie, 1999.

Szymański, Józef. "Biskupstwa polskie w wiekach średnich. Organizacja i funkcje" [Polish bishoprics in the Middle Ages: organization and functions]. In Kłoczowski, *Kościół*, 1:127–236.

—. *Kanonikat świecki w Małopolsce od końca XI do połowy XIII wieku* [Canons secular in Little Poland from the end of the eleventh to the mid-thirteenth century]. Lublin: Agencja Wydawniczo-Handlowa AD, 1995.

Tabuteau, Emily Z. *Transfers of Property in Eleventh-Century Normandy*. Chapel Hill: University of North Carolina Press, 1988.

Tazbirowa, Julia. "Początki organizacji parafialnej w Polsce" [Origins of the parish organization in Poland]. *Przegląd Historyczny* 5 (1963), 369–86.

Thomas, Alfred. "Czech–German Relations as Reflected in Old Czech Literature." In Bartlett and MacKay, *Frontier Societies*, 199–215.

Topolski, Jerzy. *An Outline History of Poland*. Warsaw: Interpress, 1986.

Tymieniecki, Kazimierz. "Majętność książęca w Zagościu i pierwotne uposażenie klasztoru joannitów na tle dorzecza dolnej Nidy. Studium z dziejów gospodarczych XII w." [The ducal estate in Zagość and the original endowment of the house of the Hospitallers of St. John in the context of the settlement of the lower Nida river system: A study in twelfth-century economic history]. In Tymieniecki, *Pisma wybrane* [Selected writings], 35–126. Warsaw: Państwowe Wydawnictwo Naukowe, 1956.

van Houts, Elisabeth M. C. *Local and Regional Chronicles*, Typologie des sources du moyen âge occidental 74. Turnhout: Brepols, 1995.

–, ed. *Medieval Memories: Men, Women, and the Past, 700–1300*. Harlow: Longman/ Pearson Education, 2001.

Walker, David. "The Organization of Material in Medieval Cartularies." In *The Study of Medieval Records: Essays in Honour of Kathleen Major*, ed. D. A. Bullough and R. L. Storey, 132–50. Oxford: Clarendon Press, 1971.

Walkówski, Andrzej. *Najstarszy kopiarz lubiąski* [The earliest Lubiąż cartulary]. Wrocław: Wydawnictwo Uniwersytetu Wrocławskiego, 1985.

Wasilewski, Tadeusz. "Poland's Administrative Structure in Early Piast Times." *Acta Poloniae Historica* 44 (1981), 5–31.

Waśko, Anna. "Bernard Zwinny" [Bernard the Agile]. In *Piastowie*, 425.

–. "Henryk IV Prawy (Probus)" [Henry IV the Righeous]. In *Piastowie*, 427–431.

White, Stephen D. *Custom, Kinship, and Gifts to Saints: The Laudatio Parentum in Western France, 1050–1150*. Chapel Hill: University of North Carolina Press, 1988.

–. "Tenth-Century Courts at Mâcon and the Perils of Structuralist History." In Brown and Górecki, *Conflict*, 37–68.

Wiśniowski, Eugeniusz. "Rozwój organizacji parafialnej w Polsce do czasów reformacji" [The development of the parish organization in Poland until the Reformation]. In Kłoczowski, *Kościół*, 1:237–274.

–. "Parish Clergy in Medieval Poland." In Kłoczowski, *Christian Community*, 119–48.

Wroniszewski, Jan. "*Proclamatio alias godło*. Uwagi nad genezą i funkcją zawołań rycerskich w średniowiecznej Polsce" [*Proclamatio alias godło*: remarks on the origins and function of the knightly battle cry in medieval Poland]. In *Społeczeństwo Polski średniowiecznej* [The society of medieval Poland], ed. Stefan Kuczyński, vol. 4, 147–70. Warsaw: Państwowe Wydawnictwo Naukowe, 1990.

Wünsch, Thomas, and Alexander Patschovsky, ed. *Das Reich und Polen: Parallelen, Interaktionen und Formen der Akkulturation im hohen und späten Mittelalter*. Vorträge und Forschungen 59. Ostfildern: Jan Thorbecke Verlag, 2003.

Wyrozumski, Jerzy. *Kazimierz Wielki* [Casimir the Great]. Wrocław: Zakład Narodowy im. Ossolińskich, 1982.

–. *Dzieje Krakowa* [A history of Kraków]. Vol. 1: *Kraków do schyłku wieków średnich* [Kraków until the end of the Middle Ages]. Kraków: Wydawnictwo Literackie, 1992.

Wyrwa, Andrzej Marek. "Cystersi. Geneza, duchowość, organizacja życia w zakonie (do XV wieku) i początki fundacji na ziemiach polskich" [The Cistercians: origins, spirituality, and organization of life in the Order (through the fifteenth century), and the beginnings of foundations in the Polish lands]. In Olszewski, *Cystersi*, 11–39.

–. "Powstanie zakonu cystersów i jego rozwój na ziemiach polskich w średniowieczu" [The origins of the Cistercian Order and its development in the Polish lands during the Middle Ages]. In Wyrwa, Strzelczyk, and Kaczmarek, *Monasticon*, 1:27–54.

–, Jerzy Strzelczyk, and Krzysztof Kaczmarek, ed. *Monasticon Cisterciense Poloniae*. 2 vols. Poznań: Wydawnictwo Poznańskie, 1999.

– and Józef Dobosz, ed. *Cystersi w społeczeństwie Europy Środkowej* [Cistercians in the society of Central Europe]. Poznań: Wydawnictwo Poznańskie, 2000.

Yates, Frances A. *The Art of Memory*. Chicago: University of Chicago Press, 1966.

Zaremska, Hanna. *Niegodne rzemiosło. Kat w społeczeństwie Polski XIV–XVI w.* [The unworthy craft: the executioner in Polish society between the fourteenth and the sixteenth centuries]. Warsaw: Państwowe Wydawnictwo Naukowe, 1986.

–. *Banici w średniowiecznej Europie* [Outlaws in medieval Europe]. Warsaw: Semper, 1993.

Zawadzka, Józefa. "Fundowanie opactw cysterskich w XII i XIII wieku" [The founding of Cistercian monasteries in the twelfth and thirteenth centuries]. *Roczniki Humanistyczne* 7 (1958), 121–50.

Zdrójkowski, Zbigniew. "Miasta na prawie średzkim (materiały)" [Towns established according to the law of Neumarkt – the sources]. *Sobótka* 41 (1986), 343–51.

Żerelik, Rościsław. "*Ego minimum fratrum*. W kwestii autorstwa drugiej części 'Księgi Henrykowskiej'" [*Ego minimum fratrum*: concerning the authorship of the second portion of the *Henryków Book*]. *Nasza Przeszłość* 83 (1994), 63–75.

–. "Średniowieczne archiwa cysterskie na Śląsku" [Medieval Cistercian archives in Silesia]. In Wyrwa and Dobosz, *Cystersi*, 353–62.

–. "Dzieje Śląska do 1526 roku" [The history of Silesia until 1526]. In *Historia Śląska* [History of Silesia], ed. Marek Czapliński, 14–116. Wrocław: Wydawnictwo Uniwersytetu Wrocławskiego, 2002.

Zientara, Benendykt. *Henryk Brodaty i jego czasy* [Henry the Bearded and his times]. Warsaw: Państwowy Instytut Wydawniczy, 1975. 2nd ed. Warsaw: Wydawnictwo TRIO, 1997.

–. "Socio-Economic and Spatial Transformation of Polish Towns during the Period of Location." *Acta Poloniae Historica* 34 (1976), 57–83.

–. "Walloons in Silesia in the Twelfth and Thirteenth Centuries." *Quaestiones Medii Aevi* 2 (1981), 127–50.

Zimmermann, Michel. "Ouverture du colloque." In Zimmermann, *Auctor*, 7–14.

–, ed. *Auctor et auctoritas. Invention et conformisme dans l'écriture médiévale*. Paris: École des Chartes, 2001.

Żmudzki, Paweł. *Studium podzielonego królestwa. Książę Leszek Czarny* [A study in a divided kingdom: Duke Leszek the Black]. Warsaw: Wydawnictwo NERITON, 2000.

Żytkowicz, Leonid. "Trends of the Agrarian Economy in Poland, Bohemia and Hungary from the Middle of the Fifteenth to the Middle of the Seventeenth Century." In Mączak, Samsonowicz, and Burke, *East-Central Europe*, 59–83.

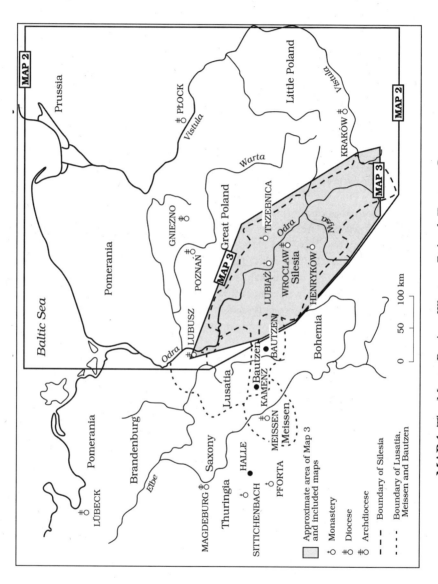

MAP 1 The Macro Region: Western Poland, Eastern Germany

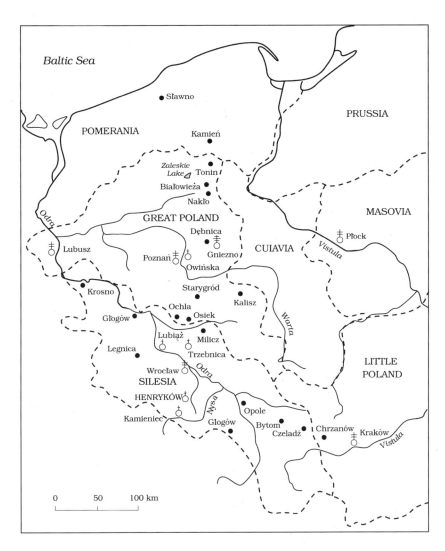

MAP 2 Western Poland

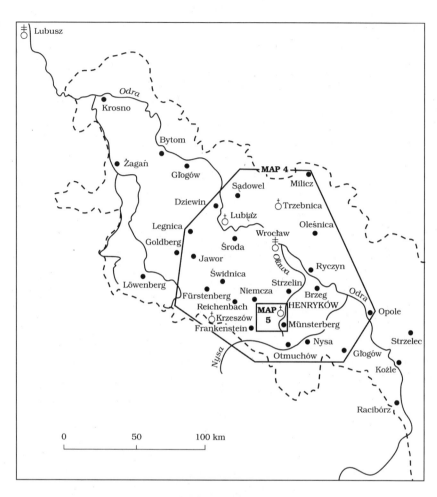

MAP 3 Silesia

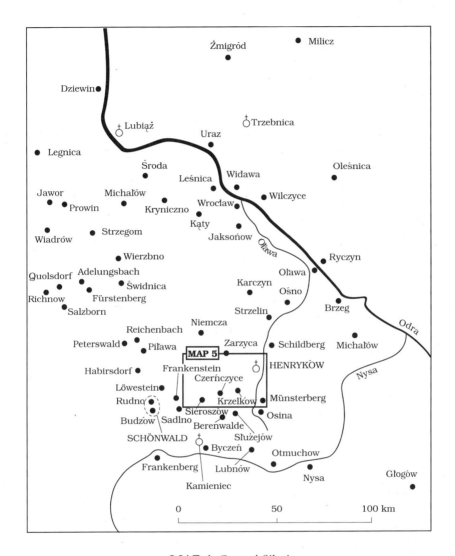

MAP 4 Central Silesia

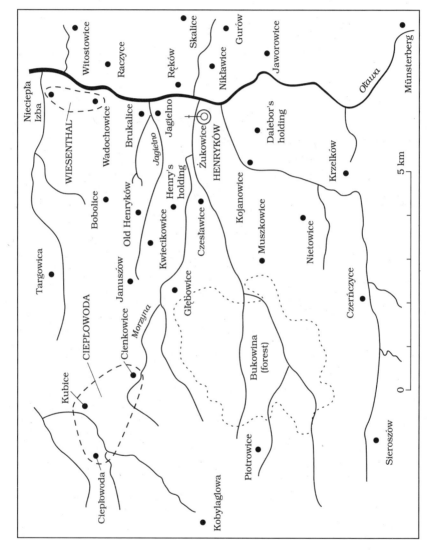

MAP 5 The Henryków Region

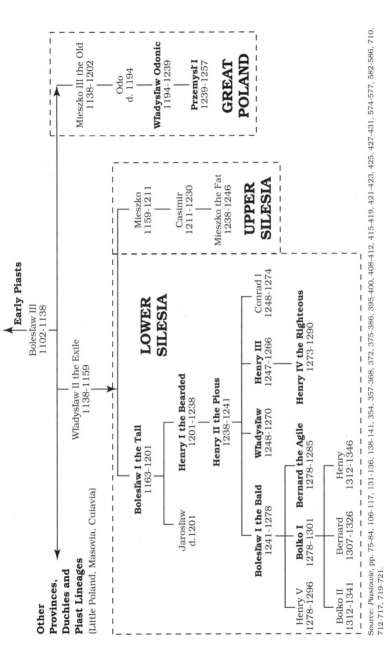

Genealogical Chart The branches of the Piast dynasty documented in the *Henryków Book*
(Dukes mentioned by name are indicated in bold.)

Source: *Piastowie*, pp. 75-84, 106-117, 131-136, 138-141, 354, 357-368, 372, 375-386, 395-400, 408-412, 415-419, 421-423, 425, 427-431, 574-577, 582-586, 710, 712-717, 719-721.

Other Provinces, Duchies and Piast Lineages
(Little Poland, Masovia, Cuiavia)

Early Piasts

Bolesław III
1102-1138

Władysław II the Exile
1138-1159

LOWER SILESIA

Bolesław I the Tall
1163-1201

Jarosław
d. 1201

Henry I the Bearded
1201-1238

Henry II the Pious
1238-1241

Bolesław I the Bald
1241-1278

Władysław
1248-1270

Henry III
1247-1266

Conrad I
1248-1274

Henry V
1278-1296

Bolko I
1278-1301

Bernard the Agile
1278-1285

Henry IV the Righteous
1273-1290

Bolko II
1312-1341

Bernard
1307-1326

Henry
1312-1346

UPPER SILESIA

Mieszko
1159-1211

Casimir
1211-1230

Mieszko the Fat
1238-1246

GREAT POLAND

Mieszko III the Old
1138-1202

Odo
d. 1194

Władysław Odonic
1194-1239

Przemysł I
1239-1257

Index